The Comprehensive PTSD and Complex PTSD Recovery Guide

Published by Talking Therapies UK

www.TalkingTherapies.co.uk

First Edition: 2025

Important Disclaimer

This book is intended for educational and informational purposes only. It is not intended to be a substitute for professional medical advice, diagnosis, or treatment. The information provided in this guide should not replace consultation with qualified healthcare professionals, including psychiatrists, psychologists, psychotherapists, counsellors, or other mental health practitioners.

If you are experiencing symptoms of post-traumatic stress disorder (PTSD), complex PTSD, or any other mental health condition, please seek appropriate professional help. If you are in crisis or experiencing thoughts of self-harm or suicide, please contact emergency services immediately or reach out to a crisis helpline in your country.

The author, publisher, and any associated parties make no representations or warranties of any kind, express or implied, regarding the completeness, accuracy, reliability, suitability, or availability of the information contained within this book. Any reliance you place on such information is strictly at your own risk.

The techniques, strategies, and exercises described in this book are based on established therapeutic approaches. However, individual responses to therapeutic interventions vary, and what works for one person may not work for another. Always work with a qualified mental health professional when addressing trauma-related conditions.

Case examples presented in this book are composite illustrations based on clinical experience and do not represent any specific individual. Any resemblance to actual persons is coincidental.

In the United Kingdom:

Samaritans: 116 123 (free, 24 hours)

NHS Mental Health Crisis Line: 111 (option 2)

Emergency Services: 999

Dedication

For Isabella James, Paul James, and Russell King

With love and gratitude

Contents

COLOUR CODING GUIDE

This guide uses colour highlighting to help you navigate important information and engage with practical skills at your own pace.

YELLOW – Important Learning Points & Key Concepts

Yellow highlighting indicates crucial information about how PTSD works, why symptoms persist, or core concepts that are foundational to your recovery. (Herman, 2015)

MAGENTA – Case Studies & Recovery Stories (Herman, 2015)

Magenta highlighting identifies stories of individuals who have recovered from PTSD, woven throughout this guide.

ORANGE – Practical Skills & Worksheets

Orange highlighting marks step-by-step techniques, worksheets, and exercises you can implement immediately.

BLACK – Main Body Text

The majority of this guide remains in standard black text, providing supportive narrative and context.

ABBREVIATIONS AND KEY TERMS

This guide uses several important abbreviations. Understanding these terms will help you navigate the content and communicate with healthcare providers.

Therapeutic Approaches:

- • CBT = Cognitive Behavioural Therapy (the general therapeutic approach for PTSD)
- • CT-PTSD = Cognitive Therapy for PTSD (based on Ehlers & Clark model; for adults)
- • TF-CBT = Trauma-Focused Cognitive Behavioural Therapy (specific protocol for children and adolescents)
- • PE = Prolonged Exposure (Foa's evidence-based treatment for adults)
- • CPT = Cognitive Processing Therapy (combined exposure and cognitive approach)
- • EMDR = Eye Movement Desensitization and Reprocessing (bilateral stimulation therapy) (Shapiro, 2018)

Diagnostic and Classification Systems:

- • DSM-5 = Diagnostic and Statistical Manual of Mental Disorders, Fifth Edition (USA classification system)
- • ICD-11 = International Classification of Diseases, 11th Revision (World Health Organization system)
- • PTSD = Post-Traumatic Stress Disorder

- • C-PTSD = Complex PTSD (recognised in ICD-11)

Other Important Terms:

- • Trauma-focused CBT = umbrella term for any cognitive behavioural therapy specifically designed to address trauma (Bisson et al., 2013; NICE, 2018)

INTRODUCTION: About This Guide

Welcome to this comprehensive guide on Post-Traumatic Stress Disorder (PTSD) and Complex PTSD. Whether you are a trauma survivor seeking understanding and healing, a loved one supporting someone with PTSD, or a clinician treating trauma patients, this guide offers evidence-based information, practical strategies, and hope for recovery. With over 112,000 words across 23 chapters and 10 appendices, this resource represents one of the most comprehensive guides to PTSD recovery available.

WHAT IS PTSD?

Post-Traumatic Stress Disorder is a mental health condition that develops after experiencing or witnessing a traumatic event.

Trauma involves actual or threatened death, significant injury, or sexual violence.

PTSD affects approximately 7–8 per cent of the population at some point in their lives, with higher rates among certain groups like combat veterans, sexual assault survivors, and first responders. (Seal et al., 2007)

PTSD is not a weakness or a character flaw; it represents a normal response to abnormal experiences, reflecting how the brain and body respond to overwhelming threat.

- PTSD involves four symptom clusters as defined by DSM-5: intrusion symptoms (flashbacks, nightmares, intrusive memories)
- avoidance (avoiding trauma reminders)
- negative alterations in cognitions and mood (negative beliefs, emotional numbing, detachment)
- and marked alterations in arousal and reactivity (hypervigilance, irritability, sleep problems, exaggerated startle).

These symptoms persist for at least one month after trauma, cause significant distress or functional impairment, and are not attributable to substances or other medical conditions.

Complex PTSD (C-PTSD) is a form of PTSD recognised in ICD-11 but not yet in DSM-5.

C-PTSD develops from chronic trauma, particularly during developmental years, and includes core PTSD symptoms plus additional difficulties: severe emotion dysregulation, persistent negative self-concept, and interpersonal relationship problems. (Teicher & Samson, 2016)

C-PTSD typically results from childhood abuse, domestic violence, human trafficking, prolonged captivity, or other situations involving repeated trauma and inability to escape. (Herman, 2015; Teicher & Samson, 2016)

Understanding the distinction between PTSD and C-PTSD matters because treatment approaches differ somewhat, with C-PTSD requiring more extensive stabilisation before trauma processing.

WHO THIS GUIDE IS FOR This guide serves multiple audiences, each finding relevant sections for their needs: TRAUMA SURVIVORS: If you have PTSD or suspect you might, this guide provides: an understanding of what PTSD is and how it develops; a comprehensive overview of evidence-based treatments; practical coping strategies for managing symptoms daily; guidance on relationships, parenting, work, and other life domains; recovery stories demonstrating healing is possible; and resources for accessing professional help. LOVED ONES AND SUPPORTERS: If you care about someone with PTSD, this guide offers: a clear explanation of PTSD symptoms and behaviours; guidance on how to support without enabling avoidance; communication strategies; understanding of treatment processes; self-care for supporters; and a letter template helping trauma survivors explain PTSD to loved ones. CLINICIANS AND HEALTHCARE PROVIDERS: If you treat trauma patients, this guide includes: a comprehensive chapter on clinical treatment of PTSD and C-PTSD; your relationship with your therapist challenges and solutions; treatment protocols and adaptations; managing difficult clinical situations; cultural competence guidance; vicarious traumatisation prevention; and resources for continuing education. STUDENTS AND EDUCATORS: If you are learning about trauma, this guide provides: a thorough grounding in PTSD theory and research; evidence base for treatments; understanding of trauma neurobiology; a comprehensive glossary of terminology; and extensive references to primary sources. WHAT MAKES THIS GUIDE COMPREHENSIVE This guide differs from shorter PTSD resources in the following ways: DEPTH OF COVERAGE: Twenty-three chapters cover everything from basic PTSD concepts through advanced treatment techniques, specific trauma types, relationships, parenting, sexuality, work, and more. Nothing is superficial; each topic receives thorough and nuanced exploration, acknowledging complexity while providing practical guidance. (Stamm, 2010; Pearlman & Saakvitne, 1995)

EVIDENCE-BASED APPROACH: Every treatment recommendation is grounded in scientific research. We prioritise interventions demonstrated to be effective through randomised controlled trials and meta-analyses, whilst noting when evidence is limited. References to research findings throughout establish credibility whilst helping readers understand why specific approaches are recommended. PRACTICAL APPLICATION: Theory matters, but issues of application matter more. Each chapter provides concrete strategies, examples, and guidance for applying concepts in everyday life. Worksheets in Appendix B provide fillable templates for tracking symptoms, challenging thoughts, planning safety, and more. MULTIPLE PERSPECTIVES: This guide addresses PTSD from various angles: neurobiological, psychological, social, and cultural. We incorporate the perspectives of trauma survivors, their loved ones, and clinicians. We address standard PTSD, Complex PTSD, and trauma-specific issues for combat veterans, medical trauma survivors, and first responders. ACCESSIBILITY: Despite depth, we write in clear, understandable language, minimising jargon. When technical terms are necessary, we define them. The style strikes a balance between professional authority and warmth, never condescending to readers while providing expert guidance. CULTURAL HUMILITY: We acknowledge that trauma, healing, and appropriate treatment vary across cultures. We avoid assuming Western approaches apply universally, note cultural considerations throughout, and emphasise the importance of culturally adapted treatment. REALISTIC HOPE: This guide strikes a balance between a realistic understanding of PTSD challenges and genuine hope for recovery. We never minimise trauma's impact or promise unrealistic quick fixes. However, we consistently emphasise that recovery is possible, treatment works, and many people have healed from trauma as severe as yours. (Herman, 2015; Teicher & Samson, 2016)

HOW THIS GUIDE WAS DEVELOPED This guide synthesises current PTSD research, clinical practice guidelines from organisations like the American Psychological Association and the UK Psychological Trauma Society, and wisdom from trauma survivors about what helps recovery. (Herman, 2015)

- Content draws from: peer-reviewed research on PTSD neurobiology, assessment, and treatment
- evidence-based treatment manuals for PE, EMDR, CPT, and other approaches (Shapiro, 2018)
- clinical practice guidelines from professional organisations
- trauma survivors' narratives about recovery (Herman, 2015)
- and clinical experience treating diverse trauma populations.

We prioritise evidence-based treatments with the strongest research support whilst acknowledging that individual responses vary and multiple valid paths to recovery exist. (Herman, 2015)

When evidence is mixed or limited, we note this transparently rather than overstating certainty.

When discussing controversial topics, we present multiple perspectives, enabling readers to make informed decisions in consultation with their treatment providers.

IMPORTANT TERMINOLOGY NOTE: Understanding TF-CBT and CT-PTSD (Cohen et al., 2016)

As you read this guide, you may encounter references to "Trauma-Focused Cognitive Behavioural Therapy" and related terms. These can be confusing because they are closely related but refer to different things. This note clarifies the distinction.

The Umbrella Term: "Trauma-Focused CBT" (Bisson et al., 2013; NICE, 2018)

"Trauma-focused CBT" is a broad category that describes any cognitive behavioural therapy specifically designed to address trauma. This includes Prolonged Exposure (PE), Cognitive Processing Therapy (CPT), Eye Movement Desensitization and Reprocessing (EMDR), and the Cognitive Therapy model developed by Ehlers and Clark. (Resick & Schnicke, 2016)

The Specific Protocol: TF-CBT® (Cohen et al., 2016)

When you see "TF-CBT" with emphasis, this refers to a specific, standardized protocol designed by Drs. Cohen, Mannarino, and Deblinger. This particular version is specifically designed for children and adolescents aged 3–18 and their non-offending caregivers. It follows a structured protocol known by the acronym PRACTICE. (Cohen et al., 2016)

The Adult-Focused Protocol: CT-PTSD

This guide primarily focuses on "Cognitive Therapy for PTSD" (CT-PTSD), which is based on the cognitive model developed by Ehlers and Clark. This approach is specifically designed for adults. Unlike the TF-CBT protocol, CT-PTSD does not follow the PRACTICE acronym and typically does not involve caregivers in the same structured way.

Why This Matters for Your Care

If you are an adult seeking treatment, a clinician will likely recommend CT-PTSD (Ehlers & Clark model), Prolonged Exposure (PE), Cognitive Processing Therapy (CPT), or EMDR. You would not typically be offered the specific TF-CBT protocol because that is designed for children. However, clinicians may use the general term "trauma-focused CBT" to describe any of these adult-focused approaches. (Resick & Schnicke, 2016)

HOW TO USE THIS GUIDE

The length of this guide may feel overwhelming initially. You do not need to read it cover-to-cover immediately. Instead, use it as a reference resource throughout recovery, focusing on sections most relevant to current needs. FOR TRAUMA SURVIVORS, SUGGESTED READING PATH: If Newly Diagnosed or Questioning Whether You Have PTSD: Start with Chapter 1 (Understanding PTSD), complete PCL-5 screening in Chapter 2, and read Chapter 3 (Causes and Risk Factors). This foundation helps you understand what you are experiencing. Then proceed to Chapter 4 (Evidence-Based Treatments) to learn about treatment options before consulting a healthcare provider. If Starting Treatment, Focus on the chapters most relevant to your specific treatment approach. Chapters on developing trauma narratives (Chapter 4), challenging unhelpful thoughts (Chapters 5 and 7), graded exposure to feared situations (Chapter 6), and managing physical symptoms (Chapter 8) provide core treatment content. Later chapters on relationships, meaning-making, and maintaining recovery support long-term healing

If you are reading this guide, you may be struggling with the aftermath of a traumatic experience.

Perhaps you have survived a serious accident, witnessed something deeply distressing, experienced violence or abuse, or lived through a natural disaster.

Maybe you have served in the military, worked as a first responder, or endured a medical emergency.

Whatever your experience, if you are finding that the trauma continues to affect your daily life, through intrusive memories, nightmares, intense anxiety, or a persistent sense of being unsafe, you may be experiencing Post-Traumatic Stress Disorder (PTSD).

The decision to pick up this guide and begin exploring recovery represents an act of courage that should not be underestimated. (Herman, 2015)

Many people who experience trauma retreat into avoidance, hoping that if they simply do not think about what happened, the pain will eventually fade on its own.

Whilst this is an understandable and very human response to overwhelming distress, research and clinical experience consistently demonstrate that avoidance, whilst providing short-term relief, maintains suffering in the long term. (Clark, 1999)

By choosing to face your trauma and engage with evidence-based treatment strategies, you are taking the first and essential step towards genuine, lasting recovery. (Herman, 2015)

Every person who has survived trauma has a unique story to tell.

Your trauma might have occurred decades ago or recently.

It might have been a single, discrete event, a car accident, an assault, a natural disaster, or it might have been prolonged and repeated, such as childhood abuse, domestic violence, or multiple combat deployments. (Herman, 2015; Teicher & Samson, 2016)

You might have clear, vivid memories of what happened, or your memories might be fragmented and unclear.

You might have developed PTSD symptoms immediately, or they might have emerged months or even years after the trauma.

Whatever your experience, the fundamental principles of trauma-focused cognitive behavioural therapy can help you recover.

It is important to acknowledge at the outset that what you are experiencing, the intrusive memories that interrupt your daily life, the nightmares that steal your rest, the hypervigilance that leaves you perpetually exhausted, the avoidance that progressively shrinks your world, all of these symptoms, whilst deeply distressing, are not signs of weakness, character flaws, or evidence that you are 'broken.' Instead, they represent your brain and body's attempt to protect you from further harm. (Van der Kolk et al., 1996)

Your nervous system, having encountered a genuine threat, has learned to be vigilant, cautious, and reactive.

The challenge is that these protective mechanisms, having served their purpose during the actual trauma, have persisted beyond their usefulness and now cause suffering in the absence of genuine danger.

Understanding this distinction, between protective responses that were once adaptive and symptoms that now maintain distress, is fundamental to recovery. (Herman, 2015)

You are not fundamentally damaged.

Your brain is working precisely as evolution designed it to work when encountering an extreme threat.

The task before you is not to fix something that's broken, but rather to help your brain and body learn that the danger has passed, that the threat is no longer present, and that you can safely engage with life again without constant vigilance and protection.

Understanding Your Symptoms: Not Broken, But Protective

Primarily, know this: you are not broken, you are not weak, and you are not alone.

PTSD is a natural response to abnormal circumstances.

Your mind and body have been through something extraordinary, and they are doing their best to protect you from further harm.

The symptoms you are experiencing, however distressing they may be, represent your brain's attempt to keep you safe.

The challenge is that these protective mechanisms, whilst well-intentioned, can become unhelpful when they persist long after the danger has passed.

Let us expand on this crucial point, because utterly understanding and internalising it can fundamentally shift how you relate to your symptoms.

When we describe PTSD symptoms as 'your brain's attempt to keep you safe,' this is not just comforting rhetoric; it is grounded in neuroscience, and our understanding of how the human threat detection system works. (LeDoux, 1998)

The human brain evolved over millions of years to prioritise survival primarily.

Our ancestors who were most vigilant, most responsive to threats, and most capable of learning from dangerous situations were the ones who survived to pass on their genes.

We are their descendants, carrying neurological systems exquisitely designed to detect, respond to, and remember threats.

Consider what happens during a traumatic event at the neurological level.

When you encounter an extreme threat, specific brain structures become highly activated, whilst others become suppressed.

The amygdala, your brain's alarm system, an almond-shaped structure deep in the temporal lobe, fires intensely, triggering the release of stress hormones like cortisol and adrenaline throughout your body. (LeDoux, 1998)

Your sympathetic nervous system activates, preparing your body for action through what is commonly known as the 'fight or flight' response, though we now recognise that 'freeze' and 'fawn' (appeasing) are equally valid survival responses.

Blood flows away from non-essential systems like digestion towards your muscles, preparing them for rapid action.

Your pupils dilate to take in more visual information.

Your heart rate increases dramatically, pumping more oxygen-rich blood to your muscles and brain.

Your breathing becomes rapid and shallow, maximising oxygen intake.

Your liver releases stored glucose to provide immediate energy.

Your blood thickens slightly to promote clotting in case of injury.

Pain perception decreases temporarily, allowing you to continue functioning even if injured.

All these changes happen automatically, without conscious thought, orchestrated by ancient brain structures that prioritise immediate survival over everything else. (LeDoux, 1998)

Simultaneously, the prefrontal cortex, the part of your brain responsible for rational thinking, planning, executive function, and contextual understanding, becomes less active. (Foa & Kozak, 1986)

This makes profound evolutionary sense: when facing an attacking predator or immediate mortal danger, you do not have time to philosophise about the nature of the threat, carefully weigh multiple response options, or consider the long-term implications of your actions.

You need to act immediately and instinctively.

Run, fight, freeze, or submit—these survival responses emerge from ancient parts of our brain that humans share with other mammals, reptiles, and even simpler organisms. (Porges, 2011; Levine, 2008)

These responses have been refined over hundreds of millions of years of evolution because they work; they keep organisms alive long enough to reproduce.

This state of heightened activation and altered brain function is entirely appropriate and adaptive during actual threat.

It is your brain's emergency response system doing exactly what it is designed to do, and it has kept humans alive as a species for millennia. (LeDoux, 1998)

The problem in PTSD is that this emergency response system does not fully stand down after the danger has passed. (LeDoux, 1998)

Your brain, having learned that the world can be dangerous in this way, remains vigilant for signs that the danger might return.

The amygdala stays sensitised, maintaining a lower threshold for activation. (LeDoux, 1998)

The threat detection system stays primed, constantly scanning the environment for potential dangers. (LeDoux, 1998)

Your body maintains a higher baseline level of arousal than it did before the trauma, never quite returning to the relaxed, parasympathetic state that characterises feeling genuinely safe. (Yehuda & Seckl, 2011)

The Neuroscience of Trauma: Why Symptoms Persist

This creates the constellation of symptoms you are experiencing.

Intrusive memories occur because a traumatic experience was not processed and stored in the same way as ordinary memories; it remains fragmented, sensory-dominated, and easily triggered. (Van der Kolk et al., 1996; Brewin et al., 2010)

During trauma, when the prefrontal cortex is suppressed and the amygdala is highly activated, memories are encoded differently. (LeDoux, 1998)

Normal memories are processed by the hippocampus, which contextualises them in time and space, creating coherent narratives with clear beginnings, middles, and ends. (Eichenbaum, 2000)

These memories are filed away in our autobiographical memory system with appropriate context markers: 'This happened at this time, in this place, and it is over now.'

Traumatic memories, by contrast, are encoded primarily by the amygdala without adequate hippocampal processing. (LeDoux, 1998)

They remain fragmented collections of sensory impressions, sights, sounds, smells, physical sensations, and overwhelming emotions, without proper narrative structure or temporal context.

These memory fragments are stored with high emotional intensity but without the contextual information that would allow your brain to recognise them as belonging to the past. (Van der Kolk et al., 1996)

When triggered, these memories are activated with full sensory and emotional force, feeling as though they are happening right now rather than being safe recollections of events that occurred in the past.

When you encounter something that reminds your brain of the trauma, even if the reminder is subtle or outside conscious awareness, these fragmented memory traces are activated.

A particular tone of voice, the angle of sunlight at a certain time of day, a specific smell, the feeling of your heart racing during exercise, or even an internal thought can trigger the memory.

Because the triggers can be so subtle and the memory lacks proper contextual markers, flashbacks and intrusive memories can feel completely random and unpredictable, adding to your sense of lacking control and safety. (Van der Kolk et al., 1996)

You might have no conscious awareness of what triggered a particular flashback, which can be profoundly disorienting and frightening.

Nightmares reflect your brain's attempt to process and integrate a traumatic experience during sleep. (Ross et al., 1989)

During rapid eye movement (REM) sleep, when most vivid dreaming occurs, the brain naturally processes emotional experiences and consolidates memories.

For people without PTSD, this processing gradually integrates difficult experiences into long-term memory with decreasing emotional intensity.

However, in PTSD, this processing often remains incomplete and distressing rather than resolution-focused.

The traumatic content is rehearsed repeatedly without being properly integrated, leading to chronic nightmares that maintain rather than resolve distress. (Ross et al., 1989)

Many people with PTSD develop a fear of sleep itself, leading to chronic sleep deprivation that exacerbates all other symptoms.

Hypervigilance, that constant scanning for danger, that inability to relax, that sense of being perpetually 'on guard', represents your threat detection system operating in overdrive. (LeDoux, 1998)

Your brain has learned that the world can suddenly become dangerous, often without warning, and it is determined not to be caught off guard again.

This makes evolutionary sense: in an environment where threats are genuinely present, heightened vigilance increases survival chances.

The problem is that this vigilance, appropriate during actual danger, persists in objectively safe environments.

Your brain hasn't updated its threat assessment to reflect current reality.

The exaggerated startle response you might experience, jumping at sudden noises, feeling panic at unexpected movements, experiencing intense distress at harmless surprises, reflects this same heightened sensitivity to potential threats.

Your nervous system maintains a hair-trigger response, interpreting neutral or mildly surprising stimuli as potential dangers requiring immediate defensive action.

This is not a conscious choice or something you can simply decide to stop doing; it is a deeply ingrained neurological pattern that requires specific therapeutic work to modify.

The Role of Avoidance in Maintaining PTSD

Avoidance, the most understandable of all PTSD symptoms, is your brain's attempt to protect you from experiencing further distress.

If certain places, people, activities, or even thoughts trigger painful memories and overwhelming emotions, of course, your brain motivates you to avoid them.

This is basic learning theory in action: organisms naturally move away from things that cause pain and towards things that provide pleasure or relief.

In the short term, avoidance works beautifully; it provides immediate relief from anxiety and distress.

The moment you decide not to go to that triggering location, not to watch that disturbing film, not to think about that aspect of the trauma, you feel a sense of relief, your anxiety decreases, and you feel safer.

This is precisely why avoidance becomes so entrenched and why PTSD persists.

Every time you avoid something, your brain feels relief; the removal of something aversive (anxiety, distress, fear) strengthens the avoidance behaviour. (Clark, 1999)

It is a powerfully effective short-term coping strategy, which is why it is so difficult to overcome.

Your brain learns: 'When I avoid this trigger, I feel better immediately; therefore, avoiding is the right strategy.' This learning happens at a deep, automatic level, often without conscious awareness. (Clark, 1999)

However, avoidance maintains PTSD through several mechanisms. (Clark, 1999; Salkovskis, 1991)

First, it prevents you from learning that these triggers are not themselves dangerous.

The reminder of the trauma, whether it is a car park where you were assaulted, a news story about an event like your trauma, or a physical sensation that resembles what you felt during the trauma, is not itself dangerous.

It is a reminder, not a repeat of the actual threat.

But if you consistently avoid these reminders, you cannot have the opportunity to gain a new experience of this crucial distinction.

Your fear remains untested and therefore unchanged. (Foa & Kozak, 1986)

In fact, avoiding it can make the fear grow stronger.

Each time you avoid, you send yourself the message: 'This must really be dangerous if I need to avoid it so carefully.'

Second, avoidance prevents you from discovering that you can tolerate the distress these triggers provoke.

Many people with PTSD believe that if they encounter a powerful trigger, they will be completely overwhelmed, lose control, fall apart, or never recover.

These catastrophic predictions feel true, which motivates desperate avoidance. (Clark, 1999)

However, these predictions are usually inaccurate.

Whilst triggers do provoke genuine distress, most people who face them (with appropriate support) discover that the distress, whilst uncomfortable, is tolerable.

It has a natural peak and then decreases.

- You do not fall apart
- you survive the experience, but you can only learn this through experience
- avoidance prevents this learning.

Third, avoidance prevents the trauma memory from being properly processed and integrated into your life story. (Foa & Kozak, 1986)

Memories need to be thought about, talked about, and approached for them to become properly filed away in your autobiographical memory system.

When you consistently avoid thinking about or discussing the trauma, the memory remains fragmented, unprocessed, and highly charged.

It stays 'stuck' in the present rather than becoming properly located in the past.

This is why trauma-focused therapy involves deliberately approaching the trauma memory, seeking to elaborate on the details of the memory, rather than avoiding it.

This allows the processing and integration that lead to genuine healing.

Fourth, avoidance progressively shrinks your life.

What often begins as avoiding specific, trauma-related situations can gradually generalise to avoiding broader categories of experience.

Someone who avoids the specific car park where they were assaulted might gradually avoid all car parks, then all enclosed spaces, and then leave home entirely.

Someone who avoids thinking about their combat trauma might avoid all military-related content, then all news coverage, then all films with conflict, then social situations where people might ask about their service.

The world of safe, available experiences becomes progressively smaller, whilst the domain of avoided experiences grows larger.

This shrinking of life is one of the most tragic aspects of PTSD.

Finally, avoidance itself confirms and reinforces negative beliefs about yourself, the world, and your capacity to cope.

Each time you avoid, you are implicitly telling yourself: 'I cannot manage this.

I am too weak/fragile/damaged to cope with this situation.

The world is too dangerous for me to engage with normally.' These beliefs then drive further avoidance, creating a self-perpetuating cycle.

Breaking this cycle requires gradually, systematically facing what you have been avoiding, not as punishment or 'exposure therapy' for its own sake, but as a way of learning new, more accurate information: that you are stronger than you think, that most situations are safer than they feel, and that you can tolerate distress without being destroyed by it.

Negative Beliefs and Thoughts in PTSD

Negative changes in thoughts and mood represent another cluster of PTSD symptoms that significantly impact quality of life and maintain the disorder.

Trauma does not just create fear and hyperarousal; it fundamentally challenges your understanding of yourself, other people, and the world.

Before trauma, most people operate with a set of generally optimistic assumptions that allow them to function: 'I am reasonably safe,' 'I am competent and capable,' 'People are generally trustworthy,' 'The world is fairly predictable and controllable,' 'Bad things probably will not happen to me.' These assumptions are not based on rigorous analysis; they are more like background beliefs that we do not consciously examine but that nevertheless guide our behaviour and emotional responses.

PAUSE POINT: Ground Yourself

PAUSE POINT: Ground Yourself in the Present

If you're feeling overwhelmed by what you're reading, stop and use the 5-4-3-2-1 grounding technique:

- • Notice 5 things you can SEE
- • Identify 4 things you can TOUCH or FEEL
- • Listen for 3 things you can HEAR
- • Notice 2 things you can SMELL
- • Identify 1 thing you can TASTE

Take three deep breaths and continue when you're ready.

Trauma shatters these assumptions.

When something terrible happens, particularly if it is unexpected or involves human malevolence, these comfortable beliefs are revealed as incomplete or false.

You discover that you are not always safe, that you cannot always prevent terrible things from happening, that the world can be cruel and random, that people can be dangerous, that you are vulnerable in ways you never fully appreciated.

This shattering of assumptions is one reason trauma is so psychologically destabilising: it is not just the event itself, but the way the event challenges fundamental beliefs about reality.

In the aftermath of trauma, people often develop persistently negative beliefs about themselves.

These might include: 'I am damaged or permanently broken,' 'I am weak or inadequate,' 'I cannot trust my own judgment,' 'I am worthless,' 'I should have been able to prevent what happened,' 'There's something fundamentally wrong with me.' These beliefs often incorporate harsh self-blame and shame.

Many trauma survivors blame themselves for the trauma, for their responses during the trauma, or for their ongoing symptoms.

This self-blame, whilst painful, can serve a function: it provides a sense of control.

If the trauma happened because of something you did or did not do, then theoretically, you can prevent future trauma by being more careful, more vigilant, or making different choices.

The alternative, accepting that terrible things can happen randomly, that you had limited control, can feel even more frightening.

Beliefs about other people often change dramatically following trauma, particularly interpersonal trauma.

You might develop beliefs like: 'No one can be trusted,' 'People will hurt me if given the chance,' 'Everyone judges me,' 'Nobody understands or cares,' 'I am alone and cannot rely on anyone.' These beliefs create social isolation, as you withdraw from relationships to protect yourself from potential hurt.

The isolation then confirms the beliefs, without meaningful connection, you feel more alone and unsupported, which reinforces the idea that you cannot rely on others.

Breaking this cycle requires taking risks in relationships, gradually testing whether trusted people can indeed be trustworthy, despite your fears.

Beliefs about the world also shift following trauma.

You might develop perspectives like: 'The world is completely dangerous,' 'Bad things happen randomly and unpredictably,' 'There's no justice or fairness,' 'Nowhere is truly safe,' 'I need to be constantly vigilant because danger could strike at any moment.' These beliefs make it difficult to relax, to take appropriate risks, or to engage fully with life.

If you believe the world is fundamentally dangerous, why would you leave your house?

Why would you trust anyone?

Why would you invest in relationships or goals that could be taken away at any moment?

Beliefs about the future often become pessimistic or hopeless: 'My life is ruined,' 'I'll never recover,' 'Nothing good will ever happen again,' 'I'll feel this way forever,' 'There's no point trying to build a life because it will just be destroyed again.' These beliefs undermine motivation to engage in recovery work. (Herman, 2015)

If you genuinely believe you will never recover, why invest effort in therapy?

Why face avoided situations?

Why challenge negative thoughts?

This hopelessness is one of the most painful aspects of PTSD and one that requires deliberate attention in treatment.

How Cognitive Behavioural Therapy Addresses PTSD

Throughout this guide, we will explore the nature of trauma and PTSD, understand how CBT can help, and work through practical exercises and techniques that have helped thousands of people recover.

You will learn how to develop your own trauma narrative, challenge unhelpful thoughts, face your fears gradually and safely, and build a life worth living beyond the trauma.

This journey requires courage, but you have already demonstrated tremendous strength simply by surviving what you have been through and by picking up this guide.

Cognitive Behavioural Therapy (CBT) for PTSD is not a single technique but rather a comprehensive evidence-based approach that targets the multiple mechanisms maintaining the disorder.

Unlike some forms of therapy that focus primarily on understanding why the trauma happened or gaining insight into your emotional patterns, trauma-focused cognitive behavioural therapy is fundamentally pragmatic and skills-based. (Cohen et al., 2016)

The question isn't primarily 'Why did this happen to me?' or 'What does this mean about me?', though these questions may be explored, but rather 'What is keeping me stuck in PTSD right now, and what can I do to help myself heal?'

CBT for PTSD typically involves several core components, each targeting a different maintaining mechanism we have discussed.

First, psychoeducation, the educational component you are engaging with right now, helps you understand PTSD from a cognitive-behavioural perspective.

This is not just information for its own sake; understanding how PTSD works changes how you relate to your symptoms.

Instead of seeing yourself as broken or crazy, you understand your symptoms as understandable responses that can be modified.

This shift in perspective reduces shame, increases hope, and motivates engagement with treatment.

Second, memory processing work involves deliberately approaching the trauma memory in a structured, therapeutic way to facilitate its proper integration into your autobiographical memory.

This might be called 'trauma narrative work,' 'imaginal exposure,' 'reliving,' or similar terms depending on the specific protocol.

The fundamental principle is the same: by repeatedly, deliberately thinking through the trauma memory in detail whilst staying grounded in the present, you allow the memory to be processed differently.

The memory becomes properly contextualised in time and space, loses some of its fragmented, sensory quality, and begins to feel more like a coherent narrative of something that happened in the past rather than something happening in the present.

This memory work is often the most daunting aspect of treatment for people with PTSD. The idea of deliberately thinking about the worst moments of your life, in detail, repeatedly, understandably provokes anxiety. Many people worry: 'Will not this make me worse? Will not I be re-traumatised? Will not this be unbearable?' These concerns are understandable, but research and clinical experience demonstrate that structured memory processing, conducted appropriately, is not harmful, it is healing. The key is that you are approaching the memory in a very different context than the original trauma: you are safe, you have control (you can pause or stop if needed), you are with a supportive therapist or working through this guide at your own pace, and you are approaching the memory with the explicit goal of processing and integrating it rather than simply being overwhelmed by it.

Third, cognitive restructuring involves identifying and challenging the negative, unhelpful beliefs that maintain PTSD.

This is not about 'positive thinking' or forcing yourself to believe things that aren't true.

Rather, it is about examining your trauma-related beliefs carefully and considering whether they are accurate, helpful, and based on all available evidence.

Many beliefs that feel true in the grip of PTSD turn out to be overgeneralisations, distortions, or are based on incomplete information.

Through careful analysis, you can develop more balanced, accurate perspectives that reduce distress and support recovery. (Herman, 2015)

The Evidence Base: Why CBT Works for PTSD

This guide offers hope grounded in evidence.

Cognitive Behavioural Therapy (CBT) for PTSD is one of the most thoroughly researched and effective treatments available.

Numerous clinical trials and decades of practice have demonstrated that CBT can help people recover from even the most severe trauma.

Recovery does not mean forgetting what happened or pretending it didn't occur. (Herman, 2015)

Rather, it means reaching a place where the trauma no longer controls your life, where you can remember what happened without being overwhelmed, where you can move forward with purpose and meaning, and where you can reclaim the life you deserve.

When we say this approach is 'evidence-based,' we are referring to a substantial and growing body of rigorous scientific research demonstrating the effectiveness of trauma-focused CBT. (Bisson et al., 2013; NICE, 2018)

This is not anecdotal evidence or individual testimonials; whilst these have their place, they are not sufficient for establishing whether a treatment works.

Instead, the evidence comes from randomised controlled trials (RCTs), the gold standard for evaluating treatment effectiveness.

In these studies, participants with PTSD are randomly assigned to receive either trauma-focused CBT, another treatment, or a control condition (such as being on a waiting list).

Outcomes are measured systematically using validated assessment tools.

This rigorous methodology allows researchers to determine whether improvements are due to the specific treatment or to other factors like time passing, attention from a therapist, or expectation of improvement.

Meta-analyses, comprehensive studies that combine results from multiple individual RCTs using sophisticated statistical methods, consistently show that trauma-focused CBT produces large, clinically significant improvements in PTSD symptoms. (Bisson et al., 2013; NICE, 2018)

Effect sizes (a statistical measure of treatment impact that allows comparison across studies) for CBT-based treatments typically range from 1.0 to 2.0, which in clinical terms represents a substantial, meaningful difference between treated and untreated groups.

To put this in perspective, effect sizes above 0.8 are considered 'large' in psychological treatment research.

Trauma-focused CBT does not just produce modest improvements; it produces transformative change for many people. (Bisson et al., 2013; NICE, 2018)

A landmark meta-analysis published in 2007 by Bisson and colleagues in the British Journal of Psychiatry examined 38 RCTs of psychological treatments for PTSD.

The analysis found that trauma-focused CBT and Eye Movement Desensitisation and Reprocessing (EMDR) were the most effective treatments, both producing significantly better outcomes than waitlist controls, usual care, and several other psychological interventions. (Shapiro, 2018)

Subsequent meta-analyses have consistently confirmed these findings, with trauma-focused psychological therapies emerging as first-line treatments. (Bisson et al., 2013)

The National Institute for Health and Care Excellence (NICE) in the United Kingdom, which provides evidence-based guidance on effective healthcare interventions, conducted a comprehensive review of PTSD treatment research and issued clinical guidelines in 2018.

Based on their analysis of the available evidence, NICE recommends trauma-focused psychological therapies, specifically trauma-focused CBT and EMDR, as first-line treatments for PTSD in adults. (Shapiro, 2018)

This recommendation is based on the strength and consistency of evidence demonstrating their effectiveness.

Similar recommendations come from treatment guidelines developed by the American Psychological Association, the U.S.

Department of Veterans Affairs and Department of Defence, the Australian Centre for Post-traumatic Mental Health, and other respected organisations internationally. (Seal et al., 2007)

Long-term follow-up studies demonstrate that the benefits of trauma-focused CBT tend to be maintained over time. (Bisson et al., 2013; NICE, 2018)

Unlike some interventions that produce short-term improvements followed by relapse, CBT appears to produce durable change.

Studies following participants for six months, one year, two years, or even five years after treatment completion typically show maintained improvements, with some participants continuing to improve even after active therapy has ended.

This suggests that CBT does not just provide temporary symptom relief; it teaches skills and facilitates psychological changes that continue to benefit people long after therapy concludes.

Importantly, trauma-focused CBT has been demonstrated to be effective across diverse trauma types. (Bisson et al., 2013; NICE, 2018)

Whether your trauma involved combat, sexual assault, serious accidents, natural disasters, childhood abuse, medical trauma, terrorist attacks, or other experiences, the fundamental principles of trauma-focused CBT apply. (Bisson et al., 2013; NICE, 2018)

Whilst specific applications may be tailored to particular trauma types or populations, for example, combat-related PTSD might involve specific content about military experiences, whilst childhood abuse-related PTSD might address developmental impacts, the core elements remain consistent: processing traumatic memories, challenging unhelpful beliefs, and facing avoided situations. (Herman, 2015; Teicher & Samson, 2016)

Research demonstrates beneficial outcomes regardless of trauma type.

Research also demonstrates that CBT-based approaches work across different demographic groups, including different ages, genders, cultural backgrounds, and socioeconomic statuses.

Studies have been conducted with veterans, assault survivors, accident victims, refugees, first responders, and many other populations. (Seal et al., 2007)

Whilst cultural adaptations may enhance engagement and relevance, for example, by incorporating culturally appropriate metaphors, examples, or therapeutic approaches.

The fundamental CBT model has shown effectiveness internationally, across Western and non-Western cultures.

This suggests it taps into universal human psychological processes rather than being narrowly applicable to specific cultural groups.

A particularly important finding from research is that CBT appears to work not just for recently traumatised individuals but also for people with chronic, longstanding PTSD.

Some people worry that if they have had PTSD for years or even decades, it is too late to benefit from treatment.

Research contradicts this concern.

Studies including participants with PTSD of many years' duration show a significant improvement with trauma-focused CBT. (Bisson et al., 2013; NICE, 2018)

Whilst chronic PTSD may require longer or more intensive treatment than acute PTSD, recovery is possible even decades after the trauma. (Herman, 2015)

The brain retains its capacity to learn and change, with neuroplasticity, throughout life, which means that psychological change remains possible regardless of how long symptoms have persisted.

It is worth acknowledging that not everyone responds to CBT, and not everyone who responds experiences complete symptom resolution.

Research suggests that approximately 60-70% of people who complete a full course of trauma-focused CBT will no longer meet diagnostic criteria for PTSD at the end of treatment, a remarkably effective rate for any psychological intervention. (Foa & Rauch, 2004; Powers et al., 2010)

However, this also means that 30-40% continue to experience significant symptoms despite treatment. (Schoenfeld et al., 2016)

If you are in this latter group, this does not mean you have failed or that recovery is impossible; it may mean you need additional support, a different treatment approach, more intensive intervention, or attention to complicating factors such as ongoing life stressors, substance use, or physical health problems. (Herman, 2015)

Additionally, amongst those who do respond, many continue to experience some residual symptoms.

Complete absence of all PTSD symptoms is less common than a significant improvement to a manageable level.

This is important to understand so you can set realistic expectations.

Recovery typically means that symptoms are reduced to a level where they no longer significantly impair your functioning or quality of life, rather than complete symptom elimination. (Herman, 2015)

You might still occasionally have a nightmare or intrusive memory, particularly under stress, but these become manageable rather than overwhelming. (Raskind et al., 2007; Ross et al., 1989)

The goal is living well despite occasional symptoms, not achieving a state of perfect psychological health with zero symptoms.

How to Use This Guide Effectively

Remember, you do not have to walk this path alone.

Whilst this guide provides comprehensive information and exercises you can work through independently, many people find it helpful to collaborate with a qualified therapist.

Professional support can provide accountability, help you navigate difficult moments, offer personalized guidance, and ensure you are implementing techniques correctly.

If you would like professional support as you use this guide, organisations such as Talking Therapies UK (www.TalkingTherapies.co.uk) offer specialist trauma-focused CBT delivered by experienced therapists who understand what you are going through.

Many areas also have NHS Talking Therapies services that provide evidence-based psychological therapy, often free at the point of access.

This guide is designed to be both comprehensive and practical.

You will find detailed explanations of PTSD and how CBT addresses it, providing the theoretical foundation for understanding why particular techniques work.

You will find step-by-step instructions for therapeutic techniques, broken down into manageable components so you know exactly what to do.

You will find worksheets and exercises you can complete at your own pace, allowing you to apply concepts personally rather than just reading passively.

You will find real-world examples throughout, drawn from clinical practise but with identifying details changed to protect confidentiality, to illustrate concepts and demonstrate how techniques work in practise.

You will find regular opportunities for reflection and self-assessment, helping you track your progress and identify areas needing more attention.

And you will find suggestions for tailoring the approach to your specific needs, because recovery is not one-size-fits-all. (Herman, 2015)

Take your time with this material. Recovery is not a race, and there is no prize for rushing through. Some sections may feel emotionally challenging; that is normal. If you find yourself becoming overwhelmed, it is absolutely fine to take a break, practise some self-care, and return when you feel ready. This guide will still be here. You are in control of the pace. Some people work systematically, spending time with each chapter before moving on. Others prefer to skim through initially to get an overview, then return to work through exercises in detail. Still others dip in and out, focusing on chapters that feel most relevant to current struggles. There is no single 'right' way to use this guide. (Herman, 2015)

However, we do recommend that everyone read the foundational chapters on understanding PTSD and the CBT model before moving into the practical exercises. These chapters provide important context for the work ahead. Understanding why PTSD develops, what maintains it, and how CBT targets these maintaining factors will help you make sense of the exercises and implement them more effectively. It also provides motivation. When you understand why a particular exercise works, you are more likely to persist with it even when it feels difficult.

- Genetic factors play a role. Studies of twins show that PTSD has a heritable component
- people with family histories of anxiety, depression, or PTSD are more vulnerable. This does not mean PTSD is predetermined or inevitable
- genetics influence vulnerability but do not determine outcomes. Environmental factors and treatment can override genetic vulnerability.

Peritraumatic factors, what happens during the trauma itself, matter significantly. Peritraumatic dissociation (feeling detached, numb, or unreal during the trauma) predicts higher PTSD risk. This is paradoxical dissociation might seem protective in the moment, but it interferes with proper memory processing, leaving memories more fragmented and less integrated. Strong peritraumatic emotions, particularly horror, fear, helplessness, or shame, also predict higher PTSD risk.

Post-traumatic factors are particularly important and more modifiable than pre-trauma or peritraumatic factors.

Social support is one of the most powerful protective factors against PTSD.

People with strong, supportive relationships recover better than those who are isolated or whose relationships are strained.

This support does not require people to fully understand what you went through; simply having people who care, who are willing to listen without judgment, who provide practical help, and who maintain connection makes an enormous difference.

Conversely, negative social responses after trauma increase PTSD risk.

Being blamed for the trauma, having your experience minimised or dismissed, being told to 'just get over it,' experiencing judgment or stigma, or losing important relationships in the aftermath all worsen outcomes.

This is particularly problematic for certain trauma types.

Sexual assault survivors often face victim-blaming, combat veterans may encounter incomprehension or judgment from civilians, and people who have experienced mental health crises may face stigma. (Seal et al., 2007)

Chapter One: Understanding Post-Traumatic Stress Disorder

FAST TRACK - What You Will Learn

- Understanding PTSD helps you recognise your experience is a normal response to trauma
- PTSD affects millions of people worldwide—you are not alone
- Recovery is possible through evidence-based treatment (Herman, 2015)
- Knowing the facts about PTSD reduces shame and self-blame

Post-Traumatic Stress Disorder represents one of the most significant mental health conditions affecting millions of people worldwide. Understanding PTSD begins with recognising what trauma is, how it affects the brain and body, and why some people develop PTSD whilst others do not. This chapter provides comprehensive foundational knowledge about PTSD, establishing the groundwork for understanding treatment approaches discussed in subsequent chapters. Whether you are experiencing PTSD symptoms yourself, supporting someone with PTSD, or working as a clinician, this foundational understanding proves essential for effective recovery. (Herman, 2015)

What Constitutes Trauma? Defining Traumatic Events

Not all distressing experiences constitute trauma in the clinical sense.

Trauma, as defined in diagnostic criteria, involves exposure to actual or threatened death, serious injury, or sexual violence.

This exposure can occur through directly experiencing the traumatic event yourself, witnessing the event happening to others, learning that the event happened to a close family member or friend (particularly when the event was violent or accidental), or experiencing repeated or extreme exposure to aversive details of traumatic events, as often occurs with first responders, emergency service personnel, and professionals who work with trauma survivors.

This definition distinguishes trauma from other stressful or distressing life events that, whilst difficult, do not typically lead to PTSD.

Divorce, job loss, academic failure, or financial difficulties can certainly cause significant distress and might contribute to depression or anxiety, but they do not usually produce the specific constellation of symptoms characterising PTSD.

The key distinguishing feature involves threat to life or physical integrity, events that overwhelm normal coping mechanisms and fundamentally challenge assumptions about safety, control, and predictability in the world.

Common traumatic events that can lead to PTSD include:

- Combat exposure and military service in war zones
- Physical assault, including mugging, robbery, or being attacked
- Sexual assault and rape
- Serious accidents, such as car crashes, industrial accidents, or falls
- Natural disasters like earthquakes, floods, hurricanes, or wildfires
- Terrorist attacks or mass violence events
- Childhood abuse, including physical, sexual, or severe emotional abuse
- Domestic violence and intimate partner violence
- Serious medical trauma, such as life-threatening illness, intensive care unit experiences, or medical procedures experienced as traumatic
- Witnessing violence, death, or serious injury to others
- Being held captive, kidnapped, or imprisoned

This list is not exhaustive; any event meeting the criterion of actual or threatened death, serious injury, or sexual violence can potentially lead to PTSD. (Herman, 2015; Teicher & Samson, 2016)

Diagnostic Criteria for PTSD: Understanding the DSM-5 Definition

The Diagnostic and Statistical Manual of Mental Disorders, Fifth Edition (DSM-5), published by the American Psychiatric Association, provides the most widely used diagnostic criteria for PTSD in clinical practice and research.

Understanding these criteria helps you recognise whether symptoms you or someone you know experiences constitute PTSD versus normal distress following trauma.

PTSD requires meeting specific criteria across several domains, not simply feeling upset after a traumatic event.

The diagnosis includes exposure to trauma, intrusion symptoms such as flashbacks and nightmares, persistent avoidance of trauma-related stimuli, negative alterations in cognitions and mood, and marked alterations in arousal and reactivity. (Van der Kolk et al., 1996)

These symptoms must persist for more than one month, cause clinically significant distress or impairment, and not be attributable to substances or other medical conditions.

Prevalence and Risk Factors: Who Develops PTSD?

PTSD affects approximately 7 to 8 per cent of people in the United Kingdom and United States at some point in their lives.

However, prevalence varies dramatically across populations depending on exposure to different types of trauma.

Combat veterans experience PTSD at rates of 10 to 30 per cent. (Seal et al., 2007)

Sexual assault survivors develop PTSD at particularly high rates, approximately 50 per cent.

First responders, including police, firefighters, paramedics, and emergency department staff, experience elevated PTSD rates due to repeated trauma exposure. (Haugen et al., 2012)

Understanding risk factors helps explain why some people develop PTSD whilst others recover naturally.

Pre-trauma risk factors include previous trauma exposure, pre-existing mental health conditions, family history of mental health problems, and personality characteristics.

Peri-trauma factors involve trauma severity, interpersonal violence, perceived life threat, and peri-traumatic dissociation.

Post-trauma factors include lack of social support, additional life stressors, and ongoing exposure to trauma reminders.

The Course of PTSD Over Time

Understanding PTSD's typical course helps set realistic expectations for recovery. (Herman, 2015)

Immediately following trauma, most people experience acute stress reactions that resemble PTSD symptoms but do not yet constitute a disorder.

For many people, these symptoms gradually decrease over weeks and months as the brain naturally processes the trauma.

This natural recovery occurs in approximately half of trauma-exposed individuals, with symptoms resolving within three months. (Herman, 2015)

However, for others, symptoms persist or worsen beyond the first month, meeting criteria for PTSD.

Without treatment, chronic PTSD often follows a fluctuating course with periods of relative stability punctuated by symptom exacerbations triggered by reminders, stressors, or anniversaries.

With evidence-based treatment, significant symptom reduction and functional improvement occur for the majority of PTSD sufferers, demonstrating that recovery is achievable. (Herman, 2015)

Chapter Two: The Cognitive Behavioural Understanding of PTSD

- The CBT model explains how trauma memories become stuck
- Your brain's threat system becomes overly sensitive after trauma
- Understanding why symptoms persist gives hope for recovery (Herman, 2015)
- Cognitive Behavioural Therapy directly targets the problem

How Does PTSD Develop and Persist?

To understand how CBT helps with PTSD, we first need to understand how PTSD develops and, crucially, what keeps it going. The CBT model of PTSD, developed by researchers such as Anke Ehlers and David Clark at the University of Oxford, provides a comprehensive framework for understanding this. This model has been refined over decades of research and clinical practice and forms the theoretical foundation for trauma-focused CBT. (Bisson et al., 2013; NICE, 2018)

During a traumatic event, our brain operates in survival mode.

The threat-detection parts of our brain, particularly the amygdala, a small almond-shaped structure deep in the temporal lobe, become highly activated, whilst the parts responsible for logical thinking and contextual processing, particularly areas of the prefrontal cortex, become relatively less active. (LeDoux, 1998)

This makes profound evolutionary sense: when facing immediate danger, you need to react quickly rather than ponder philosophically.

Survival depends on rapid, automatic responses rather than careful, deliberate reasoning.

As a result of this survival-mode processing, traumatic memories are encoded differently from ordinary memories.

Normal autobiographical memories are processed by the hippocampus, which provides temporal and spatial context, when and where events occurred, the sequence of events, and how the experience fits into your life story. (Eichenbaum, 2000)

These normal memories are stored with clear context markers that tell your brain, 'This happened then, in that place, and it is over now.' When you recall a normal memory, you maintain clear awareness that you are remembering something from the past.

Traumatic memories, in contrast, are encoded primarily by the amygdala without adequate hippocampal processing. (LeDoux, 1998)

They may be fragmented, sensory-dominated (full of images, sounds, smells, physical sensations, and overwhelming emotions), and poorly integrated into your autobiographical memory, your life story.

These memories lack the proper context markers that would allow your brain to recognise them as belonging to the past.

When triggered, they are experienced with full emotional intensity and a sense of 'nowness,' as though the trauma is happening in the present moment rather than being a memory of something that occurred in the past.

The Ehlers and Clark Model: A Sense of Current Threat

The central premise of the Ehlers and Clark model is this: PTSD persists when trauma survivors process the experience in a way that creates a sense of serious current threat.

Even though the traumatic event is over, it does not feel over.

The threat feels present and ongoing.

This sense of current threat isn't a conscious belief; you might intellectually know that you are safe now, but your emotional and physiological systems respond as though danger is imminent.

This discrepancy between intellectual knowledge ('the trauma is over') and emotional/physical experience ('I am in danger right now') is central to understanding PTSD.

This sense of current threat arises from two main sources, each of which can independently maintain PTSD, but which typically interact to create a self-perpetuating cycle. Understanding both sources is crucial because an effective treatment must address both. Addressing only one source typically produces an incomplete recovery. (Herman, 2015)

The first source is the nature of the trauma memory itself. Because traumatic memories are poorly integrated into your autobiographical memory and lack proper temporal context, they can be easily triggered by stimuli in your current environment. When triggered, these memories are re-experienced with the same emotional intensity and sense of 'nowness' as the original event. You do not remember the trauma; you re-live it. The boundaries between past and present collapse.

Imagine the difference between remembering your last birthday party and re-experiencing a traumatic event.

When you remember your birthday, you know you are thinking about something that happened in the past.

You might recall pleasant feelings and specific moments, but you maintain clear awareness that you are in the present, safely remembering.

You can choose to think about it in detail or let the memory fade.

You have control.

The memory feels like a memory, contextualised in time and space, part of your life story.

With trauma memories in PTSD, this clear distinction between past and present dissolves.

The memory feels like it is happening now.

It arrives unbidden, triggered by something you may not even consciously notice.

The emotions are as intense as they were during the actual trauma, the fear, horror, helplessness, rage, or shame feel utterly real and present.

Your body responds as though you are genuinely in danger, heart racing, muscles tensing, breathing quickening, stress hormones flooding your system.

You lose awareness of your current, safe environment.

For the duration of the flashback or intrusive memory, your brain and body genuinely believe the trauma is happening again.

These memories can be triggered by obvious reminders, returning to the location where the trauma occurred, encountering the perpetrator, or seeing news coverage of similar events.

But they can also be triggered by subtle, seemingly innocuous cues that share some quality with the original trauma.

A particular tone of voice might trigger memories of your abuser, even when the current speaker means no harm.

The angle of sunlight at a certain time of day might trigger combat memories.

A fleeting smell might trigger memories of a fire or assault.

The sensation of your heart racing during exercise might trigger memories of the fear you felt during trauma.

Even internal cues, particular thoughts, emotions, or physical sensations, can trigger the memory.

Because the triggers can be so subtle and outside of conscious awareness, flashbacks and intrusive memories can feel completely random and unpredictable. (Van der Kolk et al., 1996)

You might be having a perfectly normal day when suddenly you are overwhelmed by trauma memories, with no idea what triggered them.

This unpredictability adds to your sense of lacking control and safety.

If you cannot predict when memories will strike, how can you ever feel safe?

This drives further avoidance as you attempt to eliminate potential triggers, but because triggers can be so varied and subtle, complete avoidance is impossible.

Negative Appraisals of the Trauma and Its Consequences (Ehlers & Clark, 2000)

The second major source of ongoing threat comes from the meanings you have attached to the trauma and its aftermath. These interpretations, or 'appraisals' in cognitive therapy terminology, can be about the trauma itself, your responses during the trauma, your current symptoms, other people's responses, or implications for your future. These appraisals create and maintain a sense of current threat even when you are physically safe. They are often outside of conscious awareness, operating as background assumptions that shape your emotional responses without you deliberately thinking them through. (Ehlers & Clark, 2000)

Appraisals about the trauma itself might include thoughts like: 'I should have been able to stop it,' 'The trauma happened because I am weak, bad, or unlucky,' 'I attracted this to myself somehow,' 'I deserved what happened,' 'The fact that this happened proves I am fundamentally flawed,' or 'This trauma has ruined my entire life.' These appraisals typically involve excessive self-blame, overgeneralisation (one bad event means your entire life is ruined), or drawing sweeping conclusions about yourself based on the trauma. Whilst these appraisals feel absolutely true, they are usually distorted or based on incomplete evidence.

Self-blame is particularly common and deserves special attention.

Many trauma survivors blame themselves for the trauma or for aspects of how it unfolded.

This self-blame, whilst painful, serves a psychological function: it provides a sense of control.

The alternative, accepting that terrible things can happen randomly, that you had limited or no control, that the world is fundamentally unpredictable, can feel even more frightening.

So, your mind may prefer self-blame, even though it is painful and usually inaccurate, because it maintains an illusion of control.

However, self-blame is almost always based on distorted thinking.

You might blame yourself for decisions made in the heat of the moment without full information, judging past-you by standards that are only possible with hindsight.

You might blame yourself for normal human limitations, not being strong enough to fight off an attacker, not being able to predict the future, or not being superhuman.

You might blame yourself for the perpetrator's choices, taking responsibility for another person's actions.

Challenging this self-blame is crucial for recovery, though it requires careful, compassionate exploration rather than simply telling yourself to stop blaming yourself. (Herman, 2015)

Appraisals about your reactions during the trauma create another layer of distress and perceived current threat. You might think: 'I didn't fight back enough, so I am a coward,' 'The fact that I froze means I am weak,' 'I should have done more to help others,' 'My body responded in ways I am ashamed of' (for example, experiencing physical arousal during sexual assault, which is a physiological response that does not indicate consent or enjoyment), 'I didn't react the way a strong person would,' or 'The way I responded proves something is wrong with me.'

These appraisals reflect a misunderstanding about trauma responses. (Ehlers & Clark, 2000)

As we've discussed, during extreme threat, your nervous system takes over, producing automatic survival responses: fight, flight, freeze, or fawn. (Porges, 2011; Levine, 2008)

You do not consciously choose these responses; they emerge from ancient brain structures designed to maximise survival. (LeDoux, 1998)

Freezing, for example, often occurs when fight or flight aren't viable options; it is an adaptive response that can save your life by making you less of a target or conserving energy. (Porges, 2011)

Judging these automatic responses as cowardly or weak reflects a misunderstanding of neurobiology, not an accurate assessment of your character.

Appraisals about the symptoms you are currently experiencing create additional distress and maintain the sense of current threat. You might think: 'These symptoms mean I am going crazy,' 'I am losing control of my mind,' 'I'll never be able to cope with normal life again,' 'I am permanently damaged or broken,' 'These symptoms mean I am weak,' 'I am failing because I still have symptoms,' or 'If people knew about my symptoms, they'd think I was crazy.' These appraisals about symptoms are particularly problematic because they create secondary distress; you are not just distressed by the symptoms themselves but also by what you believe the symptoms mean about you. (Ehlers & Clark, 2000)

This secondary distress can be more debilitating than the primary symptoms.

For example, having an intrusive memory is distressing, but believing that intrusive memory means you are going crazy or permanently damaged makes it much more distressing.

Similarly, experiencing intense anxiety is unpleasant, but believing that anxiety means you are weak or failing compounds the suffering.

Part of recovery involves learning that symptoms, whilst genuinely difficult, do not mean what you fear they mean. (Herman, 2015)

They are not evidence of permanent damage, weakness, or impending madness; they are understandable responses to trauma that can be modified through appropriate treatment.

Appraisals about other people's responses to your trauma and symptoms create a social-related current threat. (Ehlers & Clark, 2000)

You might think: 'Nobody understands what I went through,' 'People judge me for not being over it,' 'If people knew the details, they'd think less of me,' 'I cannot trust anyone anymore,' 'Everyone will hurt me eventually,' 'People's support is fake or will disappear,' or 'I am a burden to others with my symptoms.' These appraisals drive social withdrawal and isolation, preventing you from receiving the support that could facilitate recovery. (Ehlers & Clark, 2000)

They also create self-fulfilling prophecies.

If you believe people cannot be trusted and withdraw from relationships, you do not have opportunities to learn that some people can indeed be trustworthy and supportive.

Appraisals about implications for the future create ongoing hopelessness and maintain PTSD. (Ehlers & Clark, 2000)

You might think: 'Something terrible will happen again,' 'I'll never feel safe,' 'My life is ruined forever,' 'I'll always feel this way,' 'There's no point trying to build a life because it will just be destroyed again,' 'I cannot trust that good things will last,' or 'The future holds only more pain.' These catastrophic predictions undermine motivation to engage in treatment or rebuild your life. (Clark, 1999)

If you genuinely believe you'll never recover, why invest effort in recovery work? (Herman, 2015)

If you believe the future holds only pain, why plan or hope?

These negative appraisals maintain a sense of current threat even when you are physically safe. (Ehlers & Clark, 2000)

If you believe you are permanently damaged, the world is entirely dangerous, another trauma is inevitable, and you cannot trust anyone, then of course you'll remain in a state of high alert and distress.

These beliefs make hypervigilance seem necessary and adaptive rather than excessive. (Porges, 2011; Yehuda & Seckl, 2011)

They make avoidance seem like sensible protection rather than a maintaining factor.

They make social withdrawal seem like necessary self-protection rather than isolation that worsens suffering. (Ashton, 2002)

The Maintaining Cycle: Why PTSD Does not Just Go Away

If traumatic memories and negative appraisals were the whole story, PTSD might still naturally resolve over time as these memories were gradually processed, and beliefs were challenged through normal life experiences. (Ehlers & Clark, 2000)

However, people with PTSD often engage in understandable coping strategies that, whilst providing short-term relief, actually prevent natural recovery and maintain the disorder. (Clark, 1999)

These are called 'maintaining behaviours' or 'safety behaviours,' and understanding them is crucial because they are often the primary target of treatment. (Clark, 1999)

You cannot simply stop having intrusive memories or immediately change deeply held beliefs, but you can change your behaviour, and changing behaviour creates opportunities for memories to be processed and beliefs to be challenged. (Van der Kolk et al., 1996)

Avoidance, which we've mentioned repeatedly, is the most obvious and important maintaining behaviour.

When you avoid reminders of the trauma, you achieve temporary relief from distress.

Your anxiety decreases.

You feel safer.

This immediate reinforcement makes avoidance powerfully compelling.

However, avoidance prevents you from learning several crucial things.

First, it prevents you from learning that the reminders themselves are not dangerous.

The car park where you were assaulted is not inherently dangerous; it is a reminder, not a repeat of the actual threat.

But if you always avoid car parks, you never have the opportunity to learn this distinction.

Many people with PTSD believe that if they encounter a powerful trigger, they'll be completely overwhelmed, lose control, fall apart, or never recover.

These catastrophic predictions feel absolutely true and motivate desperate avoidance. (Clark, 1999)

Whilst triggers do provoke genuine distress, most people who face them (with appropriate support and preparation) discover that the distress, whilst uncomfortable, is tolerable.

It reaches a peak and then naturally decreases; anxiety and fear cannot stay at maximum intensity indefinitely.

Your body physically cannot maintain that level of arousal.

But you can only learn this through experience; avoidance prevents this crucial learning.

Memories need to be thought about, talked about, and approached for them to become properly filed away in your autobiographical memory system with appropriate context markers.

This is why trauma-focused therapy involves deliberately approaching the trauma memory rather than avoiding it; this allows the processing and integration that lead to genuine healing.

Fourth, avoidance progressively shrinks your life, creating a secondary problem that can become as impairing as the PTSD itself.

What often begins as avoiding specific, trauma-related situations can gradually generalise to avoiding broader and broader categories of experience.

Someone who avoids the specific car park where they were assaulted might gradually avoid all car parks, then all enclosed spaces, leaving home at night, then leaving home entirely.

Someone who avoids thinking about their combat trauma might avoid all military-related content, then all news coverage, then films with conflict, then social situations where people might ask about their service, then all social situations.

This shrinking of life is one of the most tragic aspects of PTSD; people become prisoners of their avoidance, unable to work, socialise, pursue interests, or engage with activities they once valued.

I am too weak, fragile, or damaged to cope with this situation.

The world is too dangerous for me to engage with normally.

I need to hide and protect myself because I am not capable of facing life.' These beliefs, operating at a deep, often unconscious level, then drive further avoidance, creating a self-perpetuating cycle.

You avoid because you believe you cannot cope, and the avoidance confirms that you cannot cope (because you never evaluate whether you actually can).

Safety Behaviours: Subtle Avoidance (Clark, 1999)

Safety behaviours are subtle protective actions that people take to prevent feared catastrophes when in triggering situations. Unlike outright avoidance (staying away entirely), safety behaviours involve entering situations but doing things to feel safer. These behaviours are often less obvious than avoidance and can be harder to identify, but they are equally important in maintaining PTSD because they prevent you from learning that you are safe without these precautions.

Examples of safety behaviours might include: always sitting near exits so you can escape if needed; constantly scanning your environment for threats rather than relaxing; carrying weapons or defensive items like pepper spray, alarms, or knives; only going out with trusted companions rather than venturing out alone; checking and rechecking locks repeatedly; maintaining constant contact with someone via phone when out; avoiding eye contact with people; wearing clothing designed to make you less visible or noticeable; planning escape routes before entering any building; positioning yourself with your back to walls; avoiding certain times of day even when in otherwise safe locations; or using alcohol or medication to tolerate situations. (Clark, 1999)

Whilst understandable, safety behaviours prevent you from learning that you are safe without these precautions. (Clark, 1999)

They maintain the belief that disaster is always imminent and only your vigilance and protective actions prevent it.

Consider someone who always sits near exits: they never learn that they would be perfectly safe sitting elsewhere, because they never try.

The belief 'I am only safe if I can escape quickly' remains untested.

Consider someone who constantly scans for threats: they never learn that they can relax their vigilance without dreadful things happening.

The belief 'I must stay constantly alert to prevent danger' remains confirmed.

Moreover, safety behaviours often have costs. (Clark, 1999)

They maintain anxiety and hyperarousal; you cannot truly relax when you are constantly scanning for threats or planning escape routes.

They interfere with normal activities, constantly checking your phone for safety contact interrupts conversations and activities.

They can create social difficulties, refusing to go anywhere without your trusted companion limits your independence and puts pressure on that relationship. (Lader, 2011; Ashton, 2002)

They can be expensive; always taking taxis instead of using public transport adds up.

They can reinforce unhelpful beliefs, carrying weapons confirms that the world is dangerous, and you need protection.

Part of recovery involves gradually reducing safety behaviours, not all at once but systematically, to test whether your feared catastrophes occur. This is called 'dropping safety behaviours' in CBT terminology. For example, you might experiment with sitting in the middle of a cinema rather than near the exit, or going to a familiar shop alone rather than with your companion, or reducing how often you check locks from ten times to eight times, then six, then four. These experiments allow you to gather new evidence: 'I sat in the middle of the cinema and nothing bad happened. I felt anxious initially, but the anxiety decreased as the film progressed. I coped fine without being near the exit.' This new evidence begins to challenge and modify your beliefs about danger and your capacity to cope. (Clark, 1999)

Rumination and Worry: Unhelpful Mental Processes

Many people with PTSD spend considerable time thinking about the trauma, but in unhelpful ways. This isn't the same as productive processing of the memory, rather, it is repetitive, circular thinking that maintains distress without leading to resolution. This unhelpful thinking comes in several forms.

Rumination involves repetitively thinking about the trauma, but focusing on questions that have no satisfying answers: 'Why did this happen to me?' 'What if I had done something differently?' 'What does this mean about me?' 'Why can't I just get over it?' You might endlessly analyse what you could or should have done differently, replay the worst moments repeatedly, ruminate about the unfairness or injustice, or focus repeatedly on the worst moments without processing the whole experience.

This rumination feels like you are doing something productive, trying to understand, make sense of, or resolve the trauma, but it keeps you stuck in negative thinking patterns without moving towards resolution.

It is the mental equivalent of picking at a wound without cleaning or dressing it properly.

Worry about future trauma represents another form of unhelpful thinking.

You might spend considerable time thinking about whether another trauma will occur, trying to anticipate and prevent it, imagining worst-case scenarios, or planning what you would do if something bad happened.

This worry feels protective; surely anticipating danger helps you prevent it?

However, worry typically focuses on catastrophic scenarios that are very unlikely, generates anxiety without producing practical solutions, and maintains your sense that the world is dangerous and you are vulnerable.

Worry is distinct from practical planning.

Practical planning involves identifying realistic risks, developing proportionate precautions, and then moving on.

Worry involves repeatedly imagining worst-case scenarios without resolution.

Thought suppression, trying to push away or not think about trauma-related content, is another unhelpful mental process. This might seem like an effective strategy: if thoughts about the trauma are distressing, just do not think about them. However, thought suppression typically backfires. Research demonstrates the 'rebound effect': the more you try to suppress thoughts, the more they return. Try this experiment: for the next ten seconds, try extremely hard not to think about a white bear. Do not think about what a white bear looks like, how it moves, or what it sounds like. Just do not think about it. What happens? The white bear keeps appearing in your mind. This is the rebound effect. Moreover, thought suppression prevents memory processing; memories that are consistently pushed away remain unprocessed and therefore maintain their power.

These unhelpful mental processes, rumination, worry, and thought suppression, maintain PTSD by keeping you focused on the trauma in unproductive ways, preventing proper memory processing, maintaining negative beliefs, and generating ongoing distress. Part of treatment involves recognising these patterns and learning alternative ways of relating to trauma-related thoughts, ways that involve deliberate, structured processing rather than rumination, practical problem-solving rather than worry, and mindful awareness rather than suppression.

The Complete CBT Model: Putting It All Together

We can now see the complete picture of how PTSD develops and persists according to the CBT model. Understanding this complete model is crucial because it reveals multiple points of intervention, multiple ways to break the cycle, and facilitates recovery. Effective treatment does not rely on changing just one thing; it systematically addresses all the maintaining factors. (Herman, 2015)

First, a traumatic event occurs during which your brain processes information in survival mode, creating fragmented, sensory-based memories that are not properly integrated into your life story. These memories lack the temporal and spatial context markers that would allow your brain to recognise them as belonging to the past. Instead, they remain 'stuck' in the present, ready to be triggered with full emotional intensity.

Second, you develop negative appraisals about the trauma, your responses during the trauma, your current symptoms, other people, and your future. (Ehlers & Clark, 2000)

These appraisals create a sense of ongoing current threat even though the trauma is over. (Ehlers & Clark, 2000)

They tell you: 'I am damaged,' 'The world is dangerous,' 'I cannot cope,' 'Another trauma is inevitable,' 'Nobody can be trusted,' 'I will never recover.' These beliefs, operating at both conscious and unconscious levels, maintain hypervigilance, avoidance, and distress. (Porges, 2011; Yehuda & Seckl, 2011)

Third, the nature of the trauma memory means it is easily triggered and re-experienced with full emotional intensity, feeling like it is happening now rather than being a memory of something that happened in the past.

Triggers can be obvious or subtle, conscious or outside awareness.

When triggered, you experience flashbacks, intrusive memories, or intense emotional and physical reactions. (Van der Kolk et al., 1996)

These re-experiencing symptoms confirm your sense of current threat: 'See, I am not safe, the trauma feels like it is happening again.'

Fourth, you engage in understandable but unhelpful coping strategies, avoidance, safety behaviours, rumination, worry, thought suppression, which provide short-term relief but prevent the memory from being processed and the negative appraisals from being challenged. (Ehlers & Clark, 2000)

Avoidance prevents you from learning that triggers are not dangerous, that you can tolerate distress, and from processing the memory.

Safety behaviours prevent you from learning that you are safe without constant precautions. (Clark, 1999)

Rumination keeps you stuck in negative thinking without resolution.

These strategies maintain the disorder by preventing the natural recovery processes that would otherwise occur. (Herman, 2015)

Fifth, these maintaining behaviours keep you stuck in the cycle, preventing natural recovery and confirming your negative beliefs. The avoidance confirms 'I cannot cope.' The hypervigilance confirms 'The world is dangerous.' The failure of the memory to naturally resolve confirms 'I am permanently damaged.' Each element reinforces the others in a self-perpetuating system. (Porges, 2011; Yehuda & Seckl, 2011)

This creates a self-perpetuating cycle where each element reinforces the others. The good news is that by understanding this cycle, we can identify multiple points of intervention, ways to break the cycle, and allow recovery to begin. We do not need to change everything at once. Breaking the cycle at any point begins to disrupt the entire system. (Herman, 2015)

Points of Intervention: How CBT Breaks the Cycle

CBT for PTSD systematically addresses each maintaining factor.

First, through memory processing work (also called trauma narrative work, imaginal exposure, or reliving), you deliberately approach the trauma memory in a structured, therapeutic way.

By repeatedly thinking through the memory in detail whilst staying grounded in the present, you facilitate its proper integration into your autobiographical memory.

The memory acquires proper context markers ('this happened then, in the past, and it is over now'), becomes less fragmented and more coherent, and begins to lose its overwhelming emotional charge.

It transforms from something that feels like it is happening now to something that clearly happened in the past.

Second, through cognitive restructuring, you identify and challenge the negative appraisals, maintaining your sense of current threat. (Ehlers & Clark, 2000)

This involves carefully examining beliefs like 'I am permanently damaged,' 'The world is entirely dangerous,' or 'I'll never recover,' and considering whether they are accurate, helpful, and based on all available evidence.

Often, these beliefs turn out to be overgeneralisations, distortions, or are based on incomplete information.

Through careful analysis, you develop more balanced, accurate perspectives that reduce distress and support recovery. (Herman, 2015)

Third, through behavioural experiments and graded exposure, you systematically face avoided situations.

You do not do this randomly or recklessly; you develop a hierarchy of avoided situations from least to most difficult, and work through them gradually, starting with manageable challenges.

- Through these exposures, you learn that: triggers are not themselves dangerous
- you can tolerate the distress they provoke
- feared catastrophes do not occur
- and you are more capable than you believed.

Each successful exposure provides evidence that challenges negative beliefs and builds confidence.

Fourth, you learn to recognise and modify unhelpful mental processes, rumination, worry, and thought suppression, replacing them with more helpful approaches. Instead of ruminating endlessly, you learn structured memory processing. Instead of worrying about catastrophes, you learn practical problem-solving. Instead of suppressing thoughts, you learn mindful awareness and acceptance.

Fifth, you gradually drop safety behaviours, testing whether feared catastrophes occur without constant precautions. You might experiment with sitting away from exits, going out without your companion, reducing lock-checking, or relaxing hypervigilance. These experiments provide evidence that you are safer than you feel and more capable than you believe. (Porges, 2011; Yehuda & Seckl, 2011)

Parallels with Other Trauma Models

It is worth noting that whilst this guide focuses on CBT, other therapeutic approaches conceptualise trauma in similar ways, recognising the importance of memory processing and meaning making. These approaches, whilst using different techniques, target the same underlying mechanisms. This convergence suggests that we are understanding fundamental truths about how trauma affects people and how healing occurs.

Eye Movement Desensitisation and Reprocessing (EMDR) also focuses on processing inadequately integrated traumatic memories. (Shapiro, 2018)

EMDR uses bilateral stimulation, typically side-to-side eye movements, though tapping or auditory tones can also be used, to facilitate the reprocessing of traumatic memories. (Shapiro, 2018)

During EMDR sessions, you focus on the traumatic memory whilst simultaneously tracking a moving object with your eyes or receiving other bilateral stimulation. (Shapiro, 2018)

The theory suggests this facilitates the brain's natural information processing system, allowing traumatic memories to become properly integrated and lose their emotional charge.

Both CBT and EMDR recognise that traumatic memories are 'stuck', inadequately processed and integrated, and need specific therapeutic work to become properly filed away. The techniques differ; CBT uses prolonged, detailed verbal processing of memories, whilst EMDR uses briefer memory activation with bilateral stimulation, but the underlying principle is similar. Both approaches have strong research support demonstrating effectiveness. (Shapiro, 2018)

Compassion-Focused Therapy, developed by Paul Gilbert, emphasises the role of shame and self-criticism in maintaining PTSD.

Many trauma survivors engage in harsh self-blame and self-criticism, which compounds their suffering.

Compassion-Focused Therapy teaches skills for developing self-compassion, treating yourself with the same kindness you would offer a good friend.

This complements CBT's cognitive work: whilst CBT helps you develop more accurate, balanced thoughts, Compassion-Focused Therapy helps you develop a kinder, more supportive relationship with yourself.

Chapter Three: Preparing for Recovery Work (Herman, 2015)

- Stabilisation is the foundation for successful recovery (Herman, 2015)
- Coping skills and safety planning must come before trauma processing (Stanley & Brown, 2012)
- Building support networks strengthens your resilience (Bonanno, 2004)
- This chapter provides tools you can use immediately

Managing Flashbacks: Complete Protocol (Van der Kolk et al., 1996)

Flashback management requires a comprehensive approach addressing before, during, and after episodes. Preparation prevents some flashbacks and reduces the severity when they occur. Intervention during flashbacks shortens duration and intensity. Post-flashback care supports recovery and provides learning for future prevention. Pre-flashback preparation involves identifying triggers systematically. Keep a detailed log: date, time, trigger, flashback content, intensity (0-10), duration, and what helped. Patterns emerge showing common triggers you can prepare for or avoid; warning signs preceding flashbacks; situations increasing vulnerability; and an effective intervention. This knowledge lets you anticipate flashbacks and respond more effectively when they occur. Create a flashback safety plan collaboratively with a therapist: list your common triggers; describe your typical flashback presentation (Do you freeze? Become agitated? Dissociate?); identify grounding techniques that work for you specifically; list people to contact for support; prepare flashback coping cards with grounding statements you can read; and establish recovery practices for after flashbacks. Having a plan reduces panic when flashbacks occur; you know what to do rather than scrambling. During flashbacks, implement protocol immediately: physically separate from trigger if possible; orient to present: state your name, current age, today's date, where you are aloud; engage senses intensely: touch objects noticing texture, smell strong scent, look at colours noticing details; remind yourself repeatedly: That was then, this is now, I am safe, this is flashback not current danger; control breathing to slow heart rate; and wait patiently for flashback to pass knowing it will end. Do not fight the flashback, which intensifies it. Orient, ground, wait. Complex flashbacks involving multiple sensory modalities or extended duration require additional intervention: call trusted person who can talk you through grounding; remove yourself to safe space if you are in triggering environment; use most powerful grounding techniques in your arsenal; consider taking prescribed PRN anxiety medication if you have it; and do not try to continue normal activities, give yourself permission to pause and focus entirely on managing flashback. Trying to push through typically prolongs the flashback. post-flashback care is essential yet often neglected. After flashback ends: rest, flashbacks are physiologically exhausting; practise self-compassion rather than self-criticism; debrief what happened: what triggered it, what helped, what to do differently next time; reconnect with the present through gentle activities; reach out to support person if that helps; and plan to discuss flashback with therapist next session. Processing flashbacks therapeutically prevents them from maintaining trauma rather than just managing episodes as they occur. Emotional flashbacks, intense feelings disconnected from the current situation, require a modified approach. You might not realise you are experiencing a flashback since there's no visual/sensory memory, just overwhelming emotion. Clues include emotion intensity disproportionate to the situation; feeling suddenly like a child; difficulty identifying what triggered the emotion; and a sense of being transported somewhere else emotionally. Manage by: recognising emotional flashback is occurring; asking: What does this feeling remind me of?; orienting to present whilst acknowledging past pain: I felt this during trauma, but I am here now and safe; self-soothing the part of you still feeling traumatized; and gradually reconnecting with present moment and current reality. Reducing flashback frequency long-term requires processing traumatic memories therapeutically. Flashbacks represent unprocessed trauma breaking into consciousness. Evidence-based trauma treatment, PE, CPT, EMDR, or other trauma-focused approaches, processes memories, making flashbacks less frequent and intense over time. Whilst grounding manages individual flashbacks, trauma processing addresses the root cause. Combine effective flashback management with trauma-focused treatment for optimal long-term outcomes. (Shapiro, 2018)

Sleep Optimisation for PTSD: Comprehensive Approach

Sleep disturbance in PTSD involves multiple mechanisms requiring multi-pronged intervention.

Hyperarousal keeps the nervous system activated, preventing sleep initiation.

Nightmares disrupt sleep maintenance. (Ross et al., 1989)

Avoidance of bed due to nightmare anticipation creates sleep deprivation. (Raskind et al., 2007; Ross et al., 1989)

Addressing all mechanisms simultaneously produces better outcomes than targeting any single aspect.

- Sleep hygiene basics provide foundation: consistent sleep/wake times including weekends (Perlis et al., 2005)
- bedroom used only for sleep and sex, not other activities
- comfortable sleep environment (cool temperature, dark, quiet)
- avoiding screens 1-2 hours before bed (blue light suppresses melatonin)
- avoiding caffeine after noon and alcohol before bed (disrupts sleep architecture)
- limiting daytime napping
- and establishing a relaxing bedtime routine signaling body that it is time to sleep.

These basics sound simple, but many PTSD patients violate them chronically, maintaining sleep disturbance.

Arousal reduction before bed directly addresses hyperarousal, preventing sleep.

Progressive muscle relaxation systematically releases tension accumulated throughout the day.

Starting with toes, tense the muscle group for 5 seconds, then release completely, noticing the difference between tension and relaxation.

Progress through the entire body: feet, calves, thighs, abdomen, chest, hands, arms, shoulders, neck, face.

This practice decreases physiological arousal incompatible with sleep whilst teaching body awareness of tension and relaxation.

Breathing exercises activate the parasympathetic nervous system, promoting calm. (Porges, 2011)

4-7-8 breathing: inhale through the nose for 4 counts, hold breath for 7 counts, exhale through the mouth for 8 counts, repeat 4 times.

The extended exhale activates the parasympathetic system.

Alternatively, diaphragmatic breathing: breathe deeply into the belly rather than the chest, ensuring the belly expands on inhale.

Practise nightly, creating a conditioned association between breathing practice and sleep.

Imagery for sleep uses pleasant mental imagery, replacing intrusive trauma imagery.

Develop a detailed safe place visualisation: a location where you feel completely safe, real or imaginary.

Before bed, visualise this place engaging all senses: what you see, hear, smell, feel physically, and experience emotionally.

This pleasant imagery occupies mind space that might otherwise be filled with trauma imagery whilst promoting relaxation.

Combine with breathing exercises for a powerful effect.

- Cognitive interventions address unhelpful sleep beliefs maintaining insomnia: I must sleep 8 hours or I cannot function (catastrophising)
- I'll never sleep well with PTSD (hopelessness)
- I should fall asleep immediately (unrealistic expectation)
- I must stay in bed trying to sleep (increases sleep anxiety).

- Challenge these beliefs: Many people function adequately on less than 8 hours
- sleep improves with treatment
- 20-30 minutes to fall asleep is normal
- staying in bed awake creates a conditioned association between bed and wakefulness
- If not asleep in 20 minutes, get up and do a quiet activity until sleep.

Nightmare management reduces sleep disruption from trauma dreams. (Raskind et al., 2007; Ross et al., 1989)

- Image Rehearsal Therapy (IRT) involves writing down recurrent nightmares
- changing the nightmare narrative to have a neutral or positive ending, you create (Raskind et al., 2007; Ross et al., 1989)
- rehearsing the new dream script during the day through visualisation
- and repeating nightly before sleep.

These conditions brain to modify dream content.

Research shows IRT significantly reduces nightmare frequency and intensity. (Raskind et al., 2007)

Practise consistently, and effectiveness builds over time.

Lucid dreaming techniques give some control during nightmares. (Ross et al., 1989)

Reality testing throughout the day, regularly checking: Am I dreaming?

How do I know I am awake?, creates a habit mind carries into dreams.

When a nightmare occurs, and you recognise you are dreaming, you might be able to change dream content, wake yourself up, or reduce fear by remembering it is a dream, not reality. (Raskind et al., 2007; Ross et al., 1989)

Not everyone can achieve lucid dreaming, but for those who can, it reduces nightmare distress significantly. (Raskind et al., 2007; Ross et al., 1989)

Medication for sleep should be used judiciously as an adjunct, not a primary intervention.

Prazosin specifically targets PTSD nightmares by blocking noradrenergic activity. (Ross et al., 1989)

Research shows mixed results, but many patients report reduced nightmare frequency and intensity. (Raskind et al., 2007)

Discuss with a psychiatrist if nightmares remain severe despite behavioural interventions. (Ross et al., 1989)

Avoid benzodiazepines for chronic use, tolerance, dependence, and memory impairment, making them a poor long-term choice. (Ashton, 2002; Lader, 2011; NICE, 2018)

Trazodone or mirtazapine might help sleep whilst treating comorbid depression.

Sleep tracking provides objective data about patterns and progress.

Apps like CBT-I Coach track sleep onset latency, night awakenings, total sleep time, and sleep efficiency. (Perlis et al., 2005; Riemann et al., 2009)

- Tracking shows: whether insomnia is as severe as it feels subjectively (often sleep is better than perceived)
- which interventions correlate with better sleep
- and objective improvement over time, even when subjectively sleep still feels poor.

Data contradicts negative beliefs about maintaining insomnia.

If insomnia persists despite comprehensive intervention, consider CBT for insomnia (CBT-I), a brief specialised treatment highly effective for chronic insomnia, including PTSD-related sleep disturbance.

- CBT-I includes sleep restriction (initially limiting time in bed to actual sleep time, gradually extending)
- stimulus control (strengthening bed-sleep association)
- cognitive therapy for sleep beliefs
- and sleep hygiene. (Perlis et al., 2005)

Evidence shows CBT-I produces lasting improvement, whereas medication effects disappear when discontinued. (Perlis et al., 2005; Riemann et al., 2009)

Seek a provider trained in CBT-I specifically. (Perlis et al., 2005; Riemann et al., 2009)

Nutrition, Exercise, and Physical Health in PTSD Recovery (Herman, 2015)

Physical health profoundly affects PTSD symptoms through multiple mechanisms. Poor nutrition, sedentary lifestyle, and neglected physical health maintain symptoms, whilst optimal physical health supports recovery. Understanding these connections allows you to leverage physical health as a recovery tool. Nutrition affects mood, energy, and nervous system regulation. Trauma survivors often neglect nutrition due to: depression reducing appetite or motivation; hyperarousal causing stomach upset; using food restrictively for control; or binge eating for emotional regulation. However, nutrition directly impacts recovery. Blood sugar instability from skipping meals or excessive sugar creates irritability, anxiety, and difficulty concentrating, mimicking PTSD symptoms. Nutritional deficiencies, vitamin D, B vitamins, omega-3 fatty acids, and magnesium, affect mood and anxiety. Inflammation from a poor diet affects both physical and mental health. Optimal nutrition for PTSD recovery includes: regular meals maintaining stable blood sugar; adequate protein supporting neurotransmitter synthesis; complex carbohydrates providing steady energy; colourful vegetables and fruits providing antioxidants and fibre; omega-3 fatty acids from fish, walnuts, or supplements supporting brain health; limiting processed foods, excess sugar, and alcohol which disrupt mood regulation; adequate hydration as even mild dehydration affects mood and cognition; and considering vitamin D supplementation if deficient (common in PTSD patients who avoid outdoors). Exercise represents an evidence-based intervention for PTSD independently of other treatments. Aerobic exercise: reduces anxiety and depression; improves sleep quality; decreases hyperarousal; improves body image and sense of physical agency; provides a healthy emotional outlet; and produces neurobiological changes supporting recovery, including increased BDNF (brain-derived neurotrophic factor) supporting neuroplasticity. Research shows regular exercise (3-5 times weekly, 30-60 minutes, moderate intensity) produces significant PTSD symptom reduction. Choose an exercise that you'll actually do consistently, rather than avoid optimal exercise you'll avoid. Options include: walking or jogging outdoors combining exercise with nature exposure; gym workouts if that appeals; swimming providing rhythmic movement in supportive environment; cycling either outdoors or stationary; group fitness classes providing structure and social connection; dancing combining movement, music, and expression; martial arts building sense of physical competence and safety; or yoga combining movement, breathing, and mindfulness. Experiment to find what feels sustainable and enjoyable. Exercise guidelines for trauma survivors: start gradually if sedentary, even 10-minute walks provide benefits; build slowly to avoid injury or burnout; prioritise consistency over intensity; choose activities feeling empowering not triggering (some trauma survivors avoid gyms, prefer solo exercise, or conversely prefer group settings); notice and celebrate physical achievements rebuilding sense of efficacy; and use exercise for regulation but not avoidance, exercise complements therapy, does not replace it. Mind-body exercises provide particular benefits for trauma: yoga improves body awareness, flexibility, and regulation whilst fostering mind-body connection trauma disrupted; tai chi combines gentle movement with meditation building present-moment awareness; qigong uses breath and movement for energy regulation and calm; and Pilates builds body awareness and core strength. These approaches work through enhancing interoception, awareness of internal body states, trauma typically impairs. Physical health conditions require attention as they interact with PTSD bidirectionally. PTSD increases risk for cardiovascular disease, chronic pain, gastrointestinal problems, autoimmune conditions, and metabolic syndrome. These conditions worsen PTSD symptoms, whilst PTSD exacerbates physical conditions. Do not neglect physical health, focusing only on psychological symptoms; address both simultaneously. Regular medical care, appropriate treatment of physical conditions, and a healthy lifestyle support both physical and mental health. Sleep, nutrition, and exercise form an interconnected triad of physical health supporting recovery. Each affects others: good sleep supports exercise motivation and healthy eating; regular exercise improves sleep quality; healthy nutrition provides energy for exercise and affects sleep. Poor functioning in any area undermines others: sleep deprivation increases cravings for unhealthy food and reduces exercise motivation; poor nutrition depletes energy for exercise; a sedentary lifestyle worsens sleep quality. Target all three simultaneously for synergistic benefits rather than waiting to perfect one before addressing others.

Social Support and Connection in Recovery (Herman, 2015)

Social support represents one of the strongest predictors of PTSD recovery outcomes. (Herman, 2015)

Robust social support predicts faster recovery, better treatment response, lower symptom severity, and reduced risk of chronic PTSD. (Herman, 2015)

Conversely, social isolation maintains and exacerbates symptoms.

Understanding types of support, how to build a support network, and how to utilize support effectively optimizes this crucial recovery factor. (Herman, 2015)

Types of social support serve distinct functions.

Emotional support involves empathy, caring, and validation, people who listen without judgment, offer comfort during distress, and demonstrate they care about you.

Instrumental support includes practical assistance: help with childcare, transportation to appointments, financial support, and help with tasks when overwhelmed.

Informational support provides guidance, advice, and knowledge: people who have recovered from trauma sharing strategies, a therapist providing psychoeducation, and friends researching resources.

Companionship involves spending time together in positive activities, reducing isolation through shared experience.

Building a support network requires intentional effort, as trauma often destroys or prevents social connections.

Start by identifying existing supports: who currently provides any type of support?

This might include family members, friends, romantic partner, coworkers, religious or spiritual community, a support group, healthcare providers, or online communities.

Evaluate the quality of each support: Is this person trustworthy?

Do they respond helpfully?

Do they respect boundaries?

Not all relationships provide good support; some might be harmful or inadequate.

- Strengthen existing positive supports by: communicating more openly about your needs
- asking for specific help rather than hoping they'll figure it out
- expressing appreciation for support received
- reciprocating when you are able
- and deepening relationships through increased contact and vulnerability.

Many people want to help but do not know how; clear communication about what helps empowers them to provide effective support.

- Develop new supports through: trauma support groups (in-person or online), connecting with others who understand
- community activities aligned with interests, providing natural friendship opportunities
- volunteering, creating connections whilst contributing meaningfully
- classes or groups teaching new skills whilst meeting people
- religious or spiritual communities if that resonates
- and online forums for trauma survivors offering 24/7 peer support.

Building new connections takes time and repeated exposure; do not expect instant friendships, but gradually relationships develop.

Support groups specifically for trauma survivors offer unique benefits.

Shared experience reduces isolation; you are not alone in struggling.

Witnessing others' recovery provides hope. (Herman, 2015)

Learning how others cope provides strategies.

The group provides a safe place to practise social connection.

Hearing your story witnessed and validated by people who understand is profoundly healing.

- Options include therapy groups facilitated by professionals, peer-led support groups
- diagnosis-specific groups (combat trauma, sexual assault survivors, first responders)
- and online groups providing accessibility and anonymity.

Online communities provide support, particularly valuable when an in-person connection feels overwhelming or isn't available.

- Benefits include accessibility 24/7 from home
- anonymity, allowing sharing without in-person vulnerability
- connecting with people worldwide who have experienced similar trauma
- and learning from collective wisdom.
- Cautions include maintaining boundaries around time spent online
- avoiding triggering content
- verifying information before following advice
- and recognising online support complements but does not replace in-person connection and professional treatment.

Quality online communities enforce respectful communication and provide peer moderation.

Asking for help challenges trauma survivors who learned not to rely on others.

- Practise with low-stakes requests, building up to more significant asks: ask a neighbour to water plants while you are away
- Request a friend to accompany you to a difficult appointment
- Ask a family member for specific practical help
- Ask a romantic partner for particular emotional support.

Notice anxiety about asking decreases with positive experiences.

Most people genuinely want to help; giving them specific requests allows them to support you effectively.

Reciprocity maintains healthy relationships long-term.

Whilst friends and family may understand you need more support during acute trauma recovery, relationships cannot sustain indefinite one-way support. (Herman, 2015)

- As you improve, reciprocate by offering support when they face difficulties
- contribute to the relationship in ways you can manage (even just being present)
- express gratitude explicitly
- and balance talking about trauma with discussing other aspects of life.

Balanced reciprocity over time maintains sustainable support relationships.

Recognise toxic or unhelpful support responses and limit contact appropriately.

- Unhelpful responses include minimising your experience (others have it worse)
- blaming you for trauma
- pressuring you to get over it quickly
- sharing your trauma story without permission
- making trauma about their feelings
- offering unwanted advice
- or being inconsistently available.

Limit time with people providing these responses.

You do not owe explanations; protect yourself by reducing contact with unhelpful people whilst investing in genuinely supportive relationships.

Cultural considerations affect support seeking and provision.

Collectivist cultures might emphasise family support and view seeking outside help as bringing shame to the family.

Individualist cultures might emphasise self-sufficiency, discouraging dependency.

Men often receive messages that seeking support is weak.

LGBTQ+ individuals might lack family support due to rejection.

Cultural humility means understanding how culture shapes support experience whilst recognising within-culture variation.

Work with what's available whilst recognising cultural factors affecting support access and utilisation.

Meaning-Making and Post-Traumatic Growth (Tedeschi & Calhoun, 2004)

Meaning-making, constructing an understanding of trauma's significance and integrating it into life narrative, represents a crucial aspect of long-term recovery. Trauma shatters fundamental assumptions about the world, self, and future. Recovery involves either rebuilding these assumptions or constructing a new worldview integrating the trauma experience. This process isn't about justifying trauma or claiming it was good. Trauma is always harmful and shouldn't have occurred. Rather, meaning-making involves finding purpose, growth, or positive change despite trauma. Post-traumatic growth (PTG) describes positive psychological change experienced following trauma. Research identifies five domains of growth: increased appreciation for life, recognising its fragility and preciousness; closer relationships developing deeper connections through shared vulnerability; greater personal strength, recognising I survived therefore I am stronger than I thought; new possibilities discovering opportunities or paths you wouldn't have pursued without trauma; and spiritual or existential development deepening faith or meaning systems. PTG does not mean you are glad trauma happened, but that despite a terrible experience, some positive changes emerged. PTG develops through specific processes. Cognitive processing, actively thinking about trauma, discussing it, and writing about it, facilitates meaning-making. Ruminating without progress does not produce growth; constructive processing, examining how trauma affected you, what you learned, and how you changed does. Social support provides validation and alternative perspectives, supporting meaning-making. Time allows processing; PTG typically emerges months to years post-trauma, not immediately. Personality factors like optimism and openness predict PTG but aren't requirements; anyone can experience growth. Common forms of meaning-making include: finding purpose through helping others experiencing similar trauma (becoming counsellor, peer supporter, or advocate); spiritual or religious interpretation integrating trauma into faith worldview; believing trauma revealed important truths about self, relationships, or life; viewing trauma as a catalyst for positive life changes you wouldn't have made otherwise; or creating legacy or memorial honouring loss. Your meaning-making is individual; what provides meaning to you matters, not conforming to the expected narrative. Challenges in meaning-making include: pressure to find a silver lining before you are ready, meaning-making cannot be forced; others dismissing your pain if you report growth (growth and pain coexist); survivor guilt if you experience growth while others didn't survive or do not recover; or conflicting meanings (it taught me I am strong but I wish I'd never needed that lesson). These challenges are normal. Meaning emerges gradually through organic processing, not through forced positive thinking. Narrative therapy approaches support meaning-making explicitly. Constructing a coherent trauma narrative incorporating what happened, how it affected you, how you responded, and who you are now integrates trauma into a broader life story. Trauma is a chapter in your life, not an entire book. Narrative therapy questions include: How has this experience shaped who you are? What strengths did you discover? How have your priorities changed? What do you want your life to reflect now? What do you want people to know about your story? Answering these questions over time creates an integrated narrative, reducing trauma's power to dominate identity. Contributions and advocacy transform personal pain into social benefit, providing meaning through preventing others' suffering. This might involve raising awareness about trauma type you experienced; advocating for policy changes; supporting organisations preventing trauma; volunteering with trauma survivors; sharing your recovery story publicly; or professional work in the trauma field. However, you are not obligated to contribute or find meaning through helping others; your recovery itself is sufficient. Choose a contribution if it brings meaning to you, not from obligation. Spirituality and meaning intersect complexly. Trauma challenges faith for many. How could God allow this? Why didn't prayer protect me? Some people lose faith entirely, others find faith deepens, and others develop a different spiritual understanding. All responses are valid. If spirituality matters to you, exploring trauma's spiritual meaning with a clergy member, spiritual director, or therapist comfortable with spirituality can support integration. For non-religious people, existential meaning-making addresses similar questions about purpose and significance without a religious framework. Meaning-making does not erase trauma or make it acceptable. You can simultaneously believe trauma was terrible and never should have happened, AND I grew in ways I value. These are not contradictory. Trauma caused suffering that was not worth any growth, yet growth occurred, nonetheless. This both/and thinking allows you to acknowledge the full complexity of trauma's impacts without minimising either harm or growth. Recovery involves holding both pain and growth, loss and gain, what was destroyed and what was built from ruins. (Tedeschi & Calhoun, 2004)

Recovery Milestones and Progress Markers (Herman, 2015)

Recognising recovery progress provides motivation and hope, yet PTSD recovery is a gradual, nonlinear process, making progress difficult to see day-to-day. (Herman, 2015)

Understanding typical recovery milestones helps you recognise improvements even when recovery feels stagnant. (Herman, 2015)

Remember: these are general patterns, not a rigid timeline.

Your recovery follows its own pace. (Herman, 2015)

Early recovery milestones (weeks to months): recognising you have PTSD and seeking information; engaging with treatment despite fear; beginning to distinguish triggers from current threats; using grounding techniques at least sometimes effectively; having some days better than your worst days; reduced avoidance in one area; sleeping slightly better occasionally; brief moments of feeling okay; reduced substance use if present; and decreased suicidal ideation intensity if present.

These early gains seem small but represent significant shifts from acute trauma response.

Middle recovery milestones (months to year+): consistent treatment engagement; using coping skills reliably during distress; reduced flashback frequency or intensity; improved sleep quality most nights; engaging in previously avoided activities gradually; challenging negative trauma-related beliefs at least sometimes; improved emotion regulation, emotions still intense but not constant overwhelm; rebuilding or building social connections; returning to work or improved functioning at work if working; reduced hypervigilance noticing you can relax sometimes; and experiencing pleasure or joy occasionally despite symptoms.

Middle recovery involves symptoms decreasing from severe to moderate while developing skills to manage remaining symptoms. (Herman, 2015)

Advanced recovery milestones (year+ to several years): symptom severity in mild range; functioning at or near pre-trauma levels; healthy relationships or working on relationship patterns consciously; trauma memories accessible without overwhelming distress, can remember without reliving; integrated trauma narrative placing trauma in life context without defining entire identity; pursuit of meaningful activities and goals; generally positive self-concept despite occasional negative thoughts; rarely experiencing flashbacks or nightmares or managing them quickly; comfortable with emotions across range; and ability to support others beginning to give back.

Advanced recovery does not mean complete symptom absence but rather symptoms no longer significantly impairing life. (Herman, 2015)

- Long-term recovery characteristics (years): trauma is part of your history, you can discuss without crisis
- symptoms are minimal or absent most of the time
- fulfilling relationships
- satisfaction with life overall
- resilience when facing new stresses (Bonanno, 2004)
- post-traumatic growth evident (Tedeschi & Calhoun, 2004)
- wisdom gained from experience
- helping others if chosen
- and living authentic life aligned with values.

Long-term recovery means trauma no longer dominates your present or limits your future. (Herman, 2015)

You have integrated experience into your identity whilst building life beyond it.

Non-linear progress is normal and expected.

- You'll have: setbacks following periods of improvement, often around anniversaries, additional stressors, or without clear trigger

- plateau periods where progress seems stalled, continued treatment during plateaus often precedes the next improvement phase
- rapid gains followed by slower progress, some people improve quickly initially, then progress slows
- fluctuations where symptoms vary significantly day-to-day or week-to-week.

Non-linear progress does not indicate treatment failure or that you are backsliding permanently; it is a normal recovery pattern. (Herman, 2015)

Measuring progress objectively supplements subjective assessment.

Use standardised questionnaires (PCL-5 for PTSD symptoms, PHQ-9 for depression, WSAS for functional impairment) monthly.

- Track: symptom frequency and intensity
- avoidance behaviours
- quality of life indicators
- sleep quality
- social connection
- and functioning in major life domains (work, relationships, self-care).

Objective tracking reveals progress you might miss subjectively.

Reviewing scores over time shows the overall trajectory despite daily fluctuations.

Celebrating progress, even little progress, supports continued motivation.

- When you notice improvement, acknowledge it explicitly. I used to be unable to leave the house, but now I can go to the shops.
- share progress with supporters who can validate it
- record progress in journal, creating visible record
- reward yourself for achievements treating yourself kindly
- and recognise the effort involved, progress reflects your hard work in treatment and daily coping.

Do not dismiss gains as insignificant or minimise accomplishments.

Each improvement matters.

Progress in one domain affects others even when not obviously connected.

Better sleep improves emotion regulation.

Reduced avoidance decreases isolation and improves mood.

Improved relationships provide support,, enhancing resilience. (Bonanno, 2004)

Better coping skills reduce crisis frequency, allowing focus on growth.

Physical health improvements support mental health.

Recognise that gains accumulate and reinforce each other, creating a positive upward spiral over time.

When progress stalls, troubleshoot rather than despair: Are you attending treatment consistently?

Is treatment evidence-based and appropriate?

Do substance use or other behaviours maintain symptoms?

Are current stressors overwhelming your coping capacity?

Is medication optimised if using medication?

Do you need more intensive treatment?

Is a different treatment approach needed?

Are you practicing skills between sessions?

Consult with the treatment team to identify and address obstacles.

Stalled progress indicates a need for adjustment, not that recovery is impossible. (Herman, 2015)

Remember that recovery isn't returning to the pre-trauma self if trauma occurred during development, it is becoming a healthy version of the current self. (Herman, 2015)

You might be a different person than before the trauma.

That's okay.

- Recovery means building a life you find meaningful (Herman, 2015)
- relationships that support you
- effective emotion regulation
- adequate functioning
- and general satisfaction.

You do not need to become who you were before trauma; you need to become who you can be now, integrating trauma experience whilst living fully.

That's recovery's goal. (Herman, 2015)

Comprehensive Crisis Management and Safety Planning (Stanley & Brown, 2012)

Crisis situations, severe symptom exacerbation threatening safety, require prepared response. Creating comprehensive crisis plan before crisis occurs provides roadmap when thinking is impaired. Effective crisis management prevents hospitalisation, self-harm, and treatment disruption whilst ensuring safety during most difficult periods. Crisis identification involves recognising warning signs before a full crisis develops. Early warning signs might include increased flashback frequency; worsening sleep disruption; intensified irritability or anger; increased substance use; rising suicidal thoughts; social withdrawal accelerating; neglecting self-care; engaging in risky behaviours; or sensing loss of control. Identifying your personal warning signs, patterns preceding previous crises allows intervention before the situation deteriorates completely. Safety planning starts with immediate crisis response: remove means of self-harm from environment, medications locked or removed, weapons secured elsewhere, sharp objects limited; identify internal coping strategies you can use without contacting others, distraction techniques, grounding, sensory tools, safe place visualization, coping cards with helpful statements; identify social supports you can contact for distraction or support, friends' phone numbers, support hotline numbers; identify adults who can help in crisis, therapist contact info, crisis team numbers, trusted family; and identify safe environments, places you can go for safety if home feels unsafe. Write this plan when stable, keep copies accessible, and share with supports. Crisis hotlines provide 24/7 professional support: Samaritans (116 123) offers confidential emotional support for anyone in distress; Crisis Text Line (text SHOUT to 85258) provides text-based crisis support particularly useful if talking feels overwhelming; Combat Stress (0800 138 1619) specifically supports veterans; Rape Crisis (0808 802 9999) supports sexual violence survivors; or specific local crisis services your area provides. Save numbers in phone, post visibly at home. These services exist specifically for crises; using them is appropriate and encouraged. Grounding intensive protocol for crisis: rapid grounding sequence every 10 minutes until crisis reduces: say aloud your name, age, date, location; engage all 5 senses intensely: touch multiple textures, smell a strong scent, look at multiple colours naming them, listen to music or nature sounds, taste something strong; complete physical grounding: stamp feet hard feeling floor, apply pressure to pressure points, hold ice, splash cold water on face; repeat coping statements: This feeling is temporary, I have survived crises before, I will survive this, Help is available, I am safe right now; and check SUDs (distress level 0-10) noting if it is decreasing even slightly. Continue the cycle until distress becomes manageable. Distraction during a crisis serves an important function despite seeming like avoidance. When overwhelmed, sometimes you need to step back from crisis temporarily to regulate somewhat before addressing issues. Effective crisis distraction includes: intense physical activity, burning off distress energy; engaging tasks requiring concentration, puzzles, games, detailed crafts; social contact even if not discussing crisis, talking to friend about neutral topics; strong sensory experiences, very cold shower, very spicy food, loud music; or absorbing media, films, books, or podcasts. Distraction does not solve crisis but creates temporary relief, allowing recovery before addressing the situation. When to seek emergency help: imminent plans to harm self or others with means accessible; severe dissociation leaving you unable to function or at risk; psychotic symptoms like command hallucinations or severe paranoia; medical emergencies including overdose, self-harm injuries, or medication interactions; or complete breakdown of normal functioning where you cannot care for basic needs. Call 999, go to A&E, or call the crisis team. A serious crisis requires professional immediate intervention; do not try to manage alone beyond your capacity. Psychiatric hospitalisation serves specific functions: providing safe environment when you cannot maintain safety; intensive treatment when outpatient insufficient; medication adjustments requiring monitoring; or respite when outpatient resources are exhausted. Hospitalisation isn't failure; it is an appropriate intervention for a serious crisis. If hospitalised: participate actively in treatment; be honest with staff about symptoms; develop a discharge plan before leaving; arrange follow-up care immediately; and process experience with an outpatient therapist afterwards. Brief hospitalisation can prevent chronic deterioration by addressing the crisis effectively. Post-crisis processing with a therapist prevents future crises: What triggered the crisis? What warning signs preceded it? What helped and did not help? What changes might prevent a similar crisis? How can the safety plan be improved? What additional supports are needed? Processing the crisis therapeutically transforms it into a learning experience rather than simply a traumatic episode. Each crisis managed successfully, with recovery and learning, builds confidence in your capacity to survive difficult periods. Reducing crisis frequency long-term requires: consistent, evidence-based treatment addressing core symptoms; medication optimisation if using medication; adequate stabilisation before intensive trauma processing; building robust coping skills; maintaining a strong support network; addressing substance use if present; managing life stressors where possible; practicing excellent self-care; and recognising warning signs early. Crisis frequency typically decreases as recovery progresses; early recovery might involve frequent crises, whilst advanced recovery involves rare, manageable, difficult periods. Recovery from crisis involves rebuilding after an acute episode: gradually resuming normal activities rather than immediately returning to full functioning; processing the crisis emotionally without shame or self-blame; reconnecting with supports you may have withdrawn from; implementing lessons learned about triggers and effective coping; celebrating survival through a difficult period; and recommitting to recovery work. Crisis represents a temporary setback, not permanent deterioration. Recovery continues after crisis passes. (Stanley & Brown, 2012)

Advanced Cognitive Restructuring Beyond Basic Techniques

While Chapter Five covered foundational cognitive restructuring, advanced techniques provide additional tools for challenging deeply entrenched trauma-related beliefs. These approaches address complex stuck points resisting basic cognitive interventions. Core belief modification addresses underlying schemas rather than surface thoughts. Surface thought: He will hurt me as my abuser did. Underlying core belief: All relationships lead to harm. Surface interventions challenge specific thoughts, but the core belief regenerates similar thoughts endlessly. Identify core beliefs by asking repeatedly: If that thought is true, what does it mean about me/others/world? Continue asking until reaching the fundamental assumption. Then challenge core belief directly through examining evidence across the entire life, not just trauma; identifying exceptions contradicting the belief; considering alternative core beliefs fitting evidence equally well; behavioural experiments testing belief validity; and gradually building evidence supporting a healthier core belief through positive experiences. The continuum technique addresses absolutist thinking. Trauma creates black-

and-white beliefs: I am completely worthless versus I am valuable. Reality exists on a continuum. Draw a line representing 0-100 scale. At extremes: 0 = completely worthless, 100 = completely valuable. Where would you place someone who: has flaws but also strengths; sometimes fails but also succeeds; has been hurt but also experienced care; contributes in some ways even if not perfectly? Most people place them mid-range, 40-60. Now, where do you place yourself honestly? If you placed yourself at extreme (0-10), examine evidence: What strengths do you have, even if imperfect? What do people appreciate about you? What have you contributed? This exercise reveals that absolutist thinking does not match reality's nuance. practise placing self and situations on continuums rather than extremes. The responsibility pie technique addresses excessive self-blame. Trauma survivors often assume total responsibility for trauma or its consequences. Draw a circle representing 100% responsibility for the outcome. List all factors contributing: your actions, perpetrator's actions, circumstances, others' actions, chance. Assign a percentage to each factor proportional to its actual contribution. Often, survivors assign themselves 100% initially, but recognising other factors' contributions reveals their responsibility is a smaller piece, perhaps 20-30% for any choices they made, while perpetrator, circumstances, and other factors comprise the remaining 70-80%. This does not eliminate responsibility for your part but accurately attributes causation, preventing excessive self-blame. Behavioural experiments test belief validity through real-world experience. Belief: If I show vulnerability, people will reject me. Experiment: Share something moderately vulnerable with a trusted person, observe response. Hypothesis: They'll reject me. Alternative hypothesis: They will respond supportively. Experiment and evaluate the outcome. Most experiments disconfirm catastrophic predictions, providing evidence contradicting negative beliefs more powerfully than pure cognitive work. Design experiments that: test specific beliefs; are feasible and safe; have clear observable outcomes; and are processed afterwards, examining what happened versus what you predicted. Imagery rescripting directly modifies traumatic memories' emotional meaning. This differs from exposure (which processes memory as-is) by altering memory itself in imagination. In imagery: revisit traumatic memory but introduce change, adult self enters to protect child self, needed help arrives, you respond differently, outcome changes. This does not change historical facts but changes memory's emotional charge by adding adult perspective, resources, or alternative endings. Research shows imagery rescripting reduces traumatic memory distress and challenges the meanings derived from trauma. practise with a therapist initially, as this technique activates emotion significantly. Mindfulness-based cognitive therapy integrates mindfulness with cognitive work. Rather than challenging thoughts directly, observe them non-judgmentally: Notice thoughts arise, label it as thoughts, watch it pass without engaging. This creates distance from thoughts; they are mental events, not facts about reality. With practise, thoughts lose power because you are not believing them automatically; you respond rather than react; and you recognise thoughts come and go whilst you remain constant. MBCT particularly helps when cognitive challenges feel exhausting or create arguments with self. Simply observing thoughts breaks their hold without requiring active debate. Socratic dialogue goes beyond challenging questions to genuine inquiry. Instead of: What evidence contradicts this belief? (which clients often resist), try: Help me understand your perspective, why does this belief make sense to you? What experiences led you to this conclusion? If someone you care about believed this about themselves, how would you respond? This collaborative approach respects the client's logic whilst gently introducing alternative perspectives. Good Socratic questioning involves genuine curiosity, not disguised arguing. (Clark, 1999)

Acceptance and Commitment Therapy (ACT) approaches offer an alternative to changing thoughts, instead changing the relationship with thoughts.

- ACT teaches accepting thoughts and feelings rather than fighting them
- being present in the current moment
- identifying values
- and committing to value-based action despite difficult thoughts and feelings.
- When thought arises, I am worthless. ACT does not argue whether it is true, but rather notices that thought exists.
- recognises it, though not a fact
- asks: Is acting on this thought moving me towards my values?

and takes value-based action regardless of thought's presence.

This approach particularly helps when cognitive challenges create unhelpful arguing with oneself or when thoughts are partially understandable given a trauma history, but prevent valued living.

Accepting thoughts exist whilst choosing behaviour based on values rather than thoughts creates freedom, trauma-related cognitions otherwise prevent.

Schema mode work integrates cognitive and experiential approaches addressing developmental trauma. (Teicher & Samson, 2016)

Early maladaptive schemas, pervasive beliefs like I am defective or I cannot trust anyone, developed during childhood, creating modes or states: Vulnerable Child (experiencing unmet needs), Angry Child (protesting unmet needs), Punitive Parent (harsh internal critic), Detached Protector (emotional avoidance), and Healthy Adult (balanced, effective).

When triggered, you shift into modes unconsciously.

- Mode work involves identifying which mode you are in
- understanding each mode's purpose and origin
- developing a compassionate relationship with child modes
- limiting Punitive Parent mode
- strengthening Detached Protector's flexibility
- and building Healthy Adult to manage needs effectively.

This framework helps complex trauma survivors understand internal experience and develop an integrated self rather than being controlled by childhood adaptations that no longer serve them.

Compassion-focused techniques directly address shame, central to trauma.

- Develop a compassionate mind through: understanding your struggles result from circumstances not character defects, you did the best you could with the resources available
- recognising all humans struggle and make mistakes, you are not uniquely flawed
- treating yourself as you would treat a dear friend facing similar difficulties, with kindness, not contempt
- and cultivating a compassionate inner voice, replacing harsh self-criticism.
- Practices include: compassionate letter writing (what would a compassionate other say to you?)
- self-compassion break during distress (recognising suffering, noting common humanity, offering kindness)
- and compassionate imagery (imagining compassionate presence supporting you).

Research shows self-compassion strongly predicts recovery outcomes, whilst self-criticism maintains symptoms. (Herman, 2015)

Developing compassion for yourself is not self-indulgence or letting yourself off the hook; it is an essential healing practise, creating an internal environment supporting recovery rather than maintaining suffering. (Herman, 2015)

These advanced cognitive restructuring techniques, core belief modification, continuum thinking, responsibility pies, behavioural experiments, imagery rescripting, mindfulness-based approaches, Socratic dialogue, ACT methods, schema mode work, and compassion-focused practices, provide a comprehensive toolkit for addressing complex trauma-related cognitions.

Different techniques resonate with different people, and different stuck points require different approaches.

Collaborate with a therapist to identify which techniques match your specific difficulties.

Practise consistently, as cognitive change requires repeated application over time.

Initial attempts might feel awkward or ineffective, but with continued practise, these techniques become natural tools you can deploy automatically when trauma-related thoughts arise.

Remember that changing cognitions developed over years or decades through trauma requires patience and sustained effort.

Each time you challenge negative thoughts, each behavioural experiment disconfirming catastrophic predictions, each moment of self-compassion rather than self-criticism, you are rewiring neural pathways and building healthier thought patterns that support rather than hinder recovery. (Herman, 2015)

The cognitive work is difficult but immensely worthwhile.

Your thoughts powerfully affect your emotions and behaviours, meaning cognitive change creates ripple effects, improving multiple life domains simultaneously.

Trauma and Work: Managing PTSD in Professional Settings

PTSD affects work performance and workplace relationships in multiple ways.

Concentration difficulties impair productivity.

Hypervigilance creates exhaustion. (Porges, 2011; Yehuda & Seckl, 2011)

Interpersonal problems affect colleague relationships.

Avoidance might lead to absenteeism or avoiding certain work situations.

Yet employment provides structure, financial stability, purpose, and social connection, supporting recovery. (Herman, 2015)

Balancing work demands with PTSD management requires specific strategies and sometimes workplace accommodations under disability legislation.

Workplace accommodations under the Equality Act 2010 in the UK (or Americans with Disabilities Act in the US) protect employees with PTSD.

- Reasonable accommodations might include a flexible schedule for therapy appointments
- a private workspace reducing sensory triggers
- a modified break schedule for managing symptoms
- a reduced workload during treatment intensification
- the ability to work from home occasionally
- noise-canceling headphones
- clear written instructions supplementing verbal ones
- or regular check-ins with a supervisor providing feedback and support.

Request accommodations through a formal process requiring medical documentation supporting the need for specific accommodations.

You aren't required to disclose specific diagnosis details; documentation can simply note a mental health condition requiring accommodations.

- Managing PTSD symptoms at work involves: using grounding techniques discreetly during workday
- taking micro-breaks for regulation
- communicating boundaries professionally without detailed disclosure
- planning around triggers when possible
- utilising employee assistance programmes if available providing free counselling
- building supportive relationships with trusted colleagues who can provide understanding during difficult periods
- separating work and home life maintaining boundaries that protect recovery time (Herman, 2015)
- practicing self-compassion when symptoms affect performance rather than harsh self-criticism
- and recognising that some days will be harder than others, requiring flexibility in expectations.

Returning to work after leave requires a gradual reintegration; consider a phased return, starting part-time and gradually building up to full-time as tolerated.

If the current job is incompatible with recovery because of a triggering environment, unsupportive management, or excessive demands, exploring alternative employment may be necessary, despite the difficulty of a job transition. (Herman, 2015)

Your health and recovery must be prioritised; no job is worth sacrificing your wellbeing permanently. (Herman, 2015)

Many people successfully work whilst managing PTSD through a combination of treatment, accommodations, symptom management strategies, and a supportive workplace environment.

Employment supports recovery by providing structure, purpose, financial stability, and a sense of competence, making it a valuable goal worth pursuing while ensuring it does not overwhelm your capacity to heal. (Herman, 2015)

This comprehensive coverage of PTSD and employment demonstrates that recovery and professional success are compatible goals. (Herman, 2015)

Thousands of people manage PTSD successfully whilst maintaining fulfilling careers across all industries and professions.

With an appropriate treatment, workplace supports, symptom management strategies, and self-compassion, you can work productively while healing.

Your PTSD does not disqualify you from professional achievement, meaningful work, or career advancement.

It simply means you navigate work whilst managing an additional challenge that appropriate support and strategies can address effectively.

Recovery is achievable, professional success is possible, and comprehensive support makes both goals attainable for trauma survivors. (Herman, 2015)

Your healing journey matters immensely.

Military Culture and Treatment Barriers

Military culture profoundly affects help-seeking and treatment engagement. Cultural values emphasising strength, self-reliance, mission accomplishment, and emotional stoicism create barriers to acknowledging mental health difficulties. Admitting psychological struggle might feel like weakness incompatible with warrior identity; letting down the unit or brothers/sisters in arms; professional liability threatening career; or failure to tough it out as trained. Stigma within the military remains significant despite institutional efforts. Service members fear: judgment from peers and superiors; negative fitness reports or security clearance impacts; being seen as unreliable; removal from preferred duties; or medical discharge ending career. These fears, though sometimes overestimated, have a basis in real experiences of others who faced discrimination after disclosing mental health struggles. Overcoming cultural barriers requires: normalising PTSD as an expected outcome of combat exposure, not character weakness; education that seeking treatment demonstrates strength and commitment to wellness; leadership modelling appropriate help-seeking; confidential treatment pathways; peer support from other veterans in recovery demonstrating treatment compatibility with military identity; and explicit career protection policies preventing discrimination based on mental health treatment. Treatment adaptations for military culture include: therapists understanding military culture, rank structure, and deployment experiences; using military-specific terminology and examples; respecting chain of command whilst maintaining therapeutic boundaries; acknowledging loss of military identity as genuine grief; addressing survivor guilt and loss of comrades as distinct grief process; and providing an evidence-based treatment whilst working within military worldview rather than against it. A therapist's credibility with military populations is often enhanced by military experience themselves or extensive veteran treatment experience. Transition from military to civilian life, especially if medically discharged due to PTSD, creates an additional challenge. Veterans lose unit cohesion and brotherhood; clear mission and purpose; structured environment; shared understanding among those who have experienced combat; and core identity as a service member. Treatment should address this transition grief whilst building a new civilian identity and meaning. (Seal et al., 2007)

Treatment Approaches for Combat PTSD (Seal et al., 2007)

Standard evidence-based PTSD treatments (PE, CPT, EMDR) effectively treat combat PTSD when appropriately adapted. (Shapiro, 2018)

- Modifications for military trauma include: addressing multiple traumas sequentially (Seal et al., 2007)

- incorporating moral injury treatment as an adjunct
- allowing flexible pacing given complex trauma exposure
- addressing comorbid substance use and TBI common in veterans (Seal et al., 2007)
- and integrating with physical rehabilitation if combat injuries present.

Prolonged Exposure adapted for veterans involves processing multiple combat memories, starting with moderately distressing ones before approaching the most traumatic. (Foa et al., 2007; Powers et al., 2010)

In vivo exposure addresses civilian situations avoided because they resemble combat: crowded places, driving, and noisy environments.

Treatment helps veterans discriminate: a crowded shopping centre isn't a hostile fire zone even though the physiological response feels similar. (Seal et al., 2007)

- Cognitive Processing Therapy addresses stuck points common in combat trauma: I should have saved them (overestimating personal control)
- Their deaths are my fault (excessive responsibility)
- I am irreparably damaged (overgeneralization from combat experiences)
- The world is completely dangerous (appropriate threat detection in combat, but not in civilian life)
- or I can never forgive myself for what I did (moral injury component requiring specific intervention beyond standard CPT).

EMDR efficiently processes multiple combat memories, particularly helpful for veterans with complex combat exposure histories. (Shapiro, 2018)

Modified protocols address dissociation common in military trauma and moral injury components, requiring adapted targeting. (Seal et al., 2007)

EMDR's emphasis on dual attention (memory whilst remaining grounded in present) helps veterans who struggle with verbal trauma narratives. (Shapiro, 2018)

Group therapy provides unique benefits for veterans. (Seal et al., 2007)

Shared military experience reduces isolation and increases the credibility of fellow group members.

Processing trauma alongside others who have experienced similar events validates experience whilst providing multiple perspectives on stuck points.

Skills training groups (anger management, stress reduction, family communication) provide a practical tool while building connections with the veteran community.

Many veterans prefer group to individual therapy, finding shared experience more acceptable than one-on-one disclosure to a civilian therapist. (Seal et al., 2007)

- Complementary approaches beneficial for combat veterans include: trauma-sensitive yoga addressing hyperarousal and body disconnection (Seal et al., 2007)
- equine therapy providing connection and purpose
- wilderness therapy reconnecting with nature whilst building skills
- art therapy processing trauma nonverbally
- and service dog programmes providing companionship, security, and concrete support for hypervigilance and nightmares. (Ross et al., 1989)

These adjuncts complement rather than replace an evidence-based treatment.

Chapter Four: Developing Your Trauma Narrative

- Creating a trauma narrative helps your brain process what happened
- Telling your story in a safe way reduces its power over you
- Memory processing is challenging but essential to recovery (Karatzias et al., 2019)
- Guidance here supports you through this important work

Understanding Memory Processing Work

Memory processing work, also called trauma narrative work, imaginal exposure, reliving, or written exposure, is a core component of trauma-focused CBT. (Bisson et al., 2013; NICE, 2018)

This work involves deliberately and repeatedly thinking through the trauma memory in detail, with the explicit goal of facilitating its proper processing and integration into your autobiographical memory.

For many people, this is the most daunting aspect of PTSD treatment, and understandably so.

The idea of deliberately thinking about the worst experience of your life, in detail, repeatedly, naturally provokes anxiety and resistance.

- However, memory processing work is not harmful
- it is healing. This isn't torture or re-traumatisation
- it is therapeutic processing conducted in a controlled, supportive context that's fundamentally different from the original trauma. The key differences are crucial: You are safe now. The trauma isn't actually happening
- you are deliberately recalling and processing a memory. You have control
- you can pause, slow down, or stop if needed, which you couldn't do during the actual trauma. You are approaching the memory with a specific therapeutic goal rather than being overwhelmed by it. If working with a therapist, you have support throughout the process. Even if working independently through this guide, you can prepare yourself, use coping strategies, and approach the work at your own pace.

The rationale for memory processing work is grounded in how traumatic memories maintain PTSD.

As we discussed, traumatic memories are encoded differently from normal memories; they are fragmented, sensory-dominated, and lack proper temporal and spatial context. (Van der Kolk et al., 1996; Brewin et al., 2010)

They are not integrated into your autobiographical memory with appropriate context markers telling your brain, 'This happened then, in that place, and it is over now.' Instead, they remain 'stuck' in the present, easily triggered, and experienced with full emotional intensity as though the trauma is happening now rather than being safely in the past.

Memory processing work facilitates the transformation of these fragmented, present-tense traumatic memories into properly contextualised past-tense autobiographical memories.

By repeatedly thinking through the memory in a structured way, whilst staying grounded in the present, you allow your brain to process and integrate the memory properly.

The memory acquires the context markers it was missing: 'This happened then, on that date, in that location.

It was terrible, but it is over now.

I am here, in the present, and I am safe.' The memory becomes more coherent and less fragmented.

The overwhelming emotions become less intense and more manageable.

The memory begins to feel like a memory rather than a current experience.

This transformation does not happen instantly; it requires repeated processing over multiple sessions or writing exercises.

Each time you think through the memory, your brain processes it a bit more thoroughly.

Fragmented details begin to cohere into a narrative.

Overwhelming emotions become gradually more manageable as your brain learns that thinking about what happened does not make it happen again.

The gap between your intellectual knowledge ('the trauma is over') and your emotional experience ('I feel like I am in danger') begins to close.

Research demonstrates that this memory processing work is highly effective.

Studies show that after completing trauma narrative work, people experience significant reductions in intrusive memories, nightmares, emotional reactivity to reminders, and overall PTSD symptoms. (Van der Kolk et al., 1996)

The memory becomes less intrusive because it is properly filed away rather than being 'stuck' and easily triggered.

When the memory does arise, it is less distressing because it feels like a memory rather than a current experience.

This isn't about forgetting or minimising what happened; the memory remains accessible when appropriate, but it no longer dominates your experience or interrupts your daily life unbidden.

It is worth addressing common concerns about memory processing work directly because these concerns can prevent people from engaging with this crucial component of treatment.

Many people worry: 'Will not this make me worse?

Will not deliberately thinking about the trauma increase my symptoms?

Will not I be re-traumatised?' These are entirely understandable concerns.

However, research and clinical experience demonstrate that properly conducted memory processing work does not make people worse; it makes them better.

Yes, you may experience a temporary increase in symptoms during work, intrusive memories may increase, you may feel more anxious or sad, and nightmares may occur. (Van der Kolk et al., 1996)

This temporary increase is normal, expected, and actually indicates that you are engaging with material that needs processing.

Within days or weeks of completing the work, symptoms typically decrease significantly below their starting level.

The temporary increase is the price of admission for longer-term improvement.

Another common concern is: 'I will not be able to cope with the emotions that come up.

I'll fall apart.' This fear is understandable; the emotions associated with trauma are indeed intense and overwhelming.

However, this prediction is usually inaccurate.

Whilst memory processing does evoke strong emotions, most people discover that these emotions, whilst difficult, are tolerable.

You do not fall apart.

You do not lose control permanently.

The emotions peak and then naturally decrease.

Moreover, you develop confidence in your ability to tolerate distress, which is itself therapeutic.

Before processing work, you might believe, 'I cannot handle thinking about this; it will destroy me.' After completing processing work, you know, 'I can handle difficult emotions.

They are painful, but they pass, and I survive them.' This confidence is invaluable.

Some people worry: 'Talking about the trauma will make it more real or give it more power.' This reflects a common but mistaken belief that avoiding something makes it less powerful.

The opposite is true with trauma memories.

Avoiding the memory keeps it powerful; it remains this terrible, overwhelming thing that you cannot face.

Processing the memory reduces its power.

By facing it deliberately and discovering you can survive that facing; by transforming it from a fragmented present-tense experience into a coherent past-tense narrative, you take power away from the memory.

It becomes something that happened to you rather than something that defines you and controls your present.

Preparing for Memory Processing: What You Need to Know

Before beginning memory processing work, several preparatory steps can help ensure the work is as effective and manageable as possible. These preparations aren't obstacles or delays; they are foundations that make the work more likely to succeed.

First, ensure you have adequate coping resources in place. Review the coping strategies discussed in the previous chapter, grounding techniques, breathing exercises, self-soothing activities, distraction when needed, physical activity, and social support. practise these strategies before you need them urgently. You want them to be familiar and readily accessible when distress increases during memory work. Think of this like a pilot practicing emergency procedure in a simulator before potentially needing them in flight; you are preparing for situations you hope will not arise but might.

Second, identify a safe, private location for this work. You need somewhere you will not be interrupted, where you feel secure, where you can express emotions if they arise without concern about being overheard or disturbed. For many people, this is their bedroom or another private room in their home. If you do not have private space at home, consider whether a therapist's office, a trusted friend's home, or another location might work. The key is feeling safe and private.

Third, schedule the work at times when you have space afterward for processing and self-care.

Do not schedule memory processing right before important work meetings, difficult family obligations, or other demanding situations.

Give yourself time and space afterward, ideally at least a few hours, preferably an evening or a day, to process emotions, use coping strategies, and engage in self-care.

Many people find it helpful to schedule memory work for weekend mornings, giving them the whole day to process and recover before returning to work responsibilities.

Fourth, consider whether you want to work through the memory alone or with support.

If you are working with a therapist, they'll guide you through this process.

If you are working through this guide independently, consider whether having a trusted friend or family member nearby (not necessarily in the room, but available) would be helpful.

Some people prefer to do this work entirely alone; others find it reassuring to have support available.

There's no single right answer; choose what feels right for you.

Fifth, prepare for the practical aspects of the work. You'll need paper and pen, or a computer if you prefer typing. You will need tissues. You might want water or tea available. You might want a blanket or comfort object. Think about what would make the space more comfortable and supportive for difficult emotional work.

The Memory Processing Method: Step by Step

There are several specific methods for processing trauma memories, but we'll focus on written narrative exposure, writing out your trauma memory in detail, repeatedly, to facilitate its processing and integration.

- This method has several advantages: you can work at your own pace
- you have a written record of your progress
- you can see how your narrative changes over repeated writings
- and many people find writing less overwhelming than speaking aloud, particularly when working independently.

The method involves writing out the trauma memory in as much detail as possible, including sensory details, thoughts, emotions, and physical sensations, in the present tense as though it is happening now.

The present tense is important because traumatic memories in PTSD already feel like they are happening now; that is the problem.

By writing in the present tense, you are matching how the memory is currently encoded.

As you repeatedly process the memory through writing, it gradually transforms from feeling present-tense to clearly being past-tense.

You start by writing 'I am in the car and I see the other vehicle coming towards me' and, over repeated writings, it transforms into 'I was in the car and I saw the other vehicle coming towards me, that happened on a specific date, it is over now, and I survived it.' This transformation is the goal of the work.

Here's the step-by-step process: First, settle into your safe, private space with your writing materials. Do some grounding, notice where you are, what you can see and hear, and remind yourself you are safe now. Do some breathing to regulate your nervous system. Remind yourself why you are doing this work: to process the memory so it no longer controls your life, to facilitate your recovery, to reclaim your future. (Lewis et al., 2020)

Second, begin writing the trauma memory from the beginning, not the moment of the worst trauma, but from when things were still normal before the trauma began.

If you were assaulted, start with what you were doing that day before the assault.

If you had a car accident, start with where you were driving and why.

Starting before the trauma itself provides context and makes the writing less overwhelming.

- Write in as much detail as possible, what you could see, hear, smell, and feel
- what you were thinking
- what emotions you were experiencing.

Write in the present tense: 'I am driving to work.

It is a Tuesday morning.

The sun is bright.

I am thinking about the meeting I have later.' This detailed, sensory writing helps engage with the memory properly.

Third, continue writing through the entire trauma, including the worst moments. This is the hardest part, and you may need to pause, use breathing techniques, remind yourself where you are, and then continue. Do not rush through the worst parts; they are precisely the parts that need most processing. Describe what happened, what you thought, what you felt, and what physical sensations you experienced. Include details about what you could see, hear, and smell. If you dissociated during the trauma, write about that: 'I feel disconnected from my body. Everything seems far away and unreal.' If you felt terror, write about that: 'I am terrified. I think I am going to die. My heart is racing so fast I think it will burst.'

Fourth, continue writing through to the aftermath of the trauma, when the immediate danger passed, what happened next, and how the trauma ended.

Include your thoughts and feelings after the worst was over: relief, shock, confusion, numbness, or whatever you experienced.

Write until you reach a point of relative safety or normalcy.

For example, if writing about an assault, continue through being helped, getting to safety, going to the hospital, or going home.

If writing about an accident, continue through being rescued, receiving medical care, or reaching safety.

This completion of the narrative is important; you are not leaving yourself stuck in the worst moment, but rather processing through to safety.

Fifth, after completing the narrative, take a break.

Notice where you are now.

Do grounding exercises.

Use breathing techniques.

Remind yourself: 'That was then.

I am here now.

I am safe.

I survived.

I am processing this memory, so it no longer controls me.' Allow yourself to feel whatever emotions are present without judging them.

Use self-soothing strategies.

Reach out for support if needed.

Many people feel exhausted after this work; that's expected.

You have done something difficult and important.

Be kind to yourself.

Sixth, after some time has passed, perhaps later that day or the next day, re-read what you have written. This re-reading is itself part of the processing. As you read, you might notice details you didn't include, emotions that weren't fully expressed, or thoughts you had that you didn't write down. Make notes about these. Re-reading helps consolidate the processing work and prepares you for the next writing session.

Seventh, repeat the entire process.

Yes, repeat it.

You'll write the same trauma narrative again, in the same level of detail, in the present tense.

This repetition is crucial; the therapeutic benefit comes from repeated processing, not from a single writing.

Most people need to write their trauma narrative 3-5 times, sometimes more, for optimal processing.

- Each time you write it, you'll likely notice changes: the narrative becomes more coherent and less fragmented
- you remember additional details or notice connections you missed before
- the emotions, whilst still present, become somewhat less overwhelming
- the memory begins to feel more like a past event rather than a present experience
- and you develop greater confidence in your ability to tolerate engaging with the memory.

What to Expect During and After Memory Processing

Understanding what's normal during memory processing helps you persist with the work even when it is difficult.

During the writing itself, expect strong emotions.

You might cry, feel intense fear or anger, experience physical tension or shaking, or feel numb and disconnected.

All of these responses are normal.

You are engaging with traumatic material; of course, it provokes strong responses.

The key is that you are doing so deliberately, in safety, with a therapeutic purpose, rather than being overwhelmed unexpectedly by flashbacks. (Van der Kolk et al., 1996)

You might find that time seems to pass strangely during writing; what feels like a long time might only be 15 minutes, or conversely, you might write for an hour that passes quickly. This temporal distortion is normal when engaging with traumatic material. You might dissociate to some degree, feeling somewhat disconnected or unreal. If this happens, pause, do grounding exercises, and reconnect with the present before continuing. Some dissociation is normal, but you want to remain adequately present to do the processing work effectively.

After completing a writing session, expect to feel emotionally and physically exhausted.

You have done demanding work.

Many people feel drained, want to sleep, or need quiet time alone.

This is appropriate self-care, not avoidance.

Give yourself permission to rest and recover.

Some people experience a temporary increase in PTSD symptoms after beginning memory processing work, more intrusive memories, more nightmares, and increased anxiety. (Van der Kolk et al., 1996)

This is normal, expected, and actually indicates that you are engaging with material that needs processing.

The symptoms typically peak during the first few processing sessions and then begin to decrease as the work progresses.

By the time you have completed several writings, symptoms are usually significantly reduced compared to baseline.

You might notice that your narrative changes over repeated writings.

Early writings might be quite fragmented and chaotic, jumping around in time, missing details, or having significant gaps.

This fragmentation reflects how the memory is currently encoded.

Over repeated writings, the narrative typically becomes more coherent, linear, and complete.

Details fill in.

The sequence of events becomes clearer.

This increasing coherence reflects the memory being processed and integrated properly.

You might also notice that the emotions, whilst still present, become less overwhelming.

The first writing might be intensely distressing throughout.

The fifth writing might still be sad or disturbing, but more manageable; you can write through it without becoming as overwhelmed.

Crucially, you might notice shifts in the meaning you attribute to the trauma.

Early writings might be dominated by self-blame, shame, or beliefs about permanent damage: 'I should have fought back.

This happened because I am weak.

I'll never recover from this.' Later writings often show more balanced, compassionate perspectives: 'I did what I could in an impossible situation.

This wasn't my fault.

I was hurt, but I am recovering.' These shifts in meaning, which often occur naturally through the processing work, though they can also be deliberately cultivated through cognitive restructuring, are an important part of recovery. (Bisson et al., 2019)

Some people find that writing their trauma narrative in stages, building up the layers of their story is helpful approach. Starting with an initial draft, outlining just the facts, then re-writing the narrative to include thoughts and emotions, before continuing to elaborate further on 'hot spots', which are the worst moments.

Working with "Hot Spots": The Worst Moments

Within any trauma, there are typically particular moments that are most distressing, sometimes called 'hot spots' or 'stuck points.' These are the moments that you most want to avoid thinking about, the moments that trigger the strongest emotional responses, the moments that appear most frequently in intrusive memories and nightmares. (Van der Kolk et al., 1996)

Hot spots often involve moments of greatest threat, helplessness, horror, or shame.

They might be the moment you thought you were going to die, the moment you saw someone else be killed or severely injured, the moment you felt most powerless, or the moment something particularly shameful or degrading occurred.

These hot spots require particular attention in memory processing. It is tempting to rush through them in writing, to skim over the worst moments with brief, vague descriptions. This is understandable avoidance, but it prevents proper processing. The hot spots are precisely the parts of the memory that are most stuck, most fragmented, and most in need of processing. To process them effectively, you need to slow down and write about them in detail, despite the distress this provokes.

When you reach a hot spot in your writing, deliberately slow down.

Spend more time on this part.

Write in even more detail about what you could see, hear, smell, feel, think, and experience emotionally and physically.

If the hot spot involves something you feel ashamed of, perhaps you froze when you believed you should have fought, or your body responded in ways you find shameful, or you did something to survive that you feel guilty about, write about this, too.

The shame loses its power when brought into the light and examined.

What feels shameful in isolation often becomes understandable when viewed with compassion and full context.

For example, if a hot spot involves the moment you froze during an assault, write in detail: 'I want to fight back, but I cannot move.

My body will not respond.

I feel paralysed.

I am terrified and confused about why I cannot move.

I think I should be fighting, but I am just frozen.

I feel ashamed that I am not fighting back.' Then, in reflecting on this hot spot later, you can recognise that freezing is a normal, automatic survival response, not a choice or a failure.

Many assault survivors freeze, and research shows that freezing is often the response that keeps people safest in situations where fighting or fleeing aren't viable. (Porges, 2011; Levine, 2008)

But you can only challenge the shame and self-blame if you first fully acknowledge and express them.

Some therapists recommend specific techniques for hot spots.

One approach is to write the hot spot moment repeatedly within a single session, writing that particular moment 3-4 times in succession, with brief breaks between each writing.

This intensive processing of the most difficult moment can be highly effective, though it is also very demanding.

If attempting this, ensure you have adequate support and coping resources available.

Another approach is to spend extra time on hot spots during each full narrative writing, slowing down, adding more detail, staying with the moment longer, rather than rushing through.

Both approaches can be effective.

Including Thoughts, Emotions, and Physical Sensations

Effective trauma narrative work includes not just the external events (what happened) but also your internal experience (what you thought, felt, and experienced physically).

Many people, when first writing trauma narratives, focus primarily on the external events: 'The car hit me.

I went to the hospital.

I had surgery.' Whilst this captures the objective sequence, it misses the internal experience that makes the trauma traumatic.

A more complete narrative includes the subjective experience: 'The car is coming at me.

I think I am going to die.

I am terrified.

My heart is pounding so hard it hurts.

Everything goes into slow motion.

I hear the impact, a terrible crunching sound.

I feel intense pain in my leg.

I think I am dying.

I am scared and confused.'

Including thoughts means writing what you were thinking during the trauma. These thoughts might be clear and verbal, 'I am going to die' or 'I need to get away', or they might be more fragmented impressions. Even thoughts you feel ashamed of or that seem irrational deserve inclusion: 'I think this is my fault,' 'I think I deserve this,' 'I wish I could just disappear,' 'I think I should fight back, but I am too scared.' These thoughts are part of your experience and need processing.

Including emotions means identifying and naming what you were feeling.

This can be challenging because trauma often involves overwhelming, complex emotions that are hard to articulate.

You might have felt terror, horror, helplessness, rage, disgust, shame, guilt, betrayal, or confusion, possibly multiple emotions simultaneously or in rapid succession.

Do your best to identify and name these emotions in your writing: 'I feel terrified,' 'I am so angry I want to scream,' 'I feel disgusted and dirty,' 'I am ashamed.' If you cannot identify specific emotions, describe the experience: 'I feel overwhelmed,' 'Everything feels unreal,' 'I feel like I am disconnecting from my body.'

Including physical sensations means describing what you felt in your body, both the physical impacts of the trauma itself and your body's responses to threat.

Physical impacts might include pain, pressure, temperature changes, or injury sensations.

Body responses to threat might include rapid heartbeat, difficulty breathing, trembling, muscle tension, nausea, dizziness, or feeling frozen.

These physical sensations are an important element of traumatic memory and deserve detailed description: 'My heart is racing so fast I think it will explode.

I cannot breathe properly.

My whole body is shaking.

I feel sick to my stomach.

There's intense pain in my arm where he's gripping me.'

Working with Dissociation During Trauma

Many people dissociate during trauma, experiencing feelings of unreality, disconnection from their body, emotional numbness, or feeling like they are watching events from outside themselves.

Dissociation is a protective response to overwhelming threat: when you cannot physically escape, your mind escapes by disconnecting from the experience.

Whilst protective in the moment, dissociation during trauma predicts higher PTSD risk, partly because it interferes with memory processing.

Memories formed during dissociation are often particularly fragmented and poorly integrated.

If you dissociated during your trauma, include this experience in your narrative writing.

Describe what dissociation felt like: 'Everything feels far away and unreal.

I feel like I am watching this happen to someone else.

I feel disconnected from my body.

I am numb.

I can see terrible things happening, but I do not feel anything.

Time feels strange, I do not know if this lasts seconds or hours.' Including dissociative experiences in your narrative helps process them.

You are acknowledging the full reality of your experience rather than glossing over dissociation.

- However, you also want to avoid dissociating during the memory processing work itself. Dissociating while writing the narrative interferes with the processing

- you need to be adequately emotionally engaged for the work to be effective. If you notice yourself dissociating during writing, feeling numb, disconnected, or emotionally distant from what you are writing, pause, do grounding exercises, reconnect with the present, and then continue. You are aiming for a middle ground: emotionally engaged enough to process the material (which means feeling emotions, sometimes strongly), but not so overwhelmed that you dissociate. This balance can be challenging to achieve, and it is one reason why working with a therapist can be helpful
- they can help you maintain this optimal engagement zone.

Working with Multiple Traumas

Many people with PTSD have experienced multiple traumatic events. You might have multiple distinct traumas, a car accident, an assault, and a natural disaster, for example, or you might have experienced repeated similar traumas, such as ongoing childhood abuse or multiple combat deployments. Working with multiple traumas requires some modification of the approach. (Cusack et al., 2016; Teicher & Samson, 2016)

If you have multiple distinct traumas, you will typically need to process each one separately.

Start with the trauma that feels most manageable rather than jumping straight to the worst trauma.

Building your skills and confidence with a less overwhelming trauma helps prepare you for processing more difficult memories.

This does not mean avoiding the worst trauma indefinitely, eventually, you'll need to process all significant traumas that contribute to your PTSD, but it means approaching them strategically rather than randomly.

If you have experienced repeated similar traumas, such as ongoing abuse or multiple combat incidents, you might process one representative incident in detail, which often reduces distress related to other similar incidents.

Alternatively, you might create a narrative that captures the general pattern while also focusing on specific worst incidents.

Some people find adopting a timeline approach helpful, outlining the sequence of events in the order they occurred throughout their life.

A therapist can help determine the best approach for your particular situation.

Common Challenges in Memory Processing and How to Address Them

Memory processing work, whilst highly effective, presents several common challenges. Understanding these challenges and having strategies to address them helps you persist with the work even when difficulties arise.

Challenge 1: Difficulty starting or persistent avoidance.

You know you should write the narrative, but you keep putting it off, finding reasons to delay, or starting but stopping after a few sentences.

This avoidance is completely understandable; your brain is trying to protect you from distress.

However, this avoidance maintains PTSD. (Clark, 1999; Salkovskis, 1991)

Strategy: Start with the easiest part, the beginning, before the worst moments.

Commit to writing for just 10 minutes.

You can always stop after 10 minutes if it is genuinely unbearable, but you'll often find that once you start, you can continue.

Use the '10-minute rule': promise yourself you'll write for 10 minutes and then reassess.

Another strategy is to write with support, having someone nearby (not necessarily in the room) who knows what you are doing and can provide comfort afterwards.

Reward yourself after completing difficult work, and plan something enjoyable for after the writing session.

Challenge 2: Becoming overwhelmed during writing and needing to stop.

You start writing, but the emotions become so intense that you cannot continue.

You freeze, dissociate, panic, or simply shut down. (Porges, 2011; Levine, 2008)

Strategy: This indicates you are moving too fast or jumping straight to the worst moments.

Slow down.

Start with earlier parts of the trauma sequence, before the worst moments.

Write more slowly, taking breaks to ground yourself and breathe.

If you become overwhelmed, stop, use grounding and breathing techniques, and then continue from an earlier point in the narrative rather than from where you stopped.

Some people find it helpful to write in stages, perhaps writing only the first third of the narrative in one session, the middle third in another session, and the final third in a third session, before writing the complete narrative all at once.

Challenge 3: Feeling nothing, emotional numbing or dissociation during writing.

You write the narrative, but you feel detached, numb, or like you are just reporting facts without emotion.

This lack of emotional engagement interferes with processing.

Strategy: Slow down you are writing.

Add more sensory detail, what you could see, hear, smell, and feel physically.

Explicitly write about emotions, even if you do not feel them strongly right now: 'I was terrified,' 'I felt helpless and trapped.' Read the narrative aloud after writing it, hearing yourself say the words can increase emotional engagement.

Consider whether you are at a safe enough point in life to engage with this material, sometimes dissociation during processing indicates that you are not yet in a position to do this work safely, and you might need more stabilisation first.

Challenge 4: Difficulty with specific parts, you can write most of the narrative but get stuck at particular moments.

Strategy: These stuck points are likely hot spots that need extra attention.

Do not skip them, they are precisely the parts that need most processing.

If you absolutely cannot write about a particular moment initially, write everything up to that point and everything after it, marking the gap: 'Something terrible happens here that I am not ready to write about yet.' Then, in subsequent writings, try to gradually fill in more detail about that moment.

You might start with very brief, general descriptions and gradually add detail over multiple writings.

The goal is eventually to process the whole memory, including the worst parts, but you can build up to this gradually if needed.

Challenge 5: Memories feel unclear or fragmented, you are not sure what happened in what order, or significant parts are missing.

Strategy: Write what you do remember, even if it is fragmentary.

Over repeated writings, more details often emerge as the memory becomes less fragmented.

Include the fragmentation in your writing: 'Things are unclear here.

I remember seeing X, but I am not sure what happened next.

Then I remember being in Y location.' This honesty about fragmentation is part of the processing.

Do not try to force memories or fill in gaps with guesses, work with what you actually remember.

As processing progresses, fragmented memories often become more coherent naturally.

Challenge 6: Symptom spikes after writing, intrusive memories, nightmares, or anxiety increase significantly after memory processing sessions. Strategy: This is normal, especially in early sessions, and typically indicates you are engaging with material that needs processing. However, you can manage symptom spikes through several strategies: Schedule writing sessions when you have time afterward for self-care and recovery. Use your coping toolkit extensively after writing, grounding, breathing, self-soothing, physical activity, social connection. Consider whether you are processing too much too quickly, perhaps shorter sessions or slower progression would be more manageable. Remind yourself that symptom spikes are temporary and will decrease as processing progresses. If symptoms become unmanageable, pause the memory work and consult with a therapist before continuing. (Van der Kolk et al., 1996)

Knowing When Memory Processing Is Complete

How do you know when you have done enough memory processing work? Several indicators suggest the memory has been adequately processed, and you can move on to other aspects of treatment.

First, the narrative has become coherent and complete. You can write or think through the entire trauma in a logical sequence, from beginning to end, without significant gaps, confusion, or fragmentation. The narrative hangs together as a story, a terrible story, but a comprehensible one, rather than being a collection of disconnected fragments.

Second, the emotional intensity has reduced. The memory is still sad, disturbing, or upsetting; it would be strange if it weren't, given that trauma is objectively terrible, but you are not overwhelmed by emotions when thinking about or writing about it. You can engage with the memory without becoming so distressed that you cannot function. The emotions feel more like sadness or appropriate distress about a past event rather than the overwhelming terror, horror, or shame of reliving it.

Third, the memory feels clearly located in the past.

When you think about the trauma, you have a clear awareness that you are remembering something that happened then, not experiencing something happening now.

The temporal boundaries between past and present are clear.

You might think: 'That terrible thing happened to me on that date, in that place.

It was awful, but it is over now.

I am here, in the present, and I am safe.' This sense of pastness is crucial, it indicates the memory has acquired proper temporal context markers.

Fourth, intrusive memories and nightmares have decreased significantly. The memory no longer intrudes into your consciousness unbidden multiple times per day. You can think about other things. Nightmares, if they occur, are less frequent and less distressing. The memory is accessible when you choose to think about it, but it does not dominate your mental life uninvited. (Van der Kolk et al., 1996)

Fifth, triggers provoke less intense reactions. When you encounter reminders of the trauma, you might still feel uncomfortable or sad, but you do not experience overwhelming panic, complete flashbacks, or intense physical symptoms. You can recognise 'This reminds me of the trauma' without being thrown back into that experience fully. (Van der Kolk et al., 1996)

Sixth, the meanings you have attached to the trauma have shifted. You no longer believe, or believe as strongly, that the trauma defines you, that you are permanently damaged, that you are to blame, or that you cannot cope with life. You might have developed more balanced, compassionate perspectives: 'That terrible thing happened, and it changed me, but it does not define me. I am recovering. I am stronger than I realised.' These shifts in meaning often occur naturally through memory processing, though they can also be cultivated through cognitive restructuring, which we'll discuss in the next chapter.

When several of these indicators are present, you have likely done sufficient memory processing work on that particular trauma. This does not mean you'll never think about the trauma again or never feel distressed by it, but it means the memory has been adequately processed and integrated. You can then move on to other components of treatment, such as cognitive restructuring or behavioural exposure, confident that you have addressed this crucial foundation.

In Vivo Exposure: Reclaiming Your Life from Avoidance

Whilst memory processing work addresses the trauma memory itself, another critical component of trauma-focused treatment involves gradually facing the situations, places, activities, and experiences you have been avoiding since the trauma. This is called in vivo exposure, meaning 'in real life' exposure, or graded exposure. Alongside imaginal exposure through trauma narrative work, in vivo exposure forms the second essential pillar of exposure therapy for PTSD.

Understanding the Role of Avoidance in Maintaining PTSD

Avoidance is one of the hallmark features of PTSD, and understandably so. After experiencing trauma, you naturally want to avoid anything that reminds you of what happened, as these reminders trigger intense distress, anxiety, memories, and overwhelming emotions. Avoidance provides immediate relief; when you avoid a trauma reminder, you do not experience the distress it would trigger. In the short term, this feels protective and necessary.

However, avoidance maintains and strengthens PTSD in the long term through several mechanisms. (Clark, 1999; Salkovskis, 1991)

First, avoidance prevents you from learning that the situations you are avoiding are actually safer than you believe.

If you avoid driving after a car accident, you never discover that most journeys end safely.

If you avoid crowded places after an assault, you never learn that most crowded places pose no threat.

Your brain cannot update its threat assessment if you never gather new, disconfirming evidence.

The situation remains categorised as dangerous because you never experience evidence to the contrary.

Second, avoidance strengthens the association between neutral cues and danger in your mind.

Each time you avoid something because it reminds you of the trauma, you reinforce the message to your brain that this thing is indeed dangerous and must be avoided for safety.

The association grows stronger rather than weaker.

If you avoid cars because they remind you of an accident, avoiding strengthens the belief that cars are dangerous, even though cars themselves are neutral objects that are statistically quite safe.

Third, avoidance prevents natural habituation to distress.

When you first encounter a trauma reminder, anxiety spikes intensely.

However, if you remain in the situation without fleeing, anxiety naturally decreases over time as your nervous system realises no actual threat is present.

This process, called habituation, teaches your brain that the trigger is not dangerous, and the anxiety response is unnecessary.

Avoidance interrupts this natural learning process.

You flee before habituation can occur, which maintains the intense anxiety response indefinitely.

Fourth, avoidance progressively restricts your life.

What begins as avoiding specific trauma-related situations often expands to avoiding entire categories of experiences.

If you were assaulted at night, you might initially avoid going out after dark.

Over time, this might expand to avoiding going out alone at any time, then avoiding certain types of locations entirely, then rarely leaving home at all.

Each avoided situation makes future avoidance more likely because you have not built confidence in your ability to cope.

Your world shrinks progressively, and the trauma continues to control your life even though the actual traumatic event is long past.

Fifth, avoidance prevents you from engaging in meaningful activities and relationships. If you avoid situations that matter to you, driving to visit family, attending social events, going to work, pursuing hobbies, you lose access to sources of meaning, connection, and joy. This deprivation contributes to depression, isolation, and a sense that life is not worth living. The trauma has already taken enough from you; you do not need to surrender additional territory through avoidance.

The purpose of in vivo exposure is to reverse these processes systematically.

By gradually, deliberately facing avoided situations in a structured way, you can learn that these situations are safer than your trauma-influenced brain believes, discover that you can tolerate and cope with anxiety better than you thought, weaken the associations between neutral cues and danger, reclaim activities and experiences that matter to you, and rebuild a full, meaningful life.

In vivo exposure is not about being reckless or exposing yourself to genuine danger; it is about facing situations that are objectively safe but feel dangerous because of their association with trauma.

Creating Your Exposure Hierarchy: Mapping the Landscape of Avoidance

Before beginning in vivo exposure, you need to identify what you are avoiding and create a systematic plan for gradually facing these avoided situations. This plan, called an exposure hierarchy, lists avoided situations from least to most anxiety-provoking, allowing you to build skills and confidence progressively rather than attempting the most difficult situations first.

Start by creating a comprehensive list of everything you avoid because it reminds you of the trauma or triggers PTSD symptoms. Be thorough and specific. Include places you avoid, activities you no longer do, people you stay away from, objects or situations you find difficult, and subtle avoidances you might not have fully recognised. Many people discover they are avoiding more than they initially realised once they start listing systematically.

For each avoided situation, rate how much anxiety or distress thinking about doing this creates. Use a 0-100 scale where 0 represents no anxiety at all, completely comfortable, and 100 represents the maximum anxiety imaginable, absolute terror or panic. This rating is subjective; there is no right or wrong answer. The ratings help you understand the relative difficulty of different situations for you personally.

Consider the example of Sarah, who was assaulted whilst walking home alone at night.

Her comprehensive avoidance list might include: Going out after dark (any distance), Walking alone during daytime (long distance), Walking alone during daytime (short distance, familiar routes), Walking with someone else after dark, Being in car parks (especially when quiet), Using public transport at peak times, Using public transport at quiet times, Going to shops alone, Going to busy social events, Making eye contact with strangers, Wearing certain types of clothing, Taking certain routes that pass near the assault location.

Each situation receives an anxiety rating based on how distressing Sarah finds the thought of doing it.

Once you have your comprehensive list with ratings, organise the items from lowest to highest anxiety rating. This becomes your exposure hierarchy. The hierarchy typically contains 10-15 items, though it can be shorter or longer depending on the scope of your avoidance. If you have many avoided situations, you might create separate hierarchies for different domains, perhaps one for driving-related avoidances, another for social situations, and another for specific locations.

Your hierarchy should be personalised to your specific avoidances and trauma.

Two people with PTSD from similar traumas will have different hierarchies based on their individual patterns of avoidance and anxiety triggers.

There is no standard hierarchy; yours should reflect your unique experience.

Additionally, the hierarchy is a working document that you can modify as you progress.

You might discover that something you rated 60 actually feels more like 40 once you start exposure work, or you might identify new avoided situations to add.

Flexibility and ongoing adjustment are appropriate and encouraged.

Conducting Graded Exposure: The Systematic Process

With your hierarchy established, you begin exposure work by starting with the lowest-rated item, the situation that provokes the least anxiety. This graduated approach allows you to build skills, confidence, and evidence that you can cope before tackling more difficult situations. Attempting the most difficult situations first typically results in overwhelming anxiety, potential failure experiences, and increased avoidance rather than progress.

Before conducting your first exposure, ensure you have adequate coping resources in place.

Review grounding techniques, controlled breathing, and other anxiety management strategies discussed earlier in this guide.

You want these skills readily accessible if anxiety becomes intense during exposure, though the goal is not to use these strategies to eliminate anxiety but rather to manage it if it becomes overwhelming.

Some anxiety during exposure is normal, expected, and actually necessary for the learning process to occur.

Plan your exposure. Identify specifically what you will do, when you will do it, where exactly you will go, how long you will stay, and what support you will have available if needed. This preparation reduces uncertainty and makes the exposure more manageable. For your first few exposures, consider having a support person available, perhaps waiting nearby or reachable by phone, though as you build confidence, you will conduct exposures independently.

When conducting the exposure, approach the situation deliberately and stay in the situation long enough for anxiety to decrease naturally.

This is crucial.

If you enter the situation, feel anxiety spike, and immediately flee, you reinforce the avoidance pattern and the belief that the situation is dangerous.

Instead, you need to remain in the situation whilst anxiety is elevated and discover that it decreases over time without anything catastrophic occurring.

This habituation process typically requires 30-60 minutes, though the time varies depending on the situation and your individual response pattern.

During exposure, monitor your anxiety level using the same 0-100 scale you used for your hierarchy.

This is called your Subjective Units of Distress Scale or SUDS rating.

Check your SUDS every 5-10 minutes throughout the exposure.

You will typically observe that anxiety starts at a moderate to high level when you first enter the situation, peaks within the first 10-15 minutes, and then gradually decreases if you remain in the situation.

This decrease, the habituation response, is the learning experience you are aiming for.

Your brain discovers: 'I am in this situation.

I feel anxious.

But nothing terrible is happening.

The anxiety is decreasing.

I can cope with this.'

After completing the exposure, record what happened. Note the situation you practised, how long you stayed, your peak SUDS rating, your SUDS at the end, what you learned from the experience, and any difficulties encountered. This record serves multiple purposes. It tracks your progress, provides evidence of improvement over time, helps you identify patterns in your anxiety responses, and allows you to plan subsequent exposures more effectively.

Repeat each exposure multiple times before progressing to the next item on your hierarchy.

A single exposure to a situation might produce some anxiety reduction, but repeated exposures consolidate the learning much more effectively.

Research suggests that conducting the same exposure 3-5 times, until your peak anxiety rating decreases substantially, perhaps by 50 per cent or more from your first attempt, is optimal.

You should reach a point where the situation that initially felt quite anxiety-provoking now feels manageable and does not trigger intense distress.

This demonstrates that your brain has learned the situation is safe.

Once you have habituated to the lowest item on your hierarchy, progress to the next item.

Work through your hierarchy systematically, spending adequate time on each level before advancing.

Do not rush to tackle the most difficult items too quickly.

Building solid foundations at each level makes subsequent levels more manageable.

Think of this as building physical fitness; you would not attempt to run a marathon without first building up your capacity through progressively longer runs.

Similarly, psychological exposure requires graduated progression.

The Principles of Effective Exposure: Maximising Learning

Several principles maximise the effectiveness of in vivo exposure and should guide your practise throughout this process.

First, exposure should be prolonged rather than brief.

Brief exposures, entering a situation for just a few minutes and then leaving, do not allow sufficient time for habituation to occur.

You experience the anxiety spike but leave before the decrease, which reinforces rather than reduces anxiety.

Aim for exposure sessions lasting at least 30-60 minutes for most situations, longer if needed for anxiety to decrease substantially.

The session ends when anxiety has decreased notably from its peak, not when anxiety first spikes or when you reach a predetermined time limit.

Second, exposure should be repeated rather than one-off. A single exposure might produce temporary anxiety reduction, but repeated exposures consolidate learning more deeply. Your brain needs multiple opportunities to gather evidence that the situation is safe and that anxiety decreases naturally. Think of learning any skill; you would not expect to master it from a single practise session. Similarly, anxiety reduction and avoidance reversal require repeated practise.

Third, exposure should be systematic and planned rather than haphazard.

Random, unplanned encounters with trauma reminders often feel overwhelming because you are unprepared mentally and might not stay in the situation long enough for habituation.

In contrast, planned exposures allow you to approach situations deliberately, with appropriate preparation, adequate time, and coping resources available if needed.

This planned, systematic approach produces better outcomes than simply hoping you will encounter and face avoided situations spontaneously.

Fourth, exposure requires full engagement rather than distraction or avoidance.

Whilst in the exposure situation, you want to be fully present and engaged with the experience, not using distraction or mental avoidance to reduce anxiety artificially.

If you enter a feared situation but spend the entire time distracting yourself with your phone or dissociating mentally, your brain does not learn that the situation itself is safe.

The learning occurs when you are present, aware of the situation, experiencing the anxiety, and discovering it decreases naturally.

Subtle avoidances, such as wearing sunglasses to avoid eye contact, bringing a companion when the goal is to practise alone, or planning escape routes obsessively, similarly interfere with the learning process.

Identify and eliminate these subtle avoidances as you progress.

Fifth, exposure should target situations based on their trauma association rather than their objective danger level.

The goal is not to expose yourself to genuinely dangerous situations to prove you can tolerate them.

Rather, the goal is to face situations that are objectively safe but feel dangerous because they remind you of the trauma or trigger anxiety.

This distinction is crucial.

If you were assaulted in a car park, visiting a well-lit, busy car park during daytime is appropriate exposure; visiting a deserted car park in a high-crime area at night is not therapeutic exposure, it is genuine risk.

Always apply common sense about actual safety whilst recognising that your trauma-influenced threat assessment often overestimates danger in objectively safe situations.

Sixth, exposure should be self-paced within reason.

Whilst it is important to challenge yourself and not avoid indefinitely, exposure works best when you progress at a pace that feels challenging but not overwhelming.

If you attempt situations that are too difficult too quickly, you risk becoming overwhelmed, having a negative experience, and increasing avoidance.

Conversely, if you progress too slowly, staying at very easy levels indefinitely, you do not build the confidence and skills needed for more difficult situations.

The optimal pace involves stretching yourself, facing situations that create moderate anxiety rather than only minimal anxiety, whilst ensuring you do not become completely overwhelmed.

You should feel some discomfort during exposure; that discomfort indicates you are working in the growth zone where learning occurs.

Troubleshooting Common Challenges in Exposure Work

In vivo exposure, whilst highly effective, presents several common challenges. Understanding these challenges and having strategies to address them helps you persist with the work even when difficulties arise.

Challenge 1: Anxiety does not decrease during exposure.

You enter the situation, anxiety spikes, but even after 45-60 minutes, anxiety remains high rather than decreasing.

This lack of habituation is frustrating and can make exposure feel pointless.

Strategy: Consider whether you are using subtle avoidances or distractions that interfere with learning.

Are you present and engaged with the situation, or are you mentally avoiding or dissociating?

Eliminate these subtle avoidances and fully engage with the experience.

Additionally, ensure you are staying in the situation long enough; some situations require longer than 60 minutes for anxiety to decrease, particularly early in exposure work.

If anxiety genuinely does not decrease despite prolonged, engaged exposure over multiple attempts, consider whether this situation is too difficult currently and whether starting with an easier step might be more productive.

Occasionally, lack of habituation indicates that the situation genuinely triggers responses that require additional preparation or professional guidance.

Challenge 2: Anxiety decreases during exposure but returns to high levels next time.

Your first exposure goes well, anxiety decreases substantially by the end.

However, when you attempt the same situation again a few days later, anxiety is just as high as the first time, as though no learning occurred.

Strategy: This is frustratingly common and does not indicate that exposure is not working.

Initial anxiety reduction within a session (within-session habituation) typically precedes anxiety reduction between sessions (between-session habituation).

Continue with repeated exposures to the same situation.

Over multiple repetitions, you will notice that whilst anxiety might still be elevated at the start of each exposure, the peak is lower, the anxiety decreases more quickly, and eventually, the starting anxiety level decreases too.

This progression from within-session habituation to between-session habituation is the normal learning trajectory.

Patience and repeated practice are essential.

Challenge 3: Exposure feels too difficult, and you keep avoiding or cancelling planned exposures.

You create your hierarchy, plan exposures, but when the time comes, you find reasons to postpone, cancel, or avoid actually doing them.

This avoidance of exposure itself is common, understandable, and problematic.

Strategy: First, ensure your hierarchy is graduated appropriately.

If even the lowest item feels too difficult, break it down into smaller steps.

There is no exposure that is too easy as a starting point.

If driving feels too overwhelming, perhaps sitting in a parked car with the engine off is your starting point.

If going to shops alone feels impossible, perhaps going to a shop with someone else is your first step.

Start wherever you can, and build from there.

Second, schedule exposures as concrete appointments with yourself, specific day, time, and plan, rather than vaguely intending to do them sometime.

Concrete plans are more likely to be followed through.

Third, identify and challenge thoughts that maintain avoidance: 'This won't work,' 'It's too dangerous,' 'I'm not ready yet.' Use cognitive restructuring techniques to evaluate whether these thoughts are accurate.

Fourth, consider using commitment strategies.

Tell someone else about your exposure plans so you have external accountability.

Alternatively, if working with a therapist, conduct initial exposures with them present for support.

The first step is always the hardest; momentum builds once you begin.

Challenge 4: Panic attacks during exposure.

You enter the situation, anxiety spikes to overwhelming levels, you experience a panic attack with intense physical symptoms, and you feel you must escape immediately.

Strategy: First, recognise that panic attacks, whilst terrifying, are not dangerous.

They peak within 10-15 minutes and then decrease naturally.

You cannot have a panic attack indefinitely; it is physiologically impossible.

If you experience a panic attack during exposure, try to stay in the situation if at all possible.

Use breathing exercises, grounding techniques, and remind yourself: 'This is a panic attack.

It is intensely unpleasant but not dangerous.

It will pass in minutes.

I can get through this.' If you absolutely must leave the situation, leave briefly, use coping strategies to reduce panic, and then return to the situation as soon as you can, even if only for a short time.

Leaving and not returning reinforces the panic response and avoidance.

Returning demonstrates to yourself that you can cope and that the situation is survivable.

If panic attacks occur repeatedly during exposures, this might indicate you are progressing too quickly up your hierarchy.

Return to easier steps and build more gradually.

Additionally, ensure you have learned and practised anxiety management techniques thoroughly before attempting exposure situations likely to trigger intense anxiety.

Challenge 5: External events undermine progress.

You are making good progress with exposure work when an external event occurs that triggers significant symptoms or makes exposure temporarily impossible.

Perhaps news coverage of a similar trauma triggers intense distress, a stressful life event increases overall anxiety, or lockdowns prevent you from accessing certain situations.

Strategy: External disruptions to exposure work are inevitable over the course of recovery. (Watkins et al., 2018)

Do not interpret them as total failure or loss of all progress.

Some temporary setback is normal.

When the disruption has passed, return to exposure work, perhaps stepping back one or two levels on your hierarchy to rebuild confidence before progressing again.

You have not lost all your progress; the learning is still present in your brain, even if temporarily inaccessible due to heightened distress.

With some practice after a disruption, you will often find you regain ground more quickly than you initially built it.

This is because the learning was consolidated previously; you are reactivating it rather than starting from scratch.

Challenge 6: Difficulty generalising learning across contexts.

You successfully habituate to a specific situation, perhaps driving to your local supermarket, but anxiety remains high for similar situations, such as driving to other shops or other locations.

The learning does not generalise as broadly as you hoped.

Strategy: Generalisation of learning across contexts varies between individuals.

Some people find that exposure to one example of a feared situation reduces anxiety across all similar situations.

Others require exposure to multiple different examples before generalisation occurs.

If you fall into the latter category, this does not indicate failure; it simply means you need to practise exposure across varied contexts.

Once you have habituated to your local supermarket, deliberately practise driving to different shops, different locations, at different times of day.

This varied practice promotes broader generalisation.

Over time, as you accumulate extensive exposure experiences across diverse contexts, generalisation improves, and you find that novel situations provoke less anxiety because your brain has learned that this entire category of situations is safe.

Integrating In Vivo Exposure with Imaginal Exposure and Cognitive Work

In vivo exposure works most effectively when integrated with the other components of trauma-focused CBT discussed in this guide. The three core components, imaginal exposure through trauma narrative work, in vivo exposure to avoided situations, and cognitive restructuring of unhelpful thoughts, work synergistically to produce optimal outcomes. (Bisson et al., 2013; NICE, 2018)

Imaginal exposure and in vivo exposure target different aspects of PTSD and complement each other.

Imaginal exposure addresses the trauma memory itself, processing and integrating it so it becomes a past event rather than a present experience.

In vivo exposure addresses the behavioural avoidance and anxiety that maintain PTSD in daily life.

Many people find that as they progress with trauma narrative work, in vivo exposures become easier because processing the memory has reduced the general anxiety and distress that fuel avoidance.

Conversely, successfully conducting in vivo exposures often makes trauma narrative work easier because you have built confidence in your ability to tolerate distress and discovered that facing feared experiences does not destroy you.

Cognitive restructuring supports exposure work by challenging the thoughts that maintain avoidance.

Before exposure, you might think: 'If I go to that place, something terrible will happen,' 'I won't be able to cope with the anxiety,' or 'Avoiding is the only way to stay safe.' These thoughts maintain avoidance and make exposure feel impossible.

Using cognitive restructuring to evaluate and challenge these predictions, what is the actual evidence that something terrible will happen?

What is the probability?

Have I coped with difficult things before?

What would happen if I tried this exposure and discovered I could handle it?

This cognitive work provides motivation and reduces resistance to beginning exposure.

During and after exposure, you gather evidence that challenges unhelpful thoughts.

If your thought was 'I can't cope with anxiety in crowded places,' and you then successfully visit a crowded shop, stay for 45 minutes whilst anxious, and discover that anxiety decreases and nothing terrible happens, you have powerful evidence contradicting your original thought.

This evidence-gathering through behavioural experiments, which in vivo exposure essentially provides, often produces cognitive change that purely cognitive techniques alone do not achieve.

Your brain updates its predictions based on actual experience.

Therefore, effective trauma-focused treatment involves working on all three components concurrently or in close succession.

You might spend some sessions on trauma narrative work, some on in vivo exposure, and some on cognitive restructuring, with each component informing and supporting the others.

This integrated approach addresses PTSD comprehensively, targeting the trauma memory, the avoidance behaviours, and the unhelpful thoughts simultaneously rather than addressing only one element in isolation.

Knowing When In Vivo Exposure Work Is Complete

How do you know when you have completed sufficient in vivo exposure work? Several indicators suggest you have adequately addressed avoidance and can confidently navigate situations that previously triggered intense anxiety.

First, you can engage in activities and situations that matter to you without prohibitive anxiety.

You might still feel some nervousness or awareness of potential triggers; this is normal and does not indicate incomplete exposure work.

However, the anxiety is manageable, does not prevent you from doing what you want to do, and decreases relatively quickly when you enter the situation.

You are no longer making life decisions based primarily on avoiding anxiety triggers.

You can go to work, socialise, pursue hobbies, maintain relationships, and engage with life fully.

Second, your avoidance list has shortened dramatically. Activities that were on your original avoidance list are now things you do regularly without significant anticipatory anxiety. You might have avoided dozens of situations initially; now, most of these situations no longer trigger avoidance impulses. Your world has expanded rather than remaining constricted.

Third, you have developed confidence in your ability to cope with anxiety and distress.

You know from repeated experience that anxiety, whilst unpleasant, is tolerable and temporary.

You have successfully navigated dozens of anxiety-provoking situations and discovered that you can handle them.

- This confidence generalises beyond specific situations
- you approach novel potentially challenging situations thinking: 'This might be difficult, but I've handled difficult things before, and I can handle this too,' rather than: 'I can't cope with this
- I need to avoid it.'

Fourth, unexpected encounters with trauma reminders provoke manageable rather than overwhelming responses.

You unexpectedly encounter something that reminds you of the trauma, a smell, a location, a similar situation.

Instead of experiencing intense panic, complete avoidance, or being thrown into a flashback, you notice: 'This reminds me of the trauma.

I feel uncomfortable.

But I can handle this feeling.' You can use coping strategies effectively, and the distress passes relatively quickly.

These spontaneous exposures, which are inevitable in daily life, have become manageable rather than catastrophic.

Fifth, you have reclaimed meaningful activities that matter to you personally.

Exposure is not merely about reducing anxiety in abstract situations; it is about rebuilding a life worth living.

When you can engage in work, relationships, hobbies, and activities that bring meaning and joy, activities that were restricted by avoidance, you have achieved the central goal of exposure therapy.

Your life is no longer dominated by trauma and avoidance but is instead full of chosen activities and experiences.

When these indicators are present, you have likely completed sufficient in vivo exposure work.

This does not mean you will never feel anxious again or that all trauma-related distress has disappeared completely.

Recovery from PTSD is not about achieving a state of perpetual calm or complete elimination of all symptoms. (Ozer et al., 2003)

Rather, it is about reducing symptoms to manageable levels, reclaiming your life from avoidance, and developing confidence in your ability to cope with challenges.

When you have achieved these goals, exposure work has served its purpose, and you can focus on other aspects of recovery and life beyond trauma. (Guay et al., 2006)

In vivo exposure requires courage, persistence, and systematic effort.

Facing situations you have been avoiding for months or years is genuinely difficult work.

However, this work is also genuinely liberating.

Each exposure you complete is an act of reclaiming your life from trauma, demonstrating to yourself that you are not as fragile as you feared, and building evidence that the world is safer than your trauma-influenced brain believes.

The temporary discomfort of exposure work purchases long-term freedom from the prison of avoidance.

This is an investment worth making.

Combined with imaginal exposure and cognitive restructuring, in vivo exposure provides a path to comprehensive PTSD recovery and a life no longer dominated by trauma and fear. (Charuvastra & Cloitre, 2008)

Chapter Five: Challenging Unhelpful Thoughts and Beliefs

- Unhelpful thoughts about yourself and the world maintain PTSD
- Challenging these thoughts doesn't mean positive thinking

- Small shifts in thinking create significant emotional changes
- You can learn to notice and modify stuck thought patterns

This chapter focuses on cognitive restructuring techniques to challenge and modify the unhelpful thoughts and beliefs that maintain PTSD symptoms. You will learn to identify negative thought patterns, evaluate their accuracy, and develop more balanced, realistic perspectives. The techniques in this chapter are fundamental to cognitive behavioural therapy and form a core component of trauma recovery. (Neff & Germer, 2018)

Understanding the Cognitive Model of PTSD (Ehlers & Clark, 2000)

At the heart of cognitive behavioural therapy for PTSD lies a simple yet powerful principle: it is not events themselves that determine how we feel, but rather how we interpret and think about those events. This does not mean trauma is not real or that you imagined its impact. Rather, it recognises that two people experiencing similar traumatic events may develop different beliefs about what happened, and these differing beliefs lead to different emotional and behavioural responses.

Consider the cognitive triangle: thoughts, feelings, and behaviours are intimately connected.

When you have a thought such as 'the world is completely dangerous', this thought triggers feelings of fear and anxiety.

These feelings then drive behaviours like avoidance, hypervigilance, and isolation. (Porges, 2011; Yehuda & Seckl, 2011)

The behaviours, in turn, reinforce the original thought, creating a self-perpetuating cycle.

Breaking this cycle at any point, but particularly at the level of thoughts, can create positive ripple effects throughout the entire system.

Following trauma, people commonly develop excessively negative beliefs about themselves, others, and the world. These beliefs feel utterly true and are maintained by selective attention to confirming evidence whilst discounting contradictory information. Cognitive restructuring helps you examine these beliefs more objectively, consider alternative perspectives, and develop more balanced, realistic ways of thinking that reduce distress and support recovery. (Gilbert, 2014)

Common Cognitive Distortions in PTSD

Trauma typically generates predictable patterns of distorted thinking. Recognising these patterns in your own thoughts represents the first step towards challenging them. The most common cognitive distortions in PTSD include:

Overgeneralisation: Drawing broad conclusions from single incidents. After one traumatic event, one may conclude that 'nowhere is safe' or 'everyone will hurt me'. This distortion extends one negative experience to all similar situations, creating excessive fear and avoidance. You might think, 'because I was assaulted once, I will always be a victim' or 'since I failed to prevent what happened, I will always fail at everything important'.

Catastrophising: Automatically assuming the worst possible outcome. When experiencing a reminder, immediately jumping to 'something terrible is about to happen' even when the current situation is objectively safe. This distortion keeps you in a constant state of alarm, interpreting minor stressors as major threats. You might think 'if I go out alone, I will definitely be attacked' or 'if I try to work through this trauma memory, I will have a complete breakdown'.

All-or-nothing thinking: Viewing situations in extreme, dichotomous terms without acknowledging the middle ground. Believing you are either completely safe or in mortal danger, completely in control or totally helpless, entirely strong or pathetically weak. This black-and-white thinking eliminates nuance and creates unnecessary distress because most of life exists in shades of grey.

Personalisation and self-blame: Taking excessive responsibility for traumatic events beyond your actual control. Believing 'if only I had done something differently, this would not have happened' when in reality you had limited options in a dangerous situation. This distortion maintains guilt and shame whilst ignoring the perpetrator's responsibility or the role of circumstances beyond your control.

Mind reading: Assuming you know what others think about you, usually in negative ways. Believing others see you as weak, damaged, or contaminated by trauma without actual evidence. This distortion leads to social withdrawal based on feared judgements that may not exist. You might think 'everyone can tell something is wrong with me' or 'they all think I'm pathetic for not being over this'. (Ashton, 2002)

Emotional reasoning: Believing that because you feel something intensely, it must be true. 'I feel terrified, therefore I am in danger' or 'I feel worthless, therefore I am worthless'. Whilst feelings provide important information, they are not always accurate reflections of reality, particularly when the traumatic stress response has been triggered.

Should statements: Rigid rules about how you, others, or the world should be. 'I should have fought back', 'they should have protected me', 'the world should be fair and just'. These thoughts create guilt when directed at yourself and anger or disappointment when directed at others or the world, whilst changing nothing about what actually occurred.

The Thought Record: Your Primary Cognitive Restructuring Tool

The thought record provides a structured method for identifying, examining, and challenging unhelpful thoughts. Whilst it may seem cumbersome initially, with practice it becomes more natural, eventually happening almost automatically in your mind without needing to write everything down. Initially, however, writing provides crucial structure and helps you slow down the automatic thinking process enough to examine it objectively.

A complete thought record includes several columns capturing the full sequence of situation, thoughts, feelings, and alternative perspectives. You can find a blank thought record template in Appendix B, but the basic structure includes:

Situation: What was happening when the distressing thought occurred? Where were you? Who was present? What were you doing? Be specific and factual, describing the objective situation without interpretation. For example, 'sitting at home watching television' rather than 'trying to relax but failing as usual'.

Moods/Emotions: What did you feel? List all emotions present and rate their intensity from 0 to 100. Be as specific as possible with emotion words. Rather than just 'bad', identify whether you felt anxious, sad, angry, guilty, ashamed, or some combination. The same thought can trigger multiple emotions simultaneously.

Automatic Thoughts: What went through your mind when you started to feel this way? What does this situation mean to you? What does it say about you, others, the world, or the future? Capture thoughts as they occurred, even if they seem irrational or extreme. Often the most distressing thoughts are images rather than words. If an image occurred, describe it in detail.

Evidence For: What facts or experiences support this thought? Be careful to distinguish between actual evidence and further interpretations. 'I felt terrified' is not evidence that danger was present, though it is evidence that your fear response was activated. Look for concrete, observable facts.

Evidence Against: What facts or experiences contradict this thought? This is often the most difficult column because selective attention means you automatically notice confirming evidence whilst filtering out contradictory information. Force yourself to look for evidence against the thought, even if it feels forced initially. What would a defence lawyer argue if trying to disprove this thought?

Alternative Thought: Based on all the evidence, what is a more balanced, realistic way to think about this situation? The alternative thought should acknowledge valid concerns whilst being less extreme and more nuanced than the original thought. It should feel believable rather than like empty positive thinking. Rate how much you believe this alternative thought from 0 to 100.

Re-rate Moods: After generating the alternative thought, re-rate the intensity of each emotion. Often emotions reduce significantly when you develop a more balanced perspective, though they may not disappear entirely, which is perfectly normal. Even a 20 to 30 per cent reduction in emotional intensity represents meaningful progress.

Socratic Questioning: Examining Thoughts Through Inquiry

Socratic questioning provides a gentler alternative to directly challenging thoughts, using curious inquiry to help you discover alternative perspectives for yourself rather than having them imposed from outside. This method asks open-ended questions that encourage examination of evidence, consideration of alternatives, and exploration of the implications of different beliefs.

When a distressing thought arises, ask yourself questions such as: What is the evidence for and against this thought? Am I confusing a thought with a fact? What is the worst that could happen? What is the best that could happen? What is most realistically likely to happen? What cognitive distortions might I be engaging in? If a friend had this thought, what would I tell them? What would be a more balanced way to look at this situation? What action could I take if my thought were true? What has my experience been in similar situations previously?

These questions help you step back from automatic thoughts and examine them more objectively. The goal is not to eliminate negative thoughts entirely, which would be unrealistic, but rather to develop a more balanced, nuanced perspective that includes both difficulties and strengths, both real dangers and genuine safety, both painful realities and hopeful possibilities.

Addressing Core Beliefs in PTSD

Beneath automatic thoughts lie deeper core beliefs, fundamental assumptions about yourself, others, and the world that shape how you interpret experiences. Following trauma, core beliefs often become excessively negative: 'I am defective', 'other people are dangerous', 'the world is completely unpredictable and unsafe'. These beliefs feel like absolute truths because they have been reinforced repeatedly through selective attention and confirmation bias.

Core beliefs are more difficult to change than automatic thoughts because they are broader, more deeply held, and more resistant to contradictory evidence. However, persistent work examining and challenging core beliefs can produce profound shifts in how you experience yourself and the world. The process involves identifying core beliefs through downward arrow technique, gathering evidence for and against them, and developing more balanced alternative core beliefs.

The downward arrow technique identifies core beliefs by repeatedly asking 'if that thought were true, what would it mean about me?' For example, the automatic thought 'I should have fought back' might lead to 'that would mean I was weak', which leads to 'that would mean I am fundamentally defective', revealing the core belief 'I am worthless and defective'. Once identified, this core belief can be examined more systematically.

Challenging core beliefs requires gathering evidence from your entire life, not just the trauma.

Create a detailed log of experiences that contradict the negative core belief.

If your core belief is 'I am completely helpless', document times you successfully handled difficult situations, solved problems, or influenced outcomes.

If your core belief is 'everyone is dangerous', list people who have been kind, supportive, and trustworthy.

The evidence must be specific and detailed to counter the core belief's broad, absolute nature.

Developing alternative core beliefs requires crafting statements that are believable, balanced, and genuinely helpful.

Rather than swinging to the opposite extreme ('I am perfect and nothing bad will ever happen'), develop nuanced beliefs that acknowledge both strengths and limitations: 'I have both strengths and weaknesses like everyone else', 'whilst some people are untrustworthy, many others are genuinely caring', 'whilst bad things can happen, I have resources to cope with difficulties'.

These balanced beliefs better reflect reality's complexity.

Chapter Six: Facing Your Fears—Advanced Graded Exposure Strategies

Whilst the foundational principles of in vivo exposure covered in Chapter Four provide the essential framework for addressing avoidance, many people with PTSD encounter situations that require more sophisticated exposure strategies. This chapter explores advanced techniques for managing complex exposure challenges, working with specialised types of avoidance, integrating exposure with other treatment components, and maximising the effectiveness of your exposure work. These approaches build upon the basic graded exposure methodology and offer additional tools for situations where straightforward exposure proves insufficient or requires modification.

Advanced Exposure Hierarchy Development: Beyond the Basics

Creating a basic exposure hierarchy, as discussed in Chapter Four, involves listing avoided situations and rating their anxiety levels. However, more sophisticated hierarchy development can identify subtle patterns of avoidance, incorporate multiple dimensions of fear simultaneously, and create more targeted exposure plans.

Consider dimensionalized hierarchies, where you analyse avoidance across multiple fear dimensions rather than treating each situation as simply more or less anxiety-provoking.

For example, if you avoid driving after a car accident, your avoidance might vary based on several dimensions: distance (short trips vs long journeys), traffic density (quiet roads vs motorways), time of day (familiar daylight driving vs night), weather conditions (clear vs rainy), passenger presence (alone vs with others), and route familiarity (known routes vs unfamiliar areas).

Each dimension contributes independently to anxiety levels.

Rather than creating a simple linear hierarchy, you create a multi-dimensional matrix.

This allows you to vary one dimension whilst holding others constant, building skills systematically in each domain.

You might start with short-distance, daylight, familiar routes with a passenger present, then progressively vary each dimension independently.

Perhaps you increase distance whilst maintaining daylight and passenger presence, then once comfortable with longer distances, you practise alone whilst maintaining daylight and familiar routes.

This systematic variation across dimensions provides more granular control over difficulty levels and helps identify which specific elements most powerfully drive anxiety.

Contextual factors also merit consideration in hierarchy development.

The same situation might provoke vastly different anxiety depending on context.

Going to a shopping centre at 10 a.m.

on a quiet Tuesday might be moderately anxiety-provoking, whilst the same shopping centre on a busy Saturday afternoon might be substantially more difficult.

Including varied contexts for the same basic situation in your hierarchy acknowledges this reality and ensures exposure encompasses the range of contexts you will encounter in real life.

Additionally, consider incorporating predictability as a hierarchy dimension.

Many people find unpredictable situations substantially more anxiety-provoking than predictable ones.

You might tolerate a crowded space if you know exactly when you will leave, but find it overwhelming if the duration is uncertain.

Building tolerance for unpredictability, starting with short unpredictable durations and gradually increasing uncertainty, can be valuable exposure work. (Ashton, 2002)

This might involve staying in a situation for a flexible time ("I will stay between 20 and 40 minutes and decide in the moment when to leave") rather than always having a fixed predetermined duration.

Finally, hierarchies should evolve as you progress rather than remaining static.

You initially might rate driving on a motorway as 90 on your anxiety scale, but after completing extensive exposure to easier driving situations, you might reassess and find it now feels more like 60.

Regularly reviewing and updating your hierarchy ratings reflects your actual current anxiety levels rather than outdated pre-exposure predictions.

Additionally, as you complete items on your hierarchy, you might identify previously unrecognised avoidances to add.

The hierarchy is a living document that grows and changes alongside your recovery progress. (ISTSS, 2019)

Interoceptive Exposure: Facing Physical Sensations

Many people with PTSD avoid not just external situations but also internal physical sensations that remind them of trauma or trigger anxiety.

Rapid heartbeat, shortness of breath, dizziness, trembling, and other physiological sensations can become conditioned triggers for panic or flashbacks. (Van der Kolk et al., 1996)

If your heart raced during the trauma, subsequent episodes of elevated heart rate, even from benign causes like exercise, might trigger trauma memories and intense anxiety.

This creates a vicious cycle: you avoid activities that produce these sensations, which maintains fear of the sensations and restricts your life further.

Interoceptive exposure specifically targets fear of internal physical sensations through deliberately inducing these sensations in safe, controlled circumstances and discovering that they are harmless. This technique, developed originally for panic disorder treatment, proves valuable for PTSD when physical sensations have become conditioned triggers.

To conduct interoceptive exposure, you first identify which specific physical sensations you fear and avoid.

Common feared sensations include rapid heartbeat, breathlessness, dizziness, feeling faint, chest tightness, trembling, sweating, and feelings of unreality.

For each feared sensation, you then identify safe activities that reliably produce this sensation.

For a rapid heartbeat, running on the spot, climbing stairs repeatedly, or doing jumping jacks produces an elevated heart rate safely.

For breathlessness, hyperventilating for 30-60 seconds, breathing through a straw, or holding your breath produces the sensation.

For dizziness, spinning in a chair or shaking your head vigorously creates this feeling.

The goal is not to recreate the exact intensity experienced during trauma but rather to produce a milder version of the same sensation category.

You then engage in these sensation-inducing activities deliberately and repeatedly, whilst staying present with the sensations rather than distracting yourself or fleeing.

The procedure follows standard exposure principles: you rate your anxiety before inducing the sensation, engage in the activity for sufficient duration to produce the sensation clearly, rate anxiety during and after the sensation, and repeat multiple times until anxiety decreases substantially.

Over repeated practice, you learn that these physical sensations, whilst uncomfortable, are not dangerous and do not inevitably lead to catastrophe or loss of control.

The sensation becomes uncoupled from trauma memories and perceived threat.

Interoceptive exposure is particularly valuable when physical sensations have become such powerful triggers that you avoid any activity that might produce them.

If you avoid exercise because elevated heart rate triggers panic, or avoid coffee because increased arousal feels dangerous, interoceptive exposure can break this pattern.

By deliberately producing these sensations repeatedly in safe contexts, you desensitise your fear response and reclaim activities you have been avoiding due to associated physical sensations.

However, interoceptive exposure requires careful application.

Certain medical conditions make some sensation-inducing activities genuinely inadvisable.

If you have cardiovascular problems, respiratory conditions, or vestibular disorders, consult with medical professionals before engaging in activities that stress these systems.

Additionally, interoceptive exposure can be intensely distressing initially, as you are deliberately producing sensations strongly associated with trauma or panic.

Starting with very brief durations, perhaps 10-15 seconds initially, and gradually increasing duration as tolerance builds makes this work more manageable. (Ashton, 2002)

Having a therapist guide initial interoceptive exposure sessions can provide essential support whilst you build confidence in this technique.

Imaginal Exposure Combined with In Vivo: Integrated Approaches

Whilst imaginal exposure (trauma narrative work) and in vivo exposure (facing avoided situations) are often described as separate components of trauma-focused treatment, combining them strategically can produce particularly powerful results for certain presentations.

One integration approach involves conducting imaginal exposure immediately before in vivo exposure.

You spend 15-20 minutes engaging with the trauma memory through narrative work, allowing trauma-related emotions and cognitions to become activated, and then immediately proceed to an in vivo exposure situation whilst these emotions are still present.

This technique, sometimes called 'in vivo exposure with emotional engagement', ensures you are processing trauma-related affect in real-world situations rather than solely in imaginal work.

The combination can be particularly effective when in vivo situations trigger trauma memories; by activating the memory before entering the situation, you can process the memory-situation connection more directly.

Alternatively, you might conduct in vivo exposure first and then immediately process whatever trauma-related content arose through narrative work or cognitive restructuring.

Perhaps you visit a location similar to where your trauma occurred, note the thoughts, memories, and emotions this triggers, and then spend 30 minutes after leaving the situation writing about or processing this activated content.

This approach captures 'hot' cognitions, the thoughts and beliefs present when you are actually anxious, which are often more therapeutically relevant than 'cold' cognitions generated when you are calm and removed from triggering situations.

Some people benefit from exposure to trauma reminders combined with memory processing simultaneously.

You might visit the actual location where trauma occurred whilst simultaneously engaging in trauma narrative work, either verbally with a therapist present or through writing in the location.

This intensive combined approach can produce rapid habituation but requires careful implementation.

The intensity of combining both memory activation and situational exposure simultaneously can be overwhelming.

This technique is typically reserved for later in treatment, after you have built substantial tolerance through separate imaginal and in vivo work, and is often best conducted with professional support initially. (Ashton, 2002)

The key principle underlying these integrated approaches is that emotional processing occurs most effectively when trauma-related affect is activated. (Foa & Kozak, 1986)

Simply going through the motions of exposure whilst emotionally numb or disconnected produces limited benefit.

Similarly, processing memories whilst completely removed from any situational triggers might not generalise well to real-world situations.

Strategic combination of imaginal and in vivo exposure ensures that processing occurs whilst you are emotionally engaged with trauma-related content in contexts where this material naturally arises.

Working with Safety Behaviours and Subtle Avoidance (Clark, 1999)

Safety behaviours, actions you perform to feel safer in anxiety-provoking situations, often maintain rather than reduce anxiety in the long term. (Clark, 1999)

These behaviours prevent you from learning that the situation is safe without these precautions.

Common safety behaviours in PTSD include: always staying near exits, constantly scanning the environment for threats, avoiding eye contact, wearing particular types of clothing to be less noticeable, gripping objects tightly, keeping your back to walls, maintaining minimum distances from other people, having escape routes planned, keeping weapons or defensive items accessible, and relying on companions to feel safe. (Clark, 1999)

Safety behaviours create problems because they maintain the belief that safety depends on these behaviours rather than that the situation itself is safe. (Clark, 1999)

If you always stay near exits and nothing bad happens, your brain concludes: 'Nothing bad happened because I stayed near the exit,' rather than: 'Nothing bad happened because this situation is safe.' The situation remains categorised as dangerous, requiring protective measures.

Additionally, safety behaviours often restrict your behaviour and quality of life almost as much as complete avoidance. (Clark, 1999)

If you can only go to restaurants if you sit facing the door with your back to the wall and are prepared to leave at any moment, you are severely limiting your dining experiences and maintaining constant vigilance.

Effective exposure work requires progressively reducing and ultimately eliminating safety behaviours. (Clark, 1999)

This does not mean suddenly abandoning all precautions before you have built any confidence.

Rather, it involves a graduated reduction as exposure progresses.

Early in exposure work, using some safety behaviours whilst you build initial tolerance is acceptable and often necessary. (Clark, 1999)

If their presence allows you to engage in exposure that you would otherwise completely avoid, they have temporary utility.

However, as you habituate and build confidence, you systematically drop safety behaviours to test whether you actually need them. (Clark, 1999)

The process involves identifying all safety behaviours you employ in a given situation, including subtle ones you might not have fully recognised. (Clark, 1999)

Then, creating a hierarchy of safety behaviours from least to most difficult to relinquish. (Clark, 1999)

Begin with the easiest safety behaviour to drop.

Perhaps you stop constantly scanning your surroundings every few seconds, or you practise making brief eye contact with strangers rather than always avoiding it.

Once comfortable without this behaviour, eliminate the next one on your list.

Gradually, you conduct exposure with fewer and fewer protective measures, discovering that your safety does not actually depend on these behaviours.

For particularly entrenched safety behaviours, conducting specific experiments can be informative. (Clark, 1999)

Perform the same exposure twice, once with the safety behaviour and once without, and compare your anxiety levels and outcomes.

Often, you will discover that anxiety is initially higher without the safety behaviour but decreases comparably over time, and nothing catastrophic occurs in either condition.

This evidence demonstrates that the safety behaviour is not actually providing the protection you believed it did.

However, distinguish between maladaptive safety behaviours and reasonable precautions. (Clark, 1999)

Some behaviours represent sensible risk management rather than excessive anxiety-driven avoidance.

Locking your doors at night, avoiding genuinely dangerous areas, and maintaining awareness of your surroundings in unfamiliar places represent reasonable caution, not safety behaviours requiring elimination. (Clark, 1999)

The distinction lies in whether the behaviour is proportionate to actual risk.

If you are avoiding all public places because you cannot sit facing the door, this is a maladaptive safety behaviour.

If you prefer sitting facing the door when in an unfamiliar place but can comfortably sit otherwise when this is not possible, this is reasonable preference.

The goal is reducing behaviours that significantly restrict your life and maintain excessive anxiety, not eliminating all caution or personal preferences.

Exposure to Ambiguous and Uncertain Situations

Many people with PTSD experience intense distress about uncertainty and ambiguity.

After trauma, the world feels dangerous and unpredictable.

You might develop strong preferences for predictability and control, struggling intensely when situations are ambiguous or outcomes are uncertain.

This intolerance of uncertainty maintains PTSD by driving excessive information-seeking, difficulty with decision-making when outcomes are uncertain, avoidance of situations where you lack complete control, and chronic worry about potential future threats. (Ashton, 2002)

Exposure work for intolerance of uncertainty involves deliberately engaging with ambiguous situations and resisting urges to seek excessive reassurance or control. This is challenging because it requires tolerating discomfort without doing anything to reduce it, which feels counterintuitive. However, learning to tolerate uncertainty is essential for PTSD recovery, as life inevitably contains substantial uncertainty regardless of precautions taken. (Ashton, 2002)

Begin by identifying situations where intolerance of uncertainty drives problematic behaviour. (Ashton, 2002)

Perhaps you call family members repeatedly to confirm their safety, or you avoid making plans unless you can control all details, or you excessively research situations before encountering them.

For each pattern, design exposures that specifically target uncertainty tolerance. (Ashton, 2002)

If you seek repeated reassurance about safety, practise refraining from asking for reassurance despite the urge to do so.

If you excessively research situations beforehand, deliberately enter situations with minimal advance preparation.

If you avoid situations lacking complete control, choose activities where outcomes are genuinely unpredictable.

These exposures often feel particularly difficult because you are not just facing external situations but also tolerating internal distress about not knowing.

The anxiety might not decrease as quickly as in standard exposure because you are not gathering evidence that a specific situation is safe; rather, you are building tolerance for the discomfort of not knowing. (Ashton, 2002)

With repeated practice, however, you learn that you can tolerate uncertainty without catastrophe occurring and that compulsive efforts to eliminate uncertainty actually increase rather than decrease distress in the long term.

Therapists sometimes employ worry exposure for intolerance of uncertainty, where you deliberately generate and sit with worrying thoughts about uncertain future events without trying to resolve or neutralise them. (Ashton, 2002)

This technique, adapted from generalised anxiety disorder treatment, can be valuable for PTSD when worry about future threats maintains symptoms.

You might spend 15-30 minutes purposefully worrying about a feared future scenario, without seeking reassurance, without generating solutions, simply allowing the worry to exist.

This demonstrates that you can tolerate uncertainty and that worrying, whilst unpleasant, is not dangerous and eventually decreases if you resist compulsive attempts to eliminate it through reassurance-seeking or excessive planning.

Working with Nightmares Through Exposure-Based Techniques (Ross et al., 1989)

Nightmares are one of the most distressing symptoms of PTSD and can significantly impair quality of life by disrupting sleep and maintaining distress about the trauma. Whilst several treatments exist for trauma-related nightmares, exposure-based approaches can be particularly effective for nightmares that repeatedly replay traumatic content. (Ross et al., 1989)

Imagery Rehearsal Therapy (IRT), whilst not strictly exposure, incorporates exposure principles.

In IRT, you identify a recurring nightmare, write down the nightmare narrative in detail, and then create a modified version of the nightmare where you change elements to reduce its distressing nature. (Raskind et al., 2007; Ross et al., 1989)

The changes can be realistic or completely fantastical; the key is creating a version you have control over that ends less traumatically.

You might change the ending so you escape danger, or introduce a protective figure, or alter the threat so it is neutralised.

Then, you mentally rehearse this modified nightmare narrative repeatedly whilst awake, typically 10-20 minutes daily. (Raskind et al., 2007; Ross et al., 1989)

Over time, rehearsing the modified version appears to alter the actual nightmare, reducing its frequency and intensity. (Raskind et al., 2007; Ross et al., 1989)

The exposure component lies in deliberately engaging with nightmare content whilst awake and safe, similar to imaginal exposure for the trauma memory itself. (Raskind et al., 2007; Ross et al., 1989)

By repeatedly thinking through the nightmare narrative in a controlled, waking context, you process the content, habituate to associated distress, and potentially reconsolidate the nightmare memory in an altered form. (Raskind et al., 2007; Ross et al., 1989)

Research demonstrates that IRT produces significant reductions in nightmare frequency and intensity for many people with PTSD, and benefits often extend to other PTSD symptoms as well. (Raskind et al., 2007)

Another approach involves direct exposure to nightmare content through deliberate waking recall and processing. (Raskind et al., 2007; Ross et al., 1989)

Upon waking from a nightmare, rather than immediately trying to forget it or distract yourself, you deliberately write the nightmare down in detail and then process it as you would a trauma memory. (Raskind et al., 2007; Ross et al., 1989)

This might include identifying hot spots in the nightmare, noting emotions and thoughts present in the dream, and potentially working through cognitive restructuring about dream content that carries unhelpful meanings. (Raskind et al., 2007; Ross et al., 1989)

Some people find that this immediate processing of nightmares upon waking reduces their impact and, over time, their frequency. (Ross et al., 1989)

For nightmares that closely mirror the actual trauma, trauma-focused treatment addressing the trauma memory itself often produces nightmare reduction as a secondary benefit. (Ross et al., 1989)

As you process the trauma memory through narrative work, nightmares frequently decrease, suggesting they represent intrusive replay of inadequately processed traumatic content. (Ross et al., 1989)

Therefore, if you experience nightmares that directly replicate traumatic events, prioritising trauma narrative work might be the most efficient approach, with nightmare reduction following naturally from memory processing. (Ross et al., 1989)

However, some nightmares in PTSD do not directly mirror the trauma but instead represent thematic variations, perhaps involving similar threats, feelings of helplessness, or betrayal themes without being literal replays. (Ross et al., 1989)

These thematic nightmares can be addressed through either IRT if they are recurring and identifiable, or through targeting the underlying themes in daytime cognitive and exposure work. (Ross et al., 1989)

If nightmares involve themes of powerlessness, developing mastery and competence in waking life might reduce nightmare intensity. (Ross et al., 1989)

If they involve interpersonal betrayal themes, processing trust issues in relationships might help.

Nightmare management sometimes requires addressing factors that exacerbate nightmares rather than solely using exposure techniques. (Ross et al., 1989)

Poor sleep hygiene, substance use, certain medications, and high evening arousal all can worsen nightmares. (Perlis et al., 2005)

Attending to these factors alongside exposure work provides the best outcomes.

Additionally, some nightmares are simply resistant to treatment and might require pharmacological interventions. (Ross et al., 1989)

Prazosin, for instance, has evidence for reducing trauma-related nightmares in some individuals. (Ross et al., 1989)

Combining medication that reduces nightmare intensity with exposure-based processing of nightmare content can be an effective integrated approach. (Raskind et al., 2007; Ross et al., 1989)

Exposure for Social Fears and Interpersonal Trauma

When PTSD stems from interpersonal trauma such as assault, abuse, or betrayal, social situations often become primary avoidance targets. You might avoid intimacy, struggle with trust, fear judgment or rejection, or withdraw from relationships entirely. Exposure work for these social fears requires modifications from standard exposure because interpersonal situations involve genuine reciprocal interactions rather than static environmental contexts.

Social exposure hierarchies might include: making small talk with strangers, making eye contact, asserting yourself in low-stakes situations, attending social events, initiating plans with acquaintances, disclosing personal information to trusted individuals, engaging in increasingly intimate interactions, setting boundaries in relationships, and expressing vulnerable emotions. The anxiety often centres not just on the situation itself but on potential negative responses from others, making prediction of outcomes genuinely uncertain in ways that exposure to places or objects is not.

Conducting social exposures requires repeatedly engaging in interpersonal situations whilst accepting that others' responses are not fully under your control.

You cannot guarantee that every social interaction will be positive.

Part of the learning process involves discovering that negative social outcomes, whilst unpleasant, are survivable and not catastrophic.

If you fear rejection and then experience mild rejection in a social exposure, this can be therapeutically valuable evidence that rejection does not destroy you, contrary to your pre-exposure prediction.

This reality testing, discovering that you can cope with realistic negative outcomes, not just that negative outcomes never occur, is crucial for interpersonal fear reduction.

However, social exposures should be conducted thoughtfully to maximise positive outcomes where possible.

Deliberately putting yourself in situations guaranteed to produce rejection or negative responses is not therapeutic exposure; it is simply exposing yourself to genuine negative experiences.

The goal is facing situations where negative outcomes are possible but not certain and discovering that most interactions go reasonably well, and when they do not, you can cope.

Choosing supportive environments for early social exposures, perhaps recovery groups, therapy groups, or carefully selected social settings, provides contexts where positive responses are more likely whilst still challenging your avoidance. (Cloitre et al., 2012)

For fears specifically about intimacy or physical closeness, graded exposure might involve a series of progressively intimate interactions, starting with impersonal but physically proximate situations and building towards intentionally intimate contexts.

This might begin with tolerating others in your personal space in crowded places, progress to appropriate physical contact in safe contexts, such as handshakes or hugs with trusted individuals, and eventually to deliberately intimate situations if appropriate for your recovery goals. (Brand et al., 2019)

Throughout, the exposure is to wanted proximity and intimacy where your trauma history makes these feel frightening, not to unwanted contact that would represent revictimisation rather than therapeutic exposure.

Combining social exposures with cognitive work about interpersonal meanings is particularly important.

You might conduct social exposures successfully but continue to interpret others' behaviours through a trauma-influenced lens, seeing threat or rejection where none exists.

PAUSE POINT: Ground Yourself

- • Notice 5 things you can SEE

Processing these interpretations through cognitive restructuring alongside exposure helps ensure that you not only face feared situations but also develop more accurate, balanced perceptions of social interactions.

This integrated approach addresses both the behavioural avoidance and the cognitive biases that maintain interpersonal fears.

Leveraging Technology for Exposure Practice

Modern technology offers tools that can enhance exposure therapy in various ways, particularly for situations that are difficult to access in real life or for building skills before conducting in vivo exposures.

Virtual Reality (VR) exposure therapy allows immersive simulated exposure to situations that might be difficult to arrange in reality or as preliminary practice before real-world exposure.

VR environments can simulate driving, flying, combat scenarios, crowds, or other situations with controllable difficulty levels.

Whilst VR exposure does not fully replace in vivo exposure for most purposes, evidence suggests it produces meaningful anxiety reduction and can serve as a useful intermediate step between imaginal exposure and full in vivo exposure.

VR's advantage lies in its ability to provide repeated, controlled practice with standardised situations that can be adjusted precisely to match hierarchy levels.

Smartphone applications can support exposure work through several mechanisms.

Anxiety tracking apps allow you to monitor SUDS ratings during exposures, record exposure logs systematically, and visualise progress over time.

These data can motivate continued practice by demonstrating improvement that might not be subjectively obvious day-to-day.

Exposure reminder apps can prompt you to conduct planned exposures, reducing the tendency to postpone or avoid practise.

Guided exposure apps provide structured exposure protocols with coaching through each step, which can be valuable when professional guidance is not accessible.

Video recordings can enhance exposure effectiveness in specific ways.

Recording yourself during social exposures and then reviewing the recording later allows you to evaluate your actual behaviour objectively rather than relying on anxious predictions about how you appeared.

Many people discover that they appeared far more composed and less anxious than they felt, which challenges beliefs about being visibly anxious or incompetent.

Additionally, reviewing recordings of exposures where you successfully coped can provide evidence countering unhelpful thoughts about your inability to handle challenging situations.

Video-based exposure to trauma reminders, watching videos that contain trauma-related content in controlled ways, can supplement direct in vivo exposure.

For example, if you were in a car accident but cannot drive yet, watching videos of driving, progressing from calm traffic to busier situations, might help begin habituation before attempting actual driving.

Similarly, watching videos of situations you avoid can familiarise you with those situations and reduce anticipatory anxiety before conducting live exposures.

However, video exposure is not a substitute for in vivo exposure; it is a supplementary tool that might ease the transition to real-world practice.

Telehealth platforms have made therapist-guided exposure more accessible. Conducting exposure with therapist support via video call, while not identical to in-person guidance, allows real-time coaching and support that can enhance exposure effectiveness. Some exposures can even be conducted during video sessions, with the therapist virtually present whilst you engage in the situation, providing a useful intermediate between independent practise and fully therapist-accompanied exposure.

However, technology should enhance rather than replace fundamental exposure work. The core mechanism, prolonged, repeated facing of avoided situations until habituation occurs, remains central regardless of technological tools employed. Use technology strategically to address specific challenges, not as an avoidance of direct exposure through over-reliance on virtual or video-based alternatives that never progress to real-world practice.

Maintaining Exposure Gains and Preventing Relapse

After completing substantial exposure work and achieving significant symptom reduction, maintaining gains requires ongoing attention. Without continued practice, avoidance patterns can re-emerge gradually, particularly if stressful life events occur or if you encounter situations that reactivate trauma-related fears.

The first maintenance strategy involves periodic exposure practice even after symptoms have improved substantially.

Rather than completely ceasing exposure work once you have completed your hierarchy, incorporate occasional exposures into your routine to maintain habituation.

This does not require the intensive daily practice of active treatment, but periodic practice, perhaps weekly or monthly, of situations you historically found difficult, helps sustain progress.

Think of this like physical fitness; you do not stop all exercise once you achieve fitness goals because fitness would decline.

Similarly, occasional exposure practice maintains psychological fitness in managing anxiety and avoidance.

Develop strategies for responding to setbacks or symptom increases without reverting to complete avoidance.

Temporary symptom increases are normal during recovery, particularly after stressful events. (Ross et al., 2017)

The key is recognising these as temporary setbacks rather than total relapse and responding constructively.

If you notice avoidance creeping back in, perhaps you start avoiding certain situations again after feeling comfortable for months, reinstate exposure practise deliberately.

Return to an easier level of your hierarchy if needed and rebuild from there.

The skills you developed during treatment are not lost; they simply require reactivation after periods of reduced practise.

Build a relapse prevention plan that specifies warning signs of increasing avoidance, triggers that might precipitate symptom increases, and concrete steps you will take if early warning signs appear.

This plan might include: specific exposures you will reinstate if you notice increased avoidance, coping strategies you will employ if anxiety increases, people you will contact for support, and criteria for seeking professional help if self-managed strategies prove insufficient.

Having this plan prepared in advance makes it more likely you will respond effectively rather than allowing gradual deterioration.

Expect that certain situations might always be somewhat anxiety-provoking without this indicating treatment failure.

Some situations are objectively more challenging than others.

The goal is manageable anxiety that does not prevent functioning, not complete absence of all anxiety in all situations.

If you find some situations consistently provoke moderate anxiety even after thorough exposure, this might simply reflect realistic appraisal of challenge rather than inadequate exposure.

Continue engaging in these situations despite moderate anxiety, which demonstrates that you are not letting trauma control your choices.

Finally, recognise that exposure work is not just about eliminating anxiety and avoidance but also about building a meaningful life.

As you reclaim activities through exposure, ensure you are engaging with activities that actually matter to you, not simply going through the motions of exposure for its own sake.

The ultimate goal is a rich, meaningful life filled with chosen activities, relationships, and experiences.

Exposure is the tool that makes this possible by removing the barriers of anxiety and avoidance.

Maintain focus on this larger goal of valued living rather than becoming preoccupied solely with anxiety levels or exposure accomplishments.

Conclusion: Exposure as Liberation

Advanced graded exposure strategies provide powerful tools for addressing the complex avoidance patterns that maintain PTSD. Whether working with subtle safety behaviours, interoceptive fears, social anxiety following interpersonal trauma, or uncertainty intolerance, these approaches share common principles: systematic, graduated facing of feared situations, prolonged engagement allowing habituation, repeated practice consolidating learning, and continuous refinement based on experience. (Clark, 1999)

Exposure work requires courage and persistence.

Facing fears is inherently difficult work, which is why avoidance feels so appealing in the short term.

However, the long-term benefits of exposure work far exceed the temporary discomfort required.

Each exposure you complete reclaims territory from trauma, demonstrating that you are not as fragile as you feared, the world is not as dangerous as your trauma-influenced brain believes, and you can cope with challenges more effectively than you thought possible.

Integrate these advanced exposure strategies with trauma narrative work and cognitive restructuring to create comprehensive treatment addressing PTSD from multiple angles simultaneously.

No single component, imaginal exposure, in vivo exposure, or cognitive work, is sufficient alone.

Rather, their combination produces synergistic effects greater than any single approach.

As you work through exposure systematically, challenging unhelpful thoughts, processing traumatic memories, and reclaiming avoided activities, you build a pathway to recovery and a life no longer dominated by trauma. (Fenster et al., 2018)

The journey of exposure therapy is one of progressive liberation.

Each small step, each exposure completed, represents an act of reclaiming your life from fear and avoidance.

The temporary distress of facing feared situations purchases lasting freedom from the constraints of PTSD.

This is difficult work, but it is also deeply meaningful work.

You are not merely reducing symptoms; you are rebuilding a life worth living.

Remain patient with yourself, trust the process, celebrate small victories, and continue practising consistently.

Recovery is possible, and exposure therapy provides a proven pathway towards that recovery. (Lanius et al., 2018)

Chapter Seven: Managing Physical Symptoms and Sleep

This chapter provides comprehensive techniques for managing PTSD's physical manifestations, including both foundational and advanced strategies for addressing chronic pain, tension, and somatic symptoms. These approaches offer additional tools for addressing chronic pain, tension, and somatic symptoms that persist despite basic interventions.

Somatic Experiencing and Body-Based Trauma Work

Somatic Experiencing (SE) focuses on releasing trauma held in the body through careful attention to physical sensations and natural completion of defensive responses that trauma interrupted. During trauma, your body mobilises defensive responses, fight, flight, freeze, but often cannot complete these responses. SE posits that this incomplete response energy remains trapped in the nervous system, maintaining chronic arousal, tension, and physical symptoms. SE helps discharge this energy safely.

SE works through tracking body sensations, noticing tension, temperature changes, trembling, pressure, and tightness, without trying to change them initially.

You learn to tolerate uncomfortable sensations long enough for them to shift naturally.

As you notice sensation, it might intensify briefly then release, often accompanied by physical discharge: spontaneous shaking, deep breathing, temperature changes, or sudden relaxation.

This discharge represents the nervous system completing interrupted defensive responses and returning to a regulated state.

SE practitioners guide you to pendulate between resources (positive sensations, safe body areas) and dysregulation (uncomfortable sensations), building capacity to tolerate distress whilst maintaining connection to safety.

This pendulation prevents overwhelming activation whilst allowing gradual processing.

SE also works with micro-movements, tiny physical actions your body wants to make, allowing completion of truncated defensive responses.

For instance, if you froze during trauma, SE might involve gradually allowing pushing away movement your body wanted to make but couldn't.

This completion reduces physical symptoms stemming from incomplete responses.

- SE should be practiced with trained practitioner initially, as working with body activation requires careful titration to avoid overwhelming nervous system. However, basic principles can be applied independently: notice body sensations without immediately trying to change them
- allow natural movements like shaking or deep breaths
- practise grounding in present safety whilst experiencing activation
- and recognise that uncomfortable sensations often shift and release when given attention and space rather than suppression or avoidance.

Chapter Eight: Rebuilding Relationships and Social Connection

- Facing fears through gradual exposure is one of the most effective treatments
- Avoidance strengthens fear; approaching it reduces fear
- You can do this at your own pace using a structured plan
- This chapter guides you through safe, effective exposure work

Understanding How PTSD Affects Relationships

PTSD does not exist in isolation, it profoundly affects your relationships with others, and these relationship impacts in turn affect your recovery. (Monson & Shnaider, 2014)

Understanding how trauma and PTSD influence relationships helps you navigate these challenges more effectively, repair important relationships, and build the social support crucial for recovery. (Foa et al., 2019)

Social connection is one of the most powerful protective factors against PTSD and one of the strongest predictors of recovery. (APA, 2017)

Yet PTSD often drives precisely the isolation that would most harm recovery. (NICE, 2018)

Trauma affects relationships through multiple mechanisms.

First, if your trauma involved interpersonal violence or betrayal, you might struggle to trust anyone.

The person who hurt you might have been someone you trusted, a partner, family member, friend, or authority figure.

This betrayal teaches the painful lesson that people cannot be trusted, that closeness leads to hurt.

You might withdraw from relationships entirely, keep everyone at emotional distance, or constantly vigilantly monitor others for signs of threat.

This protective distancing, whilst understandable, prevents the connection necessary for healing and leaves you isolated precisely when support would help most.

Second, PTSD symptoms themselves strain relationships.

Irritability and anger outbursts damage relationships when you snap at loved ones over minor issues.

Emotional numbing makes it difficult to experience or express affection, leaving partners and friends feeling unloved or unimportant.

Avoiding activities you previously shared with others erodes connection.

Hypervigilance and constant scanning for threats make others feel distrusted or uncomfortable. (Porges, 2011; Yehuda & Seckl, 2011)

Sleep disturbance affects bed partners.

The cognitive changes, difficulty concentrating, memory problems, and preoccupation with trauma make it hard to be present in relationships.

Your loved ones might feel they've lost you to PTSD, that the person they knew has been replaced by someone distant and difficult.

Third, well-meaning others often respond unhelpfully, not through malice but through misunderstanding of trauma and PTSD.

They might tell you to just get over it, minimise what you experienced, express frustration that you are not recovering faster, avoid discussing the trauma entirely, or become overly protective in ways that infantilise you.

These responses, whilst often coming from care and concern, can feel invalidating or smothering.

Understanding that these responses typically stem from others' own discomfort, ignorance, or anxiety rather than lack of care can help, though it does not erase the hurt.

Identifying and Cultivating Supportive Relationships

Not everyone in your life will be equally capable of providing helpful support during PTSD recovery. (Forbes et al., 2020)

Some people, despite good intentions, simply do not have the capacity, understanding, or emotional resources to support you through this challenging time.

Others might have their own issues that prevent them from being reliably supportive.

Identifying who can realistically provide support helps you invest your limited energy in relationships most likely to be helpful rather than pursuing support from people unable to provide it.

Consider each person in your life and ask: Do they generally respond supportively when I am struggling?

Can they listen without immediately trying to fix or minimise?

Do they respect boundaries when I need space?

Have they shown themselves trustworthy with sensitive information?

Do interactions with them generally leave me feeling better or worse?

People who consistently demonstrate these qualities are likely to be helpful sources of support.

Those who do not, who criticise, minimise your experiences, gossip, become overwhelmed by your struggles, or drain rather than replenish you, might need to remain at greater emotional distance during recovery, regardless of their nominal relationship to you. (Schnyder et al., 2015)

This discernment isn't about judging people as good or bad, but about recognising that different people have different capacities at different times. Someone who cannot support you through PTSD might be wonderful in other contexts or might develop greater capacity in the future.

For many people with PTSD, the challenge isn't identifying existing supportive relationships but rather building new ones when trauma has destroyed previous connections or when social isolation has been profound. Building new relationships requires gradual steps, starting with low-stakes interactions and progressively working towards deeper connection as trust and comfort develop.

Gradual Approaches to Building New Connections

Start with structured, time-limited social contact that does not require deep disclosure or long-term commitment.

Join a class, group, or organisation focused on an activity you enjoy or want to learn, art classes, exercise groups, book clubs, hobby groups, or volunteer activities.

These contexts provide natural conversation topics (the shared activity) and built-in structure (defined meeting times and duration) that makes socializing more manageable.

You can attend regularly without pressure for deeper connection, allowing relationships to develop naturally over time if they are going to.

Practise brief, positive interactions with acquaintances before pursuing deeper friendships.

Chat briefly with neighbours, exchange pleasantries with regular cashiers or baristas, make small talk with colleagues.

These micro-interactions rebuild social skills that might have atrophied during isolation, provide evidence that social contact can be pleasant rather than threatening, and create a foundation of comfort with people generally.

You are not trying to become best friends with everyone, you are simply practicing being around people in low-stakes ways.

When you identify someone, you might want to know better, take small, graduated steps towards deeper connection.

Extend the conversation slightly beyond the minimum required.

Share something mildly personal and notice their response.

If they respond supportively, reciprocate interest by asking about them.

Suggest a time-limited, public activity together, coffee, attending an event, walking in a park.

These lower-commitment interactions allow you to assess compatibility and trustworthiness without immediately jumping to intense friendship.

Accept that building relationships takes time and involves some risk.

Not everyone you reach out to will reciprocate.

Some attempted connections will not develop into friendships.

This isn't about you being deficient, it is simply how relationships work.

Compatibility, timing, and circumstances all influence whether connections develop.

Rejection or lack of reciprocation, whilst disappointing, does not mean you are unworthy of friendship.

It means that particular connection wasn't a good match.

Continue reaching out to different people, and eventually you'll find those who reciprocate.

Repairing Relationships Damaged by PTSD

If PTSD has damaged important existing relationships with partners, family members, and close friends, repair is often possible but requires conscious effort, communication, and willingness from both parties to work towards reconnection.

Not all relationships can or should be repaired, particularly if they were unhealthy before trauma or if the other person is unwilling to engage in repair.

However, many relationships that matter to you and that were generally positive before trauma became complicated by PTSD can be strengthened through intentional repair work.

Begin by acknowledging the impact your PTSD has had on the other person.

PTSD does not just affect you; it affects everyone close to you.

Your withdrawal, irritability, emotional unavailability, or other symptoms have likely hurt, confused, or frustrated people who care about you. (Ashton, 2002)

This acknowledgment isn't about taking inappropriate blame for having PTSD; you didn't choose to develop PTSD, and symptoms aren't character flaws.

Rather, it is recognising that your symptoms have had real impacts on others, and those impacts deserve acknowledgment.

You might say something like: 'I know my withdrawal has been hard on you. (Ashton, 2002)

I have been struggling with PTSD symptoms, and I recognise that's affected our relationship.

I want to work on repairing that.'

Explain what you are experiencing in ways the other person can understand.

Many relationship problems stem from misunderstanding.

When you withdraw, your partner might interpret it as not loving them anymore, rather than understanding it as emotional numbing from PTSD.

When you are irritable, friends might think they've done something wrong rather than recognising that hyperarousal makes you reactive.

Educating loved ones about PTSD, what symptoms you experience, why they occur, and that they are not about the other person can transform hurt and confusion into understanding and support.

Consider sharing educational materials, inviting them to therapy sessions, or simply having honest conversations about your experience.

Ask what they need from you.

Repair isn't one-directional; whilst you are working on managing symptoms, the other person might have legitimate needs that have gone unmet.

Ask directly: 'What do you need from me that you haven't been getting?

What would help you feel more connected?' Listen without defensiveness to their answer.

They might need more quality time together, more emotional expressiveness, more help with practical tasks, more consistency, or simply to understand what's happening with you.

Some requests might be immediately doable; others might need to be goals you work towards gradually as symptoms improve.

Make specific, achievable commitments and follow through.

General promises to 'do better' rarely produce change.

Instead, identify specific, concrete actions you can take to improve the relationship.

'I'll plan one date activity with you each week' is more actionable than 'I'll be more present.' 'I'll tell you when I am feeling overwhelmed rather than just withdrawing' is clearer than 'I'll communicate better.' Make commitments you can realistically keep given your current symptoms, then consistently follow through.

This follow-through rebuilds trust and demonstrates that you are genuinely invested in repair.

Communicating Your Needs Effectively

One of the most common relationship difficulties in PTSD involves unmet needs; either you are not getting the support you need, or others do not understand what would actually help.

Often, this stems from difficulty identifying or communicating your needs rather than from others' unwillingness to help. Learning to recognise and effectively communicate your needs strengthens relationships and increases the likelihood of receiving helpful support.

First, clarify your needs for yourself. When you are struggling, pause and ask: What would actually help right now? Do I need someone to talk to, or do I need solitude? Do I need practical help with tasks, or emotional support? Do I need advice and problem-solving, or just validation and understanding? Do I need physical comfort like a hug, or would touch feel overwhelming? Getting clear on what you actually need, rather than vaguely wishing someone would magically know how to help, allows you to request specific support.

Use clear, direct communication rather than hints or expectations that others should know what you need.

Others aren't mind readers, and what would help one person might not help another.

State your needs explicitly: 'I am feeling overwhelmed, and I need some space to decompress.

Can we talk later this evening?' or 'I am struggling with anxiety and it would help if you could just listen without trying to fix it' or 'I am having a difficult day and I could use company, would you be free to watch a film together?' This direct communication removes guesswork and makes it easy for others to help.

Distinguish between needs and demands. A need is a request that the other person can choose whether to meet: 'I need support right now, are you available to talk?' A demand is a requirement that does not allow choice: 'You need to drop everything and help me immediately.' Demands damage relationships by not respecting others' autonomy and limitations. Requests that honour their ability to say no when they are not available preserve goodwill whilst still allowing you to communicate needs.

Provide context when making requests. Rather than just stating what you need, briefly explain why you need it, this helps others understand and respond appropriately. 'I am feeling triggered by this conversation, can we change the subject?' provides more useful information than just 'Can we change the subject?' The brief explanation helps the other person understand the urgency and nature of your need without requiring extensive disclosure.

Thank people when they provide support, even if the support wasn't perfect. Appreciation encourages continued support and strengthens relationships. If someone made time to talk with you, helped with a task, or simply spent time with you when you needed company, acknowledge that: 'Thank you for making time for me today, it really helped.' This positive reinforcement makes people more likely to continue providing support.

Setting and Respecting Boundaries in Relationships

Boundaries, limits on what you are willing to accept, participate in, or tolerate, are essential for healthy relationships, yet many people with PTSD struggle with boundaries.

You might have overly rigid boundaries that keep everyone at distance, preventing both harm and connection.

Or you might have very porous boundaries, tolerating treatment that's harmful because you fear asserting limits will lead to abandonment.

Developing appropriate boundaries that protect you whilst allowing connection is crucial for relationship health.

Healthy boundaries are flexible rather than rigid or absent.

They allow connection with trustworthy people whilst protecting you from exploitation or mistreatment.

They recognise that different relationships appropriately have different levels of intimacy and access.

You might share deeply personal information with a close friend but maintain more professional boundaries with colleagues.

They can be adjusted based on circumstances.

You might normally enjoy socialising, but set a boundary on social contact when you are overwhelmed and need recovery time. (Resick et al., 2017)

Identifying your boundaries requires self-awareness about what feels acceptable versus uncomfortable, safe versus unsafe, energising versus draining.

Notice your emotional and physical responses in interactions.

If you consistently feel drained, resentful, anxious, or uncomfortable after interactions with someone, you might need stronger boundaries with that person.

If someone regularly crosses limits you have stated, ignores your needs, or pressures you into things you are uncomfortable with, clearer boundaries are needed.

- Common boundaries people with PTSD might need include: limits on discussions of trauma ('I am not comfortable discussing details of what happened with casual acquaintances')
- limits on physical contact ('I need you to ask before hugging me rather than assuming it is okay')
- limits on time and energy ('I can visit for two hours but then I need to leave to manage my symptoms')

- limits on types of activities ('I am not ready to go to crowded places yet')
- limits on advice-giving ('I need you to listen rather than tell me what to do')
- or limits on demands ('I cannot take on additional responsibilities right now').

Communicate boundaries clearly and directly. Use 'I' statements that express your limits without blaming: 'I need to leave now because I am feeling overwhelmed' rather than 'You are overwhelming me.' Be specific about what you need: 'Please do not discuss the accident in front of me' is clearer than 'I do not like talking about that.' Understand that stating boundaries might feel uncomfortable initially, many people with PTSD have learned that asserting limits is dangerous, but in healthy relationships, reasonable boundaries are respected.

Managing Unsupportive or Harmful Responses from Others

Despite your best efforts at communication and boundary-setting, some people will respond in unhelpful or actively harmful ways. Understanding common unhelpful responses and how to manage them protects you whilst maintaining realistic expectations about others' limitations.

Minimisation occurs when others downplay the severity of your trauma or its impact: 'It wasn't that bad,' 'Others have had it worse,' 'You should be over it by now.' This minimisation often stems from discomfort; acknowledging the full horror of your experience would be distressing for them, so they minimise it to manage their own discomfort.

Understanding this motivation does not make minimisation okay, but it helps you not internalise it.

Respond by asserting your reality without arguing: 'It was serious to me and continues to affect me.

I need you to accept that or simply disengage from the conversation if they persist.

Advice-giving, whilst usually well-intentioned, can feel dismissive when you need validation more than solutions.

People often offer advice because they want to help and feel uncomfortable with your distress.

However, unsolicited advice ('You should just think positively!' 'Have you tried yoga?') can imply your struggles result from not trying hard enough.

Redirect by stating your need: 'I appreciate you wanting to help, but what I need right now is someone to listen rather than advise.' If they persist with advice, you might need to limit how much you share with that person.

Overprotection can be as problematic as under-support.

Some people respond to your PTSD by trying to shield you from all difficulty, making decisions for you, or treating you as fragile.

This infantilization, whilst coming from care, undermines your autonomy and reinforces beliefs that you cannot cope.

Assert your capability: 'I appreciate your concern, but I need to make this decision myself' or 'I understand you are trying to protect me, but I need to face this challenge as part of my recovery.' (Maercker et al., 2022)

- Some responses are actively harmful rather than merely unhelpful: blaming you for the trauma ('What did you expect would happen?')
- using your PTSD against you in arguments ('You are just overreacting because of your issues')
- or refusing to respect boundaries after you have clearly stated them.

These responses indicate relationships that might not be worth preserving.

Consider whether the relationship provides more benefit than harm.

If someone consistently responds harmfully despite your clear communication, distance or ending the relationship might be necessary for your wellbeing.

The Role of Support Groups in Recovery (Hyland et al., 2021)

Support groups, gatherings of people who share similar experiences, typically facilitated by a professional or trained peer, provide unique benefits that complement individual therapy and personal relationships. Understanding what support groups offer and how to find appropriate ones can help you decide whether group support might benefit your recovery. (Karatzias et al., 2017)

Support groups reduce isolation through shared experience.

Meeting others who have experienced trauma and developed PTSD demonstrates viscerally that you are not alone, that your symptoms are normal responses to abnormal events, and that recovery is possible. (Courtois & Ford, 2013)

Other people in the group are at various stages of recovery, providing hope and practical models. (Brewin et al., 2017)

This normalisation is powerful in ways that intellectual understanding ('I know PTSD is common') often isn't.

Seeing someone describe experiences almost identical to yours, or hearing how someone managed a symptom you are struggling with, provides both validation and practical guidance.

Groups provide opportunities to give support as well as receive it.

As you progress in recovery, you can offer understanding, encouragement, and practical suggestions to others who are earlier in their journey. (Ford et al., 2019)

This shift from being solely a recipient of support to also being a provider of support rebuilds self-efficacy and purpose.

You are not just someone damaged by trauma; you are someone with valuable experiences and insights that can help others.

This contribution feels meaningful in ways that simply receiving help does not.

Different types of support groups exist, and finding the right fit matters.

General PTSD support groups welcome anyone with PTSD, regardless of trauma type.

These provide broad peer support and shared understanding of PTSD symptoms.

Trauma-specific groups focus on particular trauma types, combat veterans, sexual assault survivors, survivors of childhood abuse, first responders, or survivors of specific events. (Cloitre et al., 2020; Teicher & Samson, 2016)

These offer a connection with people who have faced very similar experiences and understand context-specific challenges.

Some groups are peer-led, run by trained individuals with lived experience.

Others are professionally facilitated by therapists or counsellors.

Both can be effective, though professionally facilitated groups often have more structure and clinical guidance.

Finding support groups involve research and trial.

Ask your therapist for recommendations.

Contact local mental health organisations, hospitals, or community centres that often host groups.

Search online for groups in your area.

Many organisations maintain directories of support groups.

In the UK, organisations like Mind, Combat Stress, Rape Crisis, and Victim Support services often provide or can recommend groups.

Try different groups to find the right fit; group culture and composition vary significantly, and what works for one person might not work for another.

Give any group several sessions before deciding whether it is helpful; initial discomfort is normal and often diminishes with familiarity.

Online Communities and Support

- Online forums, communities, and a support group provide alternative avenues for connection when in-person options are unavailable or inaccessible. Online support offers particular advantages: accessibility from home, which is crucial if avoidance, physical limitations, or geographical isolation prevent in-person attendance
- anonymity, allowing sharing without revealing your identity
- asynchronous participation, letting you read and contribute when you have energy rather than at scheduled meeting times
- and access to diverse perspectives from people worldwide rather than just your local area.

However, online support also has limitations and risks to navigate thoughtfully.

Quality varies enormously; some online communities are well-moderated, evidence-based, and supportive, whilst others spread misinformation, encourage unhelpful coping strategies, or foster negative thinking patterns.

Screen communities carefully before investing time and emotional energy.

- Look for communities that: encourage professional treatment rather than replacing it
- have active moderation that maintains supportive, respectful discourse
- discourage detailed trauma descriptions that could trigger others
- promote evidence-based recovery strategies (Watts et al., 2013)
- and maintain appropriate boundaries.

Be cautious about over-reliance on online communities as your sole source of support.

Online connections cannot fully replace in-person relationships and professional support.

It can supplement but shouldn't substitute for comprehensive treatment.

Additionally, spending excessive time in trauma-focused communities can sometimes maintain focus on trauma and symptoms rather than supporting broader life engagement.

Use online support thoughtfully as one component of recovery rather than allowing it to consume disproportionate time and attention. (van Dis et al., 2020)

Protect your privacy and safety online.

Be judicious about what personal information you share, even in supportive communities.

Use screen names rather than real names.

Do not share identifying details that could allow others to find you.

Be alert to anyone who seems to be grooming you for exploitation, people who push for private contact, request personal information, or make you uncomfortable.

Trust your instincts; if someone or something feels off, disengage.

Remember that not everyone online is who they claim to be, and vulnerable populations can attract predatory individuals.

Intimate Relationships and Sexual Intimacy After Trauma

PTSD particularly affects intimate relationships and sexual intimacy, especially when trauma involved sexual violence or betrayal by a partner. Even when trauma was unrelated to sexuality, PTSD symptoms, emotional numbing, hypervigilance, dissociation, and body disconnection interfere with sexual intimacy. Understanding these impacts and working to address them with patience and communication can help preserve or rebuild intimate connections. (Porges, 2011; Yehuda & Seckl, 2011)

If your trauma involved sexual violence, reclaiming comfortable sexuality requires addressing specific trauma-related associations between sex and danger.

Your nervous system learned that sexual contact means threat, making arousal and intimacy feel dangerous even with a safe, consensual partner.

This isn't about 'not trusting' your partner intellectually; it is about trauma-based associations in your nervous system that require relearning.

- This relearning happens gradually through ensuring you feel genuinely safe with your partner
- maintaining absolute control over all sexual contact (nothing happens without your explicit, ongoing consent)
- moving extremely slowly and stopping immediately if you feel uncomfortable
- and gradually building positive associations between intimacy and safety through accumulated positive experiences.

Communication with your partner is crucial.

They likely feel confused, rejected, or frustrated by changes in your sexual relationship.

They might not understand why you have withdrawn or why formerly enjoyable activities now trigger distress.

Explain what you are experiencing: 'The trauma has affected how I experience touch and intimacy.

It is not about you; my body's stress response gets triggered.

I need us to go very slowly and for you to check in with me frequently.' Help them understand that rebuilding comfort with intimacy takes time and that pressuring them will be counterproductive.

Establish clear, explicit consent protocols rather than assuming ongoing consent.

Many couples operate with implied consent; if you are in bed together, touch is assumed okay unless someone objects.

After trauma, explicit checking works better: 'Is it okay if I touch you here?' 'Do you want to continue?' This checking might feel awkward initially, but it provides safety and control crucial for reducing trauma responses.

Your partner might worry this feels clinical, but explain that it is necessary for your comfort and actually allows more intimacy than pushing through discomfort would.

Focus on non-sexual physical intimacy while rebuilding comfort.

Holding hands, hugging, cuddling, massage, these forms of physical connection that do not involve sexuality can maintain closeness whilst being less triggering.

They allow you to slowly recalibrate your nervous system's response to touch with your partner.

Some people find it helpful to create zones: certain types of touch are comfortable, others aren't certain body areas are okay, others are off-limits for now.

Communicate these boundaries clearly and revise them as comfort increases.

Building a Sustainable Social Support Network

Comprehensive recovery involves cultivating multiple sources of support rather than relying entirely on one person or one type of connection. (Ehring et al., 2014)

- A sustainable support network might include: one or two close confidants who know your story in detail and provide emotional support
- several friends for social activities and companionship
- family members who provide practical help and care
- professional support through therapy
- peer support through groups
- and broader community connections through work, hobbies, or organisations.

This diversification means you are not overwhelming any single person, and you have various sources to turn to for different needs.

Regularly assess and tend to your relationships.

Are there connections that consistently drain rather than replenish you?

Consider whether those relationships need boundaries or distance.

Are there relationships you have been neglecting that deserve more attention?

Prioritise investing in those.

Are you getting the support you need, or are needs going unmet?

Identify what's missing and consider how to address that, asking existing connections for what you need, building new relationships, or accessing professional or group support.

Chapter Nine: Rebuilding Meaning, Purpose, and Identity

How Trauma Affects Sense of Self and Meaning

Beyond the specific symptoms of PTSD, the flashbacks, hypervigilance, and avoidance, trauma often produces profound existential impacts, affecting your sense of who you are, what life means, and what purpose you are working towards. (Van der Kolk et al., 1996)

These meaning-level impacts can be as distressing as symptoms themselves, yet they are often overlooked in favour of addressing more immediately urgent symptoms.

Understanding and addressing trauma's effects on meaning, purpose, and identity is crucial for complete recovery and building a life worth living beyond mere symptom reduction. (Coventry et al., 2020)

Trauma can shatter previously held assumptions about yourself, others, and the world, assumptions so fundamental you might not have consciously recognised them until trauma violated them.

You might have assumed you were invulnerable or that bad things happen to other people but not you.

Trauma demonstrated viscerally that you are vulnerable, that terrible things can happen to anyone.

You might have assumed you are competent.

Trauma might have involved experiences where you couldn't act effectively, leaving you questioning your capability.

You might have assumed the world is generally just or that good behaviour protects you from harm.

Trauma often involves profound injustice; you didn't deserve what happened, yet it happened anyway.

These shattered assumptions create what's sometimes called a crisis of meaning.

The frameworks you used to understand your life and make decisions no longer work.

Questions that seemed settled become painfully open: Who am I?

What can I trust?

What's the point of anything if terrible things can happen randomly?

Is there any justice or order in the world?

What do I value?

What's worth working towards?

These questions, whilst philosophically interesting in the abstract, become urgently personal and distressing when trauma forces you to confront them directly.

Identity, your sense of who you are, can feel fractured or lost after trauma.

You might feel you are not the person you were before trauma, yet you do not know who you are now.

- The characteristics you identified with might have changed: if you were confident, trauma might have introduced self-doubt
- if you were trusting, trauma might have created suspicion
- if you were optimistic, trauma might have brought pessimism.

Some people describe feeling like trauma killed who they were, leaving a stranger inhabiting their body.

This identity disruption is painful; you are grieving the loss of your pre-trauma self whilst struggling to understand and accept who you are now.

Your sense of purpose, what you are living for, what gives life meaning, might feel lost or invalidated.

Goals you were working towards might seem pointless.

Activities you found meaningful might feel empty.

The future you imagined might no longer feel attainable or desirable.

This loss of purpose creates existential emptiness; you are surviving day to day without a clear sense of why or what you are moving towards.

Depression often accompanies this meaning loss, not just as a symptom of PTSD but as a natural response to life feeling purposeless.

Understanding Post-Traumatic Growth (Tedeschi & Calhoun, 2004)

Whilst the focus of PTSD treatment is appropriately on reducing suffering and restoring functioning, research has identified another phenomenon: post-traumatic growth, or positive changes that can emerge from struggling with trauma. (Tedeschi & Calhoun, 2004)

This concept is sometimes misunderstood or misused; it absolutely does not mean trauma is good or that you should be grateful for it.

Trauma is terrible.

No one should have to experience it.

The growth comes not from trauma itself but from the struggle to cope with trauma's aftermath.

Understanding post-traumatic growth can help you recognise possible positive changes without invalidating the very real suffering trauma caused. (Tedeschi & Calhoun, 2004)

Post-traumatic growth occurs in several domains. (Tedeschi & Calhoun, 2004)

Many people report deeper, more authentic relationships.

Having faced a crisis, superficial connections feel less appealing whilst meaningful connections feel more precious.

You might have discovered who truly supports you, deepening those relationships.

You might have developed greater empathy for others who suffer, enhancing connection.

Some people report increased compassion, patience, and the ability to be present with others' pain without needing to fix it.

Greater appreciation for life and changed priorities are common.

Trauma's confrontation with mortality or suffering often clarifies what truly matters.

Things you once stressed about might seem trivial.

Experiences you took for granted, health, safety, loved ones, simple pleasures, might feel more precious.

You might make different choices about how to spend time, prioritising meaning and connection over achievement or acquisition.

This shift isn't about toxic positivity or pretending everything is fine; it is about genuine reorientation towards what matters most to you.

Many people discover inner strength they didn't know they had.

Surviving trauma and working through recovery demonstrates resilience and capability. (Mavranezouli et al., 2020)

You might have endured things you thought would destroy you, but discovered you are stronger than you believed.

This isn't about dismissing ongoing struggles; you can recognise your strength whilst also acknowledging difficulties.

The recognition is empowering: 'I do not want to have gone through this, but having gone through it, I have discovered I am more resilient than I knew.'

Some people develop new possibilities or paths they wouldn't have otherwise discovered.

This might involve career changes, becoming a therapist, counsellor, or advocate because of understanding trauma personally.

It might involve creative expression, writing, art, or music that processes trauma and connects with others.

It might involve activism or volunteering that gives meaning to suffering by helping prevent others' suffering or supporting other survivors.

These new paths do not justify trauma, but they can provide meaning derived from trauma.

Identifying Your Core Values

Values, the principles and qualities that matter most to you, that you want your life to reflect, provide direction for rebuilding meaning and purpose. Unlike goals (specific outcomes you work towards), values are ongoing directions of travel, like compass points guiding your journey. Clarifying your values helps you make decisions aligned with what truly matters to you rather than defaulting to what you think you should value or what you valued before trauma forced reconsideration.

Common value domains include: relationships and connection (being a loving partner, supportive friend, engaged family member); personal growth and learning (developing skills, understanding, self-awareness); health and wellbeing (physical fitness, mental health, self-care); creativity and expression (making art, writing, music); contribution and service (helping others, making positive impact); justice and fairness (standing against injustice, protecting vulnerable people); pleasure and enjoyment (experiencing joy, fun, beauty); spirituality or meaning (connecting to something larger, exploring existential questions); achievement and competence (excelling at work, mastering skills); autonomy and freedom (making own choices, living independently); security and safety (building stability, protecting yourself and loved ones); or legacy (creating something lasting, influencing future).

To clarify your values, consider these reflection questions: What matters most to you in life? When you imagine looking back at your life, what would make you feel it was well-lived? What do you want to be remembered for? What causes you to feel most alive or engaged? If you had unlimited resources and no fear of failure, what would you do? What do you most appreciate about yourself when you are at your best? What qualities do you admire in others? What would you want written in your obituary beyond facts about your life?

After identifying potential values through reflection, prioritise them.

You likely identified many things that matter, but not everything can have equal priority.

If you try to pursue all values equally and simultaneously, you'll scatter your energy without making meaningful progress in any direction.

Instead, identify 3-5 core values that feel most important right now; these become your primary compass points for decision-making and goal setting.

Other values remain important but are secondary focus areas.

It is important to distinguish between values you genuinely hold versus values you think you should hold, or values imposed by others.

Trauma and PTSD recovery can create pressure to adopt certain values; you might feel you should value forgiveness, or positivity, or activism. (Karatzias et al., 2019)

Question whether these are authentic to you or external expectations.

Your values should feel personally meaningful rather than obligatory.

If a value feels like 'should' rather than genuine importance, question whether it belongs on your list.

Understand that values can change over time, and that's okay. Values you held before trauma might no longer feel relevant. New values might have emerged through your trauma experience. What mattered at age 20 might not matter at 40. Periodically, perhaps annually, revisit your values and assess whether they still resonate or whether they need updating. This flexibility allows your values to evolve as you grow and change through recovery and life more broadly. (Lewis et al., 2020)

- For example, if one of your core values is connection and relationships, living this value might involve: calling a friend weekly
- planning one social activity per month
- showing up for important events in loved ones' lives
- expressing appreciation to people who matter
- or making time for meaningful conversations rather than just superficial interaction. These are concrete, doable actions that reflect the value of connection, even if PTSD symptoms make them somewhat challenging.
- If personal growth is a core value, living it might involve: reading for learning rather than just distraction
- taking a class or course in something interesting
- practicing a skill regularly
- reflecting on experiences to extract lessons
- seeking feedback and using it constructively
- or engaging with ideas that challenge your thinking. Again, these are specific actions that can be incorporated into life despite PTSD.
- If contribution or helping others is central, this might involve: volunteering for causes you care about

- mentoring someone earlier in a journey you have travelled
- supporting friends and family practically when they need help
- advocating for changes that would benefit others
- or sharing your recovery story to help other trauma survivors. These actions create meaning by channelling your experience towards positive impact. (Bisson et al., 2019)

The key to effective values-based goal setting is making goals specific, manageable, and achievable despite PTSD symptoms.

Do not set goals that require complete symptom resolution to accomplish, this creates a situation where you cannot make progress until you are already recovered, which is backwards.

Instead, identify what you can do now, with current symptoms, which moves you towards your values.

Small, consistent actions aligned with values create more meaningful change than grand plans that never materialise because they feel overwhelming.

Break larger values-based aspirations into smaller steps.

If your value is creativity and your aspiration is writing a book, that might feel overwhelming.

- Break it down: write for 15 minutes three times per week
- complete a short story
- join a writing group
- take a writing course.

Each step is achievable and moves you towards the larger aspiration whilst reflecting the value of creativity.

Progress through accumulated small steps feels more sustainable than attempting giant leaps that might lead to frustration and abandonment.

Distinguish between goals (specific outcomes with endpoints) and committed actions (ongoing behaviours reflecting values).

A goal might be 'Complete a 5K run' with a specific finish line.

A committed action is 'Exercise three times per week' with no endpoint, it is something you commit to doing ongoing basis because it aligns with values around health.

Both are useful, but committed actions create sustained values-consistent living, whereas goals create specific achievements.

Balance in your life.

Reconstructing Identity After Trauma

The identity disruption trauma creates, feeling you are not who you were and not knowing who you are now, requires conscious work to address.

You are not trying to resurrect your pre-trauma self, which is likely impossible and perhaps not even desirable.

Rather, you are constructing a new, integrated identity that acknowledges trauma's impact whilst not being entirely defined by it.

This new identity incorporates both continuity (aspects of yourself that survived trauma) and change (how trauma has transformed you).

Begin by identifying aspects of yourself that remain continuous despite trauma.

What characteristics, interests, values, or quirks persisted through trauma?

Perhaps your sense of humour survived, or your love of animals, or your curiosity about science, or your loyalty to friends.

These continuities provide anchors, evidence that you are still you in important ways despite profound changes.

They connect your pre-trauma and post-trauma selves, preventing the sense that trauma destroyed who you were.

Simultaneously, acknowledge and explore the changes trauma produced.

How are you different now?

Some changes might be losses you grieve, lost innocence, lost sense of invulnerability, lost trust, lost time.

Name these losses explicitly and allow yourself to grieve them.

Other changes might be neutral or even positive, increased compassion, deeper appreciation for life, clearer priorities, and greater resilience. (Bonanno, 2004)

Acknowledge these without invalidating the suffering that produced them.

The goal isn't toxic positivity ('Everything happens for a reason!') but honest recognition ('Trauma was terrible AND I have developed some strengths through surviving it').

Consider who you want to become moving forward.

Identity isn't fixed; it is constantly evolving throughout life.

Trauma forced evolution, often in unwanted directions.

But you are not helpless in shaping your identity going forward.

What qualities do you want to develop?

What kind of person do you want to be?

What would you like others to say about you?

These aspirational elements of identity provide direction for growth.

You are not a passive victim of trauma's changes; you are an active agent in who you become.

Write your own narrative about who you are now.

This might be literal writing, a description of yourself, your story, what you have been through and who you are becoming.

Or it might be reflected conversation with trusted others about your identity and journey.

The act of articulating your story helps consolidate identity.

Rather than feeling fragmented, bits of pre-trauma you, trauma memories, struggling present you, the narrative creates coherence: 'I was this person, trauma happened and changed me in these ways, I am now this person who's working on recovery, and I am becoming this person.' (Cusack et al., 2016)

Discovering Purpose Through and Despite Trauma

Having a purpose, the sense that your life has meaning and direction, that you are living for something beyond just getting through each day, is crucial for wellbeing and often feels lost or unclear after trauma.

Discovering or rediscovering purpose isn't about forcing artificial meaning ('Everything happens for a reason' or 'Trauma made me stronger').

Rather, it is about finding genuine meaning in your life as it is now, incorporating trauma as part of your story without letting it be the only story.

Purpose can come from multiple sources.

For some people, relationships provide a primary purpose; being a good parent, partner, friend, or family member gives life meaning.

For others, work or career provides purpose through contribution, achievement, or creativity.

Some find purpose through causes they care about, environmental protection, social justice, and helping specific populations.

Others find purpose through personal growth, spiritual or religious practices, creative expression, or experiencing and appreciating beauty and life.

There's no single right source of purpose; what matters is that it feels genuinely meaningful to you.

Many trauma survivors find particular purpose in helping other survivors through peer support, advocacy, professional work in trauma fields, or sharing their recovery stories. (Watkins et al., 2018)

This transformation of suffering into service can feel deeply meaningful.

Your trauma, whilst terrible, becomes something that helps you understand and support others facing similar struggles.

This does not require becoming a therapist or formal helper; even being the friend who truly understands when someone else faces trauma can provide this meaning.

However, this path isn't for everyone, and there's no obligation to find purpose this way.

If helping others feels meaningful, pursue it; if it does not, that's equally valid.

- Purpose does not require grand gestures or life-changing missions. Modest, everyday purposes are equally valid: being reliably present for your children (Cohen et al., 2016; Cohen & Mannarino, 2008)
- doing your work with care and competence
- maintaining your garden
- creating art that expresses your experience
- volunteering at a local organisation
- being the person who checks in on elderly neighbours
- or simply living with integrity and kindness. These ordinary purposes create meaningful lives without requiring extraordinary achievements.

If purpose feels completely absent, you are surviving day-to-day without a sense of why or direction.

Start by engaging in various activities and noticing what creates even moments of engagement or meaning.

What activities absorb your attention?

When do you feel most like yourself?

What feels worth doing even when difficult?

These observations provide clues about potential sources of purpose.

Purpose isn't usually discovered through thinking alone; it emerges from engagement with life and reflection on what resonates.

Behavioural Activation: Re-engaging with Life

One of PTSD's most insidious effects is withdrawal from activities and life engagement. (Ashton, 2002)

Depression, avoidance, and low energy create a vicious cycle: you withdraw from activities, which increases depression and a sense of meaninglessness, which further reduces motivation for engagement, leading to more withdrawal. (Ashton, 2002)

Breaking this cycle requires behavioural activation, deliberately engaging in activities despite not feeling motivated, to rebuild the motivation and positive experiences that sustain engagement.

Behavioural activation is based on a counterintuitive truth: action precedes motivation more often than motivation precedes action.

We tend to think: 'When I feel motivated, I'll do things.' But with depression and PTSD, that motivation might never arise spontaneously.

Instead: 'I'll do things, and motivation and positive feelings will follow from engagement.' This does not mean forcing yourself to do everything constantly; that's neither possible nor healthy.

It means strategically engaging in specific activities likely to improve mood and meaning, even when you do not feel like it, because the engagement itself generates benefits that restore motivation.

- Create an activity schedule that includes three types of activities: necessary activities (work, hygiene, basic life maintenance)
- pleasurable activities (things you used to enjoy or might enjoy, done purely for pleasure)
- and meaningful activities (things aligned with your values that create sense of purpose).

The balance matters, if your life is all necessity with no pleasure or meaning, wellbeing suffers.

Aim for daily inclusion of at least one pleasurable and one meaningful activity, however brief.

Start with activities that have low barriers to completion. If exercise feels overwhelming, start with a 10-minute walk. If socializing feels impossible, start with a brief text exchange with a friend. If creative projects feel too demanding, start with 15 minutes of doodling or writing. These small starts overcome the inertia of inactivity whilst being manageable even when motivation is low. Success with small activities builds momentum and confidence for larger engagements.

Track your activities and mood.

Use a simple log: what activity you did, when you did it, how much effort it required (0-10), how much pleasure or satisfaction it provided (0-10), and your mood before and after (0-10).

- This tracking reveals patterns you might not notice otherwise: which activities most reliably improve mood
- which pleasure means
- how your mood varies throughout the day or week
- and what activities require so much effort relative to benefit that they are not sustainable.

Use these patterns to refine your activity schedule, doing more of what helps and reconsidering what does not.

Expect resistance and plan for it.

Your mind will generate countless reasons why you shouldn't do activities: 'I am too tired,' 'I do not feel like it,' 'It will not help anyway,' 'I'll do it later.' These thoughts are normal products of depression and avoidance patterns, not accurate assessments.

Acknowledge them without automatically obeying them: 'I notice I am thinking I am too tired.

That's a common thought pattern.

I am going to do this brief activity anyway and see how I actually feel afterwards.' Often, engagement itself reduces the resistance; once you start, continuing is easier than anticipating the start.

Creating Sustainable Routine and Structure

PTSD often disrupts life structure.

Sleep disturbance disrupts daily rhythms.

Avoidance eliminates activities that previously structured your days.

Depression saps motivation for maintaining routines.

This lack of structure worsens symptoms; without an external scaffold, you are left to manage PTSD with no support from predictable rhythms.

Deliberately building routine and structure into your days provides this scaffold, reducing the constant decisions about what to do and creating momentum through established patterns.

Start with basic routines around sleep, meals, and hygiene.

These fundamentals often deteriorate with PTSD, but they are also most amenable to structure.

Set consistent bed and wake times.

Schedule three meals at regular times.

Build a morning routine that signals the start of the day, showering, dressing, breakfast, perhaps brief physical activity or reading.

Build an evening routine that transitions towards sleep, dinner at a consistent time, limited screen exposure, calming activities, and bedtime preparation.

These simple routines create a daily structure that supports functioning.

Add structure for activity engagement.

Rather than waiting to spontaneously feel like doing things, which might never happen, schedule specific activities at specific times.

Tuesday and Thursday evenings are exercise time.

Sunday morning is for calling family.

Wednesday is for working on your hobby.

This scheduling removes repeated decision-making (should I do this now?

Maybe later?) that drains energy and often results in avoidance.

When Tuesday evening arrives, you exercise because that's what Tuesday evening is for, not because you carefully weighed options and felt motivated.

Balance structure with flexibility.

Too rigid a structure creates stress when disruption occurs; too little structure provides no support.

Aim for a framework that guides without being tyrannical.

If your scheduled exercise time coincides with genuine illness or an emergency, skip it without guilt.

If you are having a particularly difficult PTSD Day, adjust expectations while maintaining some structure, perhaps a shorter walk instead of full exercise, or a brief check-in call instead of extended social time.

Structure serves you; you do not serve structure.

Regular Review and Adjustment of Goals and Values

Values, goals, and a sense of meaning shouldn't be set once and forgotten. They benefit from regular review and adjustment as you progress in recovery, as life circumstances change, and as you learn what actually brings satisfaction versus what you thought would. Schedule periodic reviews, perhaps quarterly, where you explicitly assess your values-based goals and adjust course as needed. (Ozer et al., 2003)

During reviews, ask: Are my current goals still aligned with my values, or have they become disconnected? Am I making progress towards goals, or do they need to be broken down into smaller steps? Have my values shifted? Do different things matter more or less than they did when I last assessed? What's working well that I should continue? What's not working needs changing? What new goals might I set? This regular assessment prevents drift, where you continue pursuing goals that no longer matter or avoid updating approaches that aren't working.

Celebrate progress during reviews, not just identify problems.

PTSD recovery is long and difficult; it is easy to focus entirely on what remains difficult and overlook improvement. (Guay et al., 2006)

Deliberately note what you have accomplished: goals you have met, values you have lived according to, activities you have reclaimed, skills you have developed, and symptoms that have reduced.

This acknowledgment isn't self-congratulatory hubris; it is accurate recognition of genuine achievement that builds motivation and counters the hopelessness that can plague recovery. (Charuvastra & Cloitre, 2008)

Accepting Limitations While Pursuing Growth

Complete recovery from PTSD, returning to exactly how you were before trauma, with no residual symptoms or difficulties, is unrealistic for many people. (Neff & Germer, 2018)

Some degree of ongoing vulnerability, occasional symptoms, or lasting changes is common even with excellent treatment and substantial recovery. (Gilbert, 2014)

- This reality requires difficult balance: accepting limitations without giving up on improvement
- acknowledging ongoing difficulties without letting them define you
- adjusting expectations without abandoning hope.

Acceptance does not mean resignation or giving up.

It means acknowledging reality as it is, including limitations, whilst still working towards improvement within that reality.

You might accept: 'I will probably always be somewhat more anxious than I was before trauma' whilst still working to reduce anxiety to manageable levels.

You might accept: 'Some activities will always require more effort for me than for others' whilst still engaging in those activities because they matter.

Acceptance and effort coexist; they are not opposed.

Distinguish between limitations you can potentially change versus limitations that appear fixed.

Some PTSD impacts, certain avoidances, unhelpful thought patterns, and self-imposed isolation are changeable with sustained effort.

Working to address these makes sense.

Other impacts might be more enduring despite effort; perhaps you'll never be quite as trusting as before betrayal, or never be completely comfortable in situations similar to your trauma.

Recognising which is which helps you invest effort where it is likely productive, whilst not exhausting yourself trying to change the unchangeable.

Build a life that works within your limitations rather than waiting for limitations to disappear before living.

If crowds remain somewhat uncomfortable, plan social activities in smaller settings rather than avoiding all socialising.

If certain topics trigger distress, establish boundaries around those topics whilst engaging fully in conversations about other subjects.

If you tire more easily, structure your schedule with regular rest rather than pushing through exhaustion.

This accommodation isn't defeat; it is wisdom, you are building the best life possible with the reality you have, not with the reality you wish you had.

Rebuilding meaning, purpose, and identity after trauma is ongoing work rather than a task you complete and finish.

- Your values might continue evolving
- your sense of purpose might shift as life circumstances change
- your identity will keep developing throughout your life.

This ongoing nature isn't a failure; it is how human meaning-making works.

What you establish during PTSD recovery provides a foundation, but you'll continue building on that foundation indefinitely. (ISTSS, 2019)

The skills you develop, clarifying values, translating them into action, setting meaningful goals, adjusting course when needed, balancing acceptance with growth, serve you not just in recovery but throughout life. (Cloitre et al., 2012)

Chapter Ten: Maintaining Recovery and Preventing Relapse (Brand et al., 2019)

- Physical symptoms of PTSD are treatable
- Sleep problems, pain, and tension respond to targeted strategies
- Addressing physical symptoms improves your overall recovery (Ross et al., 2017)
- Practical techniques here provide relief you can use today

Understanding the Nature of Recovery and Relapse (Fenster et al., 2018)

After investing substantial effort in PTSD recovery, processing traumatic memories, challenging negative thoughts, facing avoided situations, managing symptoms, rebuilding relationships and meaning, an important question arises: How do I maintain these gains? How do I prevent sliding back into old patterns? Understanding the nature of recovery and relapse, developing specific maintenance strategies, and knowing how to respond effectively to setbacks helps ensure that your hard-won progress persists and continues to build over time. (Lanius et al., 2018)

First, it is crucial to understand that PTSD recovery is not a linear progression from sick to cured with a clear endpoint. (Monson & Shnaider, 2014)

Rather, recovery is better conceptualised as a process of developing skills, changing patterns, and reducing symptoms to manageable levels whilst building a meaningful life. (Foa et al., 2019)

'Recovered' does not mean never experiencing any symptoms again; it means symptoms are significantly reduced, manageable when they occur, and do not prevent you from living the life you want.

This realistic understanding prevents the disappointment and demoralisation that can occur if you expect perfect, permanent symptom elimination.

Second, fluctuation in symptoms is normal, not evidence of relapse.

Everyone, trauma survivors and non-traumatised people alike, experiences variation in mood, stress, and functioning.

You'll have better days and worse days, easier weeks and more difficult weeks.

Temporary increases in PTSD symptoms during times of stress, around anniversary dates, or when encountering powerful reminders do not mean you have lost all progress or that recovery has failed. (APA, 2017)

They mean you are human and vulnerable to normal stress responses.

The difference between these temporary fluctuations and genuine relapse is duration and severity: fluctuations are brief, and symptoms return to baseline within days or weeks; relapse involves sustained return to severe symptoms for extended periods.

Third, relapse, if it occurs, is not a catastrophic failure requiring starting over from zero.

You retain the skills you have learned, the insights you have gained, and much of the progress you have made, even if symptoms temporarily increase.

Think of relapse like falling off a bicycle whilst learning to ride, it is a setback, but you do not unlearn everything and revert to complete inability.

You get back on the bicycle with knowledge of what caused the fall and how to adjust.

Similarly, if PTSD symptoms return to problematic levels, you have the tools and knowledge to address them more quickly than you could initially.

You know what works for you, what strategies to employ, and that recovery is possible because you have achieved it before. (NICE, 2018)

Recognising Early Warning Signs

Catching potential relapse early, before symptoms become severe and entrenched, makes intervention far easier and more effective. This requires developing awareness of your personal early warning signs: the subtle changes that indicate you are beginning to struggle before full symptom return occurs. These warning signs vary between individuals, but common patterns exist.

Behavioural warning signs often appear first.

You might notice yourself beginning to avoid situations you would previously reclaimed.

Perhaps you have been successfully grocery shopping but now find yourself making excuses not to go or ordering delivery instead.

You might notice withdrawal from social contact, declining invitations, not initiating contact, cancelling plans. (Ashton, 2002)

You might let self-care slide, skipping showers, eating irregularly, neglecting exercise, staying up late despite knowing sleep is crucial.

You might stop practicing coping strategies you would been using regularly, no longer doing relaxation exercises, abandoning thought records, discontinuing journaling.

Cognitive warning signs include return of negative thought patterns you would previously challenge. You might notice more catastrophic thinking, increased self-blame, heightened pessimism about recovery, or return of beliefs you would work to modify ('Nobody can be trusted,' 'I am permanently damaged,' 'Nothing will ever be okay'). You might notice yourself ruminating more, getting stuck in repetitive negative thinking that goes nowhere productive.

Emotional warning signs include increased irritability, feelings of hopelessness, emotional numbness, or general increase in anxiety or depression. Physical warning signs might include return of sleep disturbance, increased tension and pain, changed appetite, or fatigue. Interpersonal warning signs include increased conflict in relationships, withdrawal from loved ones, or difficulty communicating needs. (Ashton, 2002)

Develop your personal warning sign list by reflecting on what changed when you were most symptomatic compared to when you are functioning better.

What specific behaviours, thoughts, feelings, or physical symptoms reliably indicate you are struggling?

Write these down explicitly.

Share them with trusted others who can notice changes you might miss.

Check in with yourself regularly, perhaps weekly, against this list: 'Am I seeing any of my warning signs?' This regular monitoring allows early intervention before symptoms escalate.

Essential Maintenance Strategies

Preventing relapse requires ongoing implementation of strategies that supported your recovery, even after symptoms improve significantly. Many people make the mistake of abandoning helpful strategies once they feel better, assuming they are no longer needed. However, these strategies often need to continue indefinitely, not as intensive treatment but as ongoing maintenance that preserves gains and prevents symptom return. (Forbes et al., 2020)

Continued practise of cognitive skills is essential. You do not need to complete formal thought records constantly, but you do need to maintain awareness of your thinking patterns and challenge unhelpful thoughts when they arise. Notice when negative thinking increases and deliberately examine evidence rather than automatically believing catastrophic thoughts. The cognitive skills you developed become more automatic with continued use but atrophy without practise.

Continued engagement with previously avoided situations prevents avoidance from re-establishing.

You do not need to seek out triggers constantly, but you do need to maintain normal life engagement that involves encountering reminders in the natural course of activities.

If you have successfully worked through avoidance of specific situations, continue engaging with those situations as part of regular life rather than reverting to avoiding them now that you feel better.

Each avoidance strengthens fear associations; each continued engagement maintains your learning that these situations are manageable.

Continued attention to physical health and symptom management supports recovery maintenance. Continue prioritising sleep through good sleep hygiene and consistent schedules. Maintain regular physical activity. Continue using relaxation and stress management techniques regularly rather than only when in crisis. These foundational health behaviours buffer against stress and reduce vulnerability to symptom return. (Perlis et al., 2005)

Continued engagement with values-based living provides meaning that sustains motivation for maintaining recovery. Regularly review your values and ensure your daily life reflects them. Continue pursuing goals aligned with what matters most to you. This ongoing values-consistent living creates positive reasons to maintain recovery beyond just avoiding symptoms, you are living well, not just avoiding illness. (Schnyder et al., 2015)

Maintain social connections that supported your recovery. Continue investing in relationships with supportive others. Attend a support group if they've been helpful, even after symptoms improve. Do not isolate yourself once you feel better, assuming you no longer need support. Social connection remains protective against relapse and enhances quality of life whether or not you are struggling with symptoms. (Resick et al., 2017)

Periodic booster sessions with a therapist can be valuable even after completing formal treatment. Rather than waiting until you are in crisis to seek help, schedule occasional check-in sessions, perhaps every few months, to review progress, address emerging difficulties before they escalate, and refine strategies. Think of these like routine dental checkups: preventive maintenance that catches small issues before they become major problems.

Managing High-Risk Situations and Anniversary Reactions

- Certain situations predictably increase vulnerability to symptom return: anniversary dates of the trauma
- times of year associated with the trauma
- major life stressors
- significant losses
- physical illness

- or returning to locations associated with the trauma. Recognising these high-risk periods and planning increased self-care and support prevents them from triggering relapse.

Anniversary reactions, increased symptoms around the anniversary of the trauma, are common and normal.

Your mind and body remember the trauma even if you are not consciously tracking the date.

In the weeks approaching the anniversary, you might notice increased intrusive memories, nightmares, anxiety, or emotional reactivity. (Van der Kolk et al., 1996)

Rather than being surprised or discouraged by anniversary reactions, anticipate them and plan accordingly.

Mark the anniversary date explicitly in your calendar.

In the weeks before, increase self-care, reach out for support, use coping strategies more deliberately, and remind yourself that temporary symptom increases are expected and will pass.

Consider commemorating the anniversary in meaningful ways, spending time with supportive others, engaging in self-care activities, or participating in rituals that feel appropriate.

Major life stressors, job loss, relationship breakup, financial crisis, health problems, death of loved ones, and taxing your coping resources and can trigger symptom increases.

During these periods, be particularly vigilant about maintenance strategies.

Do not abandon coping practices because you are busy with the crisis; instead, these are precisely the times you most need them.

Reach out for support rather than trying to manage everything alone.

Allow yourself to temporarily reduce non-essential commitments to conserve energy for managing both the stressor and PTSD symptoms.

Use all the skills you have developed, cognitive restructuring, exposure when needed, physical symptom management, social support, actively during stressful periods.

If you are returning to locations associated with the trauma, perhaps moving back to a city where the trauma occurred, or attending an event that requires going to the trauma location, plan this carefully.

Use exposure principles: prepare mentally using cognitive strategies, plan concrete coping resources, have support available, and process the experience afterwards.

These returns can be emotionally challenging even after substantial recovery, but with preparation, they are manageable and can actually reinforce your recovery by demonstrating your capacity to handle difficult situations. (Maercker et al., 2022)

Learning from Setbacks to Strengthen Future Resilience (Bonanno, 2004)

Whilst setbacks are unwelcome, they provide valuable information that can strengthen your long-term recovery if you extract and apply the lessons they offer. Each setback reveals something about your vulnerabilities, warning signs, effective and ineffective strategies, or circumstances that challenge your coping. Treating setbacks as learning opportunities transforms them from pure negative experiences into information that enhances future resilience. (Hyland et al., 2021)

After managing a setback and returning to stable functioning, conduct a systematic review. What triggered this setback? Were there early warning signs you missed or ignored? What strategies were most helpful in recovering from the setback? What strategies didn't help or made things worse? What would you do differently if faced with similar circumstances in future? Write down your conclusions explicitly; memory fades, and explicit notes ensure the learning persists beyond the immediate experience.

Update your relapse prevention plan based on setback learning.

If you discovered new warning signs, add them to your list.

If certain strategies were particularly helpful, make a note to prioritise those in future difficulties.

If specific circumstances reliably trigger symptoms, develop explicit plans for managing those circumstances preventively.

Your relapse prevention plan should be a living document that evolves based on accumulated experience, not a static plan created once and never revised.

- Share learning with your support system. If you have a therapist, discuss setbacks and what you learned in sessions. If you have trusted friends or family, let them know what helped during the difficult period and what to watch for in future. This sharing serves multiple purposes: it cements the learning through articulation
- it helps others understand how to support you effectively
- and it makes you accountable for applying the lessons rather than forgetting them once the crisis passes.

Building Long-Term Wellness Beyond Symptom Management

Whilst preventing relapse and managing symptoms remain important indefinitely, full recovery involves building positive wellbeing rather than just avoiding illness. The goal isn't merely to not be symptomatic; it is to actively thrive and experience satisfaction, meaning, and joy. This shift from problem-focused to growth-focused orientation characterises movement from surviving to thriving. (Karatzias et al., 2017)

Invest in activities that actively build wellbeing rather than just reducing distress.

Pursue genuine interests and passions.

Develop skills in areas that fascinate you.

Cultivate relationships that bring joy and meaning.

Engage with beauty through nature, art, music, or whatever resonates with you.

Contribute to causes larger than yourself.

Experience pleasure deliberately, savouring good meals, enjoying entertainment, and playing.

These positive investments create life satisfaction that goes beyond symptom absence.

Continued personal growth and development after symptom reduction provides an ongoing sense of progress and accomplishment.

Set goals unrelated to PTSD, learning new skills, advancing career, pursuing creative projects, deepening relationships, exploring new interests.

Your identity needn't remain cantered on being a trauma survivor working on recovery. (Courtois & Ford, 2013)

PAUSE POINT: Ground Yourself

- • Notice 5 things you can SEE

As symptoms reduce, you can increasingly identify with other aspects of yourself and your life.

This does not mean denying trauma's impact; it means not allowing trauma to define you entirely.

Regular engagement with gratitude and appreciation, noticing and acknowledging positive aspects of life, enhances wellbeing.

This isn't about forced positivity or denying difficulties.

Rather, it is deliberately directing attention to what's good alongside acknowledging what's difficult.

Keep a gratitude journal where you note daily what you appreciate, however small.

Share appreciation with others regularly.

Notice moments of beauty, kindness, humour, connection, or pleasure as they occur.

This practice does not eliminate difficulties but provides balance and perspective.

Consider ways trauma has contributed to growth without romanticising the trauma itself. You might have developed qualities, resilience, compassion, clarity about priorities, and deeper connections through struggling with trauma. Acknowledging these does not mean being grateful for trauma or thinking it was worth it. It means recognising that, from terrible experiences, some positive developments can emerge. This recognition provides meaning without invalidating suffering. (Bonanno, 2004)

Recognising When Additional Professional Help Is Needed

Most people experience temporary symptom fluctuations that they can manage independently using the skills and strategies developed during treatment. However, certain situations warrant seeking professional help rather than trying to manage alone. Knowing when to reach out prevents minor difficulties from becoming major crises and ensures you get support when you need it.

Seek professional help if symptoms remain severe despite consistent application of coping strategies for several weeks.

If you are using all your strategies diligently, cognitive restructuring, exposure, physical symptom management, social connection, behavioural activation, and symptoms aren't improving or are worsening, professional assessment can identify what's maintaining symptoms and suggest alternative approaches.

Do not persist with strategies that aren't working indefinitely; get expert input.

Seek help immediately if you are experiencing thoughts of harming yourself or others. Suicidal or homicidal thoughts require urgent professional intervention, not self-management. Contact emergency services, go to an emergency department, call a crisis helpline, or contact your therapist urgently. These thoughts indicate severe distress that needs immediate professional support.

Seek help if you are developing new problems beyond PTSD, significant substance use, severe depression requiring medication assessment, dangerous behaviours, or other mental health concerns. These complications require professional evaluation and specialised treatment that self-help strategies cannot provide.

Seek help if life circumstances are overwhelming your coping capacity, multiple major stressors are simultaneously present, inadequate practical or social support, or circumstances requiring resources beyond what you currently have. Therapists can help problem-solve overwhelming circumstances, connect you with resources, and provide intensive support during crisis periods. You do not need to manage everything alone.

Finally, seek help proactively for booster sessions even when not in crisis. Periodic check-ins with a therapist, perhaps every few months or annually, can reinforce skills, address emerging difficulties before they escalate, update strategies based on life changes, and provide reassurance that you are on track. These preventive sessions are valuable even when you are functioning well.

Lifestyle Factors That Support Long-Term Recovery (Brewin et al., 2017)

Beyond specific PTSD-focused interventions, general lifestyle factors significantly influence long-term recovery stability. These foundational health behaviours create resilience against stress, reduce overall symptom severity, and enhance quality of life. Attending to lifestyle isn't an optional 'nice to have' addition to treatment; it is fundamental to sustainable recovery. (Ford et al., 2019)

Sleep remains critically important throughout recovery and beyond. (Cloitre et al., 2020)

Poor sleep maintains PTSD symptoms; good sleep supports recovery. (Watts et al., 2013)

Continue prioritising consistent sleep schedules, good sleep hygiene, and addressing sleep disturbance promptly when it occurs. (Perlis et al., 2005)

If nightmares persist despite trauma-focused treatment, consider specific nightmare interventions like imagery rehearsal therapy. (Ross et al., 1989)

If insomnia remains problematic, work with healthcare providers on cognitive-behavioural treatment for insomnia or medication options if appropriate.

Do not accept severe chronic sleep disturbance as inevitable; it can and should be addressed.

Regular physical activity provides multiple benefits, reduces anxiety and depression, improves sleep, enhances mood through endorphin release, provides a sense of accomplishment, creates opportunities for social connection if done in groups, and helps regulate the chronic physiological arousal characteristic of PTSD.

Aim for at least 150 minutes of moderate aerobic activity or 75 minutes of vigorous activity weekly, plus strength training twice weekly.

This does not require gym membership or elaborate routines; walking, cycling, swimming, home exercise, yoga, dancing, sports, or any activity that gets you moving regularly provides benefits.

Find activities you genuinely enjoy or can at least tolerate, increasing the likelihood of maintenance.

Nutrition influences mood, energy, and physical health.

Whilst no specific diet cures PTSD, general healthy eating supports recovery: (van Dis et al., 2020)

- Whilst no specific diet cures PTSD, general healthy eating supports recovery: regular meals to maintain stable blood sugar (Ehring et al., 2014)
- adequate protein, healthy fats, and complex carbohydrates
- abundant fruits and vegetables
- adequate hydration
- limited caffeine, particularly in the afternoon and evening
- and minimal alcohol.

Alcohol deserves particular attention, whilst it might seem to provide short-term anxiety relief, it disrupts sleep, worsens depression, impairs judgment, and can lead to dependence. (Lader, 2011; Ashton, 2002)

If you are using alcohol regularly to manage PTSD symptoms, this warrants discussion with a healthcare provider.

Substance use, both illicit drugs and misuse of prescription medications, frequently complicates PTSD. Substances might provide temporary symptom relief but maintain symptoms long-term, prevent effective processing of trauma, create additional problems, and increase suicide risk. If you are using substances to cope with PTSD, address this with professional help. Integrated treatment addressing both PTSD and substance use simultaneously produces better outcomes than treating either in isolation.

Creating Your Personal Relapse Prevention Plan

A written relapse prevention plan consolidates everything discussed in this chapter into a concrete, personalised document you can reference during difficult periods. Creating this plan whilst stable provides a roadmap for managing difficulties before they escalate. The plan should be detailed enough to be genuinely useful but not so complex that it is overwhelming to implement.

Your plan should include several key components.

First, list your personal warning signs, the specific behavioural, cognitive, emotional, physical, and interpersonal changes that indicate you are beginning to struggle.

- Be as specific as possible: not just 'I feel more anxious' but 'I notice myself making excuses to avoid grocery shopping
- my sleep deteriorates to less than 6 hours nightly
- I start catastrophizing more frequently
- I become more irritable with family.' These specific indicators allow clear self-monitoring.
- Second, identify your high-risk situations, circumstances that predictably increase vulnerability. This might include anniversary dates and surrounding weeks

- specific times of year
- certain locations
- particular types of stressors
- returning to trauma-related places
- periods of high work stress
- relationship difficulties
- or physical illness. Note these explicitly so you can plan increased self-care during these periods.

Third, list your most effective coping strategies organised by category.

Under cognitive strategies: specific types of thought-challenging that work for you, helpful reframes you have developed, and evidence that counters your negative beliefs.

Under behavioural strategies: exposure exercises that remain important, activities that improve mood reliably, and routines that provide structure.

Under physical strategies: relaxation techniques you find helpful, exercise routines you maintain, sleep hygiene practices that work. (Perlis et al., 2005)

Under social strategies: who to contact for support, how to reach them, and what specifically helps from different people.

Fourth, create specific action plans for different severity levels of difficulty.

For mild warning signs: implement which specific strategies, how frequently, for how long before reassessing.

For moderate difficulties: which additional strategies to add, who to contact for support, and whether to schedule therapy appointments.

For severe difficulties: immediate actions to take, emergency contacts, when to seek urgent professional help, and crisis resources.

This tiered approach matches response intensity to problem severity.

Fifth, identify your values and meaningful activities. During difficult periods, it is easy to lose sight of what matters and what keeps you engaged with life. Having your core values explicitly written, along with specific activities that reflect those values, provides direction when you are struggling. These positive pulls towards meaningful engagement complement the push away from symptoms.

Supporting Others in Their Recovery Journey (Coventry et al., 2020)

As you progress in recovery, you might find yourself in a position to support others who are earlier in their PTSD journey, friends, family members, fellow support group participants, or people you encounter through advocacy or professional work. Understanding how to provide helpful support whilst maintaining appropriate boundaries benefits both the person you are supporting and your own continued recovery. (Mavranezouli et al., 2020)

The most powerful support you can offer is presence and validation.

Simply being there, listening without judgment, acknowledging that their experiences are real and significant, communicating that they are not alone, provides profound support.

You do not need to have all the answers or fix their problems.

Resist the urge to immediately offer solutions or advice unless specifically requested.

Often, people need to feel heard and understood before they can effectively engage with suggestions.

Your willingness to listen without dismissing, minimising, or rushing to fix communicates respect and support.

Share your own experience selectively and appropriately. Your lived experience with PTSD can provide hope and practical insights but avoid making every conversation about your story. Ask what would be helpful: 'Would it be useful to hear how I managed similar symptoms?' Rather than assuming your experience maps directly onto theirs, acknowledge differences whilst highlighting commonalities. Your recovery demonstrates possibility without prescribing exactly how they should recover. (Karatzias et al., 2019)

Encourage professional treatment whilst respecting autonomy.

If someone isn't receiving professional help, you might gently suggest it: 'Have you considered working with a therapist who specialises in trauma?

It really helped me.' However, respect their decisions even if you disagree.

You can provide information about treatment options and resources whilst acknowledging that choosing treatment is their decision.

Pushing too hard can create resistance; providing information and stepping back allows them to choose when ready.

Maintain appropriate boundaries in supportive relationships.

You are not a therapist (unless that's your actual profession), and you shouldn't position yourself as such.

Be clear about what you can and cannot offer: 'I am happy to share my experience and provide support, but I cannot provide therapy or professional guidance.' Do not take responsibility for their recovery; they need to do their own work. (Lewis et al., 2020)

Set limits on the time and energy you invest, and you can be supportive without being available 24/7 or sacrificing your own well-being.

If supporting someone is triggering your own symptoms or compromising your recovery, pull back and prioritise your own stability. (Bisson et al., 2019)

Recognise when someone needs more help than you can provide. If they are expressing suicidal thoughts, engaging in dangerous behaviours, experiencing severe symptoms that aren't responding to current treatment, or struggling with additional serious problems like severe substance use or psychosis, encourage urgent professional help. Provide crisis resources, but do not attempt to manage serious crises alone. Your role is a supportive peer, not a crisis interventionist. (Stanley & Brown, 2012)

Maintaining recovery from PTSD requires ongoing attention and effort, but it becomes less intensive and more integrated into normal life over time. (Cusack et al., 2016)

The strategies that initially require conscious, deliberate effort become increasingly automatic.

The vigilance needed to catch early warning signs becomes second nature rather than constant work.

You develop confidence in your ability to manage difficulties as they arise because you have successfully navigated challenges before.

Recovery maintenance shifts from being a central focus of life to being background awareness, you are living your life with ongoing attention to maintaining wellness, not living primarily to maintain recovery. (Watkins et al., 2018)

This integration represents the ultimate goal: PTSD and its management remain part of your story but do not define your entire life.

Chapter Eleven: Special Considerations and Complex Presentations

- Complex presentations require individualised approaches
- Comorbid conditions (anxiety, depression) are common
- Your treatment plan adapts to your unique needs
- Understanding special considerations improves your care

Understanding Complex PTSD and Developmental Trauma (Teicher & Samson, 2016)

The PTSD discussed throughout this guide primarily reflects the 'classic' presentation following a discrete traumatic event or series of events.

However, many people experience trauma in more complex circumstances, particularly repeated, prolonged trauma occurring during childhood or in contexts of captivity, abuse, or ongoing threat.

These circumstances can produce a somewhat different presentation called Complex PTSD (C-PTSD), which includes the core PTSD symptoms plus additional difficulties in emotional regulation, sense of self, and relationships.

Understanding these distinctions helps those with complex presentations recognise their experiences and access appropriate support.

Complex PTSD typically develops from prolonged, repeated trauma, particularly when escape isn't possible, and the trauma is interpersonal. (Ozer et al., 2003; Teicher & Samson, 2016)

- Common causes include childhood abuse or neglect, particularly when occurring over years (Guay et al., 2006; Teicher & Samson, 2016)
- domestic violence, especially when prolonged and severe
- human trafficking or sexual exploitation
- being a prisoner of war or held captive
- experiencing ongoing torture or persecution
- or sustained childhood exposure to violence, chaos, or emotional neglect.

The key factors are chronicity (trauma lasting months or years rather than single incidents), interpersonal nature (trauma inflicted by people, particularly caregivers or those in positions of power), and lack of escape or safety.

In addition to standard PTSD symptoms, Complex PTSD involves disturbances in self-organisation across three domains. (Charuvastra & Cloitre, 2008; Teicher & Samson, 2016)

- First, severe problems with emotional regulation, emotions feel overwhelming and unmanageable
- you might experience intense rage, despair, or emotional numbness
- you might struggle with self-destructive behaviours used to manage unbearable emotions
- and you might dissociate frequently.
- Second, negative self-concept, pervasive feelings of shame, guilt, or worthlessness (Teicher & Samson, 2016)
- sense of being fundamentally damaged or defective
- difficulty maintaining coherent sense of identity.
- Third, disturbed relationships, difficulty trusting anyone
- problems maintaining closeness or constantly seeking closeness inappropriately
- difficulty setting boundaries
- repeated entry into exploitative relationships.

Complex PTSD particularly affects people traumatized during childhood when personality, sense of self, and relationship patterns are still forming. (Neff & Germer, 2018; Teicher & Samson, 2016)

Early chronic trauma disrupts normal development of emotional regulation, identity formation, and relational capacities.

You might never have learned these skills because your developmental environment didn't support learning them.

Treatment for Complex PTSD therefore involves not just processing trauma memories but building fundamental capacities that should have developed in childhood but didn't. (Gilbert, 2014; Teicher & Samson, 2016)

Modified Approaches for Complex PTSD (ISTSS, 2019; Teicher & Samson, 2016)

Treatment for Complex PTSD follows similar principles as for standard PTSD, but with important modifications to address the additional difficulties and the often more fragile stability of people with complex presentations. The standard trauma-focused approaches remain important but may need to be preceded or accompanied by additional stabilisation and skill-building work. (Herman, 2015; Teicher & Samson, 2016)

Phase-based treatment is typically recommended for Complex PTSD. (Herman, 2015; Teicher & Samson, 2016)

- Phase one focuses on stabilisation: establishing safety (physical and emotional)
- developing affect regulation skills
- addressing self-destructive behaviours
- building basic self-care capacities
- establishing a therapeutic relationship
- and creating life stability sufficient to engage in trauma processing.

This phase might take weeks to many months, depending on current life circumstances and symptom severity.

The goal isn't perfect stability but 'good enough' stability to proceed.

You'll never feel completely ready, but you need sufficient resources to tolerate the distress trauma processing generates.

Phase two involves trauma processing, similar to approaches described earlier in this guide but often proceeding more gradually. Processing might involve many traumatic memories rather than a single event. The work might need to proceed more slowly with more attention to maintaining stabilisation throughout. Therapist and client work together to identify which memories to process first, often starting with less overwhelming events and building capacity before addressing the most severe traumas.

Phase three focuses on integration and rebuilding life: consolidating gains, addressing residual symptoms, building identity beyond trauma survivor, developing meaningful relationships, and pursuing valued directions in life. This phase involves applying everything learned to building the life you want.

Skills training is crucial for Complex PTSD and is often integrated throughout treatment. (Cloitre et al., 2012; Teicher & Samson, 2016)

- Key skill domains include emotion regulation (identifying, tolerating, and modulating intense emotions without destructive behaviours)
- distress tolerance (managing crises without making them worse) (Linehan, 2015)
- interpersonal effectiveness (communicating needs, setting boundaries, maintaining relationships)
- and mindfulness (being present without becoming overwhelmed).

Dialectical Behaviour Therapy (DBT) provides excellent skills in these domains and is often incorporated into Complex PTSD treatment. (Linehan, 2015)

Managing Dissociation and Fragmentation

Dissociation, feeling disconnected from yourself, your body, your surroundings, or reality, is particularly prominent in Complex PTSD, though it occurs in standard PTSD as well. Dissociation exists on a spectrum from mild zoning out to severe detachment, where you lose time or do not recognise yourself. Understanding and managing dissociation is crucial for effective treatment, as severe dissociation can interfere with trauma processing and daily functioning. (Brand et al., 2019; Teicher & Samson, 2016)

- Mild dissociation includes experiences like feeling spacey or foggy
- difficulty concentrating
- feeling like you are watching yourself from outside
- things feeling unreal or dreamlike
- or emotional numbness.
- Moderate dissociation might involve losing track of time
- not remembering how you got somewhere
- finding evidence of things you did but not remembering doing them
- or significant detachment from physical sensations.
- Severe dissociation includes losing substantial periods of time
- feeling like different parts of yourself are separate people
- not recognising yourself in the mirror
- or having no memory of traumatic periods.

Dissociation served an important protective function during trauma; it allowed you to psychologically escape when physical escape wasn't possible.

By disconnecting from overwhelming experiences, you survived situations that might otherwise have been psychologically annihilating.

However, dissociation that persists after trauma ends becomes problematic rather than protective.

It prevents you from fully processing trauma, interferes with engaging fully in life, and can create amnesia that complicates understanding your own history.

Learning to recognise when you are dissociating is the first step in managing it.

Notice your personal dissociation signs: what does it feel like when you begin dissociating?

Do you zone out?

Feel disconnected?

Lose time?

Become foggy?

Developing awareness allows intervention before dissociation becomes severe.

Keep a dissociation log noting when dissociation occurred, how severe it was, what triggered it, how long it lasted, and what helped reduce it.

These patterns reveal your particular dissociation triggers and an effective intervention.

Grounding techniques help reduce dissociation by bringing you back into present moment awareness.

- Physical grounding includes pressing feet firmly into the floor and noticing sensations
- holding ice cubes and focusing on the cold sensation
- splashing cold water on the face
- doing physical movement like stretching or walking
- or eating something with a strong taste (sour candy, peppermint).
- Mental grounding includes naming five things you see, four things you hear, three things you can touch, two things you smell, and one thing you taste
- describing your surroundings in detail
- counting backwards from 100
- or reciting memorised information.

Emotional grounding involves connecting with present emotions and needs rather than trauma-related feelings.

Building Emotion Regulation Capacities

- Many people with Complex PTSD struggle profoundly with emotion regulation (Ross et al., 2017; Teicher & Samson, 2016)
- emotions feel overwhelming, unmanageable, and terrifying. This isn't a personal weakness
- it reflects the disrupted development of regulatory capacities during childhood trauma. Building these capacities through deliberate practice is essential for both stability and successful trauma processing.

Emotion regulation involves several component skills.

First, identifying emotions: being able to name what you are feeling with some precision.

This sounds simple but is genuinely difficult if you learned to suppress all emotion or if different emotions were punished.

Practice using emotion words: am I angry?

sad?

afraid?

ashamed?

hurt?

disappointed?

frustrated?

The more precisely you identify emotions, the better you can understand what you need.

Keep an emotion diary, noting situations and corresponding emotions to build this identification skill.

Second, understanding the function of emotions: emotions provide information about your needs and situation.

Anger often signals boundary violations or injustice.

Fear signals a potential threat.

Sadness signals loss.

Shame signals belief you have violated important values.

Understanding emotional function helps you respond appropriately: if anger signals boundary violation, an appropriate response is asserting boundaries, not attacking yourself for feeling angry.

If fear signals threat, evaluate whether the threat is real or trauma-based and respond accordingly.

Third, tolerating uncomfortable emotions without immediately acting to eliminate them.

Many problematic behaviours, substance use, self-harm, disordered eating, and impulsive decisions serve to escape unbearable emotions.

However, emotions, whilst uncomfortable, aren't actually dangerous.

They rise, peak, and decline naturally if you do not escalate them through avoidance or maladaptive coping.

Practice sitting with uncomfortable emotions for brief periods, noticing them without judgment, allowing them to exist without immediately trying to fix or eliminate them.

Start with mild emotions and brief periods (5 minutes), gradually building tolerance for more intense emotions and longer periods.

Fourth, modulating emotional intensity when needed.

Whilst tolerating emotions is important, sometimes emotions are so intense that they interfere with functioning or threaten to overwhelm coping capacity.

Having skills to reduce emotional intensity in these moments prevents a crisis.

- These skills include intense physical exercise to burn off activation
- cold water exposure
- deep breathing
- progressive muscle relaxation
- distraction using engaging activities
- changing body position or facial expression (forcing a smile actually reduces distress slightly)
- or using opposite action (acting opposite to emotional urges can reduce emotional intensity).

Understanding Attachment Disruption and Relational Healing

When trauma occurs in childhood, particularly trauma inflicted by caregivers, it disrupts normal attachment development, the formation of secure bonds with primary caregivers that provide a foundation for all future relationships. This disrupted attachment affects adult relationships profoundly, but understanding these patterns allows conscious work towards more secure relating.

Secure attachment develops when caregivers consistently respond to children's needs with sensitivity and reliability. The child learns: (Cohen et al., 2016; Cohen & Mannarino, 2008)

- Secure attachment develops when caregivers consistently respond to children's needs with sensitivity and reliability. The child learns: 'I am worthy of care (Cohen et al., 2016; Cohen & Mannarino, 2008)
- others are trustworthy
- relationships are safe
- I can cope with distress because help is available.' This foundation supports healthy adult relationships characterised by trust, appropriate closeness, the ability to seek support, and the capacity for intimacy.

Insecure attachment develops when caregivers are inconsistent, neglectful, or abusive.

Different patterns emerge: Anxious attachment develops when caregiving is inconsistent, sometimes responsive, sometimes rejecting.

You learn that relationships are unpredictable, and you must work hard to maintain them, leading to clinginess, fear of abandonment, and difficulty with partner autonomy.

Avoidant attachment develops when caregivers are consistently rejecting or neglectful.

You learn that depending on others is dangerous, leading to emotional distance, discomfort with intimacy, and compulsive self-reliance.

Disorganised attachment develops when caregivers are frightening or their behaviour is chaotic.

You learn that relationships are simultaneously needed and terrifying, leading to contradictory relationship patterns, desperately seeking closeness, then pushing people away, or remaining in harmful relationships despite wanting safety.

Insecure attachment isn't a permanent destiny.

Adult attachment can shift towards greater security through corrective relationship experiences, relationships where you experience consistent responsiveness, safety, and appropriate boundaries over time.

Therapeutic relationships often provide first experiences of a consistently safe connection.

Romantic partners, friends, or other significant relationships can also gradually provide experiences that challenge negative relationship expectations.

Through accumulated positive experiences, you can learn that some people are trustworthy, that closeness does not inevitably lead to hurt, and that your needs for connection are legitimate.

Working towards secure attachment involves several deliberate practices.

First, notice your attachment patterns: do you tend towards anxious seeking of reassurance?

Avoidant self-sufficiency?

Disorganised approach-avoidance?

Understanding your patterns helps you recognise when you are acting from attachment anxiety rather than responding to actual relationship dynamics.

Second, practice asking for support even when it feels uncomfortable.

If you tend towards avoidance, deliberately sharing needs and accepting help challenges the 'I cannot depend on anyone' belief.

Third, practice tolerating appropriate distance in relationships if you tend towards anxious attachment.

Your partner or friend needing space does not mean the relationship is ending; it means they need autonomy, which secure relationships accommodate.

Fourth, choose relationships with people who demonstrate consistency, respect boundaries, and respond with appropriate care.

Repeatedly choosing unavailable or harmful partners maintains insecure patterns; choosing differently creates opportunity for change.

Managing Comorbid Mental Health Conditions

PTSD frequently co-occurs with other mental health conditions, which clinicians call comorbidity. Understanding and addressing these co-occurring conditions is important for comprehensive treatment, as they can maintain PTSD symptoms and impair recovery if untreated. (Najavits, 2002)

Depression is the most common comorbid condition, occurring in approximately half of people with PTSD.

The relationship is bidirectional: PTSD increases risk for depression through mechanisms like loss of meaning, social withdrawal, and cognitive distortions; depression maintains PTSD by reducing motivation for treatment engagement, increasing negative thinking, and impairing the active coping necessary for recovery. (Ashton, 2002)

Treatment approaches that address both simultaneously, like cognitive-behavioural therapy, effectively reduce both depression and PTSD.

If depression is severe, antidepressant medication might be recommended alongside psychological treatment. (NICE, 2018)

Anxiety disorders beyond PTSD are common, including generalised anxiety disorder, panic disorder, social anxiety, or specific phobias.

These often share maintaining factors with PTSD, avoidance, threat overestimation, safety behaviours, and respond to similar interventions. (Clark, 1999)

Exposure therapy, cognitive restructuring, and anxiety management techniques help across anxiety conditions.

Treatment can often address multiple anxiety conditions simultaneously rather than requiring separate treatments for each.

Substance use disorders occur at elevated rates in PTSD.

People use substances to manage unbearable PTSD symptoms, alcohol to sleep or numb emotions, cannabis to reduce hyperarousal, stimulants to combat numbness, and opioids for both physical and emotional pain.

However, substance use maintains PTSD by preventing effective emotion processing, disrupting sleep despite seeming to help, creating additional life problems, and interfering with trauma-focused treatment.

Integrated treatment that addresses both PTSD and substance use simultaneously produces better outcomes than treating either alone.

This might involve trauma-focused CBT modified to include substance use interventions, or addiction-focused treatment that incorporates trauma-informed principles. (Bisson et al., 2013; NICE, 2018)

Eating disorders or disordered eating occur more frequently in trauma survivors, particularly those with histories of sexual trauma or childhood abuse. (Fenster et al., 2018; Teicher & Samson, 2016)

- Eating disorder behaviours might serve multiple functions related to trauma: controlling the body when you couldn't control what happened to it
- numbing emotions
- attempting to make the body less sexually attractive to prevent further assault
- or managing traumatic memories.

Treatment needs to address both the eating disorder and underlying trauma, typically involving specialised eating disorder treatment integrated with trauma-focused work.

Cultural Considerations in Trauma and Recovery (Lanius et al., 2018)

Culture profoundly shapes how trauma is experienced, expressed, and addressed. The symptoms emphasised in diagnostic manuals reflect Western cultural contexts and might not capture how PTSD manifests across different cultural backgrounds. Understanding cultural factors helps ensure trauma treatment is respectful and effective across diverse populations.

Different cultures have varying conceptualisations of trauma, mental health, and an appropriate response to suffering.

Some cultures emphasise collective over individual experiences, and trauma might be understood as affecting the family or community rather than primarily an individual experience.

Some cultures place greater emphasis on somatic symptoms (physical manifestations) than psychological symptoms.

Some cultures have a strong stigma against mental health treatment, viewing it as shameful or weak.

Others have rich traditions of community healing that should be respected and potentially integrated with professional treatment.

Expression of distress varies culturally.

Some cultures encourage emotional expressiveness; others value restraint and emotional control.

What looks like emotional numbing in one cultural context might be appropriate emotional regulation in another.

Some cultures express psychological distress primarily through physical symptoms, headaches, fatigue, and pain, rather than emotional symptoms.

Healthcare providers need cultural competence to distinguish between pathological symptoms requiring treatment and culturally normative expressions of distress.

Specific traumas have cultural dimensions that affect recovery. (Monson & Shnaider, 2014)

For example, sexual trauma in cultures with a strong emphasis on virginity or sexual purity creates particular shame and stigma.

War trauma for refugees involves not just combat exposure but loss of homeland, culture, and identity.

Persecution and discrimination based on race, religion, sexual orientation, or gender identity create ongoing traumatisation rather than discrete events.

Historical trauma, the cumulative effects of colonisation, slavery, genocide, or systematic oppression across generations, affects entire communities and requires understanding beyond individual symptom treatment.

PAUSE POINT: Ground Yourself

- • Notice 5 things you can SEE

Trauma-Focused Cognitive Behavioural Therapy (TF-CBT) is specifically designed for children and adolescents with PTSD, though principles apply across ages.

It combines cognitive-behavioural techniques, trauma processing, and parent involvement.

Treatment addresses trauma memories, unhelpful cognitions, and associated behavioural problems whilst teaching coping skills and involving caregivers in supporting recovery. (Foa et al., 2019)

TF-CBT typically involves 12-16 sessions and has strong research support for treating traumatized youth. (Cohen et al., 2016)

Narrative Exposure Therapy (NET) was developed for survivors of multiple traumas, particularly refugees and survivors of organised violence.

Rather than processing single traumatic events, NET involves constructing a comprehensive life narrative that contextualises a traumatic experience within the person's full life story.

This approach acknowledges the cumulative impact of multiple traumas whilst helping create coherent autobiographical memory.

NET typically involves 4-10 sessions and has good evidence for complex trauma presentations.

Written Exposure Therapy (WET) is a briefer trauma-focused intervention involving writing about the trauma in detail over five sessions without therapist-guided processing.

You write continuously for 30 minutes about a traumatic experience, including sensory details, thoughts, and emotions.

Each session, you write about the same trauma, which naturally produces exposure to the memory.

WET has emerging research support and offers advantages of brevity and simplicity, potentially increasing accessibility.

Acceptance and Commitment Therapy (ACT) approaches PTSD differently than traditional trauma-focused treatments.

Rather than focusing primarily on reducing symptoms, ACT emphasises accepting uncomfortable internal experiences whilst committing to valued actions.

You learn psychological flexibility, the ability to be present with difficult thoughts and feelings whilst engaging in meaningful life activities.

ACT has growing research support for PTSD and might be particularly useful when emotional avoidance is prominent or when standard trauma-focused treatments haven't been successful.

Compassion-Focused Therapy (CFT) addresses the shame, self-criticism, and difficulty with self-compassion common in PTSD, particularly following interpersonal trauma. CFT helps develop self-compassion as an antidote to shame and self-blame whilst also addressing trauma memories. This approach has particular application for Complex PTSD, where shame and negative self-perception are prominent. Research support is growing, with promising findings particularly for trauma survivors with high shame.

Medication Options for PTSD

Whilst psychological therapy is considered first-line treatment for PTSD, medication can play an important supporting role, particularly when symptoms are severe, when psychological treatment alone hasn't been sufficient, or when comorbid conditions like severe depression require pharmacological intervention. Understanding medication options helps you make informed decisions about whether medication might benefit your recovery. (APA, 2017)

Selective Serotonin Reuptake Inhibitors (SSRIs) are the most commonly prescribed medications for PTSD and the only medications specifically approved for PTSD treatment in many countries. (Stein et al., 2006)

SSRIs like sertraline and paroxetine can reduce PTSD symptoms, including intrusive thoughts, avoidance, negative mood, and hyperarousal. (NICE, 2018; Baldwin et al., 2014)

They typically require 4-6 weeks before benefits emerge and several months of treatment for full effect.

- Response varies
- some people experience significant symptom reduction, others experience modest benefit
- some experience no benefit or problematic side effects.

SSRIs also effectively treat comorbid depression and anxiety, making them particularly useful when these conditions co-occur with PTSD. (NICE, 2018; Baldwin et al., 2014)

Other antidepressants, including venlafaxine (an SNRI), and mirtazapine, have research support for PTSD, though less extensive than SSRIs. These might be tried when SSRIs aren't effective or aren't tolerated. Tricyclic antidepressants and MAO inhibitors have some evidence for PTSD, but are prescribed less frequently due to side effects and safety concerns. (Spiegel et al., 2009)

Prazosin, an alpha-blocker originally developed for blood pressure, shows effectiveness for trauma-related nightmares and sleep disturbance in PTSD. It is typically taken at bedtime and can significantly reduce nightmare frequency and intensity, improving sleep quality. This targeted effect makes prazosin valuable even when other symptoms respond to psychological treatment, since nightmares can persist despite overall improvement. (Raskind et al., 2007)

Benzodiazepines are sometimes prescribed for PTSD-related anxiety, but are generally not recommended. Whilst they provide short-term anxiety relief, they do not reduce core PTSD symptoms, can interfere with trauma-focused psychological treatment, carry risks of dependence and withdrawal, and are associated with worse PTSD outcomes long-term. If you are prescribed benzodiazepines, discuss with your prescriber whether alternative approaches might be more appropriate for your situation. (Ashton, 2002; Lader, 2011; NICE, 2018)

Antipsychotic medications are occasionally used in PTSD, typically when symptoms are very severe, when there are psychotic features, or when other treatments haven't been effective. Evidence for their effectiveness in PTSD is limited, and they carry significant potential side effects, so they are generally reserved for specific situations rather than routine use.

Emerging treatments under investigation include MDMA-assisted psychotherapy, which has shown promising results in clinical trials and recently received approval in some jurisdictions for treatment-resistant PTSD. Ketamine and psychedelic-assisted therapies are also being researched. These remain experimental and should only be pursued through legitimate clinical trials or approved treatment programmes with proper medical supervision.

If considering medication for PTSD, work with a psychiatrist or other prescriber knowledgeable about trauma treatment.

Discuss your specific symptoms, treatment goals, previous medication trials, other medical conditions, and medications you are taking to identify appropriate options.

Understand that medication typically works best when combined with psychological treatment rather than used alone, medication can reduce symptom intensity making psychological work more manageable, but does not replace the processing and skill-building that psychological treatment provides.

Monitor your response carefully, including both symptom improvement and side effects.

Give medications adequate trial periods before concluding they are ineffective; most require weeks to months for full benefit.

Never discontinue psychiatric medications abruptly without medical guidance, as some can cause dangerous withdrawal effects. (Ashton, 2002)

Regular follow-up with your prescriber ensures appropriate dosing, monitoring for side effects, and adjustment of treatment as needed.

Choosing the Right Treatment Approach

With multiple evidence-based treatments available, how do you choose which one to pursue?

Several factors influence this decision.

First, consider what's available in your area; the best treatment is one you can actually access.

Research which trauma therapists near you are trained in which approaches.

Second, consider your preferences.

- Some people prefer highly structured exposure-based approaches
- others prefer more cognitive-focused work
- still others prefer approaches emphasising acceptance over symptom reduction.

All evidence-based treatments are effective, so choosing one that resonates with you increases the likelihood of engagement and completion.

Third, consider practical factors like session frequency, total duration, and whether treatment is available in group format if that's preferable.

Fourth, discuss options with potential therapists; they can help you understand which approach might best fit your specific presentation and circumstances.

Do not hesitate to try a different approach if the first one does not work well for you.

Treatment non-response does not mean you cannot recover; it often means you need a different approach or therapist.

Remember that an evidence-based treatment is just that, evidence-based, not universally effective for everyone. Most people significantly improve, but response varies. If you do not respond to one approach, alternatives exist. Stay hopeful and persistent.

The comprehensive research supporting these treatments provides strong confidence that effective help exists for PTSD recovery across diverse presentations and populations. (NICE, 2018)

Recovery is achievable with appropriate professional support and an evidence-based intervention. (Forbes et al., 2020)

Finding a Qualified Trauma Therapist

Finding a skilled trauma therapist is one of the most important steps in recovery, yet it can feel daunting, particularly when you are already struggling with PTSD symptoms. Understanding what to look for, where to search, and how to evaluate potential therapists helps you find appropriate professional support more efficiently. (Schnyder et al., 2015)

Qualifications matter significantly for trauma treatment.

- Look for therapists who are: properly licensed in their profession (Psychotherapist, psychologist or counsellor)
- specifically trained in evidence-based PTSD treatments (PE, EMDR, CPT, or other trauma-focused approaches) (Shapiro, 2018)
- experienced working with trauma survivors
- and ideally specialised in your particular trauma type if relevant (combat trauma, sexual assault, childhood abuse).

Do not hesitate to ask potential therapists directly about their training and experience with PTSD treatment.

Qualified therapists expect these questions and answer them readily.

Finding therapists can occur through multiple channels.

Ask your GP or primary care physician for referrals to trauma specialists.

Contact Talking Therapies UK (www.TalkingTherapies.co.uk), local mental health clinics or counselling centres that specialise in trauma.

Use therapist directories that allow filtering by speciality.

In the UK, the BABCP (British Association for Behavioural and Cognitive Psychotherapies) maintains a directory of accredited CBT therapists.

Contact professional organisations related to specific treatments (EMDR UK and Ireland for EMDR therapists, for example). (Shapiro, 2018)

Ask for recommendations from support groups or other survivors, though remember that a good fit varies individually.

Search online therapist platforms that allow filtering by specialty, though verify credentials independently.

If you are in the NHS system, discuss accessing trauma-focused psychological therapy through your GP.

NICE guidelines recommend trauma-focused CBT or EMDR for PTSD, and these should be available through NHS psychological therapy services, though waiting times vary by region. (Shapiro, 2018)

If NHS waiting times are prohibitive and you have resources, private therapy provides faster access.

Many private therapists offer sliding scale fees based on income.

Some charities provide free or low-cost trauma therapy for specific populations, combat veterans, sexual assault survivors, and domestic violence survivors. (Seal et al., 2007)

Evaluating Fit During Initial Consultations

Most therapists offer initial consultation sessions where you can discuss your needs, learn about their approach, and assess whether you feel comfortable working together. Use these consultations strategically to find the best fit rather than committing to the first therapist you contact.

Questions to ask during consultations include: What training and experience do you have treating PTSD? Which specific treatment approach do you use? How many sessions does treatment typically involve? What will sessions be like? What happens during a typical session? Have you worked with people who experienced trauma similar to mine? What's your approach to someone very anxious about starting trauma-focused work? How do you measure progress? What happens if the treatment isn't working? These questions help you understand their expertise, approach, and compatibility with your needs.

Beyond credentials and approach, assess the therapeutic relationship.

Do you feel heard and understood?

Does the therapist communicate in ways that make sense to you?

Do they seem warm and genuine whilst also maintaining appropriate professional boundaries?

Do you sense they respect your autonomy and will work collaboratively rather than dictating treatment?

The therapeutic relationship significantly predicts treatment outcomes; the best evidence-based treatment delivered by a skilled therapist will not help if you do not feel safe and understood enough to engage fully.

Trust your instincts about fit whilst also recognising that some initial anxiety about therapy is normal and does not necessarily indicate poor fit.

Do not feel obligated to continue with a therapist who does not feel right, even if they are highly qualified. It is appropriate to say: 'I appreciate your time, but I do not think we're the right fit' and continue searching. Most therapists understand that fit matters and will not take offence. Similarly, if you start treatment and realise the fit isn't working, you can change therapists. You are not locked in permanently after one session.

It is also worth considering challenging your own assumptions and biases about therapists based upon their age, gender, culture and allowing the therapist to demonstrate their ability to support you throughout treatment, you may be pleasantly surprised. For example, some people report having a new experience of a healing, therapeutic relationship with a person of the same gender as a perpetrator of harm to be an important part of the therapeutic process.

What to Expect During Trauma-Focused Treatment

Understanding what happens during trauma-focused treatment reduces anxiety about starting and helps you engage more effectively. Whilst specific treatments differ, common elements exist across evidence-based approaches.

Early sessions typically focus on assessment, psychoeducation, and preparation.

Your therapist will conduct a thorough assessment of your trauma history, current symptoms, life circumstances, and treatment goals.

They'll provide education about PTSD, explain how the treatment works, and address your questions and concerns.

They might teach preliminary coping skills to support you through later trauma processing.

This foundation-building typically occupies 1-3 sessions before intensive trauma work begins.

Do not rush through this phase, adequate preparation supports more effective trauma processing.

The trauma processing phase involves directly engaging with trauma memories and their meanings.

This looks different across treatments: in PE, you recount the trauma memory repeatedly in session whilst your therapist supports you in staying present with it.

PAUSE POINT: Ground Yourself

- • Notice 5 things you can SEE

In CPT, you write trauma accounts and work to identify and challenge unhelpful beliefs about the trauma.

In EMDR, you recall trauma memories whilst engaging in bilateral stimulation. (Shapiro, 2018)

Regardless of specific method, this phase involves deliberately confronting what you have been avoiding, which is anxiety-provoking by design.

The anxiety is purposeful, it is part of how the treatment works.

Your therapist guides you through this process, helping you tolerate distress whilst processing the memories.

Homework is typical in most evidence-based PTSD treatments.

You might write trauma accounts between sessions, conduct exposure exercises, complete thought records, practise coping skills, or engage in other activities supporting treatment.

This between-session work is crucial; therapy sessions alone aren't sufficient.

Much of the therapeutic benefit comes from practising skills and continuing exposure work outside sessions.

Expect to invest several hours weekly between sessions doing homework assignments.

This time investment produces results.

Sessions are typically weekly, though some intensive treatments might involve more frequent sessions. Standard treatments range from 8-20 sessions, depending on the approach and your needs. Sessions usually last 60-90 minutes. Treatment follows a structured protocol rather than open-ended discussion; your therapist has a specific agenda for each session based on the treatment model. This structure keeps treatment focused and time-limited.

Managing Common Treatment Challenges

Even when you have found an excellent therapist and are committed to an evidence-based treatment, challenges commonly arise. Understanding and preparing for these challenges helps you persist through difficulties rather than abandoning treatment prematurely.

Increased distress early in treatment is normal and expected.

When you begin deliberately confronting trauma memories and avoided situations, anxiety often intensifies before it improves.

This temporary worsening does not mean treatment is harming you or failing; it means you are doing the difficult work of facing what you have been avoiding.

The distress decreases with continued practice.

Discuss your distress with your therapist rather than quietly suffering or dropping out.

They can help you distinguish between expected therapeutic distress and concerning symptom increases, adjust the pace if needed, and provide additional support during difficult phases.

Avoidance of therapy itself can emerge, missing sessions, not completing homework, minimising symptoms in sessions, or finding reasons to quit.

These avoidance patterns mirror the avoidance of maintaining your PTSD.

Notice when you are tempted to avoid therapy and identify what's driving the avoidance: is the content becoming more challenging?

Are you afraid of what you might experience?

Is shame about the trauma making disclosure difficult?

Understanding the avoidance allows you to address it directly rather than acting on it.

Commit to attending even when you do not want to, completing homework even when it is uncomfortable, and being honest with your therapist about what's difficult.

Feeling worse before feeling better is common, particularly in the middle phase of treatment when you are actively processing trauma but haven't yet experienced significant symptom relief.

This middle phase can feel discouraging; you are working hard and feeling distressed without yet seeing a payoff.

Trust the process and continue practicing.

Most people experience a significant improvement in the latter half of treatment after persisting through this difficult middle phase.

Track your symptoms formally using measures your therapist provides, sometimes progress is occurring even when it does not feel like it, and objective tracking reveals improvements you haven't noticed subjectively.

Relationship strain or rupture with your therapist might occur.

Perhaps they said something that felt hurtful or misunderstood.

Perhaps you feel judged or not truly heard.

Perhaps differences in approach or expectations create friction.

Address these issues directly with your therapist rather than silently withdrawing or quitting.

Say: 'I felt hurt when you said X' or 'I do not feel like you understand my situation.' Most skilled therapists welcome this feedback and work to repair the relationship.

These ruptures and repairs can actually strengthen the therapeutic relationship and model how to address relationship difficulties generally.

If you raise concerns and the therapist is defensive or dismissive rather than responsive, that's information suggesting you might need a different therapist.

Overcoming Barriers to Accessing Professional Treatment

Many people with PTSD face substantial barriers accessing professional treatment, practical obstacles, systemic issues, or internal resistances that prevent engagement with care despite recognising the need. Understanding common barriers and strategies for addressing them helps more people access the treatment that could help them.

- Cost is a major barrier in systems without universal healthcare or when accessing private treatment. Strategies for managing cost barriers include: accessing NHS services through your GP, which are free at point of use
- seeking therapists who offer sliding scale fees based on income
- contacting charities that provide free trauma therapy for specific populations

- investigating employee assistance programmes through your workplace that might provide limited free counselling
- asking therapists about reduced-fee slots they reserve for lower-income clients
- or considering group therapy, which is typically less expensive than individual therapy whilst still being effective.

Waiting times, particularly in NHS services, can be lengthy, sometimes months between referral and first appointment.

- Whilst waiting, utilise self-help resources: read books and guides about PTSD (like this one)
- use self-help apps for PTSD that provide structured interventions
- access online support groups
- practice coping strategies independently
- and work on building general stability in life.

Self-help does not replace professional treatment, but can provide benefit whilst waiting and might improve your capacity to engage effectively when treatment becomes available.

Some areas have waiting list initiatives where you receive brief support whilst waiting for full treatment.

Ask about these when you are referred.

Geographical barriers affect people in rural or remote areas where trauma specialists are scarce.

- Consider: online therapy (teletherapy), which has been demonstrated effective for PTSD and increases access regardless of location, many qualified trauma therapists offer remote sessions
- travelling periodically for treatment, perhaps scheduling intensive therapy over several days rather than weekly appointments spread over months
- or working with a local therapist who receives consultation from a trauma specialist to ensure evidence-based treatment even if they are less experienced with PTSD.

Talking Therapies UK (www.TalkingTherapies.co.uk) is a specialist provider of remote therapies and can offer cost-effective, evidence-based treatment.

- Work and schedule conflicts create barriers
- you cannot attend appointments during business hours when you work, or childcare obligations prevent attendance. Solutions include seeking therapists who offer evening or weekend appointments
- using online therapy that allows more flexible scheduling
- requesting workplace accommodations for medical appointments
- coordinating with partners or family members for childcare during appointments

- or inquiring whether therapists offer any childcare arrangements (some practices provide childcare during parent sessions).

Addressing Stigma and Internal Barriers to Seeking Help

Beyond practical barriers, internal resistances, often rooted in stigma, shame, or fear, prevent many people from seeking help even when it is accessible. These psychological barriers can be as powerful as practical obstacles but are less often acknowledged or addressed.

Mental health stigma, the belief that having mental health difficulties indicates weakness, failure, or fundamental deficiency, stops people from seeking the help they need.

You might think: 'I should be able to handle this myself,' 'Needing therapy means I am weak,' or 'Only crazy people need psychiatrists.' These beliefs reflect stigma rather than reality.

PTSD is a normal response to abnormal events, not a character flaw.

Seeking professional help for PTSD is no different than seeking medical help for physical injury; it is responsible self-care, not weakness.

The strongest, most resilient people recognise when they need help and pursue it actively.

Shame about the trauma itself, what happened, how you responded, or what it means about you, can prevent disclosure even to therapists.

You might fear judgment, disgust, or rejection if you reveal what occurred.

Understand that qualified trauma therapists have heard extensive trauma accounts and respond with professional compassion rather than judgment.

What feels shameful to you is, to them, evidence of what you survived and overcame.

They are trained to respond supportively to any disclosure.

Many traumata survivors report that the anticipated judgment never materialized, their therapist responded with kindness and normalisation of their experiences.

Fear of the treatment process itself, worries about confronting trauma memories, experiencing intense distress, or facing overwhelming emotions, creates avoidance of therapy.

These fears are understandable but often exaggerated.

Yes, trauma-focused treatment involves some distress, but therapists pace the work to match your capacity, provide support throughout, and ensure you are never overwhelmed beyond your coping ability.

The temporary distress of treatment is generally less than the ongoing distress of untreated PTSD.

Most people who feared treatment report afterward that it was more manageable than they expected, and that short-term discomfort was worth the long-term relief.

- Cultural factors might create barriers, in some cultures, discussing personal problems with strangers is taboo
- mental health treatment is stigmatized
- or family involvement in healthcare decisions is expected but family opposes treatment. Navigate these by seeking culturally matched therapists who understand your cultural context
- educating family about PTSD and treatment if appropriate
- framing treatment as medical care for health condition rather than as mental health treatment if that reduces stigma
- or accessing treatment independently if family opposition is strong whilst recognising this creates additional stress.

Teletherapy: Remote Treatment for PTSD

Teletherapy, psychological treatment delivered remotely via video conferencing, phone, or digital platforms, has expanded dramatically in recent years, particularly following the COVID-19 pandemic. Research demonstrates that teletherapy can be as effective as in-person treatment for PTSD, making it a valuable option particularly for those with access barriers.

- Advantages of teletherapy include: elimination of travel time and costs
- access to specialists regardless of your location
- greater scheduling flexibility
- reduced barriers for people with mobility limitations or health conditions making travel difficult
- ability to attend from your own home, which some find more comfortable
- and continuation of treatment if you move or travel. For people whose PTSD involves avoidance of leaving home, teletherapy can enable treatment engagement that might otherwise be impossible.

Evidence-based treatments like , PE, and EMDR have all been successfully delivered via teletherapy with outcomes comparable to in-person delivery. Therapists adapt techniques as needed; for example, in EMDR, therapists might guide you in self-administering bilateral stimulation rather than physically moving their hand in front of you. Most major treatment components translate well to remote delivery. (Shapiro, 2018)

- Practical considerations for successful teletherapy include: ensuring you have private, quiet space for sessions where you will not be interrupted or overheard
- having reliable internet connection and functional device with camera and microphone

- familiarizing yourself with the video platform being used
- having a backup plan if technology fails (phone number to call, etc.)
- and creating appropriate session boundaries, treat teletherapy sessions with same seriousness as in-person appointments rather than casually attending whilst doing other activities.
- Limitations of teletherapy exist: some people find it harder to connect emotionally through screens
- technical issues can disrupt sessions
- crisis management is more complicated remotely
- and not all therapists or all treatment modalities are well-suited to remote delivery.

If you try teletherapy and find it does not work well for you, that does not mean therapy itself will not help; you might simply need in-person treatment.

However, many people find teletherapy highly effective and prefer it to in-person treatment even when both are available.

Navigating Mental Health Services and Healthcare Systems

Understanding how to navigate mental health services, whether NHS, private providers, charity services, or combinations, helps you access appropriate care more efficiently and advocate for your needs effectively within often complex systems.

In the NHS, accessing psychological therapy for PTSD typically begins with your GP.

Book an appointment, explain your trauma history and symptoms, and request a referral to psychological therapy services.

GPs can refer to IAPT (Improving Access to Psychological Therapies) services, which provide evidence-based psychological treatments including trauma-focused CBT and EMDR. (Shapiro, 2018)

IAPT services can also be accessed via self-referral in many areas; you do not always need a GP referral.

For more severe or complex PTSD, your GP might refer to secondary mental health services (Community Mental Health Teams), which provide more intensive specialist support.

Understanding the assessment process helps you prepare.

After referral, you'll typically have an initial assessment appointment where a clinician evaluates your symptoms, trauma history, current functioning, risk factors, and treatment needs.

Be honest and thorough; this assessment determines what treatment you are offered.

If you are nervous about discussing trauma, it is okay to say: 'I am uncomfortable discussing details, but I experienced [type of trauma] and I am having [symptoms].' You do not need to recount graphic details during assessment; a general description suffices.

If the treatment offered does not match your needs, advocate for yourself.

If you are offered general counselling but need trauma-focused treatment, say: 'NICE guidelines recommend trauma-focused CBT or EMDR for PTSD. (Shapiro, 2018)

Can I access those specifically?' If waiting times are extremely long, ask: 'Are there any shorter waiting lists I could be referred to?

Are there any urgent referral pathways given my symptoms?' You have the right to access appropriate, evidence-based treatment, though availability varies by location.

- If your initial request isn't met, consider asking your GP to make the case more strongly in the referral
- contacting PALS (Patient Advice and Liaison Service) for support navigating the system
- or raising concerns with local mental health commissioners about access to NICE-recommended treatments.
- Keep records of your journey through services: dates of appointments
- whom you saw
- what was discussed and decided
- referrals made
- and treatments offered.

This documentation helps if you need to escalate concerns, provides continuity if you see multiple providers, and tracks whether promised treatments materialise.

If treatment isn't helping, communicate this clearly: 'I have completed 8 sessions and my symptoms haven't improved.

What are the next steps?' Do not silently accept ineffective treatment; the system should be responsive to your needs.

Chapter Twelve: Advanced Coping Skills for Daily Management

- Advanced coping skills provide relief in daily life
- These techniques work alongside formal treatment
- Building your personal coping toolkit increases resilience (Bonanno, 2004)
- Mastering these skills supports long-term recovery (Resick et al., 2017)

This expanded section provides advanced coping strategies beyond foundational techniques, offering a comprehensive toolkit for managing PTSD symptoms in daily life across multiple domains.

Advanced Grounding Techniques for Severe Dissociation

When basic grounding techniques prove insufficient for severe dissociation, advanced approaches provide stronger interventions.

- The 5-4-3-2-1 technique with intensification involves traditional sensory grounding amplified: name 5 things you see whilst touching them physically
- name 4 things you hear whilst closing eyes to focus entirely on sound
- name 3 things you can touch whilst applying firm pressure noticing texture deeply
- name 2 things you smell whilst taking deep deliberate breaths
- name 1 thing you taste whilst fully experiencing the sensation.

This intensified version provides stronger sensory input, pulling you into the present more effectively than the basic version.

Ice water immersion offers powerful physiological grounding.

When severely dissociated, plunge hands or face into ice water for 30 seconds.

The intense cold activates the dive reflex, a physiological response that reorients the nervous system, slows heart rate, and brings immediate present-moment awareness.

This technique works when nothing else does because it bypasses cognitive processing and directly affects physiology.

Keep ice water or cold packs available for severe dissociative episodes.

- Strong physical sensations ground through the body: hold ice cubes until they melt completely
- snap a rubber band against the wrist (gently, not self-harm)
- bite into lemon or smell an ammonia capsule
- do intense exercise like sprints or burpees, creating powerful physical sensations
- or apply strong pressure to pressure points.

These techniques work through the intensity of sensation, overwhelming dissociative disconnect.

Use judiciously, intensity matters, but safety does too.

Opposite action for dissociation involves deliberately creating a connection when dissociation creates distance.

- If you feel floaty and unreal, ground yourself: sit on the floor feeling the floor's solidity beneath you

- press hands firmly against the wall feeling its resistance
- lie down feeling body's weight
- or squeeze objects tightly feeling their substance.

The physical anchoring counteracts the floating disconnection characteristic of dissociation.

- Structured activity interrupts dissociation through engaging the mind actively: count backwards by 7s from 100
- recite a poem or song lyrics aloud
- describe surroundings in minute detail, speaking continuously
- complete a complex mental task like planning a meal, including every step
- or engage in conversation requiring attention and response.

Dissociation involves decreased prefrontal activity; structured cognitive engagement reactivates it.

- Combination techniques layer multiple grounding methods simultaneously for maximum effect: hold ice whilst reciting grounding statements aloud whilst stamping feet rhythmically
- smell a strong scent whilst doing jumping jacks whilst saying name and date aloud
- or apply pressure to pressure points whilst describing surroundings in detail whilst listening to music.

Multiple simultaneous inputs overwhelm dissociation more effectively than single technique.

Chapter Thirteen: Moving Forward, Living Beyond Trauma

- Moving beyond PTSD opens possibilities for thriving
- Your identity extends beyond your trauma
- Building a life of meaning and purpose is achievable
- This chapter guides your transition to recovery (Herman, 2015)

Reflecting on Your Journey

If you have worked through this guide, reading the chapters, practising the strategies, and engaging in professional treatment, you have invested substantial effort in your recovery. Whether you are at the beginning of your PTSD journey or well along the path to recovery, take time to acknowledge the courage and persistence required to face trauma rather than continuing to avoid it. Recovery work is genuinely difficult, and engaging with it demonstrates strength rather than weakness. (Herman, 2015)

Your journey with PTSD is uniquely yours.

Your trauma, your symptoms, your circumstances, your strengths, and your recovery path differ from anyone else's. (Herman, 2015)

Resist comparing your progress to others or to idealised timelines.

Some people recover relatively quickly; others require years of sustained effort.

Neither timeline reflects on your worth, your effort, or your ultimate capacity for recovery. (Herman, 2015)

What matters is that you are moving forward, however gradually, rather than remaining trapped in avoidance and suffering.

- Recovery from PTSD does not mean forgetting trauma or returning exactly to who you were before it occurred. Trauma changes people (Herman, 2015)
- That's simply reality. Recovery means: symptoms reduce to manageable levels rather than dominating your life (Herman, 2015)
- you reclaim activities and relationships trauma took from you
- you develop a sense of meaning and purpose that transcends trauma
- and you build a life worth living despite what you experienced. You integrate trauma into your life story without letting it be the only story. The trauma remains part of who you are, but it is one chapter among many rather than the entire book.

As you reflect on your journey, notice changes you have made: What symptoms have improved, even if they are not completely gone? What situations can you now manage that previously felt impossible? What skills have you developed? What have you learned about yourself, about resilience, about what matters most to you? What relationships have strengthened, or new connections have formed? These changes, however modest they might feel, represent genuine progress worth acknowledging. Do not dismiss your accomplishments by focusing solely on what remains difficult. (Bonanno, 2004)

Redefining Yourself Beyond Trauma Survivor

An important aspect of recovery involves expanding your identity beyond 'trauma survivor' or 'person with PTSD.' Whilst these might be accurate descriptors, they needn't be your primary identity. As recovery progresses, you can increasingly identify with other aspects of yourself: your roles (parent, partner, friend, professional), your interests and passions, your values and commitments, your personality characteristics, your accomplishments, and your ongoing development as a person.

This does not require denying trauma occurred or pretending PTSD does not affect you.

Rather, it is about the appropriate placement of trauma within your larger identity.

Trauma is something that happened to you and continues to affect you to some degree, but it is not all you are.

You contain multitudes: you are someone who experienced trauma AND someone who loves music, or makes people laugh, or cares deeply about justice, or is learning to cook Thai food, or volunteers with animals, or is working to be a better partner, or any number of other aspects of human life.

Trauma can coexist with these other identities without overshadowing them entirely.

- Actively cultivate non-trauma identities by: engaging regularly in activities unrelated to trauma or recovery (Herman, 2015)
- pursuing interests and hobbies that absorb your attention
- developing expertise or skills in domains you care about
- contributing to causes or communities connected to your values rather than solely to trauma
- building relationships where trauma isn't the primary topic
- and setting goals and working towards achievements that reflect interests beyond recovery. These investments in non-trauma aspects of life do not compete with recovery, they support it by providing positive reasons for living well beyond just avoiding symptoms. (Herman, 2015)

Some people experience transformation through trauma recovery, not just returning to baseline but actually developing in positive directions. (Herman, 2015)

This post-traumatic growth isn't universal, isn't required for recovery, and does not make trauma worthwhile. (Tedeschi & Calhoun, 2004)

- But for some people, the process of struggling with trauma's aftermath produces: deeper relationships characterised by greater authenticity and appreciation
- increased compassion and empathy for others who suffer
- clarified priorities and values
- enhanced personal strength and confidence in their capacity to handle adversity
- greater appreciation for life and what matters most
- new possibilities and directions they wouldn't have discovered otherwise
- or spiritual or philosophical development as they grapple with existential questions trauma raises.

If you experience these changes, acknowledge them without guilt.

You can recognise growth emerged from struggle whilst still wishing the struggle hadn't been necessary.

Closing Thoughts: Your Recovery Continues (Herman, 2015)

This guide has provided comprehensive information about PTSD and evidence-based strategies for recovery. (Herman, 2015)

You have learned about trauma's effects on brain and body; how PTSD develops and what maintains it; cognitive restructuring to challenge unhelpful thoughts; exposure approaches to overcome avoidance; physical symptom management; relationship rebuilding; meaning reconstruction; relapse prevention; special considerations for complex presentations; professional treatment options; and moving forward beyond trauma.

This knowledge base equips you for recovery journey ahead. (Herman, 2015)

However, reading this guide isn't recovery itself, it is preparation for recovery. (Herman, 2015)

- The actual work happens when you apply these strategies consistently: when you notice negative thoughts and challenge them
- when you face avoided situations despite anxiety
- when you reach out for support despite discomfort
- when you practise coping skills regularly
- when you engage in trauma-focused therapy even when it is difficult
- when you persist through setbacks
- and when you gradually rebuild life reflecting your values.

Knowledge matters, but application of knowledge creates change.

Start where you are, do what you can manage, and build from there.

Small consistent actions compound into substantial change over time.

Recovery isn't solitary journey. (Herman, 2015)

While this guide focuses on what you can do independently, professional support dramatically improves outcomes for most people.

If you haven't yet accessed professional treatment, prioritise finding a qualified trauma therapist who can provide an evidence-based intervention.

If professional treatment isn't currently accessible, use this guide's strategies as a foundation whilst working to access professional support eventually.

Connect with other survivors through support groups, both giving and receiving support, facilitates recovery. (Herman, 2015)

Build relationships with people who understand trauma and can provide appropriate support.

You do not have to recover alone, and attempting to do so makes the journey much harder than necessary.

Be patient with yourself throughout recovery. (Herman, 2015)

Change takes time, probably more time than you would prefer.

You'll have better days and worse days, periods of clear progress and periods where nothing seems to improve.

This variability is normal; not evidence of failure.

Recovery isn't a linear upward trajectory but a messy process with advances, plateaus, and temporary setbacks. (Herman, 2015)

What matters is the overall direction over months and years, not day-to-day fluctuations.

Continue moving forward even when progress feels imperceptible.

Trust that consistent effort produces results even when those results aren't immediately visible.

Finally, know that recovery is possible. (Herman, 2015)

Thousands of people have recovered from PTSD, reduced their symptoms significantly, reclaimed their lives, built meaningful existence despite what they experienced.

The research is clear: with appropriate treatment and sustained effort, most people improve substantially.

You are not doomed to suffer indefinitely.

PTSD is treatable condition, not unchangeable life sentence.

The path forward might be difficult, but it exists and leads somewhere better than where you are now.

Take the first step, then the next, then the one after that.

Keep moving forward.

Recovery awaits. (Herman, 2015)

You can do this. Your recovery matters. Your life matters. Begin. (Herman, 2015)

What Recovery Looks Like: Setting Realistic Expectations (Herman, 2015)

Before beginning the practical work of recovery, it is important to clarify what recovery means and does not mean. Unrealistic expectations can lead to disappointment, unnecessary distress, or premature abandonment of treatment. Conversely, accurate expectations help you recognise and celebrate genuine progress whilst maintaining motivation during difficult phases of treatment. (Herman, 2015)

Recovery from PTSD does not mean forgetting what happened. (Herman, 2015)

The traumatic event occurred; it is part of your history, part of your life story.

Recovery does not involve erasing the memory or developing amnesia. (Herman, 2015)

You will remember what happened.

The difference is that you will be able to remember without being overwhelmed.

The memory will feel like a memory, something that happened in the past, rather than something happening now.

You will be able to think about what happened when appropriate without experiencing the same level of distress.

The memory will be integrated into your life story rather than dominating it.

Recovery does not mean never feeling any distress about what happened. (Herman, 2015)

It is entirely appropriate and normal to feel sad, angry, or disturbed when thinking about traumatic events.

These emotions do not indicate failed recovery; they indicate that you are a human being with normal emotional responses to abnormal events. (Herman, 2015)

If someone you cared about told you about experiencing a trauma like yours, you would feel sad or angry on their behalf.

It is appropriate to feel those emotions about your own experience, too.

The difference in recovery is that these emotions become manageable rather than consuming, and they do not prevent you from living your life. (Herman, 2015)

You can feel sad about what happened while also feeling joy in the present.

You can be angry about the injustice whilst also moving forward.

Emotions become guests that visit rather than tyrants that rule.

Recovery does not mean returning to exactly who you were before the trauma. (Herman, 2015)

Trauma changes people: this is simply reality.

Some of these changes may be losses you grieve: lost innocence, lost sense of invulnerability, lost trust, lost relationships, lost time.

These losses are real and deserve acknowledgment.

However, some changes may be neutral or even positive, greater appreciation for life, deeper compassion for others who suffer, clearer priorities about what matters, increased resilience, stronger relationships with people who supported you, or new meaning and purpose derived from your experience. (Bonanno, 2004)

Recovery means integrating these changes into your sense of self rather than desperately trying to resurrect a pre-trauma version of yourself who no longer exists. (Herman, 2015)

You are not trying to go backward; you are creating a new version of yourself that acknowledges what happened while also embracing possibility.

Recovery does not mean being 'cured' in the sense that you will never experience any symptoms again. (Herman, 2015)

PTSD recovery is more accurately described as symptom management and life reclamation rather than a cure. (Herman, 2015)

Most people who recover from PTSD will occasionally experience mild symptoms, particularly under stress or when encountering powerful reminders.

You might have an occasional nightmare, particularly when stressed or during anniversary periods. (Raskind et al., 2007; Ross et al., 1989)

You might experience a brief intrusive memory when encountering an unexpected trigger.

You might feel temporarily more anxious when hearing about a trauma like yours.

These occasional, mild symptoms are normal and do not indicate treatment failure or relapse.

The difference is that these symptoms are brief, manageable, and do not significantly impair your functioning.

You have tools to manage them effectively, and you trust in your ability to cope.

Recovery does not mean never being triggered. (Herman, 2015)

Triggers do not completely disappear in recovery. (Herman, 2015)

What changes is your relationship with triggers and your response to them.

Instead of triggers causing overwhelming distress and compelling avoidance, they become manageable reminders that you can notice, contextualise ('This is a reminder of what happened, not a current threat'), and move through without being derailed.

You might feel uncomfortable when triggered, but you are not overwhelmed.

You can continue with your activities rather than being stopped in your tracks.

The trigger activates your memory without dominating your experience.

Recovery does not mean having no bad days. (Ross et al., 2017)

Everyone, trauma survivors and non-traumatised people alike, has difficult days.

You will have days when you feel more anxious, more irritable, more tired, more troubled by memories, or more pessimistic.

This is part of being human, not evidence of relapse.

The difference is that you can recognise difficult days as temporary fluctuations rather than permanent states.

You can implement coping strategies, reach out for support if needed, and trust that you will feel better tomorrow or next week.

Bad days do not erase your progress; they are just bad days.

Rather, recovery means several specific, achievable things. Recovery means the trauma no longer controls your daily life. Whilst the trauma is part of your history, it is not the organising principle of your present. You make decisions based on your values and goals rather than based on avoidance and fear. You can engage with lifework, relationships, activities, and interests, rather than being consumed by managing symptoms. Your life has meaning and purpose beyond just surviving PTSD. (Fenster et al., 2018)

Recovery means you can remember what happened without being overwhelmed. (Lanius et al., 2018)

The memory is accessible when appropriate; you can think about or discuss the trauma if needed, but it does not intrude constantly.

When you do think about it, you can tolerate the emotions that arise.

You do not experience panic, dissociation, or complete emotional collapse.

The memory feels like a memory.

Sad or disturbing, but clearly located in the past, rather than feeling like it is happening now.

You have integrated the memory into your life story: 'This terrible thing happened to me, and it shaped me, but it does not define me or determine my future.'

Recovery means symptoms are significantly reduced and manageable. (Monson & Shnaider, 2014)

You may still experience some symptoms occasionally, but they are less frequent, less intense, and less impairing than they were.

When symptoms do arise, you have effective strategies for managing them, and you trust in your ability to cope.

For example, if you have a nightmare, it is distressing, but you can use grounding techniques to reorient yourself, remind yourself it was a dream, and return to sleep or start your day. (Raskind et al., 2007; Ross et al., 1989)

You are not left terrified and unable to function.

If you experience an intrusive memory, you can acknowledge it, use breathing techniques to manage anxiety, and refocus on your current activity.

The symptom does not derail your entire day.

Recovery means you have reclaimed activities, relationships, and experiences. (Foa et al., 2019)

You are engaging with life again, working or studying, socialising with friends and family, pursuing interests and hobbies, maintaining relationships, experiencing pleasure and joy, and planning for the future.

You are not avoiding entire categories of experience to manage symptoms.

Yes, you might make some thoughtful choices, you choose not to watch certain films because they are unnecessarily triggering, or you plan self-care around anniversary dates.

But these are conscious, values-based choices rather than fear-driven avoidance.

You are choosing how to engage with life rather than having your choices dictated by PTSD.

Recovery means you have confidence in your ability to cope with difficulties. (APA, 2017)

The most important aspect of recovery is the psychological shift from 'I am fragile and cannot manage distress' to 'I am resilient and can cope with challenges.' This confidence comes from repeated experiences of facing difficulties and discovering you can manage them. (NICE, 2018)

You have faced and avoided situations and survived.

You have sat with distressing emotions, and they have passed.

You have experienced setbacks and recovered.

This accumulated evidence builds genuine confidence, not bravado or false positivity, but earned trust in your capabilities.

When difficulties arise, your first thought is 'This is hard, but I can manage it' rather than 'This will destroy me.'

Recovery means you are building a meaningful life that includes, but isn't defined by, the trauma. (Forbes et al., 2020)

Your identity isn't 'PTSD sufferer' or 'trauma victim.' Whilst the trauma is part of your story, you are also many other things: partner, parent, friend, professional, and a person with interests, values, dreams, quirks, strengths, and limitations.

You are building a life oriented towards what matters to you rather than a life oriented around avoiding what frightens you.

You have goals and plans.

You have relationships that bring connection and meaning.

You have activities that provide purpose or pleasure.

You are thriving, not just surviving.

Understanding the Non-Linear Nature of Recovery (Schnyder et al., 2015)

This realistic understanding of recovery helps you recognise genuine progress without expecting perfection and helps you distinguish between normal fluctuations and concerning regression. (Resick et al., 2017)

It is crucial to understand that recovery is not linear; it does not proceed smoothly from bad to good in a straight line. (Maercker et al., 2022)

Rather, recovery involves advances, plateaus, and occasional setbacks. (Hyland et al., 2021)

Progress might look like two steps forward, one step back, sideways shuffling, leaps forward, and temporary retreats.

This is normal.

Many people imagine recovery as a steady upward trajectory: feeling terrible at the start, gradually improving week by week, and eventually reaching 'recovered' status. (Karatzias et al., 2017)

Whilst this narrative is appealing, it is not accurate.

Real recovery involves fluctuation. (Courtois & Ford, 2013)

You might have several good weeks where symptoms are minimal and you feel hopeful, followed by a difficult week where symptoms spike and you feel discouraged.

This does not mean you have lost your progress or that treatment is not working; it means you are experiencing the normal variability of recovery. (Brewin et al., 2017)

Several factors contribute to this non-linearity. First, life involves ongoing stressors unrelated to trauma. When you are stressed by work deadlines, relationship conflicts, financial concerns, physical illness, or other life challenges, your vulnerability to PTSD symptoms increases. This does not erase your progress; it is a temporary increase in symptoms due to increased overall stress. When the stressor resolves, symptoms typically decrease again.

Second, certain times may be predictably more difficult. Anniversary dates of the trauma often trigger increased symptoms. Seasons or times of year associated with the trauma may be challenging. Life transitions, even positive ones like moving house, changing jobs, or getting married, can temporarily increase vulnerability. Anticipating these predictable difficult periods allows you to plan increased self-care and support rather than being blindsided by symptom increases.

Third, the therapeutic work itself can temporarily increase symptoms.

This might seem paradoxical; shouldn't treatment reduce symptoms?

It does, overall and over time.

But the process involves temporarily approaching what you have been avoiding, which naturally increases distress in the short term.

When you begin memory processing work, you are deliberately thinking about traumatic content, which can increase intrusive memories, nightmares, and emotional distress temporarily. (Van der Kolk et al., 1996)

When you begin exposure work, facing avoided situations, you will experience increased anxiety.

This temporary increase is a sign that treatment is working; you are engaging with the material that needs processing rather than continuing to avoid.

The distress peaks and then decreases as the work produces its benefits.

Fourth, recovery involves learning and consolidation processes that take time. (Ford et al., 2019)

After a therapy session or a particularly intensive period of work, you might initially feel worse as you have stirred up difficult content.

But over the following days and weeks, as your brain processes and integrates this material, you typically feel better.

Sometimes insight or improvement comes not during the work itself but afterward, as the benefits consolidate.

This delayed benefit can be frustrating; you want to feel better immediately, but it reflects how psychological change works.

Understanding this non-linear pattern helps you maintain hope during difficult periods.

When you are having a bad week, you can remind yourself: 'This is a temporary fluctuation, not permanent regression.

I have had bad weeks before and recovered.

This does not erase my progress.

I can implement coping strategies, and this will pass.' Conversely, understanding the non-linear pattern prevents overconfidence during good periods.

When you are feeling great, you can enjoy it whilst also remaining realistic: 'I am having a good period, which is wonderful.

I should enjoy this whilst also maintaining my coping strategies and being prepared for normal fluctuations.'

Ensuring Safety and Stabilisation Before Beginning Trauma Work

Before beginning the intensive work of trauma processing, it is crucial to ensure you are safe and stable. Trauma-focused work is demanding and emotionally challenging. Attempting it when you are in crisis, when you are currently in danger, or when your life circumstances are extremely unstable is likely to be unsuccessful or even harmful. This does not mean you need perfect life circumstances; few people have those, but you need a foundation of basic safety and stability.

First and most importantly, you must be physically safe.

If you are currently in an abusive relationship, living in a dangerous environment, or experiencing ongoing trauma, your priority must be establishing safety.

You cannot effectively process past trauma whilst current trauma is occurring.

Your brain and body are correctly focused on managing current threats; they do not have resources available for processing past events.

If you are currently unsafe, reach out for help from domestic violence services, police, social services, or other relevant organisations.

Trauma processing work can begin once you are physically safe, even if your circumstances aren't perfect.

Second, you need basic life stability.

If you are homeless, if you are in immediate danger of losing your job, if you are experiencing an acute financial crisis, if you have an untreated serious physical illness, or if you are dealing with other severe life crises, trauma processing work may need to wait until these immediate concerns are addressed.

Again, this does not mean your life must be perfect; it means you need sufficient stability to engage with demanding therapeutic work.

Some people can manage trauma processing whilst dealing with moderate life stresses; others need greater stability.

This is an individual assessment you can make with your therapist if you are working with one.

Third, if you are experiencing active suicidal thinking or have engaged in serious self-harm recently, these concerns need addressing before intensive trauma work.

Suicidality and self-harm aren't absolute contraindications for trauma work; many people with PTSD experience these, but they need to be manageable and not at crisis levels.

If you are currently at risk of acting on suicidal thoughts or seriously harming yourself, reach out for immediate help: contact emergency services, crisis hotlines like Samaritans (116 123 in the UK), or present to A&E.

These services exist to help you stay safe.

Once suicidal thinking is reduced to a level where you can keep yourself safe, trauma work can proceed.

Fourth, active substance misuse needs addressing.

Many people with PTSD use alcohol or drugs to manage symptoms; this is understandable and common.

However, active substance misuse interferes with trauma processing work.

Substances can interfere with memory processing, reduce the emotional engagement necessary for trauma work, create additional instability, and prevent learning.

If you are using substances to manage PTSD symptoms, consider seeking help for this before or alongside trauma work.

This does not necessarily mean achieving complete abstinence before starting trauma work, but you do need sufficient control over substance use that it does not interfere with treatment.

Many people find that as PTSD improves through treatment, they naturally reduce substance use because they no longer need it for symptom management.

Building Your Coping Resource Toolkit

Before beginning intensive trauma work, it is helpful to build a toolkit of coping strategies you can use to manage distress. Trauma processing will temporarily increase symptoms, and you need reliable ways to manage this increased distress. Think of these coping strategies as tools in a toolbox; you will not use every tool every day, but having them available means you are prepared for whatever arises.

Grounding techniques help you stay connected to the present moment when you are feeling overwhelmed, dissociating, or experiencing flashbacks. (Van der Kolk et al., 1996)

These techniques work by engaging your senses to remind your brain where and when you actually are.

The 5-4-3-2-1 technique is particularly effective: identify 5 things you can see, 4 things you can touch, 3 things you can hear, 2 things you can smell, and 1 thing you can taste.

This systematic sensory engagement pulls your attention from internal distress to external reality.

Other grounding techniques include holding ice cubes, stamping your feet firmly on the ground, describing your current environment in detail out loud, or carrying a small object with a distinctive texture that you can touch when you need grounding.

Breathing techniques help regulate your nervous system when you are anxious or panicking.

When anxious, breathing typically becomes rapid and shallow, which maintains the anxiety response.

Deliberately slowing and deepening your breathing activates the parasympathetic nervous system, your 'rest and digest' system, counteracting the anxiety response. (Porges, 2011)

Try breathing in slowly through your nose for a count of four, holding for four, breathing out through your mouth for six, and pausing for two.

This 4-4-6-2 pattern is particularly effective.

The key is making the out-breath longer than the in-breath, which specifically activates the calming parasympathetic response.

Self-soothing techniques provide comfort and care when you are distressed.

- These might include: taking a warm bath or shower
- wrapping yourself in a comfortable blanket
- drinking warm tea or hot chocolate
- listening to calming music
- looking at comforting images or videos
- spending time with pets
- using pleasant scents like lavender or vanilla
- gentle self-massage
- or any activity that provides genuine comfort.

These aren't avoidance; you are not using them to completely block out distress, but rather, you are providing yourself with comfort whilst dealing with difficult emotions, the same way you might comfort a distressed child whilst they process something difficult.

Distraction techniques can provide temporary relief when distress is overwhelming.

These are different from avoidance; you are not using distraction to permanently avoid processing the trauma, but rather to provide temporary respite when distress reaches unmanageable levels.

- Effective distractions include engaging in absorbing activities like puzzles, games, or crafts
- watching films or shows
- reading
- exercising
- calling a friend
- doing household tasks
- or any activity that genuinely captures your attention.

The key is that you are consciously choosing to take a break from distress rather than automatically avoiding, and you plan to return to processing when you are more regulated.

Physical activity helps regulate your nervous system and manage stress.

When you are anxious or experiencing hyperarousal, your body is mobilised for action; it is prepared to run or fight.

Physical exercise allows you to complete this mobilisation response, after which your nervous system can more easily return to baseline.

This does not require intense exercise; even a 20-minute walk can significantly reduce anxiety and improve mood.

Yoga is particularly effective because it combines physical activity with breathing control and mindfulness.

Swimming, running, cycling, dancing, or any activity you enjoy can help.

Regular physical activity also improves sleep, reduces depression, and builds confidence.

Social connection provides crucial support during recovery. (Cloitre et al., 2020)

Whilst PTSD often drives isolation, connection with supportive others is one of the most powerful factors in recovery. (Watts et al., 2013)

This does not mean you need to discuss your trauma with everyone; it means maintaining relationships that provide care, acceptance, and practical support.

Even brief social contact, a phone call with a friend, coffee with a colleague, a chat with a neighbour, can reduce isolation and remind you that you are not alone.

If you do not currently have supportive relationships, consider joining a support group (many exist specifically for PTSD or for specific trauma types), engaging with community organisations, or using online communities thoughtfully.

- Developing and practicing these coping strategies before beginning intensive trauma work means you'll be prepared when distress increases. You'll have tools readily available rather than scrambling to manage overwhelming emotions without resources. Think of this as preparation: an athlete trains before competition
- a surgeon prepares instruments before surgery
- you develop coping skills before trauma processing.

Understanding the Time and Effort Required

Recovery from PTSD requires significant time and effort. This isn't a quick fix or a simple solution. Whilst brief interventions can help some people, most people with PTSD require sustained work over weeks or months to achieve meaningful recovery. Understanding this from the outset helps you commit appropriately and maintain motivation when progress feels slow. (van Dis et al., 2020)

If you are working through this guide independently, plan to dedicate regular time to the work, perhaps an hour several times per week, though more is often helpful.

Consistency matters more than duration: regular, sustained engagement produces better results than sporadic, intense work.

The total time to recovery varies enormously between individuals, depending on trauma complexity, chronicity of PTSD, life circumstances, and individual factors. (Ehring et al., 2014)

Some people notice a significant improvement within 8-12 weeks of consistent work.

Others require 6 months or longer.

Chronic, complex PTSD typically requires more time than recently developed PTSD from a single incident. (Coventry et al., 2020; Teicher & Samson, 2016)

If you are working with a therapist, trauma-focused CBT typically involves 8-16 weekly sessions, though some people need more. Each session is typically 60-90 minutes, and therapists usually assign between-session work, exercises, exposures, or reflections to complete independently. This between-session work is crucial; therapy sessions alone aren't sufficient. The real change happens through the accumulated work between sessions. (Bisson et al., 2013; NICE, 2018)

It is important to be realistic about the effort required whilst also maintaining hope.

Yes, this is demanding work.

Yes, it requires time and energy.

Yes, it will be emotionally challenging.

But it is also achievable, and thousands of people have successfully recovered using these approaches.

The effort you invest now can transform your life.

Consider the alternative: continuing to live with untreated PTSD, with all the suffering, impairment, and lost opportunities that entail.

The time and effort of treatment are significant but temporary; the benefits of recovery extend across your entire future. (Mavranezouli et al., 2020)

Chapter Fourteen: Complex PTSD, Understanding and Recovery from Developmental Trauma (Teicher & Samson, 2016)

- Complex PTSD develops from prolonged or repeated trauma (Maercker et al., 2022; Teicher & Samson, 2016)
- C-PTSD involves additional difficulties with self-perception
- Treatment approaches are modified for complex presentations
- Recovery from C-PTSD is possible and deeply transformative (Hyland et al., 2021)

Whilst earlier chapters addressed PTSD generally with some mention of complex presentations, this chapter provides a comprehensive exploration of Complex PTSD (C-PTSD), a distinct presentation resulting from prolonged, repeated trauma, particularly when occurring in childhood or contexts where escape is impossible. If you experienced chronic childhood abuse, ongoing domestic violence, captivity, or other sustained traumatic circumstances, understanding Complex PTSD helps you recognise your specific experiences and access appropriate treatment approaches.

Complex PTSD includes all core PTSD symptoms, intrusive memories, avoidance, negative cognitions and mood, and hyperarousal, plus additional disturbances in three domains: (Van der Kolk et al., 1996)

- Complex PTSD includes all core PTSD symptoms, intrusive memories, avoidance, negative cognitions and mood, and hyperarousal, plus additional disturbances in three domains: severe difficulties regulating emotions (Van der Kolk et al., 1996)
- persistent negative self-concept characterised by profound shame, guilt, and a sense of being fundamentally damaged (Teicher & Samson, 2016)

- and disturbed relationships marked by difficulty trusting, maintaining appropriate closeness, or setting boundaries. These additional features reflect how chronic trauma, particularly in childhood, disrupts the normal development of emotional regulation, identity formation, and relational capacities.

This chapter explores the origins of Complex PTSD, its distinctive features, how it differs from standard PTSD, and comprehensive treatment approaches addressing both trauma processing and building fundamental capacities that trauma disrupted. Recovery from Complex PTSD is possible but typically requires longer, more intensive treatment than standard PTSD. Understanding what you are dealing with is the first step towards an effective intervention. (Karatzias et al., 2017; Teicher & Samson, 2016)

Origins and Development of Complex PTSD (Courtois & Ford, 2013; Teicher & Samson, 2016)

Complex PTSD typically develops from a traumatic experience characterised by three key features: chronicity (trauma lasting months or years rather than discrete events), interpersonal nature (trauma inflicted by people, particularly those in caregiving or power positions), and inescapability (the victim cannot escape the traumatic situation physically or psychologically). These features distinguish Complex PTSD from standard PTSD following acute trauma.

Childhood abuse, physical, sexual, emotional, or neglect, represents the prototypical origin of Complex PTSD. (Brewin et al., 2017; Teicher & Samson, 2016)

When abuse occurs during formative developmental periods, it disrupts the acquisition of fundamental capacities normally developing through secure attachment and safe exploration.

The child learns the world is dangerous, relationships are unpredictable or harmful, their own needs do not matter, and expressing emotions leads to punishment or rejection.

These lessons become deeply ingrained beliefs, shaping all subsequent development.

The developmental timing matters profoundly.

Trauma occurring in the first few years of life, when attachment patterns form, when a sense of safety versus danger develops, and when basic trust in others emerges, has particularly pervasive effects.

The child's brain is literally forming during this period, and chronic threat fundamentally shapes neural development.

The stress response system becomes chronically activated.

The capacity to regulate emotions never fully develops.

Attachment patterns form around fear rather than security.

However, Complex PTSD isn't limited to childhood trauma. Adults can develop it from sustained domestic violence where they cannot escape, captivity situations like human trafficking or being held prisoner, ongoing persecution or torture, or repeated trauma in contexts like war zones or refugee camps. The common elements remain prolonged exposure to trauma, inability to escape, and often betrayal or harm from those who should provide safety. (Foa et al., 2007; Powers et al., 2010)

The interpersonal nature of Complex PTSD trauma is particularly damaging. (Ford et al., 2019; Teicher & Samson, 2016)

When other people inflict trauma, especially people who should protect you like parents or partners, it disrupts the ability to trust, shatters assumptions about human nature, and creates a pervasive sense of danger in relationships.

Unlike trauma from natural disasters or accidents, interpersonal trauma carries the additional burden of human cruelty, betrayal, and intentional harm.

The world is not just dangerous; people actively hurt you.

This realisation profoundly affects subsequent relationships and worldview.

The Three Domains of Disturbance in Complex PTSD (Cloitre et al., 2020; Teicher & Samson, 2016)

Beyond core PTSD symptoms, Complex PTSD involves disturbances in three interconnected domains that reflect disrupted development of fundamental psychological capacities. Understanding these domains helps you recognise your experiences and guides treatment focus. (Watts et al., 2013; Teicher & Samson, 2016)

Domain One: Emotion Dysregulation

Emotion dysregulation in Complex PTSD goes beyond the emotional numbing or irritability of standard PTSD. (van Dis et al., 2020; Teicher & Samson, 2016)

It involves pervasive difficulty identifying, tolerating, and modulating emotions across all affective states.

You might experience emotions as overwhelming, uncontrollable floods that threaten to destroy you.

Or you might feel emotionally numb most of the time with occasional breakthroughs of overwhelming affect.

The middle ground, experiencing emotions at manageable intensity that provide information without overwhelming you, feels inaccessible.

This dysregulation manifests in several ways.

- Emotional intensity that's disproportionate to triggers: minor frustrations produce rage

- small disappointments trigger devastating despair
- routine stress feels unbearable.

Rapid mood shifts where emotions change dramatically and unpredictably, making you feel out of control.

Difficulty identifying what you are feeling, you know you are distressed, but cannot name the specific emotion or its cause.

Prolonged emotional states, where once triggered, emotions last hours or days rather than minutes to hours, are typical of regulated emotional responses.

The origins of emotion dysregulation lie in disrupted early development.

Infants and young children learn to regulate emotions through co-regulation with caregivers. (Cohen et al., 2016; Cohen & Mannarino, 2008)

When distressed, the caregiver soothes them, helping them return to a calm state.

Through thousands of these interactions, children internalise the regulatory process and develop the capacity to soothe themselves. (Cohen et al., 2016; Cohen & Mannarino, 2008)

In abusive or neglectful environments, this co-regulation does not occur adequately or predictably.

The child's distress is ignored, punished, or met with the caregiver's overwhelming emotion.

They never learn regulations because no one teaches them.

Their you struggle to manage your emotions isn't a deficit they developed; it is a capacity they never acquired.

- Common coping strategies for overwhelming emotions include: substance use to numb feelings
- self-harm to release tension or create controllable pain, replacing uncontrollable emotional pain
- eating disorder behaviours to manage emotions through control of food and body
- dissociation to escape unbearable affect
- or compulsive behaviours like excessive exercise, work, or sex that distract from emotional experience. Whilst these strategies provide temporary relief, they maintain dysregulation long-term by preventing the development of genuine regulation skills and often creating additional problems.

Domain Two: Negative Self-Concept (Teicher & Samson, 2016)

Whilst people with standard PTSD might develop negative thoughts about themselves following trauma, Complex PTSD involves more pervasive, core-level disturbance in self-concept. This isn't just I made a mistake, or I should have done something differently. It is a fundamental belief: I am defective, damaged, worthless, unlovable, bad, disgusting. These beliefs feel like the truth about who you are rather than thoughts you can examine or challenge. They infuse your entire sense of identity. (Ehring et al., 2014; Teicher & Samson, 2016)

Shame is the predominant emotion characterising this negative self-concept. (Teicher & Samson, 2016)

Not guilt, feeling bad about specific actions, but shame, feeling fundamentally bad as a person.

- You might feel ashamed of: the trauma itself (the abuse happened because something is wrong with me)
- your reactions to trauma (I should have fought harder, left sooner, said no, protected others)
- your current symptoms (I am weak for struggling)
- your needs (I am burden, I shouldn't need help)
- or simply your existence (the world would be better without me).

This pervasive shame makes it difficult to seek help, accept care, or believe recovery is possible for someone as damaged as you perceive yourself to be. (Coventry et al., 2020)

The origins of negative self-concept in Complex PTSD relate to developmental timing and relational context. (Teicher & Samson, 2016)

Children naturally assume they are the centre of causation; if bad things happen, they must have caused them. (Cohen et al., 2016; Cohen & Mannarino, 2008)

If parents abuse them, they conclude they are bad rather than recognising that parents are abusive.

This developmental egocentrism means childhood trauma almost inevitably produces a distorted self-concept.

Additionally, abusers often explicitly tell children they are worthless, stupid, bad, or that the abuse is their fault. (Cohen et al., 2016; Cohen & Mannarino, 2008)

These messages, particularly from authority figures during formative years, become internalised as core beliefs.

Negative self-concept maintains itself through several mechanisms. (Teicher & Samson, 2016)

Confirmation bias leads you to notice evidence confirming you are bad, whilst dismissing evidence to the contrary.

Self-fulfilling prophecies cause you to act in ways consistent with negative beliefs, creating experiences that confirm them.

Relationship difficulties stemming from trauma get interpreted as further proof of your unworthiness rather than as symptoms.

The negative self-concept becomes a self-perpetuating system resistant to change, even when current experiences contradict it. (Teicher & Samson, 2016)

Domain Three: Disturbed Relationships

The third domain of Complex PTSD involves pervasive difficulties in relationships that extend beyond trauma-specific trust issues. These relationship difficulties reflect disrupted attachment development and include: (Mavranezouli et al., 2020; Teicher & Samson, 2016)

- The third domain of Complex PTSD involves pervasive difficulties in relationships that extend beyond trauma-specific trust issues. These relationship difficulties reflect disrupted attachment development and include: difficulty assessing trustworthiness leading to either blanket mistrust of everyone or naive trust of dangerous people (Karatzias et al., 2019; Teicher & Samson, 2016)
- problems maintaining appropriate emotional distance, either remaining rigidly distant or becoming enmeshed inappropriately quickly
- difficulty setting and maintaining boundaries, tolerating mistreatment or becoming rigid and controlling
- patterns of repeatedly entering harmful relationships that replicate trauma dynamics
- and profound fear of abandonment alongside fear of engulfment creating approach-avoidance patterns.

These relationship patterns aren't conscious choices or character flaws; they are learned adaptations to growing up in an environment where relationships were dangerous, unpredictable, or harmful.

If primary caregivers were abusive, you learned: I need relationships to survive (children depend on caregivers), but relationships hurt me.

This fundamental contradiction creates patterns where you simultaneously crave and fear closeness, pursue connection whilst pushing people away, or remain isolated despite longing for belonging.

Attachment theory provides a framework for understanding these relationship difficulties.

- Secure attachment, developed through consistent, responsive caregiving, creates an internal working model: I am worthy of love and care
- others are trustworthy and available
- relationships are safe and satisfying.

This security supports healthy adult relationships.

Insecure attachment patterns develop from inconsistent, neglectful, or abusive caregiving, creating different internal working models that shape adult relationship patterns.

Anxious attachment develops from inconsistent caregiving, sometimes responsive, sometimes rejecting.

You learn relationships are unpredictable and you must work hard to maintain them, leading to clinginess, fear of abandonment, and constant need for reassurance in adult relationships.

Avoidant attachment develops from consistently rejecting or neglectful caregiving.

You learn that depending on others is dangerous, leading to emotional distance, discomfort with intimacy, and compulsive self-reliance in adult relationships.

Disorganised attachment develops from frightening or chaotic caregiving.

You learn relationships are simultaneously desperately needed and terrifying, leading to contradictory patterns, pursuing closeness, then panicking and withdrawing, or remaining in clearly harmful relationships.

These attachment patterns aren't fixed forever, but they are deeply ingrained and require deliberate work to change.

Adult attachment can shift towards security through accumulated experiences of safe, consistent relationships that contradict early learning.

Therapy relationships often provide first experiences of truly safe connection, and romantic relationships or close friendships with secure people can gradually shift internal working models.

However, change is gradual and requires repeated experiences that challenge old patterns.

How Complex PTSD Differs from Standard PTSD (Lewis et al., 2020; Teicher & Samson, 2016)

Understanding how Complex PTSD differs from standard PTSD helps clarify why treatment approaches need modification and why recovery might take longer. These aren't completely separate conditions. Complex PTSD includes all standard PTSD symptoms plus additional features. Think of it as standard PTSD plus disturbances in self-organisation (emotion regulation, self-concept, relationships).

Trauma characteristics differ: Standard PTSD typically follows a discrete traumatic event or series of events, car accident, assault, natural disaster, or combat incident. Complex PTSD follows prolonged, repeated trauma, particularly interpersonal trauma in childhood or captivity. This difference in trauma type produces different symptom presentations. (Herman, 2015; Teicher & Samson, 2016)

Developmental impact differs: Standard PTSD occurring in adulthood affects a developed personality. Recovery involves returning to pre-trauma functioning. Complex PTSD, particularly from childhood trauma, affects personality development itself. There's no pre-trauma functioning to return to; fundamental capacities like emotion regulation, identity formation, and relational skills were never fully developed. Recovery involves building these capacities for the first time, not recovering them. (Bisson et al., 2019; Teicher & Samson, 2016)

Symptom complexity differs: Standard PTSD symptoms cluster around the trauma, intrusions about the event, avoidance of reminders, and hyperarousal in response to cues. Complex PTSD symptoms are more pervasive and less clearly trauma-linked. Emotion dysregulation, negative self-concept, and relationship difficulties affect all life areas, not just trauma-related situations. This makes Complex PTSD more impairing across broader domains of functioning. (Teicher & Samson, 2016)

Treatment approach differs: Standard PTSD often responds well to focused trauma processing,12-20 sessions of CPT, PE, or EMDR addressing the traumatic event. Complex PTSD typically requires phase-based treatment: (Shapiro, 2018)

- Treatment approach differs: Standard PTSD often responds well to focused trauma processing,12-20 sessions of CPT, PE, or EMDR addressing the traumatic event. Complex PTSD typically requires phase-based treatment: stabilisation phase building emotion regulation and safety (Shapiro, 2018)
- trauma processing phase addressing multiple traumatic memories
- and integration phase consolidating skills and rebuilding identity and relationships. Total treatment often spans months to years rather than weeks to months.

Recovery trajectory differs: Standard PTSD recovery often shows relatively rapid improvement once an effective treatment begins, and symptoms decrease substantially within 3-6 months of treatment start. (Cusack et al., 2016)

Complex PTSD recovery is more gradual, with progress in different domains at different rates. (Watkins et al., 2018; Teicher & Samson, 2016)

Emotion regulation might improve slowly over the years.

Self-concept shifts gradually through accumulated positive experiences.

Relationship patterns change incrementally as you practise new ways of relating.

This slower, more gradual recovery does not indicate treatment failure; it reflects the greater complexity of what's being addressed. (Ozer et al., 2003)

Dissociation in Complex PTSD: A Deeper Exploration (Guay et al., 2006; Teicher & Samson, 2016)

Dissociation deserves deeper exploration in the Complex PTSD context as it is more prominent, severe, and functionally impairing than in standard PTSD. (Charuvastra & Cloitre, 2008; Teicher & Samson, 2016)

Dissociation exists on a continuum from normal experiences everyone has (highway hypnosis, daydreaming) through moderate dissociation (spacing out, feeling unreal) to severe dissociation (losing time, feeling like different people, complete amnesia for periods).

Complex PTSD, particularly from severe childhood trauma, often involves more severe dissociation. (Neff & Germer, 2018; Teicher & Samson, 2016)

Structural dissociation theory provides a framework for understanding severe dissociation.

According to this model, overwhelming trauma that cannot be integrated into normal memory and identity causes personality to fragment into parts.

One part, the apparently normal part (ANP), handles daily life, goes to work, and maintains functioning.

Other parts, emotional parts (EPs), hold traumatic memories and emotions.

These parts might have different ages, beliefs about the current time, or awareness of each other.

In severe cases (dissociative identity disorder), parts become quite distinct with different names, ages, and characteristics.

Even without reaching DID severity, many people with Complex PTSD experience themselves as fragmented: I have a part that wants to recover and a part that's terrified of change. Part of me knows I am safe now, but another part still feels in danger. I feel like different people in different situations. This isn't metaphorical; neuroimaging shows different patterns of brain activation corresponding to different self-states in dissociative conditions. The fragmentation is real, not imagined. (Gilbert, 2014; Teicher & Samson, 2016)

Dissociation served a crucial protective function during overwhelming trauma.

When you could not physically escape, psychological escape through dissociation allowed survival.

Separating from the experience, it is not happening to me, I am watching from the ceiling, it is happening to someone else, which made the unbearable circumstances more bearable.

This was an adaptive response during trauma.

However, dissociation persisting after trauma becomes problematic.

It prevents trauma processing, interferes with present engagement, creates amnesia, complicating the understanding of yourself, and maintains the fragmentation of identity.

Common dissociative experiences in Complex PTSD include: (ISTSS, 2019; Teicher & Samson, 2016)

- Common dissociative experiences in Complex PTSD include: depersonalization, feeling detached from yourself, watching yourself from outside, feeling robotic or unreal (Cloitre et al., 2012; Teicher & Samson, 2016)
- derealization, surroundings feeling unreal, dreamlike, distant, or distorted
- amnesia, gaps in memory for traumatic periods or even current time
- identity confusion, uncertainty about who you are, contradictory beliefs about yourself, feeling like different people
- and identity alteration, experiencing distinct shifts into different self-states with different emotions, beliefs, or behaviours.

Working with Dissociation in Treatment

Treatment for dissociation involves several components. First, learning to recognise when you are dissociating. Many people dissociate automatically without awareness. Developing the ability to notice, I am starting to feel spacey; I am losing time, and I am feeling detached, which allows intervention before dissociation becomes severe. Keep dissociation log: when it occurs, severity, triggers, duration, what helps. These patterns reveal your dissociation triggers and an effective intervention.

Second, grounding techniques bring you back from dissociative states into present awareness. Physical grounding (cold water, ice, strong sensations), mental grounding (describing surroundings, counting, cognitive tasks), and emotional grounding (connecting with present feelings) all help. practise grounding when relatively present so skills are available when severely dissociated. Different techniques work for different people; experiment to find what's most effective for you.

Third, addressing structural dissociation requires specialised approaches.

If you experience significant fragmentation or distinct parts, work with a trauma therapist trained in treating dissociative disorders.

- Phase-oriented treatment helps stabilisation, building communication and cooperation between parts
- trauma processing, addressing memories held by different parts
- and integration, working towards a unified sense of self.

Integration does not mean parts disappear; it means they communicate, share awareness and memory, and work together rather than operating independently.

Fourth, reducing dissociation requires addressing what triggers it.

If certain therapy activities trigger severe dissociation, work with a therapist to modify the approach, proceeding more slowly, adding more grounding, and ensuring you feel safe enough to remain present.

If particular situations trigger dissociation, gradually approach them whilst practising staying present.

The goal isn't eliminating all dissociation instantly; mild dissociation is a normal stress response.

The goal is to reduce the frequency, severity, and duration of problematic dissociation whilst building capacity to remain present during difficult experiences.

Phase-Based Treatment for Complex PTSD (Herman, 2015; Teicher & Samson, 2016)

Complex PTSD treatment follows a phase-based approach, different from the focused trauma processing used for standard PTSD. (Herman, 2015; Teicher & Samson, 2016)

Attempting intensive trauma processing before adequate stabilisation often backfires, triggering overwhelming affect, severe dissociation, or a crisis that disrupts treatment.

Phase-based treatment ensures you have the necessary resources before addressing trauma directly.

- The three phases are: stabilisation and skill-building
- trauma processing
- and integration and reconnection.

Phase One: Stabilisation and Skill-Building

- Phase one establishes the foundation for trauma work. Goals include ensuring safety (addressing immediate threats like ongoing abuse, self-harm, or substance dependence)
- building emotion regulation skills (Linehan, 2015)
- reducing dissociation
- developing crisis management plans
- and creating life stability sufficient to support trauma work. This phase takes weeks to months, depending on symptom severity and life circumstances.

Safety is paramount.

If you are currently in an abusive relationship, treatment cannot effectively proceed while trauma continues.

Resources must focus on safety planning and potentially leaving the situation. (Stanley & Brown, 2012)

If you are engaging in severe self-harm or substance use, these require intervention before trauma processing; otherwise, trauma work might trigger escalation.

If you are experiencing severe suicidal ideation, stabilisation focuses on developing reasons for living and crisis intervention skills. (Stanley & Brown, 2012)

- Emotion regulation skills taught during this phase include identifying and naming emotions accurately (Linehan, 2015)
- understanding emotional triggers
- tolerating distressing emotions without immediately escaping through substances, self-harm, or dissociation
- self-soothing strategies that actually work
- and modulating emotional intensity. Skills might come from Dialectical Behaviour Therapy (DBT), which was developed specifically for severe emotion dysregulation, or other evidence-based approaches. (Linehan, 2015)
- Grounding and orientation work addresses dissociation. You learn what dissociation feels like for you specifically
- your personal triggers
- effective grounding techniques
- how to maintain dual awareness during trauma processing (knowing you are remembering trauma whilst staying aware of present safety)
- and communication with any dissociative parts if present. Without adequate dissociation management, trauma processing triggers flight into dissociation rather than processing.

Therapeutic relationship building is crucial.

Complex PTSD often involves profound difficulty trusting, particularly in relationships involving a power differential, like therapy. (Brand et al., 2019; Teicher & Samson, 2016)

- Early treatment focuses on establishing safety in the therapeutic relationship: predictable boundaries
- consistent availability
- transparent communication
- and demonstration that the therapist is trustworthy over time.

This relationship often becomes the first experience of safe connection, providing a corrective emotional experience that begins shifting internal working models of relationships.

Life stabilisation addresses practical domains affecting treatment engagement. Unstable housing, unemployment, or chaotic relationships drain energy and create ongoing stress, interfering with recovery. Whilst therapy cannot solve all life problems, addressing the most pressing practical issues creates space for psychological work. This might involve connecting with social services, addressing legal issues from trauma, or working on employment stability. (Ross et al., 2017)

Phase Two: Trauma Processing

Once stabilisation is adequate, you have emotion regulation skills, can manage dissociation, have established therapeutic trust, and have sufficient life stability, trauma processing begins. This phase addresses traumatic memories and their meanings. For Complex PTSD with multiple traumas across years, this isn't a single memory processing session. It is systematic work through trauma history, often taking months. (Linehan, 2015)

Trauma processing in Complex PTSD can use adapted versions of standard PTSD treatments. (Fenster et al., 2018; Teicher & Samson, 2016)

Prolonged Exposure can be modified: (Foa et al., 2007; Powers et al., 2010)

- Prolonged Exposure can be modified: proceeding more slowly (Foa et al., 2007; Powers et al., 2010)
- adding more emphasis on grounding and emotion regulation
- carefully titrating exposure intensity
- and ensuring adequate stabilisation before and after exposure sessions.

Cognitive Processing Therapy can address multiple trauma accounts and challenging beliefs developed across trauma history rather than a single event. (Resick & Schnicke, 2016)

EMDR can process trauma memories sequentially whilst managing dissociation and emotional overwhelm. (Shapiro, 2018)

Additional approaches useful for Complex PTSD include: (Lanius et al., 2018; Teicher & Samson, 2016)

- Additional approaches useful for Complex PTSD include: Schema Therapy, which addresses early maladaptive schemas (core beliefs) developed from childhood trauma and works to meet unmet childhood needs through therapeutic relationship and imagery
- Compassion-Focused Therapy, which explicitly addresses shame through cultivating self-compassion
- and Internal Family Systems or ego state therapy for working with dissociative parts when present.

The processing work addresses not just what happened but what it meant. Challenging stuck points like: It was my fault, I am damaged forever, I deserved it, No one can be trusted, or the world is entirely dangerous. These beliefs developed from repeatedly having a traumatic experience over the years feel true. Shifting them requires extensive work examining evidence, considering alternative explanations, and accumulating experiences that contradict them.

Pacing is crucial during this phase. Too fast risks overwhelming your capacity to process, triggering a crisis or dissociation. Too slow might feel frustrating when you want to hurry through painful material. Collaborate with your therapist to find a pace that feels manageable, challenging, but not overwhelming. Some sessions might involve intensive trauma work; others might consolidate gains or practise skills. This variable pacing prevents burnout whilst maintaining momentum.

Monitor functioning during trauma processing. Some temporary worsening is expected as you confront avoided material. However, if you experience sustained deterioration, increased self-harm, substance use, suicidal thinking, or inability to function in daily life, return to stabilisation. The trauma work is not failing; you need more foundation before proceeding. Build more skills, strengthen coping, ensure more support, then return to processing when ready.

Phase Three: Integration and Reconnection

- The final phase focuses on consolidating treatment gains and building a life beyond trauma identity. Having processed traumatic memories and developed skills, you now integrate a new understanding of yourself and trauma into a coherent narrative
- rebuilding or building for the first time healthy relationships
- pursuing meaningful activities and goals
- and transitioning from treatment whilst maintaining gains.

Integration involves constructing a coherent narrative about your life that includes trauma but is not defined entirely by it. You can tell your story, what happened, how it affected you, how you survived, what you learned, where you are now, with compassion and without being overwhelmed. The trauma becomes part of your history rather than an ongoing present experience. This integration often brings a sense of closure, even though trauma cannot be undone or forgotten.

Relationship work in this phase involves practising new relational patterns learned in therapy.

If you developed a more secure attachment through a therapeutic relationship, you now apply that learning to other relationships.

- This means assessing trustworthiness gradually rather than assuming everyone is dangerous or trustworthy
- maintaining appropriate boundaries
- communicating needs effectively
- tolerating normal relationship conflict without catastrophizing
- and allowing appropriate closeness without panic.

Meaning-making and post-traumatic growth occur during this phase. Whilst trauma is never good and shouldn't have happened, many people find meaning despite trauma: (Tedeschi & Calhoun, 2004)

- Meaning-making and post-traumatic growth occur during this phase. Whilst trauma is never good and shouldn't have happened, many people find meaning despite trauma: increased compassion for others who suffer (Tedeschi & Calhoun, 2004)
- recognition of personal strength and resilience (Bonanno, 2004)
- clarified values and priorities
- deeper appreciation for life
- or commitment to helping others through similar experiences. This meaning-making isn't about justifying trauma
- it is about finding purpose despite it.

Building identity beyond trauma survivor represents crucial work in this phase. For years or decades, your identity might have centred on trauma and survival. Recovery creates space to discover or rediscover: Who am I beyond trauma? What do I value? What brings me joy? What are my strengths? What do I want from life? Exploring these questions through activities, relationships, and reflection helps construct a fuller identity, incorporating but not limited to trauma history. (Monson & Shnaider, 2014)

Treatment termination requires careful planning.

After months or years of intensive therapy, the end feels significant.

- Work on consolidating gains and identifying ongoing practices maintaining improvement
- establishing a plan for managing setbacks without a therapist
- gradually spacing sessions rather than abrupt ending
- and processing feelings about termination, including grief about ending an important relationship.

Many people maintain occasional check-in sessions after primary treatment ends, particularly given the deep therapeutic relationship developed in Complex PTSD treatment. (Foa et al., 2019; Teicher & Samson, 2016)

Specific Therapeutic Interventions for Complex PTSD (APA, 2017; Teicher & Samson, 2016)

Beyond the phase-based framework, several specific therapeutic approaches show particular promise for Complex PTSD. Understanding these options helps you and your treatment team select interventions best suited to your needs. (Herman, 2015; Teicher & Samson, 2016)

Dialectical Behaviour Therapy (DBT) Skills (Linehan, 2015)

DBT, originally developed for borderline personality disorder, which shares many features with Complex PTSD, provides comprehensive skills for emotion regulation, distress tolerance, interpersonal effectiveness, and mindfulness. These skills directly address core Complex PTSD difficulties. Many Complex PTSD treatment programmes incorporate DBT skills training as a foundation for the stabilisation phase. (Linehan, 2015)

- Emotion regulation skills include identifying and labelling emotions accurately (Linehan, 2015)
- understanding the function of emotions
- increasing positive emotional experiences
- decreasing vulnerability to negative emotions through self-care (sleep, nutrition, exercise, treating illness)
- and checking the facts about whether emotional intensity matches the actual situation. These skills build the capacity to modulate the affect that trauma disrupted.
- Distress tolerance skills address managing crises without making them worse through impulsive action. Skills include distraction techniques (Linehan, 2015)
- self-soothing using the five senses
- improving the moment through imagery, prayer, relaxation, or vacation
- and pros-and-cons analysis of destructive urges. Whilst these skills do not solve problems, they help you survive a crisis without engaging in behaviours that create additional problems.

Interpersonal effectiveness skills teach assertiveness, boundary-setting, and relationship maintenance. For people whose relationships were consistently harmful, learning skills like asking for what you need effectively, saying no whilst maintaining relationships, maintaining self-respect in interactions, and balancing priorities in relationships provides a practical tool for healthier relating.

Mindfulness skills, observing, describing, and participating in the present moment non-judgmentally, counter dissociation and emotional avoidance characteristic of Complex PTSD. Regular mindfulness practice increases awareness of thoughts, emotions, and sensations as they occur, reducing automatic reactivity and creating space for skilful response. (NICE, 2018; Teicher & Samson, 2016)

'A Comprehensive DBT Skills Manual' is available, written by Jayden James, 2025, which can support you with understanding and learning the skills. You can purchase a copy of the manual from Talking Therapies UK (www.TalkingTherapies.co.uk) or Amazon.

Schema Therapy

Schema Therapy, developed by Jeffrey Young, specifically addresses early maladaptive schemas, broad, pervasive beliefs about self, others, and world, which develop from unmet childhood needs.

These schemas directly correspond to Complex PTSD's negative self-concept and disturbed relationships. (Teicher & Samson, 2016)

- Common schemas include abandonment/instability (people will leave me)
- mistrust/abuse (people will hurt me)
- defectiveness/shame (I am fundamentally flawed)
- failure (I cannot succeed)
- emotional deprivation (my needs will not be met)

- and social isolation (I do not belong anywhere).

Schema Therapy uses a combination of cognitive, experiential, and interpersonal techniques.

Cognitive techniques identify schemas and evidence contradicting them.

Experiential techniques like imagery rescripting involve revisiting traumatic memories in imagination but changing outcomes.

The protective adult self intervenes to protect the child self, or needs that were not met get met symbolically.

These imagery exercises create emotional corrective experiences that purely cognitive work does not provide.

Limited reparenting through therapeutic relationship involves the therapist deliberately providing (within appropriate boundaries) some of what wasn't available in childhood: consistent care, validation of needs, appropriate boundaries, and encouragement. This isn't literal parenting, but therapeutic relationship structured to meet legitimate childhood needs that went unmet, providing corrective experience that challenges schemas developed from deprivation.

- Schema mode work identifies different states or modes you shift between: Vulnerable Child mode (feeling small, frightened, overwhelmed)
- Angry Child mode (feeling rageful about unmet needs)
- Punitive Parent mode (harsh self-criticism replicating abusive caregiver messages)
- Detached Protector mode (emotional avoidance and dissociation)
- and Healthy Adult mode (integrated, compassionate, effective functioning). Therapy helps strengthen the Healthy Adult whilst compassionately addressing other modes and reducing the destructive Punitive Parent mode.

Compassion-Focused Therapy (CFT)

CFT, developed by Paul Gilbert, directly addresses shame, the predominant emotion in Complex PTSD. CFT recognises that people with trauma histories often have an overactive threat system and an underactive soothing system. Chronic threat during development means your brain became excellent at detecting danger but poor at feeling safe or soothed. CFT works to strengthen the soothing system through cultivating compassion for self and others. (Forbes et al., 2020; Teicher & Samson, 2016)

- CFT distinguishes three emotion regulation systems: threat system (detects danger, produces anxiety, anger)
- drive system (pursues goals, produces excitement, pleasure)
- and soothing system (provides safety, produces contentment, connection). Complex PTSD involves an overactive threat system responding to minimal cues, whilst an

underactive soothing system cannot calm the threat response. This imbalance maintains chronic distress even in objectively safe situations.

- Compassion training involves: understanding that your struggles aren't your fault, your brain developed under traumatic circumstances and adapted for survival
- recognising common humanity, all humans struggle, you are not uniquely defective
- and developing a compassionate mind stance, what would a wise, compassionate voice say to you? Practices like compassionate letter writing, compassionate imagery, and compassionate self-talk strengthen internal soothing capacity.

CFT directly challenges shame through compassionate reframing. Rather than being disgusted for struggling, CFT promotes that I developed these difficulties because of circumstances beyond my control as a child. I am doing my best to heal. I deserve compassion, not contempt. This reframing, practised consistently, gradually shifts internal dialogue from harsh criticism to supportive encouragement, which facilitates rather than impedes recovery. (Schnyder et al., 2015)

Medication Considerations for Complex PTSD (Resick et al., 2017; Teicher & Samson, 2016)

Medication plays a different role in Complex PTSD than standard PTSD. Whilst SSRIs can reduce core PTSD symptoms, they do not directly address emotion dysregulation, dissociation, or relationship difficulties characteristic of Complex PTSD. Medication is best viewed as an adjunct supporting psychological treatment rather than a primary intervention. However, appropriate medication can significantly improve quality of life and treatment engagement when used thoughtfully. (NICE, 2018; Baldwin et al., 2014)

SSRIs (sertraline, paroxetine, fluoxetine) remain the first-line medication for Complex PTSD, as for standard PTSD. They can reduce intrusive symptoms, decrease anxiety and hyperarousal, and help with comorbid depression, common in Complex PTSD. However, the emotional numbing side effect sometimes worsens existing you struggle to manage your emotions by further reducing emotional awareness. Work with the prescriber to monitor whether SSRIs help or hinder your specific symptom pattern. (NICE, 2018; Baldwin et al., 2014)

For severe emotion dysregulation, mood stabilisers like lamotrigine or low-dose antipsychotics like quetiapine sometimes help when SSRIs alone are insufficient. These medications can reduce emotional lability and intensity, making it easier to practise regulation skills. However, they carry more side effects than SSRIs and should be used cautiously with careful monitoring. (NICE, 2018; Baldwin et al., 2014)

Dissociation sometimes responds to medications addressing underlying anxiety or depression, but no medication directly treats dissociation.

Grounding skills and therapy remain primary interventions.

Avoid benzodiazepines for Complex PTSD, whilst they reduce anxiety short-term, they impair memory and emotional processing needed for trauma work, carry dependence risk, and can worsen dissociation. (Foa & Kozak, 1986)

If prescribed benzodiazepines previously, work towards a gradual taper whilst building alternative coping strategies. (Ashton, 2002; Lader, 2011; NICE, 2018)

Self-Care and Daily Life with Complex PTSD (Maercker et al., 2022; Teicher & Samson, 2016)

Managing Complex PTSD requires comprehensive self-care addressing multiple domains. Unlike standard PTSD, where self-care supports trauma-focused treatment, in Complex PTSD, self-care is an essential treatment component itself. The emotion dysregulation, negative self-concept, and relationship difficulties all require daily attention and ongoing practise of skills beyond therapy sessions. (Teicher & Samson, 2016)

Establishing Safety and Stability in Daily Life

- Creating external safety and stability provides a foundation for internal healing. This includes: ensuring physical safety (leaving abusive relationships if possible, securing stable housing, addressing financial crises that create ongoing stress)
- establishing predictable routines that reduce chaos and provide structure
- creating safe spaces in your environment where you can retreat when overwhelmed
- and building a support network you can access during a crisis.

Routines matter particularly for Complex PTSD. (Hyland et al., 2021; Teicher & Samson, 2016)

When childhood was chaotic and unpredictable, routines in adulthood create the predictability that supports nervous system regulation.

Simple practices like consistent sleep and wake times, regular mealtimes, scheduled self-care activities, and predictable weekly structure all help regulate arousal.

Your brain learns: life follows patterns, I can predict what happens next, I have some control.

This predictability directly counters the chaos of the traumatic past.

- Physical environment affects symptom management. Create spaces that feel safe: a comfortable bedroom supporting sleep
- a calm area for practising skills
- perhaps a creative space for expressive activities. Consider sensory elements: soft lighting rather than harsh fluorescents
- comfortable textures
- calming colours

- minimal clutter that might trigger overwhelm. Small environmental modifications accumulate to create an atmosphere supporting recovery rather than triggering symptoms. (Karatzias et al., 2017)

Managing Overwhelming Emotions in Daily Life

Between therapy sessions, you need strategies for managing intense emotions that arise unpredictably. Build an emotion regulation toolbox containing multiple strategies for different situations and emotional states. No single strategy works for everything; you need variety.

- For intense anxiety or panic: grounding techniques bringing you into the present
- progressive muscle relaxation releasing physical tension
- paced breathing slowing heart rate and activating parasympathetic nervous system (Porges, 2011)
- intense physical exercise burning off arousal
- and cold water or ice providing strong sensory input that interrupts panic cycle. practise these when relatively calm so they are accessible during actual panic.
- For overwhelming sadness or despair: opposite action (doing something contrary to depressed mood like going outside, calling friend, engaging in activity)
- self-compassion practices acknowledging pain whilst treating yourself kindly
- connecting with reasons for living
- using crisis helplines when thoughts turn suicidal
- and allowing crying when appropriate whilst also having strategies to contain it when necessary (you cannot cry indefinitely at work, you need ways to regulate even healthy emotions when timing is inappropriate).
- For rage or intense anger: physical release through intense exercise, hitting pillows, or other safe physical outlets
- opposite action like soothing activities when anger is unjustified
- timeout strategies removing yourself from triggering situations before acting impulsively
- expressing anger appropriately through assertive communication when justified
- and examining what need or hurt underlies the anger, anger often masks pain, fear, or unmet needs.
- For emotional numbness: engaging in activities that typically produce emotion even if you do not feel like it, watching emotional films, listening to music, reading poetry
- physical activities that reconnect you with your body
- creativity that accesses emotions indirectly
- connecting with others even when you feel emotionally dead
- and recognising that numbness itself is emotional state with function, it protected you from overwhelming pain. You can acknowledge its protective purpose whilst gently working to expand emotional range.

Build emotion tracking into your daily routine. Brief check-ins several times daily: What am I feeling right now? How intense is it, 0-10? What triggered it? This regular monitoring increases emotional awareness over time, helping you catch escalating emotions early when they are easier to regulate. Apps can help facilitate this tracking if you find digital tools helpful.

Addressing Negative Self-Concept in Daily Life (Teicher & Samson, 2016)
Challenging deeply ingrained negative self-concept requires daily practice, not just therapy work. Automatic thoughts like I am worthless, I am disgusting, nobody could love me arise hundreds of times daily. Without active intervention, they maintain suffering indefinitely. (Teicher & Samson, 2016)

- practise self-compassion deliberately. When you notice self-critical thought: pause
- acknowledge you are suffering (this is really painful for me)
- recognise common humanity (many people struggle with these feelings after trauma)
- and respond with kindness (what would I say to a friend thinking this about themselves?). Initially, this feels forced and false. With consistent practice over weeks and months, self-compassion becomes more natural and believable.

Keep an evidence log contradicting the negative self-concept. When you accomplish something, receive positive feedback, or manage a difficult situation, write it down. Your brain's negativity bias means you automatically notice information confirming I am worthless, whilst dismissing information contradicting it. Deliberate logging forces you to attend to contradictory evidence. Review this log regularly, especially when self-loathing intensifies. (Teicher & Samson, 2016)

Challenge absolutist language in self-talk. Notice words like always, never, completely, and totally. These words maintain a rigid negative self-concept. When you think I always fail, challenge it: Do I literally always fail at everything? What have I succeeded at? When you think I am completely worthless, ask: Is there literally nothing about me with value? What do others appreciate about me? This isn't positive thinking; it is accuracy training. (Teicher & Samson, 2016)

Engage in values-consistent behaviour regardless of feelings. You might feel worthless, but act consistently with the belief you have worth: caring for your body, pursuing goals, maintaining relationships, and setting boundaries. Behaviour change often precedes belief change. Acting as if you have worth gradually shifts actual self-concept through accumulated evidence from your actions.

Navigating Relationships with Complex PTSD (Courtois & Ford, 2013; Teicher & Samson, 2016)
Relationships present particular challenges with Complex PTSD. You might simultaneously crave connection and fear it, struggle to trust whilst desperately wanting to, or find yourself in repeatedly harmful relationships without understanding why. Conscious relationship work helps break these patterns. (Brewin et al., 2017; Teicher & Samson, 2016)

Practice assessing trustworthiness gradually rather than making all-or-nothing judgments. When meeting someone new, notice: Do they respect boundaries? Are they consistent? Do their words match their actions? How do they handle conflict? Do they take responsibility for mistakes? Trust should be earned incrementally based on evidence, not granted immediately or withheld entirely. This middle path feels uncomfortable initially, but leads to more accurate assessments.

Communicate needs and boundaries explicitly. People with Complex PTSD often assume others should know what they need or fear that expressing needs will lead to rejection. Practice stating, I need space right now, I need reassurance, I am not comfortable with that, I appreciate when you do this. Clear communication increases the likelihood that needs get met and reduces mind-reading expectations that create conflict. (Ford et al., 2019; Teicher & Samson, 2016)

Notice and interrupt trauma re-enactment patterns. Complex PTSD often involves unconsciously recreating traumatic relationship dynamics, choosing partners similar to abusive parents, remaining in harmful situations, or behaving in ways that provoke anticipated rejection. When you notice a familiar painful pattern, pause: Is this situation genuinely different from past trauma, even though it feels similar? Am I responding to an actual threat or an anticipated threat based on history? This awareness creates space for different choices. (Cloitre et al., 2020; Teicher & Samson, 2016)

Maintain relationships during difficult periods.

Complex PTSD symptoms like emotional numbness, irritability, or avoidance strain relationships. (Watts et al., 2013; Teicher & Samson, 2016)

Partners and friends might feel shut out, attacked, or confused.

Practice explaining I am struggling right now, it is not about you, I value our relationship even when I seem distant.

This communication helps people understand your behaviour stems from symptoms rather than feelings about them, reducing the likelihood they will withdraw when you most need support.

Accept that some relationships might not survive recovery. As you grow and change, some relationships based on unhealthy dynamics become incompatible with a healthier you. People who benefited from your trauma-based patterns might resist your recovery. It is painful but sometimes necessary to release relationships that cannot accommodate your healing. Grieve these losses whilst recognising they create space for healthier connections. (van Dis et al., 2020)

Specific Challenges in Complex PTSD Recovery (Ehring et al., 2014; Teicher & Samson, 2016)

Complex PTSD recovery involves unique challenges beyond those of standard PTSD. Understanding these challenges helps you prepare for them, develop appropriate strategies, and maintain realistic expectations about the recovery process. (Coventry et al., 2020; Teicher & Samson, 2016)

The Challenge of Delayed Development

When trauma occurs during formative developmental periods, it disrupts normal skill acquisition. You might have chronological adult age, but emotional development arrested at the trauma onset age. This creates a painful contradiction: you are expected to function as an adult whilst lacking capacities that typically develop in childhood through secure attachment and safe exploration.

This developmental arrest isn't your fault and does not reflect intelligence or capability in other domains. You might excel professionally while struggling with basic emotion regulation. You might manage complex tasks whilst finding simple relationships overwhelming. These contradictions confuse both you and others who wonder why someone obviously intelligent and capable struggles with things that seem basic.

Recovery involves developmental catch-up work. (Mavranezouli et al., 2020)

You are learning in adulthood what children typically learn through secure relationships: emotions are manageable, needs are valid, boundaries are acceptable, relationships can be safe, and you have inherent worth. (Cohen et al., 2016; Cohen & Mannarino, 2008)

This learning feels elementary and frustrating.

Why don't I already know this?

Everyone else seems to know this naturally.

Remember that you didn't have the opportunity to learn it at the appropriate developmental stage.

You are not behind because you are deficient; you are behind because essential learning opportunities were unavailable or actively disrupted.

Be patient with the developmental learning process. Children learn through repeated experiences over the years. Adult learning follows a similar timeline, even though you wish it could happen instantly. Grant yourself the time and repeated practise that learning these fundamental capacities requires. You are building foundational skills, and foundations take time to construct properly. (Cohen et al., 2016; Cohen & Mannarino, 2008)

The Challenge of Pervasive Impact

Unlike discrete trauma affecting specific domains, Complex PTSD from chronic childhood trauma affects everything. Your entire personality development occurred in a traumatic context, meaning recovery is not about returning to a pre-trauma self; there is no pre-trauma self to return to. This pervasive impact means recovery requires comprehensive life reconstruction rather than focused trauma processing. (Karatzias et al., 2019; Teicher & Samson, 2016)

Every relationship pattern, every belief about yourself and the world, every emotional response, every coping strategy developed within a traumatic environment bears its mark.

Changing one aspect affects everything else because everything is interconnected.

- This creates ripple effects: improving emotion regulation changes relationships
- challenging negative self-concept affects career choices (Teicher & Samson, 2016)
- reducing dissociation impacts emotional availability.

The pervasive nature means nothing exists in isolation; everything you work on influences everything else.

This pervasiveness can feel overwhelming: Is everything about me just trauma? Will I ever be more than a trauma survivor? Recovery involves distinguishing: what aspects of yourself developed because of trauma versus despite trauma? What parts represent your authentic self versus adaptive survival responses? This differentiation takes time and exploration. Through recovery, you discover: some traits you assumed were trauma responses are actually authentic personality; some behaviours you thought were just who you are actually changeable trauma adaptations. (Lewis et al., 2020)

The Challenge of Identity Confusion

Who am I? represents a fundamental question in Complex PTSD recovery. (Bisson et al., 2019; Teicher & Samson, 2016)

When your entire development occurred in traumatic circumstances, when you have organised your life around survival, when symptoms have dominated for years or decades, you genuinely might not know who you are beyond trauma and survival.

- Identity confusion involves uncertainty about your values, preferences, goals
- contradictory beliefs about yourself
- difficulty maintaining a consistent sense of self across situations
- and feeling like you are playing role rather than being your authentic self.

This confusion intensifies during recovery as the old identity as trauma victim/survivor gets challenged, but the new identity hasn't yet formed. The space between, no longer defined entirely by trauma but not yet clear who you are otherwise, feels disorienting. You might experience increased anxiety during this transition: if I am not a trauma survivor, who am I? This identity vacuum is a normal part of the recovery process, not evidence of deterioration. (Cusack et al., 2016)

Identity formation in recovery involves exploration and experimentation. Try new activities, relationships, and roles. Notice what resonates versus what feels wrong. Pay attention to what brings satisfaction, meaning, energy, versus what drains you. Through this exploration, a clearer sense of self gradually emerges. Allow yourself not to know who you are whilst actively exploring possibilities. Identity crystallizes through experience, not through thinking about it endlessly. (Watkins et al., 2018)

Therapy provides space for identity exploration. Internal Family Systems or similar approaches help you understand different parts and their purposes, working towards integration rather than fragmentation. Values clarification exercises help identify what truly matters to you versus what you thought you should value. Narrative work helps construct a coherent life story incorporating trauma, whilst not being defined entirely by it.

The Challenge of Treatment Length and Intensity

Complex PTSD treatment typically spans months to years, significantly longer than standard PTSD treatment. This extended timeline challenges motivation, tests financial resources if paying privately, and requires sustained commitment when life demands compete for attention. Unlike standard PTSD, where you can see the end of treatment within months, Complex PTSD recovery feels more open-ended and ongoing. (Ozer et al., 2003; Teicher & Samson, 2016)

The intensity of treatment, processing multiple traumas, managing severe symptoms, and addressing life circumstances can feel all-consuming. You are doing difficult emotional work in sessions, practising skills between sessions, managing daily life whilst symptomatic, and dealing with changes that recovery brings. The treatment itself becomes a major life focus, which is necessary but exhausting. (Guay et al., 2006)

- Maintaining motivation over extended treatment requires: setting small, achievable goals so you experience regular wins rather than only focusing on ultimate recovery (Charuvastra & Cloitre, 2008)
- celebrating progress even when small, three months without self-harm, expressing anger appropriately, establishing one healthy boundary all represent meaningful achievement
- connecting with reasons why recovery matters to you (Neff & Germer, 2018)
- taking breaks when needed without abandoning treatment entirely
- and adjusting expectations to match marathon rather than sprint timeline.

Financial and practical challenges of extended treatment require creative solutions.

- Options include mixing individual therapy with less expensive group therapy
- using evidence-based self-help resources to supplement professional treatment

- spacing sessions as symptoms improve (weekly, becoming fortnightly, becoming monthly)
- applying for reduced-fee services or sliding-scale arrangements
- and prioritising treatment in the budget even when difficult.

Recovery represents investment in your future; every pound or hour invested yields returns in improved quality of life. (Gilbert, 2014)

The Challenge of Grieving What Was Lost

- Recovery from Complex PTSD involves profound grief. You grieve childhood you never had (ISTSS, 2019; Teicher & Samson, 2016)
- parents who couldn't or didn't protect you
- innocence lost too early
- relationships damaged by symptoms
- opportunities missed due to impairment
- years lost to suffering
- and the person you might have been without trauma. This grief is real, valid, and often overwhelming.

Unlike grief following death with culturally recognised mourning processes, grief for lost childhood or stolen development lacks social acknowledgment. People might respond with: At least you survived, others had it worse, or dwelling on the past does not help, invalidating your legitimate grief. This disenfranchised grief complicates mourning; you need to grieve losses that others do not recognise as worthy of grief.

- Allowing grief is crucial for recovery. You cannot heal whilst denying losses. Permit yourself to mourn what trauma took from you. This mourning coexists with recovery work (Cloitre et al., 2012)
- you can grieve lost childhood whilst building skills for adult life
- you can feel angry about what you missed whilst moving forward. These are not contradictory but rather integrated aspects of comprehensive recovery. (Brand et al., 2019)

Complicated grief sometimes develops when losses feel too overwhelming to process or when grief triggers additional trauma responses. If grief becomes persistent, impairing condition preventing forward movement, specific grief therapy might help. Approaches like complicated grief treatment provide a structured process for working through profound losses whilst maintaining functioning in daily life.

Hope and Long-Term Recovery from Complex PTSD (Ross et al., 2017; Teicher & Samson, 2016)

Despite the challenges, recovery from Complex PTSD is genuinely possible. Thousands of people have recovered from even severe developmental trauma, rebuilt lives, formed healthy relationships, and found meaning and satisfaction. Your recovery is possible too, even when it feels impossible. This section addresses what successful long-term recovery looks like and how to maintain hope throughout the journey. (Teicher & Samson, 2016)

What Recovery Looks Like for Complex PTSD (Fenster et al., 2018; Teicher & Samson, 2016)

- Recovery from Complex PTSD does not mean returning to a pre-trauma state (Lanius et al., 2018; Teicher & Samson, 2016)
- there is no pre-trauma state to return to. Instead, recovery means: building capacities that trauma disrupted (Monson & Shnaider, 2014)
- reducing symptoms to manageable levels
- establishing healthy relationships
- pursuing meaningful activities
- and developing an integrated sense of self that includes trauma history without being defined entirely by it.

Successful recovery looks different for each person but common features include: (Foa et al., 2019)

- Successful recovery looks different for each person but common features include: experiencing full range of emotions at appropriate intensity rather than overwhelming floods or numbing (APA, 2017)
- maintaining stable relationships with appropriate intimacy and boundaries
- generally positive self-concept with self-compassion for struggles
- ability to regulate distress without destructive coping
- rarely experiencing dissociation or managing it quickly when it occurs
- pursuing goals and activities that provide meaning
- and generally good functioning in work, relationships, and self-care.

Complete symptom elimination isn't necessarily the goal or realistic for everyone.

Some people continue experiencing mild symptoms occasionally, brief dissociation during high stress, occasional intrusive memory, and periodic emotion dysregulation, but manage these effectively without significant impairment.

This represents successful recovery even with residual symptoms. (NICE, 2018)

The question isn't: Do I ever experience symptoms?

but rather: Do symptoms significantly impair my functioning and quality of life?

Recovery does not erase trauma or mean you are glad it happened. You will always have experienced what you experienced. Trauma remains part of your history. Recovery means trauma no longer dominates your present and future. You can remember without being overwhelmed. You can acknowledge what happened whilst living fully now. The trauma becomes part of your story rather than the entirety of your story. (Forbes et al., 2020)

Post-Traumatic Growth in Complex PTSD (Tedeschi & Calhoun, 2004)
Post-traumatic growth, positive psychological change following trauma, can occur even from severe developmental trauma. (Teicher & Samson, 2016)

This does not mean trauma was good or that you are glad it happened.

It means that, despite trauma being terrible, you developed strengths or perspectives that you value.

- Common areas of growth include greater compassion for self and others
- deeper appreciation for life and relationships
- and commitment to helping others.

People who experienced severe childhood trauma often develop exceptional empathy, intuition about others' emotions, resilience in adversity, and the capacity to hold complexity. These aren't compensations for trauma; they are genuine strengths, even though you shouldn't have had to develop them through suffering. Recognising these strengths does not minimise trauma but acknowledges your full humanity, including capacities that emerged from hardship. (Bonanno, 2004)

- Many trauma survivors find meaning through helping others. This might involve professional work in helping fields
- volunteer work with trauma survivors
- advocacy for trauma awareness and prevention
- peer support
- or simply being present for others struggling. This work provides meaning whilst honouring what you have survived. However, you are not obligated to help others or find meaning in trauma
- recovery itself is a sufficient accomplishment. (Schnyder et al., 2015)

Maintaining Hope During Long Recovery (Resick et al., 2017)
Extended recovery requires maintaining hope across months or years of difficult work. (Maercker et al., 2022)

Hope wavers; you'll have periods of optimism and periods of despair.

- Strategies for sustaining hope include: connecting with recovery stories from others who succeeded (Hyland et al., 2021)
- tracking progress objectively through symptom measures showing improvement even when you do not feel it
- celebrating small wins rather than only focusing on ultimate recovery (Karatzias et al., 2017)
- maintaining connection with why recovery matters to you (Courtois & Ford, 2013)
- and allowing yourself hope even when it feels risky after disappointment.

When hope feels absent, borrow it from others. Your therapist maintains hope when you cannot. Support group members who have progressed further demonstrate that recovery is possible. Recovery stories in books or online show people who felt exactly as hopeless as you do now and recovered anyway. You do not need unwavering personal hope; you need to stay engaged with treatment, whilst others hold hope for you. (Brewin et al., 2017)

Recognise that hopelessness itself is a symptom, not truth. Depression and trauma both produce hopelessness that feels certain but does not reflect reality. When you think recovery is impossible, recovery will never happen. I am too damaged, treat these as symptoms to note rather than facts to believe. They are trauma or depression speaking, not the truth about your actual potential for recovery. (Ford et al., 2019)

Final Thoughts on Complex PTSD Recovery (Cloitre et al., 2020; Teicher & Samson, 2016)

Complex PTSD from developmental trauma represents some of the most challenging psychological suffering. The pervasive impacts, lengthy recovery, and fundamental rebuilding required make it genuinely a difficult journey. If you are undertaking this recovery, acknowledge the courage that is required. You are facing what you spent years trying to escape. You are building capacities you should have developed naturally. You are healing wounds that should not have been inflicted. (Teicher & Samson, 2016)

Recovery is possible. The research is clear, clinical experience confirms it, and countless people demonstrate it through their own recoveries. Developmental trauma shapes you profoundly but does not determine your ultimate life trajectory. With an appropriate treatment, sustained effort, adequate support, and time, you can recover. The you that emerges from recovery might be different from who you would have been without trauma, but that person can be whole, capable, and satisfied with life. (Teicher & Samson, 2016)

Begin where you are.

Recovery does not require having everything in place first. (Watts et al., 2013)

Start by ensuring immediate safety.

Build from there.

Small steps accumulate into profound change over time.

Every practise of emotion regulation skill, every challenge to negative belief, every boundary set in a relationship, every moment of self-compassion contributes to recovery. (van Dis et al., 2020)

Trust the process, seek help, connect with others, and keep moving forward even when progress feels imperceptible.

You deserve recovery, and recovery is waiting for you. (Ehring et al., 2014)

Chapter Fifteen: Rebuilding Intimacy and Sexual Relationships After Trauma

- Sexual relationships can be rebuilt after trauma
- Intimacy difficulties are treatable symptoms, not permanent
- Communication with partners strengthens connection
- Recovery includes reclaiming sexuality and pleasure (Coventry et al., 2020)

Sexual trauma, whether a single incident or repeated abuse, profoundly impacts intimate and sexual relationships. Even non-sexual trauma can affect intimacy through hypervigilance, emotional numbing, or trust difficulties. This chapter addresses specific challenges trauma creates for intimate relationships and provides strategies for rebuilding healthy sexual intimacy. This content may be triggering; read at your own pace and skip sections if needed. (Porges, 2011; Yehuda & Seckl, 2011)

Sexual difficulties following trauma are extraordinarily common and represent a normal response to abnormal experiences, not personal deficiency.

- You might experience avoiding all sexual contact
- dissociating during sex
- flashbacks triggered by intimate touch (Van der Kolk et al., 1996)

PAUSE POINT: Ground Yourself

- • Notice 5 things you can SEE

- difficulty with arousal or pleasure
- pain during intercourse
- inability to trust partner during vulnerability of sex
- or anxiety about closeness and touch.

These responses were developed to protect you and make sense during or after trauma.

Recovery involves gradually regaining capacity for safe, pleasurable intimacy. (Mavranezouli et al., 2020)

How Trauma Affects Sexual Intimacy

Trauma impacts sexual intimacy through multiple mechanisms.

Hyperarousal and hypervigilance make relaxation, essential for pleasurable sex, nearly impossible. (Porges, 2011; Yehuda & Seckl, 2011)

You are scanning for threats even during intimate moments, unable to fully engage.

Physical sensations of arousal might feel similar to fear, confusing pleasure and danger signals.

Your body learned during trauma that physical sensations in certain contexts signal danger; it hasn't yet relearned that similar sensations in consensual, safe contexts mean something entirely different.

Dissociation during sex is a common trauma response. When intimacy triggers traumatic memories or overwhelming emotions, dissociation provides escape, you 'leave' mentally whilst your body remains physically present. Whilst protective during actual trauma, dissociation during consensual sex prevents genuine intimacy and pleasure. You are present physically but absent emotionally and psychologically, going through motions without truly experiencing or connecting.

Trust difficulties pervade sexual relationships after trauma. Sexual intimacy requires profound vulnerability, physical and emotional nakedness, relinquishing control, and trusting partner will not hurt you. When someone violated that trust traumatically, extending trust again feels terrifying even with safe partner. You might intellectually know your partner is safe, but emotionally remain guarded, unable to fully surrender to intimacy.

Body image and shame often intensify after trauma, particularly sexual trauma. You might feel your body is dirty, damaged, or disgusting. You might disconnect from your body entirely, viewing it as separate from self. These beliefs prevent comfortable embodiment during sex. How can you experience pleasure in a body you hate or feel disconnected from? Shame about trauma might extend to shame about sexuality, making healthy sexual expression feel impossible.

Trauma-related beliefs affect sexual relationships: No one would want me sexually after what happened, Sex is dangerous, I have no right to refuse, my pleasure does not matter, I must dissociate to tolerate sex, or I am damaged goods. These beliefs maintain sexual difficulties even in objectively safe relationships with caring partners. Challenging them is crucial for reclaiming healthy sexuality.

Communicating with Partners About Trauma and Intimacy

- Open communication with partners about trauma's impact on intimacy is essential but difficult. You might fear partner will judge you
- disclosing will damage the relationship
- talking about trauma will trigger you
- your partner will not understand
- or you'll burden them. Despite these fears, communication typically strengthens relationships by explaining your experiences and needs, allowing your partner to support you appropriately rather than guessing or taking difficulties personally.

Decide what and how much to disclose.

You are not obligated to share trauma details with a sexual partner, though doing so sometimes helps them understand your reactions.

- You can share that you experienced trauma affecting intimacy
- specific triggers they should know about
- what helps and does not help during sexual encounters
- and boundaries you need to be maintained.

You might share more details over time as trust deepens, or you might choose never to share specifics; both approaches are valid.

Choose timing thoughtfully. Do not disclose during sexual activity itself; have conversations when both are calm, unhurried, and able to focus. Early in the relationship, basic information about having a trauma history and needing to proceed slowly might suffice. As the relationship progresses, deeper conversations about specific needs become appropriate. Match disclosure to the relationship stage and your comfort level.

Frame conversations around what you need rather than just what happened. Partners often want to help but do not know how. Be specific: I need you to ask permission before touching certain areas, I need lights on so I can see it is you, I need to control pace, I need us to stop if I say so without questions or pressure, I need reassurance that you want me despite my difficulties. Concrete requests give partners clear ways to support you.

- Prepare for partner's reactions. Supportive partners usually respond with sadness about what happened to you
- desire to support your healing
- patience with difficulties
- willingness to adapt sexual relationship to your needs
- and questions about how to help. These responses, whilst well-intentioned, might feel overwhelming. It is acceptable to take breaks during difficult conversations, to table discussion and return to it later, or to seek couples therapy for support navigating these topics.

Practical Strategies for Rebuilding Sexual Intimacy

Rebuilding sexual intimacy after trauma requires a gradual, paced approach respecting your healing process. Rushing increases the likelihood of triggering trauma responses that create setbacks. Moving slowly with awareness and intention supports sustainable progress.

- Establish an absolute right to stop at any point without explanation. This foundational safety principle means either partner can say stop or pause at any moment
- stopping requires no justification or explanation
- the partner accepts stopping without pressure, argument, or guilt-inducing

- and you can resume if desired or not. This agreement removes pressure, allowing you to engage knowing you can exit if needed. Paradoxically, knowing you can stop often allows greater engagement than feeling trapped.

Use a gradual exposure hierarchy for sexual activities.

Start with activities, feeling completely safe, progress incrementally towards eventually comfortable full sexual intimacy.

An example hierarchy might include holding hands, sitting close together, gentle hugging, kissing, non-sexual touching like massage, sensual but non-sexual touching, gradually progressing towards sexual touching, and eventually intercourse.

Your hierarchy should reflect your specific comfort levels and triggers.

Spend whatever time needed at each level before progressing.

Weeks or months at some levels might be necessary.

- practise mindful, present-focused intimacy. During sexual activity, use grounding techniques to stay present: keep eyes open to see it is a safe partner, not a trauma perpetrator
- focus on current physical sensations, noticing what feels pleasurable or neutral
- speak and hear partner's voice, reminding you this is present, not past
- and pause if you notice dissociation beginning. Mindfulness during sex builds capacity to remain embodied and engaged rather than automatically escaping into dissociation.

Sensate focus exercises developed for sexual difficulties work well for trauma-related sexual challenges.

These structured touching exercises remove the goal of arousal or orgasm, reducing performance pressure.

You and your partner take turns giving and receiving touch, focusing on sensations without expectations.

This reintroduces physical intimacy in a low-pressure context, gradually rebuilding comfort with touch and sensual pleasure.

Many sex therapists guide couples through sensate focus specifically for trauma-related difficulties.

Create safety signals during sexual activity.

- Agree with partner on ways you will communicate during sex: verbal signals like saying your partner's name if you are becoming triggered
- nonverbal signals like tapping their shoulder
- keeping eyes open to maintain connection

- or checking in verbally at intervals.

These signals allow you to stay engaged whilst having ways to communicate needs without having to explain in detail mid-activity.

Practice signals in non-sexual contexts first so they feel natural when needed.

Address flashbacks or dissociation if they occur during intimacy. (Van der Kolk et al., 1996)

- If you flashback or dissociate: stop sexual activity immediately
- do not try to push through
- use grounding techniques to return to the present
- seek comfort from a partner if that helps or create space if you need it
- and debrief later about what triggered response and what might help prevent it next time.

Flashbacks during sex do not mean you'll never have a satisfying intimate life; they mean you need more time, preparation, or support before that particular activity feels safe. (Van der Kolk et al., 1996)

Consider working with a sex therapist specialised in trauma if difficulties persist despite effort. These specialists understand the intersection of trauma and sexuality, can provide specific techniques and exercises, work with you individually or as a couple, and help address trauma-related sexual dysfunction. Do not feel shame about needing professional help for sexual difficulties; they are legitimate trauma consequences deserving professional treatment like any other symptom.

Recognise that rebuilding sexual intimacy takes time measured in months to years, not weeks.

Progress isn't linear; you might make gains then experience setbacks, particularly around trauma anniversaries or during high stress.

Be patient with yourself and your recovery timeline. (Karatzias et al., 2019)

Each small step towards comfortable intimacy represents a significant achievement, even when progress feels frustratingly slow.

You are reclaiming an essential part of human experience that trauma tried to take from you.

That reclamation deserves however much time it requires.

When Partners Have Their Own Trauma History

When both partners have trauma histories, sexual intimacy presents unique challenges but also potential for deep understanding.

Both partners might struggle with similar issues, dissociation, flashbacks, and avoidance, requiring careful navigation to ensure both feel safe whilst building intimacy together. (Van der Kolk et al., 1996)

Communication becomes even more crucial when both partners have trauma responses that might interact unpredictably.

However, shared trauma experience also provides unique empathy and patience that partners without trauma history might not possess.

Both partners understand viscerally what trauma does, can recognise symptoms in each other, and approach difficulties with compassion born from personal experience rather than just intellectual understanding.

Couples therapy can help navigate these complex dynamics effectively for mutual healing.

Healing intimacy requires patience and compassion.

Working Through Specific Sexual Triggers

Sexual triggers, specific touches, positions, words, smells, or situations that activate trauma responses during intimacy require targeted intervention. Understanding your specific triggers and developing strategies to manage them allows gradual expansion of your comfortable sexual repertoire.

Identifying Your Triggers

- Trigger identification requires careful observation and reflection. Keep trigger journal noting what specifically triggered response (position, touch location, phrase, time of day, lighting)
- what response occurred (dissociation, flashback, panic, freeze)
- how intense the response was
- and what helped you recover. Patterns emerge over time: certain touches consistently trigger, whilst others feel safe
- specific positions are problematic
- contexts increase risk.
- Some triggers are obvious, touches mimicking assault, and positions used during trauma. Others are less apparent: certain smells triggering olfactory memory

PAUSE POINT: Ground Yourself

- • Notice 5 things you can SEE

- a partner's expression accidentally resembling the perpetrator
- time of day matching trauma

- or seemingly random details the brain associated with trauma. Do not dismiss triggers as illogical brain creates associations during trauma that might not make conscious sense, but are real for you.
- Distinguish triggers into categories: absolute triggers that reliably produce severe response requiring avoidance currently
- moderate triggers producing manageable discomfort you can work with gradually
- and mild triggers creating slight unease you can push through with grounding. This categorisation guides approach, absolute triggers need complete avoidance until processed therapeutically, moderate triggers become targets for gradual exposure, and mild triggers you practise managing in real-time.

Gradual Exposure to Triggers

Once triggers are identified, gradual exposure helps reduce their power.

This isn't about forcing yourself through triggering experiences; it is a systematic, paced approach with full control.

Start with imagination: visualise the trigger situation whilst maintaining grounding in present safety.

Progress to discussing the trigger with the partner whilst not engaged in sexual activity.

Then, approach the trigger in a modified form.

If certain position triggers, try a similar but different position.

Eventually, with preparation and support, carefully approach the actual trigger situation.

- Each exposure should be voluntary (you choose to approach it)
- planned (not a surprising encounter)
- paced (taking whatever time needed)
- escapable (you can stop immediately)
- and processed (debriefing afterwards about the experience). These conditions ensure exposure facilitates learning rather than retraumatizing. With each successful approach, the trigger loses some power as the brain learns this is a safe context, not a trauma context.

Some triggers might require therapeutic processing before sexual exposure. If a certain touch or position connects directly to trauma memory holding unprocessed material, attempting gradual exposure sexually might overwhelm. Work with the therapist to process that specific memory first, then approach exposure in an intimate relationship. Coordinate between therapy work and relationship work for optimal progress.

Managing Flashbacks During Intimacy (Van der Kolk et al., 1996)

Despite preparation, flashbacks sometimes occur during sexual activity. (Van der Kolk et al., 1996)

Having a plan for managing them reduces fear and provides concrete steps to follow.

- If flashback begins: immediately stop sexual activity, do not try to continue through flashback
- separate physically from partner if needed or maintain comforting contact if that helps
- use intensive grounding (speak aloud describing current safe environment, feel textures around you, focus on breathing)
- and remind yourself repeatedly: That was then, this is now, I am safe, I am with [partner's name], this is not the trauma.
- Partner role during flashback: follow your lead about physical contact, some people want to be held, others need space
- do not take flashback personally, it is a trauma response, not rejection
- speak calmly and reassuringly if you can hear them
- help with grounding if requested
- and wait patiently for flashback to pass without pressuring you to recover faster. Partners sometimes feel helpless during flashbacks (Van der Kolk et al., 1996)
- prepare them beforehand about what helps so they have specific actions to take.
- After flashback passes, care for yourself: do not immediately resume sexual activity that day, take time to fully recover
- practise self-compassion, flashbacks do not represent failure (Van der Kolk et al., 1996)
- debrief with partner about what happened and what might help prevent future flashbacks (Van der Kolk et al., 1996)
- and consider discussing with a therapist to process trigger memory more thoroughly. Each flashback provides information about what needs healing.

Reclaiming Your Body and Sexuality

Beyond managing symptoms, recovery involves actively reclaiming body and sexuality that trauma attempted to steal. This positive, empowering dimension of healing moves beyond just reducing problems towards building the satisfying sexual life you deserve. (Herman, 2015)

Body reconnection practices help rebuild comfortable embodiment. Progressive muscle relaxation increases body awareness. Gentle yoga cultivates present-moment physical experience. Massage (therapeutic, not sexual initially) reintroduces touch in a safe context. These practices help you reinhabit your body rather than living dissociated from it. Gradually, the body transforms from an object that trauma happened to, into a home you live in comfortably.

Exploring your own body privately, through self-touch, masturbation, or simply observing, helps reclaim sexuality for yourself, separate from partner dynamics.

- You learn what feels pleasurable
- what your body's responses are
- what you prefer

- and that your body can experience pleasure, not just pain.

This self-exploration removes performance pressure whilst rebuilding positive sexual experiences.

Some people find this easier than partner sex initially because there's no one to perform for or explain responses to.

- Redefine sexuality on your terms. Trauma might have taught sex is for someone else's pleasure
- your preferences do not matter
- you must tolerate unwanted touch
- or pleasure is impossible for you. Challenge these by discovering what you actually enjoy
- that your pleasure matters equally
- that saying no is acceptable
- and that you can experience sexual satisfaction. Your sexuality belongs to you. Recovery involves claiming it actively. (Lewis et al., 2020)

Some people find exploring sexuality through media helpful, reading erotic literature, watching ethical porn depicting consensual sexuality, or engaging with sex-positive educational content. These explorations, done at your own pace privately, help reshape understanding of sexuality from trauma-based to a broader, healthier perspective. Choose content depicting consent, mutual pleasure, and respect, and avoid material resembling your trauma or depicting coercion.

When to Seek Specialised Help

- Most trauma survivors can rebuild satisfying intimate relationships with support from a partner and general trauma therapy. However, specialised sex therapy becomes valuable when: sexual difficulties persist despite general trauma treatment
- you experience sexual dysfunction (vaginismus, erectile dysfunction, arousal difficulties) that requires specific intervention
- the relationship suffers significantly from sexual issues
- or you want structured guidance through intimacy challenges.

Sex therapists trained in trauma understand these issues intimately and provide specific techniques, exercises, and frameworks. They collaborate with individuals or couples, create customised treatment plans addressing your particular difficulties, and help navigate the complex intersection of trauma and sexuality. Do not feel shame about needing this specialised support. Sexual difficulties following trauma are legitimate health concerns deserving professional treatment.

- Finding an appropriate sex therapist: seek recommendations from a trauma therapist
- verify credentials (look for COSRT registration in the UK or AASECT certification in the US)

- ensure they have specific trauma training, not just general sex therapy training
- interview potential therapists about their approach
- and ensure you feel comfortable with them, a therapeutic relationship matters even more for intimate topics.

Hope for Healing Sexual Intimacy

Rebuilding intimate and sexual relationships after trauma represents one of the most challenging aspects of recovery, but also one of the most rewarding. Reclaiming capacity for safe, pleasurable, connected intimacy profoundly enhances quality of life and relationships. This healing is possible even after severe sexual trauma. (Bisson et al., 2019)

Thousands of trauma survivors have successfully rebuilt satisfying sexual lives. What felt impossible, trusting enough to be vulnerable, staying present during sex, and experiencing pleasure without flashbacks, becomes reality through patient, consistent work. Your intimate future isn't determined by your traumatic past. You can heal in this domain as in others, developing healthy sexuality despite trauma. (Van der Kolk et al., 1996)

Progress might be gradual and nonlinear. You will have setbacks, particularly during anniversaries or stress. Some activities might always require extra care or might remain off-limits indefinitely; that's acceptable. The goal isn't achieving some standard of normal sexuality but rather developing an intimate life that feels satisfying to you and your partner, whatever form that takes. Your sexuality is yours to define on your terms.

Many survivors report that reclaimed sexuality feels deeper and more meaningful than they imagine pre-trauma sexuality might have been.

The work required to rebuild intimacy, honest communication, mindful presence, and mutual care creates a profound connection.

Partners who successfully navigate these challenges together often develop extraordinarily strong bonds built on vulnerability, trust, and shared overcoming of difficulty.

Your path to satisfying an intimate life might differ from others, but it leads to an equally valid and fulfilling destination.

Chapter Sixteen: Parenting with PTSD and Breaking Cycles of Trauma

Age-Specific Scripts for Explaining PTSD to Children (Cohen et al., 2016; Cohen & Mannarino, 2008)

Young Children (Ages 5-8):

You might say: "Sometimes my body remembers when something scary happened, even though we're safe now. When my body remembers, I might feel scared or sad. This happens to many people. It's not your fault, and I'm getting help to feel better. You can help by being patient with me."

Children (Ages 9-12):

You might explain: "My PTSD means my brain is extra alert to danger because of something that happened. Sometimes I feel scared or upset when there's actually nothing to be scared of. I'm working with a doctor/therapist to help my brain realise we're safe now. When I'm struggling, I might need quiet time or extra support. I want you to know this isn't about anything you did."

Teenagers (Ages 13+):

You might share: "I'm dealing with PTSD, which means my nervous system learned to see threat in situations that aren't actually dangerous. My brain is essentially 'stuck' in protection mode from a past trauma. I'm working with a professional to help my nervous system learn that I'm safe now. Sometimes my mood or behaviour reflects what I'm processing, not anything to do with you."

Key Principles for All Ages:

- • Reassure children you love them and nothing was their fault (Cohen et al., 2016; Cohen & Mannarino, 2008)
- • Explain that your symptoms aren't their responsibility
- • Tell them specifically how they can support you
- • Maintain normal routines and boundaries
- • Use age-appropriate language
- • Answer their questions honestly
- • Let them know you're getting professional help

- Parenting with PTSD is challenging but manageable
- Your children can understand and support your recovery (Cohen et al., 2016; Cohen & Mannarino, 2008)
- Breaking cycles of trauma in families is possible
- Practical scripts help you explain your experiences

Parenting whilst managing PTSD presents unique challenges and rewards. You might worry: Will my PTSD harm my children? Am I passing trauma to the next generation? Can I be a good parent whilst symptomatic? These concerns are valid and common amongst trauma survivors who are parents. This chapter addresses how PTSD affects parenting, strategies for being an effective parent despite symptoms, and, most importantly, how to avoid transmitting trauma patterns to your children. (Cohen et al., 2016; Cohen & Mannarino, 2008)

First, the reassuring truth: having PTSD does not automatically make you a bad parent or doom your children to trauma. Parental PTSD does affect children, but aware, intentional parenting mitigates impacts significantly. Understanding how your symptoms affect parenting allows you to compensate, explain age-appropriately to children, and seek support. Many trauma survivors become exceptional parents precisely because they are determined to provide the safety and care they lacked. (Cohen et al., 2016; Cohen & Mannarino, 2008)

- This chapter covers: how PTSD symptoms specifically impact parenting
- strategies for managing symptoms whilst caring for children (Cohen et al., 2016; Cohen & Mannarino, 2008)
- explaining PTSD to children appropriately (Cohen et al., 2016; Cohen & Mannarino, 2008)
- breaking intergenerational trauma patterns
- and building resilience in children despite parental PTSD. Whether you are a current parent, planning to become one, or helping someone navigate parenting with PTSD, this information provides practical guidance. (Cohen et al., 2016; Cohen & Mannarino, 2008)

How PTSD Symptoms Affect Parenting

PTSD symptoms influence parenting in specific ways.

Hypervigilance might manifest as overprotectiveness, excessive worry about children's safety, restricting activities other parents allow, or constantly imagining catastrophes. (Porges, 2011; Yehuda & Seckl, 2011)

Whilst some vigilance protects children, excessive anxiety communicates to children that the world is dangerous, potentially creating anxiety in them. (Cohen et al., 2016; Cohen & Mannarino, 2008)

You might also become hypervigilant about their emotional states, overreacting to normal childhood emotions as if they signal serious problems.

- Emotional numbing affects attunement to children's needs. If you are emotionally numb, you might struggle to notice children's subtle emotional cues (Cohen et al., 2016; Cohen & Mannarino, 2008)
- respond warmly to their positive emotions
- provide emotional validation
- or engage in playful, spontaneous interaction. Children experience this as emotional unavailability even when you are physically present. They might interpret your numbing as not caring about them rather than recognising it as a trauma symptom you are struggling with. (Cohen et al., 2016; Cohen & Mannarino, 2008)

Irritability and anger can frighten children. PTSD-related irritability means you might snap at minor frustrations, yell disproportionately, or appear unpredictably angry. Children do not understand that this stems from trauma; they internalise it as something wrong with them or fear they are causing your distress. Even without physical aggression, unpredictable anger creates an atmosphere of walking on eggshells harmful to children's development. (Cohen et al., 2016; Cohen & Mannarino, 2008)

- Avoidance symptoms limit engagement. If you avoid activities triggering trauma memories, you might miss important parenting activities: avoiding playgrounds if assaulted outdoors
- avoiding school events if school was a traumatic setting
- avoiding physical affection if touched triggers. These avoidances, whilst protecting you from triggers, deprive children of the experiences and connection they need. (Cohen et al., 2016; Cohen & Mannarino, 2008)

Intrusive symptoms disrupt presence. When experiencing a flashback or intrusive memory, you are mentally elsewhere, unavailable to children in that moment. Frequent intrusions create inconsistent availability, sometimes fully present, sometimes absent mentally. Children find this inconsistency confusing and distressing. They might escalate behaviour, trying to recapture your attention or become anxiously vigilant about your mental state. (Cohen et al., 2016; Cohen & Mannarino, 2008)

Strategies for Effective Parenting with PTSD

Despite challenges, you can absolutely be an effective parent with PTSD. These strategies help compensate for symptom effects whilst protecting children's wellbeing. (Cohen et al., 2016; Cohen & Mannarino, 2008)

Prioritise your own treatment. This isn't selfish; it is an essential parenting act. Effective PTSD treatment improves your parenting capacity more than any specific parenting strategy. When symptoms decrease, you are more emotionally available, less irritable, and better able to engage. Treatment represents an investment in your children's wellbeing as well as your own. If treatment access is limited, focus on evidence-based self-help whilst working towards professional support. (Cohen et al., 2016; Cohen & Mannarino, 2008)

Practise deliberate emotional regulation before interacting with children when dysregulated. If you are irritable, angry, or overwhelmed: (Cohen et al., 2016; Cohen & Mannarino, 2008)

- Practise deliberate emotional regulation before interacting with children when dysregulated. If you are irritable, angry, or overwhelmed: take a timeout before responding to children's behaviour (Cohen et al., 2016; Cohen & Mannarino, 2008)
- use coping skills to regulate somewhat
- explain briefly: Mummy/Daddy needs a moment, I'll be right back
- and return when calmer. This prevents reacting harmfully whilst modelling healthy emotion management for children. They learn adults also have feelings they need to manage, and that's acceptable. (Cohen et al., 2016; Cohen & Mannarino, 2008)

Establish predictable routines providing stability. Even when your emotional state fluctuates, consistent routines, regular mealtimes, bedtime routines, and predictable schedules create the stability children need. Write schedules visually if your memory is affected. Use timers and reminders. Enlist a partner or support network to maintain routines when you are particularly symptomatic. Predictability in their external environment compensates somewhat for unpredictability in your internal state. (Cohen et al., 2016; Cohen & Mannarino, 2008)

- Repair ruptures when you parent sub-optimally due to symptoms. If you yell, withdraw, or respond inappropriately: return when calmer
- apologise age-appropriately: I am sorry I yelled, that wasn't about you, Mummy was feeling overwhelmed
- explain briefly without excessive detail: Sometimes adults have big feelings they are working on managing
- and reconnect warmly. These repairs prevent lasting damage from momentary failures and teach children that mistakes can be acknowledged and repaired. (Cohen et al., 2016; Cohen & Mannarino, 2008)

Build a support network, reducing isolation. Other adults in children's lives, partners, extended family, friends, and other parents, provide stability when you are struggling. Do not try to parent entirely alone with PTSD. Ask for: (Cohen et al., 2016; Cohen & Mannarino, 2008)

- Build a support network, reducing isolation. Other adults in children's lives, partners, extended family, friends, and other parents, provide stability when you are struggling. Do not try to parent entirely alone with PTSD. Ask for: help during difficult periods (Cohen et al., 2016; Cohen & Mannarino, 2008)
- respite care when symptoms intensify
- practical support with tasks you are avoiding
- and backup for maintaining routines. This support benefits both you and the children. (Cohen et al., 2016; Cohen & Mannarino, 2008)

Explaining PTSD to Your Children (Cohen et al., 2016; Cohen & Mannarino, 2008)

Children benefit from age-appropriate explanations of your PTSD. Without explanation, they create their own narratives, often that they caused your symptoms or that something is wrong with them. Honest, developmentally appropriate information prevents these misunderstandings whilst helping children make sense of their observations. (Cohen et al., 2016; Cohen & Mannarino, 2008)

For Young Children (Ages 3-7)

Young children need simple, concrete explanations focusing on observable behaviours without overwhelming details. Example explanations: Sometimes Mummy's body feels scared even when there's nothing scary right now. It is not your fault; it is just how my body is sometimes. Or: Daddy had something difficult happen before you were born, and sometimes his brain remembers it, and he feels sad or worried. But I am getting help, and I love you very much. (Cohen et al., 2016; Cohen & Mannarino, 2008)

Focus on what they observe directly: Sometimes I might seem worried or sad, that's not because of anything you did. If I need quiet time, I'll tell you, and then I'll come back to play. This concrete framing helps them understand your behaviour relates to something within you, not their actions. Reassure them frequently that they are not responsible for your feelings and that you love them.

Use simple metaphors: My brain has an alarm that sometimes goes off when there's no real danger, like a smoke alarm going off when you burn toast. Or: Sometimes big feelings get stuck in my body from something that happened before, like when you get a tummy ache. Young children understand these comparisons better than abstract explanations of trauma and PTSD. (Cohen et al., 2016; Cohen & Mannarino, 2008)

For School-Age Children (Ages 8-12)

School-age children can understand more complex explanations whilst still needing protection from overwhelming details. Example: I have something called PTSD, which stands for Post-Traumatic Stress Disorder. It happens when someone experiences something very frightening or upsetting, and their brain and body have trouble recovering from it. Sometimes I might seem jumpy, worried, or sad because of it. It is not your fault, and I am getting professional help to manage it better. (Cohen et al., 2016; Cohen & Mannarino, 2008)

Provide information about treatment: I see a therapist who helps me with PTSD, kind of like how you see the dentist for your teeth. I am working on getting better. This information reassures children that the problem is being addressed and models that seeking help for difficulties is appropriate. They learn that adults sometimes need help, and that's normal and good. (Cohen et al., 2016; Cohen & Mannarino, 2008)

Answer their questions honestly within appropriate bounds. They might ask: Will you always have PTSD? Are you okay? Did someone hurt you? Answer truthfully whilst protecting them from traumatic details: I am working on it, and it is getting better. Yes, I am okay even though I struggle sometimes. Something difficult happened, but I am safe now and getting help. Validate their questions rather than shutting down inquiry.

For Teenagers (Ages 13+)

Teenagers can handle more detailed explanations and benefit from understanding PTSD as a medical condition with a biological basis.

They are also more likely to research PTSD independently, so providing accurate information prevents misconceptions.

Example: I have PTSD from trauma I experienced.

It affects my brain's threat detection system, making me more anxious and reactive sometimes. (LeDoux, 1998)

I experience symptoms like flashbacks, hypervigilance, and sleep difficulties. (Van der Kolk et al., 1996)

I am in treatment and working on managing it, but it affects our family sometimes, and I want you to understand what's happening.

Acknowledge impact on them honestly: I know my PTSD affects you when I am irritable or withdraw, or seem anxious about your safety. I am sorry this impacts you, and I am working hard to minimise the effects. If my symptoms ever feel overwhelming to you, please tell me or talk to [another trusted adult]. This acknowledgement validates their experience whilst reinforcing that it is not their responsibility to manage your condition.

Discuss boundaries appropriately: Whilst I want you to understand PTSD, you are not my therapist. If you are concerned about me, please tell [another parent/trusted adult] rather than trying to fix it yourself. This protects teenagers from parentification, taking on an inappropriate caretaking role, whilst maintaining honest communication. They can understand without becoming responsible for your well-being.

If you experienced childhood trauma, you might worry intensely about repeating patterns. Will I abuse my children like I was abused? Am I damaging them like my parents damaged me? This fear is common and, ironically, protective. People who worry about repeating harmful patterns are least likely to do so because they are aware and intentional. Those who unthinkingly repeat patterns typically lack this self-reflection. (Cohen et al., 2016; Cohen & Mannarino, 2008)

- Breaking intergenerational trauma requires awareness of patterns you want to avoid
- deliberate practice of alternative behaviours
- healing your own trauma so it does not drive your parenting
- seeking support when struggling
- and forgiving yourself when you make mistakes whilst working to do better. You are not doomed to repeat your parents' mistakes
- you can consciously choose a different path.

Specific practices for breaking patterns: If you experienced physical abuse, commit firmly to never hitting your children and develop alternative discipline strategies. (Cohen et al., 2016; Cohen & Mannarino, 2008)

If you experienced emotional abuse or neglect, deliberately practise emotional attunement and validation even when difficult.

If boundaries were violated, maintain appropriate boundaries with your children, respecting privacy, not burdening them with adult problems, and allowing age-appropriate autonomy. (Cohen et al., 2016; Cohen & Mannarino, 2008)

Each conscious choice to parent differently breaks the pattern further.

Recognise that not repeating exact abuse does not mean you parent perfectly.

You might avoid physical abuse but struggle with emotional availability because of PTSD numbing.

Acknowledge these difficulties whilst giving yourself credit for what you are doing well.

Perfect parenting does not exist; good enough parenting that's consistent, loving, and responsive to children's needs is sufficient for healthy development. (Cohen et al., 2016; Cohen & Mannarino, 2008)

Your children do not need a perfect parent; they need a present, caring one who repairs when mistakes happen. (Cohen et al., 2016; Cohen & Mannarino, 2008)

Consider family therapy if patterns persist despite efforts. A family therapist can observe interactions, identify patterns you might not see, and teach alternative approaches. This isn't failure; it is responsible recognition that breaking deeply ingrained patterns sometimes requires professional guidance. Your willingness to seek help demonstrates a commitment to your children's well-being. (Cohen et al., 2016; Cohen & Mannarino, 2008)

Building Resilience in Your Children Despite Parental PTSD (Cohen et al., 2016; Cohen & Mannarino, 2008)

Whilst parental PTSD creates challenges, you can actively build resilience in your children that helps them thrive despite these difficulties. Resilience, the capacity to adapt successfully despite adversity, develops through specific experiences and relationships. Understanding resilience factors allows you to deliberately cultivate them in your children. (Cohen et al., 2016; Cohen & Mannarino, 2008)

Core Resilience Factors (Bonanno, 2004)

Secure attachment remains the most powerful resilience factor. (Bonanno, 2004)

Despite PTSD challenges, maintaining a warm, responsive relationship with your children, being available emotionally, responding to their needs, and providing comfort, builds secure attachment that protects against adversity. (Cohen et al., 2016; Cohen & Mannarino, 2008)

Even imperfect attachment, characterised by ruptures that get repaired, promotes resilience. (Bonanno, 2004)

Your children do not need a perfect, always-available parent; they need a good enough parent who returns after withdrawals, repairs after mistakes, and maintains an underlying loving presence. (Ashton, 2002)

Emotional coaching teaches children to understand and manage emotions. (Cohen et al., 2016; Cohen & Mannarino, 2008)

When children express emotions: validate rather than dismiss (I can see you are really frustrated), help them name the feeling (sounds like you are feeling disappointed), normalise it (everyone feels disappointed sometimes), and problem-solve if appropriate (what might help you feel better?).

This coaching, practised consistently, builds emotional intelligence that serves children throughout life. (Cohen et al., 2016; Cohen & Mannarino, 2008)

Your own emotion dysregulation makes this challenging, but not impossible; you can coach children through emotions even whilst struggling yourself. (Cohen et al., 2016; Cohen & Mannarino, 2008)

Fostering competence and mastery builds confidence. Provide age-appropriate challenges that children can master, learning new skills, taking on responsibilities, and solving problems independently. Celebrate their accomplishments. Let them experience the natural consequences of their choices when safe. These experiences teach: I can handle challenges, I have abilities, and I can affect my environment. This sense of competence buffers against stress, including stress from parental PTSD. (Cohen et al., 2016; Cohen & Mannarino, 2008)

Maintaining routines and structure provides stability. Children thrive on predictability. Regular mealtimes, bedtime routines, consistent rules, and reliable schedules create a stable framework within which they feel secure. When your emotional state fluctuates unpredictably because of PTSD, environmental predictability compensates. Enlist help maintaining routines during difficult periods; your co-parent, family members, or friends can help sustain stability when you cannot. (Cohen et al., 2016; Cohen & Mannarino, 2008)

Building a positive relationship with at least one other adult provides an additional secure base. Relationships with grandparents, aunts/uncles, family friends, teachers, or coaches create protective factors beyond the parent-child relationship. If your PTSD significantly impairs availability sometimes, these relationships become even more crucial. Facilitate connections between your children and trustworthy adults who can provide additional support and modelling of healthy adult functioning. (Cohen et al., 2016; Cohen & Mannarino, 2008)

Teaching Children About Mental Health (Cohen et al., 2016; Cohen & Mannarino, 2008)
Growing up with parent who has PTSD provides an opportunity to teach children about mental health in ways that reduce stigma and promote help-seeking. Frame lessons positively: Everyone has mental health, just like physical health. Sometimes people need help with mental health, just like they need doctors for physical health. There's no shame in struggling or seeking help; it is brave and smart. (Cohen et al., 2016; Cohen & Mannarino, 2008)

- Model healthy help-seeking. Let children know you see a therapist, take medication if you do, and practise coping skills. This normalises mental health care and demonstrates that adults seek help when needed (Cohen et al., 2016; Cohen & Mannarino, 2008)
- treatment helps

- there's no shame in having difficulties. Children who see parents managing mental health conditions learn that struggles aren't shameful secrets but addressable challenges requiring appropriate support. (Cohen et al., 2016; Cohen & Mannarino, 2008)

Teach them to recognise their own emotions and needs. Regular check-ins: How are you feeling today? What do you need? Do you need help with anything? This practise builds self-awareness and communication about internal states. If they learn to identify and express needs in childhood, they are more likely to seek help for mental health difficulties in adolescence or adulthood rather than suffering silently.

When Parental PTSD Becomes Too Impairing

Honest assessment: if your PTSD symptoms significantly impair parenting despite efforts, if you are frequently unavailable, explosive, unable to meet children's basic needs, or engaging in behaviours that frighten or harm them, additional support becomes an urgent necessity, not an optional enhancement. This does not make you a bad parent; it makes you a parent needing help. Recognise when you are beyond capacity to parent safely alone and seek intensive intervention. (Cohen et al., 2016; Cohen & Mannarino, 2008)

- Options include: increasing treatment intensity (more frequent therapy, day programmes, intensive outpatient treatment)
- temporarily increasing support (family members staying with you, paid childcare, partner taking a larger role)
- respite care allowing you treatment time
- or in severe cases, temporary arrangements where children stay with trusted relatives whilst you pursue intensive treatment. These options aren't failures (Cohen et al., 2016; Cohen & Mannarino, 2008)
- they are responsible recognition of needing support beyond your current capacity.

If you are at risk of harming yourself or children, seek immediate help: call crisis services, go to the emergency department, or contact social services yourself rather than waiting for involvement. Proactive help-seeking demonstrates parental responsibility even in crisis. Social services aren't only punitive; they can connect you with resources, provide support services, and help ensure children's safety while you access treatment. (Cohen et al., 2016; Cohen & Mannarino, 2008)

Hope for Parent-Child Relationships

Many trauma survivors become excellent parents precisely because they are determined to provide what they lacked or to prevent their children from experiencing what they endured. (Cohen et al., 2016; Cohen & Mannarino, 2008)

Your awareness of PTSD's impacts, commitment to treatment, and conscious parenting choices all protect your children. (Cohen et al., 2016; Cohen & Mannarino, 2008)

- They benefit from parents who: model resilience through recovery work (Cusack et al., 2016)
- teach emotional awareness through their own emotional processing (Foa & Kozak, 1986)
- demonstrate that difficult pasts do not determine future
- and show unconditional love despite imperfection.

Children of parents with PTSD who actively manage symptoms, maintain treatment, practice good enough parenting, and provide warm relationships typically develop normally. Research shows that parental mental illness's impact depends largely on whether the parent receives treatment and maintains relationship quality. Treated PTSD with good enough parenting produces healthy children. Your PTSD does not doom your children; your response to it determines outcomes more than symptoms themselves. (Cohen et al., 2016; Cohen & Mannarino, 2008)

Your relationship with your children can itself be healing. The unconditional love you give them, the security, validation, and care, can repair some of your own attachment wounds. Providing for them what they need creates opportunities for your own healing whilst benefiting them. This isn't using children therapeutically, which would be inappropriate, but recognising that healthy parent-child relationships benefit both parties. You deserve to experience the love and connection you create. (Cohen et al., 2016; Cohen & Mannarino, 2008)

Chapter Seventeen: Trauma, Sexual Identity, and Sexual Orientation

- Trauma and sexual identity intersect in complex ways
- LGBTQ+ individuals face unique trauma considerations
- Affirming treatment supports your whole self
- Recovery honours your identity and safety (Watkins et al., 2018)

Trauma, particularly sexual trauma, can profoundly affect how people understand and experience their sexual identity and orientation. Some trauma survivors question their sexual orientation after trauma, wondering if trauma changed them or if they are now gay, straight, bisexual, or asexual. Others experience confusion about gender identity. These questions are common, valid, and deserve thoughtful exploration rather than dismissal. This chapter addresses complex intersections between trauma and sexual identity.

Important clarification: Trauma does not cause sexual orientation.

Sexual orientation, whether you are attracted to men, women, both, or neither, develops through a complex interplay of biological, psychological, and social factors largely independent of trauma.

However, trauma can affect how you recognise, accept, express, or understand your orientation.

Trauma might suppress awareness of pre-existing orientation, create confusion about feelings, or complicate coming-out processes.

Understanding these nuances helps separate trauma effects from authentic identity.

- This chapter covers: how trauma affects sexual identity exploration
- working through sexual orientation questions after trauma
- gender identity considerations
- specific issues for LGBTQ+ trauma survivors
- and therapeutic approaches to these complex questions. Whether you are questioning aspects of your identity after trauma, supporting someone through these questions, or simply seeking to understand these connections, this information provides a framework for compassionate exploration.

How Trauma Affects Sexual Identity Understanding

Trauma, especially sexual trauma, disrupts normal sexual development and exploration. If trauma occurs during formative years when sexual identity is developing, it can interrupt or complicate natural processes of understanding attraction, desire, and identity. Even adult trauma can create confusion about a previously clear identity as trauma symptoms affect sexual functioning, desire, and intimate relationships.

Several mechanisms explain trauma's effects on identity understanding.

Avoiding sexuality entirely might prevent exploration needed to understand orientation.

If trauma involved a same-sex perpetrator, the victim might avoid same-sex relationships entirely from fear, making it difficult to recognise authentic same-sex attraction if present.

Conversely, if trauma involved an opposite-sex perpetrator, the victim might avoid opposite-sex relationships, potentially gravitating towards same-sex relationships for perceived safety rather than authentic attraction.

Dissociation during sexual activity prevents knowing what you genuinely desire or enjoy.

If you dissociate automatically during sex, you cannot accurately assess attraction or preference, and you are not present to experience these.

Only when dissociation decreases through trauma treatment can you begin understanding authentic sexual responses and preferences.

This explains why some people report sexual identity shifts during trauma recovery; they are finally present enough to recognise what was always true but inaccessible through dissociation. (Ozer et al., 2003)

Hyper-sexuality following trauma, increased sexual behaviour, often compulsive rather than pleasure-driven, can create confusion about desires and identity.

Engaging in sexual activities compulsively to manage trauma symptoms differs from authentic sexual expression.

Behaviour motivated by re-enactment, self-harm, or emotional regulation does not necessarily reflect genuine sexual orientation or preferences.

Distinguishing trauma-driven behaviour from authentic sexuality requires careful exploration and often therapeutic support.

Sexual aversion, complete avoidance of sexual activity, might lead to identifying as asexual when orientation is actually trauma-based avoidance.

Genuine asexuality, lack of sexual attraction to others, differs from trauma-induced sexual avoidance or aversion.

However, these can feel identical subjectively.

Working through trauma and observing whether sexual interest emerges helps clarify.

If interest develops with healing, it was likely trauma suppression.

If the absence of attraction persists, asexual identity might be accurate.

Sexual Orientation Questioning After Trauma

Many trauma survivors question their sexual orientation post-trauma, particularly if trauma involved sexual assault. Common questions include: Am I gay/straight now because of what happened? Did trauma change my orientation? Am I attracted to women/men because of trauma or because that's genuinely who I am? These questions deserve thoughtful exploration rather than quick answers or dismissal.

If sexual trauma involved a perpetrator of a particular gender, survivors sometimes wonder if trauma altered their orientation. A woman sexually assaulted by a man might question: Am I a lesbian now? Does my fear of men mean I am actually attracted to women? A man sexually assaulted by man might wonder: Did the assault make me gay? Am I attracted to men now because of trauma? These questions reflect common confusion about trauma effects versus authentic orientation.

Critical understanding: Trauma does not change sexual orientation. Research consistently shows that sexual orientation develops through multiple factors beginning early in life and remains relatively stable across the lifespan. Traumatic experiences, whilst profoundly impactful, do not fundamentally alter orientation. However, trauma absolutely can affect how you relate to your existing orientation, suppressing it, confusing it, or complicating the expression of it.

What might actually be happening when orientation seems to shift post-trauma: You are recognising orientation that existed before trauma, but was suppressed or unacknowledged for various reasons.

Trauma processing and increased self-awareness in therapy create space for recognising authentic orientation.

You are distinguishing trauma-based fear or attraction from genuine sexual attraction.

As trauma resolves, you can accurately assess attraction separate from fear or safety-seeking.

You are experiencing changes in who feels safe rather than who you are attracted to, gravitating towards certain people for safety reasons, whilst authentic attraction remains unchanged.

Approaching orientation questions therapeutically involves: Allowing questions without pressure for immediate answers, and identity exploration takes time.

Distinguishing safety from attraction, asking: Do I feel safe with this person/gender or genuinely attracted?

Working through trauma sufficiently to reduce dissociation, fear, and avoidance that cloud authentic experience.

Exploring attractions, fantasies, and desires when calm and safe rather than during a crisis or immediately post-trauma.

Recognising that orientation exists on a spectrum, attraction isn't always binary gay/straight but might be bisexual, pansexual, or fluid.

Working Therapeutically with Sexual Identity Questions

Therapists working with trauma survivors questioning sexual identity should: Create a safe, non-judgmental space for exploration without imposing orientation conclusions. Validate that questions are common and reasonable following trauma. Distinguish trauma effects from identity whilst acknowledging these intersect complexly. Avoid premature closure, neither insisting trauma changed orientation nor insisting it didn't. Allow the process of discovery.

Therapy explores: Timeline of attractions and identity awareness, when did various attractions first emerge? What was the trajectory before trauma? How has trauma affected this? Content of sexual fantasies and desires when safe and calm, what patterns emerge? Whom are you genuinely attracted to versus whom feels safe? How do trauma symptoms affect sexual expression and identity exploration? What fears or shame complicate authentic expression?

Specific therapeutic considerations include addressing internalised homophobia if present. LGBTQ+ individuals often internalise negative messages about same-sex attraction. Trauma might interact with pre-existing internalised homophobia, making authentic orientation even harder to recognise and accept. Therapy addresses both trauma and internalised prejudice. Similarly, addressing religious or cultural conflicts about orientation and sexuality that might predate or be complicated by trauma.

For survivors who identify as LGBTQ+, post-trauma processing, therapy supports: Coming out processes if appropriate, recognising that trauma history might complicate these. Integrating LGBTQ+ identity with trauma survivor identity. Addressing minority stress, additional stress from discrimination and prejudice, alongside trauma symptoms. Finding LGBTQ+-affirming communities and resources. Navigating relationships as an LGBTQ+ person with a trauma history.

For survivors who maintain a heterosexual identity after exploration, therapy validates that questioning was a legitimate process, not confusion or weakness. That opposite-sex relationships can be reclaimed despite trauma. That healing from trauma involving a particular gender does not require changing orientation. Those fears or difficulties with a particular gender can be worked through whilst maintaining a heterosexual identity.

Gender Identity and Trauma

Trauma can also affect gender identity understanding and expression, though, like sexual orientation, trauma does not cause gender identity. Transgender and gender diverse individuals exist across all populations regardless of trauma history. However, trauma can complicate gender identity exploration, delay recognition of authentic gender identity, or create confusion requiring careful therapeutic navigation.

For people who are transgender, trauma, particularly sexual trauma, might complicate transition processes. Questions arise: Am I transgender or just traumatised? Is my discomfort with assigned gender about trauma or genuine gender dysphoria? Should I wait until trauma is resolved before transitioning? These questions deserve nuanced exploration with providers competent in both trauma and gender identity.

Distinguishing gender dysphoria from trauma-related body disconnection is crucial. Trauma, especially sexual trauma, often produces disconnection from the body, discomfort with sexed body parts, and a desire to escape embodiment. This resembles gender dysphoria superficially but has different roots and potentially different responses to intervention. A comprehensive assessment by gender specialists and trauma specialists together provides the clearest understanding.

Key distinctions: Gender dysphoria typically predates trauma or exists independently, though trauma might obscure recognition.

Gender dysphoria persists across contexts and isn't limited to sexual situations or trauma triggers.

Alleviation of dysphoria through gender-affirming actions (social transition, medical intervention) is characteristic of genuine gender dysphoria.

Trauma-related dissociation might temporarily decrease with transition, but underlying trauma symptoms persist without trauma treatment.

Treatment approach for transgender trauma survivors involves: Simultaneous trauma treatment and gender-affirming care when appropriate; these aren't mutually exclusive.

Comprehensive assessment by both trauma specialists and gender specialists.

Recognising that transgender individuals experience trauma, including gender-based violence and discrimination, at higher rates than cisgender population.

Treating trauma does not require delaying gender-affirming care, though coordinating care optimises outcomes.

Gender-affirming care often supports trauma recovery by reducing dysphoria-related distress and affirming authentic identity. (Guay et al., 2006)

Specific Considerations for LGBTQ+ Trauma Survivors

- LGBTQ+ individuals experience trauma, including PTSD, at significantly higher rates than the heterosexual, cisgender population. Contributing factors include higher rates of childhood abuse, particularly for those rejected by families (Charuvastra & Cloitre, 2008; Teicher & Samson, 2016)
- discrimination and hate crimes
- intimate partner violence in same-sex relationships
- sexual assault
- and the cumulative effect of minority stress, chronic stress from living in a heteronormative, normative society that marginalises LGBTQ+ identities.

Minority stress theory explains how discrimination, prejudice, and stigma create chronic stress affecting LGBTQ+ mental health.

- This stress operates at multiple levels: distal stressors like direct experiences of discrimination or violence
- proximal stressors like expectations of rejection, concealment of identity, and internalised homophobia or transphobia
- and cumulative impact across the lifespan.

When LGBTQ+ individuals also experience discrete trauma, they are managing both trauma-specific PTSD symptoms and ongoing minority stress.

LGBTQ+ trauma survivors face unique treatment challenges.

Finding therapists who are both trauma-competent and LGBTQ+-affirming is crucial; lacking either creates barriers to effective treatment.

Some therapists minimise LGBTQ+ identities whilst treating trauma.

Others affirm identity but lack trauma expertise.

Comprehensive treatment requires both.

Resources like LGBTQ+ therapy directories, community mental health centres serving LGBTQ+ populations, and telehealth expand access to appropriately qualified providers.

Treatment considerations include addressing internalised homophobia or transphobia alongside trauma.

These often interact; trauma might reinforce internalised negative messages about LGBTQ+ identity, or internalised stigma might increase vulnerability to trauma.

Working with experiences of discrimination and hate crimes as traumatic events requiring processing, not just background stress.

Recognising that coming out processes themselves can be traumatic when met with rejection, violence, or loss.

Supporting connection with the affirming LGBTQ+ community as a protective factor.

Intersectionality: Multiple Marginalised Identities

Many people hold multiple marginalised identities, being LGBTQ+ and a person of colour, disabled, an immigrant, or belonging to a religious minority. These intersecting identities create unique experiences of discrimination and trauma that cannot be understood by examining each identity separately. Intersectionality recognises how multiple oppressions interact and compound.

For example, Black transgender women face astronomically high rates of violence reflecting the intersection of transphobia, misogyny, and racism. Their trauma experiences and treatment needs differ from white transgender women, Black cisgender women, or white cisgender women. Treatment must address all relevant identities and associated oppressions rather than fragmenting a person into separate demographic categories. Culturally competent care recognises these complexities.

Finding providers who understand intersectionality and can work competently across multiple identity dimensions is challenging but crucial. Seek providers with training in cultural competence, explicit affirmation of all your identities, and willingness to learn from you about your unique experiences. Community-based organisations serving specific intersectional populations often provide culturally grounded care better than mainstream services.

Moving Forward: Integration and Self-Acceptance

Whether trauma affected your understanding of sexual orientation, gender identity, or both, moving forward involves integration: bringing together trauma survivor identity, sexual/gender identity, and all other aspects of yourself into a coherent whole. You are not fragmented into separate identities but rather a complex person with multiple facets that intersect and influence each other.

Self-acceptance emerges gradually through working through trauma sufficiently to reduce its interference with authentic self-expression. Addressing internalised stigma about any marginalised identities. Building connections with communities that affirm all aspects of your identity. Recognising that questioning and exploration are valid processes, not failures or confusion. Allowing identity to be fluid when that reflects your experience, or stable when that's accurate for you.

Recovery allows reclaiming sexuality and identity that trauma obscured, suppressed, or complicated. (Neff & Germer, 2018)

As symptoms decrease, dissociation reduces, and self-understanding increases, authentic identity becomes clearer.

This might confirm what you always knew, reveal aspects of yourself you hadn't recognised, or simply allow comfortable inhabiting of identity that existed but felt inaccessible.

Trust your process, seek support, and know that authentic self-understanding is possible even after trauma profoundly affected these intimate aspects of identity.

Chapter Eighteen: Navigating Romantic Relationships During PTSD Recovery (Gilbert, 2014)

- Romantic relationships deserve attention during recovery (ISTSS, 2019)
- Partners can be sources of support and healing
- Navigating intimacy and independence is possible (Lader, 2011; Ashton, 2002)
- Healthy relationships support sustained recovery (Cloitre et al., 2012)

Romantic relationships present both challenges and opportunities during PTSD recovery. Trauma affects how you relate to partners, express intimacy, handle conflict, trust others, and maintain connection. Simultaneously, healthy relationships provide crucial support, facilitate healing, and offer corrective experiences that challenge trauma-based beliefs. This chapter provides comprehensive guidance for navigating romantic relationships whilst recovering from trauma, whether maintaining existing relationships through recovery, beginning new relationships with PTSD, or helping a partner through their recovery. (Brand et al., 2019)

- This chapter differs from previous relationship content by focusing specifically on romantic partnerships throughout the recovery process. Topics include how trauma affects specific relationship domains (Ross et al., 2017)

- communication strategies for partners
- managing triggers and symptoms within relationships
- when to pursue relationships versus focus on individual healing
- couples therapy for trauma-affected relationships
- and building healthy patterns despite trauma history. Whether single, dating, or in an established partnership, this information supports healthier relating.

How PTSD Affects Romantic Relationships: Comprehensive Overview

PTSD impacts romantic relationships through multiple interconnected mechanisms. Understanding specific effects helps both partners recognise symptoms rather than personalising difficulties or attributing them to relationship problems when they actually reflect trauma responses requiring different interventions.

Trust and vulnerability challenges: PTSD, particularly from interpersonal trauma, profoundly disrupts trust capacity.

- Even with a safe, trustworthy partner, you might: constantly question their motives
- interpret ambiguous behaviours suspiciously
- test their loyalty repeatedly
- or remain emotionally guarded despite intellectual knowledge of their trustworthiness.

This hypervigilance for betrayal protects from potential hurt but prevents intimacy from developing. (Porges, 2011; Yehuda & Seckl, 2011)

Partners often feel frustrated that, despite consistent, trustworthy behaviour, trust does not increase proportionally.

Understanding this as a trauma symptom rather than a partner statement reduces mutual frustration.

Emotional availability and intimacy: Emotional numbing, dissociation, and avoidance limit emotional intimacy.

- You might: seem physically present but emotionally distant
- struggle to share vulnerable feelings
- withdraw when your partner seeks emotional connection
- or feel uncomfortable with your partner's emotional expression towards you.

Partners experience this as rejection or disinterest, even though it is a trauma-based protective mechanism.

Explaining that emotional unavailability reflects symptom management rather than feelings about the partner helps both partners navigate this difficulty with less damage to the relationship bond.

Conflict navigation: Hyperarousal, irritability, and emotion dysregulation complicate conflict resolution.

- Arguments might: escalate rapidly beyond what the situation warrants
- trigger trauma responses like flashbacks or dissociation (Van der Kolk et al., 1996)
- lead to disproportionate reactions
- or result in withdrawal that prevents resolution. (Ashton, 2002)

Partners might walk on eggshells, avoiding normal disagreements, creating resentment and preventing healthy conflict resolution.

Learning trauma-informed conflict approaches becomes essential.

Communication patterns: PTSD affects communication directly through avoidance, difficulty identifying emotions, mind-reading expectations, or harsh criticism stemming from hypervigilance. (Porges, 2011; Yehuda & Seckl, 2011)

- You might: avoid discussing trauma or symptoms, leaving partner confused about needs
- expect partner to know what you need without stating it
- criticise or become defensive quickly
- or shut down conversations when uncomfortable.

These patterns, whilst protecting you from vulnerability, prevent effective communication necessary for relationship health.

Communication Strategies for Trauma-Affected Relationships

Effective communication becomes even more crucial in trauma-affected relationships, yet trauma makes communication more difficult. These strategies help partners navigate communication challenges whilst maintaining connection and reducing conflict.

Educating Your Partner About PTSD

- Partners cannot support effectively without understanding PTSD. Provide psychoeducation about: what PTSD is and how it develops
- specific symptoms you experience
- how these symptoms affect you and your relationship
- what helps and does not help during symptom episodes
- and your treatment plan and progress. This education prevents misunderstandings where the partner interprets symptoms as relationship problems or personal rejection.

Share information incrementally rather than overwhelming the partner with everything immediately.

Start with basics: I have PTSD from trauma I experienced.

It affects me in these ways.

I am in treatment.

Add detail as the relationship progresses and as the partner demonstrates the ability to handle information supportively.

- Some partners benefit from: reading about PTSD independently
- attending therapy sessions with you if appropriate
- connecting with support groups for partners of trauma survivors
- or speaking with your therapist about how to support you effectively.

Be specific about your needs rather than expecting the partner to infer them. Clear requests work better than hints: I need you to give me space when I am triggered, then check in after 20 minutes. I need reassurance that you are not angry when I withdraw. I need a warning before you touch me. These concrete specifics allow the partner to provide meaningful support rather than guessing.

Managing Triggers Together

Triggers will occur in relationships, certain situations, conversations, touches, or conflicts inevitably activate trauma responses.

Planning how to handle triggers together prevents them from damaging the relationship bond.

- Create a shared trigger management plan, including identifying known triggers partner should be aware of
- signals you'll use to indicate you are becoming triggered
- the partner's role during triggering, what helps and what does not
- time-out procedures allowing you to regulate
- and reconnection after the trigger passes.
- During actual triggering, the partner should: recognise signs you are triggered rather than just being difficult
- avoid taking trigger response personally
- provide space or support depending on your stated preferences
- not pressure you to explain immediately or continue difficult conversation
- and wait until you are regulated before attempting to resolve whatever prompted the trigger. Post-trigger, debrief: What triggered you? What would help prevent this trigger? What did the partner do well? What would be more helpful next time? These conversations improve management over time.

Some triggers are unavoidable in relationships; certain intimacy, vulnerability, or conflict naturally trigger trauma memories.

Rather than avoiding all triggers, work towards managing them whilst maintaining relationship engagement.

This differs from unnecessarily triggering situations that should be avoided.

Distinguish necessary relationship experiences that happen to trigger (healthy conflict, emotional vulnerability, sexual intimacy) from gratuitous situations replicating trauma that serve no relationship purpose.

Conflict Resolution with PTSD

Conflict in trauma-affected relationships requires modified approaches accounting for hyperarousal, emotion dysregulation, and potential for triggering. Standard conflict resolution advice might not work; facing conflict head-on without breaks, hashing everything out immediately, or pushing through discomfort might overwhelm trauma survivors' capacity and trigger a crisis rather than a resolution.

Trauma-informed conflict resolution includes recognising when arousal is too high for productive conversation and taking breaks.

Use time-outs with specified return time: I need 30 minutes, then let's continue.

This prevents open-ended avoidance whilst allowing regulation.

During breaks, use coping skills rather than ruminating or escalating internally.

Return as agreed, even if uncomfortable; reliability builds trust.

When reconvening, check arousal levels before continuing a difficult conversation.

Use structured communication like the speaker-listener technique during heated conflicts. One person speaks while the other only listens and reflects what they heard without defending or rebutting. Then switch roles. This structure prevents escalation common when both people speak simultaneously, defensively, or dismissively. Slowing conversation and ensuring understanding occurs before responding reduces emotional intensity, allowing productive discussion.

- Establish ground rules prohibiting name-calling or personal attacks
- bringing up past issues unrelated to current conflict
- threatening the relationship during arguments (I am leaving you, we should break up)
- physical aggression or intimidation
- or storming out without an agreed-upon time-out structure. These boundaries maintain safety, allowing conflict to strengthen rather than damage the relationship.

Repair after conflicts is crucial.

Even when conflict goes badly, someone says something hurtful, a trigger occurs, someone withdraws, and repair prevents lasting damage.

- Effective repair involves acknowledging what went wrong
- apologising for your part without excessive defensiveness
- accepting the partner's apology
- and recommitting to the relationship despite difficulty.

Research shows repair predicts relationship success more than conflict absence does; relationships that repair well after conflicts thrive, and those that do not deteriorate even with infrequent conflicts.

Common question: Should I pursue relationships now or wait until I am further along in recovery? No universal answer exists; it depends on your circumstances, symptom severity, relationship readiness, and what you want. However, some considerations help inform this decision. (Fenster et al., 2018)

Reasons to focus primarily on individual healing before pursuing relationships: If you are in crisis, actively suicidal, engaging in severe self-harm, experiencing debilitating symptoms requiring intensive treatment, relationships add stress you might not have capacity for currently.

If you are very early in trauma recovery and still highly symptomatic, building a foundation through treatment before adding relationship complexity often works better. (Lanius et al., 2018)

If you recognise patterns of entering harmful relationships and need time to work through these before repeating patterns.

Reasons relationships might support healing: Healthy relationships provide a secure base supporting recovery work. (Monson & Shnaider, 2014)

Corrective relationship experiences, being treated well, having conflicts resolved healthily, receiving consistent care, and challenging trauma-based beliefs more powerfully than therapy alone.

Connection and intimacy, whilst challenging with PTSD, are fundamental human needs; completely postponing them until recovery is complete creates unnecessary isolation. (Foa et al., 2019)

You can work on recovery whilst also pursuing relationships; these aren't mutually exclusive. (APA, 2017)

- Middle-ground approach works for many: pursue relationships whilst maintaining a strong focus on individual treatment
- be honest with potential partners about PTSD and what you are working on
- choose partners carefully, prioritising emotional safety and stability over excitement or drama
- maintain boundaries protecting recovery time and energy (NICE, 2018)
- and stay in individual therapy whilst navigating relationships to process relationship challenges through a trauma-informed lens.

Couples therapy specifically addressing trauma's impact on relationships supports both partners, improves communication, and provides a structured approach to relationship challenges. Different from individual trauma therapy, couples work focuses on relationship patterns, communication, and shared coping, whilst a trauma therapist focuses on individual trauma processing. Both can occur simultaneously for optimal outcomes.

When couples therapy is indicated: When PTSD symptoms significantly impair relationship functioning despite individual treatment progress.

When conflicts escalate repeatedly without resolution.

When one partner is burning out from supporting the other without adequate support themselves.

When communication has broken down or patterns feel entrenched.

When both partners want to improve their relationship but do not know how.

Couples therapy isn't an admission of failure; it is a proactive step towards healthier relating.

Seeking a couple's therapist with trauma expertise is essential.

General couples therapists might not understand trauma's specific impacts or might apply standard interventions that do not account for trauma symptoms.

- Trauma-informed couples' therapists understand how trauma affects attachment and relating
- when individual stabilisation is needed before couples' work
- how to manage triggering within sessions
- and the balance between addressing trauma and addressing relationship issues independent of trauma.

Common couples therapy approaches for trauma-affected relationships include Emotion-Focused Therapy (EFT) for couples, which works with attachment injuries and helps partners create a more secure emotional bond.

Cognitive-Behavioural Couples Therapy addresses unhelpful relationship patterns and builds positive interaction.

The Gottman Method focuses on friendship, managing conflict, and creating shared meaning.

Integrative approaches combining elements from multiple models tailored to your specific needs.

- Couples therapy goals typically include improving communication and reducing destructive patterns
- helping partners understand trauma and its effects

- teaching both partners coping strategies for managing symptoms within the relationship
- addressing sexual intimacy issues if present
- rebuilding trust and emotional safety
- and strengthening positive aspects of the relationship alongside addressing difficulties. Therapy supports a relationship becoming a resource for recovery rather than an additional stressor. (Forbes et al., 2020)

Supporting Your Partner Through Their Recovery (Schnyder et al., 2015)

If your partner has PTSD, this section guides supporting their recovery whilst maintaining your own wellbeing. Supporting trauma survivor demands patience, compassion, and healthy boundaries. You cannot heal your partner, but you can provide an environment supporting their healing. (Resick et al., 2017)

Essential attitudes for supportive partners: Patience with recovery timeline, healing takes time and isn't linear. (Maercker et al., 2022)

Progress might feel frustratingly slow or inconsistent.

Maintain a long-term perspective rather than expecting quick fixes.

Compassion for their struggles without enabling, distinguish between supporting through difficulties and removing all challenges that might promote growth.

Boundaries protecting your wellbeing, supporting your partner does not mean neglecting yourself.

Curiosity rather than judgment, approach their symptoms as puzzles to understand rather than flaws to criticise.

Hope for recovery even when they feel hopeless. (Hyland et al., 2021)

Sometimes, you must hold hope for both of you.

Practical support strategies: Attend therapy sessions with them when invited to better understand their treatment.

Learn about PTSD independently through reading, support groups, or consultation with mental health providers.

Provide practical assistance during difficult periods, and help with responsibilities they are struggling with temporarily.

Recognise and celebrate progress, even when small.

Maintain normalcy in the relationship with your partners, not therapist-patient.

Engage in positive activities together unrelated to trauma or treatment.

What does not help, despite good intentions: Pressuring them to get over it faster or just think positively. Demanding they explain trauma details you are curious about. Making their recovery your responsibility, you can support but cannot do it for them. Walking on eggshells avoiding all topics that might trigger, this creates inauthentic relationship. Neglecting your own needs entirely in service of theirs. Taking all their symptoms personally rather than recognising trauma origins. (Karatzias et al., 2017)

Partners' own support needs: Seek your own therapy to process feelings about your partner's PTSD and its impact on you.

Join a support group for partners of trauma survivors where you can share experiences with others in similar situations.

Maintain friendships and activities outside relationship, providing respite.

Set boundaries about what you can and cannot accommodate.

Recognise signs of compassion fatigue or caregiver burnout and address these promptly.

Your well-being matters equally; you cannot pour from an empty cup.

Building New Relationship Patterns

Recovery provides an opportunity to build healthier relationship patterns than those trauma taught you. If trauma modelled harmful relationships, abuse, neglect, and chaos, you might lack templates for healthy relating. Learning new patterns requires conscious effort, practise, and a willingness to tolerate the discomfort of unfamiliar territory. (Courtois & Ford, 2013)

Healthy relationship characteristics to cultivate: Mutual respect where both partners' needs, opinions, and boundaries matter equally.

Effective communication where both partners express needs clearly and listen empathetically.

Appropriate boundaries where each person maintains individual identity whilst sharing closeness.

Conflict resolution addressing disagreements constructively rather than destructively.

Emotional intimacy allows vulnerability without exploitation.

Physical intimacy that's consensual, pleasurable, and connecting.

Shared decision-making on important matters.

Independence alongside interdependence, supporting individual goals whilst building a shared life. (Lader, 2011; Ashton, 2002)

These patterns might feel unnatural initially if trauma normalised unhealthy dynamics.

Healthy relationships might feel boring compared to dramatic, intense relationships that trauma survivors sometimes gravitate towards.

Stability might feel uncomfortable if chaos feels normal.

Trust without constant testing might feel naive if hypervigilance feels protective. (Porges, 2011; Yehuda & Seckl, 2011)

Recognise these feelings as trauma residue rather than the truth about healthy relationships.

Healthy relating feels different, not wrong, from what trauma normalised.

Practice new patterns deliberately: When conflict arises, consciously apply healthy conflict resolution rather than defaulting to learned patterns. When a partner shows trustworthiness, acknowledge it rather than dismissing or testing further. When you notice an unhealthy pattern emerging, pause and choose a different response. These conscious choices, repeated over time, become new automatic patterns replacing trauma-based ones. Therapy supports this learning by identifying patterns, exploring origins, and practising alternatives.

APPENDIX: CLINICAL GUIDANCE FOR MENTAL HEALTH PROFESSIONALS

Chapter Nineteen: For Clinicians, Professional Guide to Treating PTSD and Complex PTSD (Watts et al., 2013; Teicher & Samson, 2016)

- Clinicians need practical guidance for PTSD treatment
- Evidence-based protocols improve outcomes
- Supervision and self-care prevent clinician burnout
- This chapter supports professional practice

This chapter provides clinical guidance for mental health professionals treating PTSD and Complex PTSD. Whether you are an experienced trauma therapist or clinician new to trauma work, this chapter offers: (van Dis et al., 2020; Teicher & Samson, 2016)

- This chapter provides clinical guidance for mental health professionals treating PTSD and Complex PTSD. Whether you are an experienced trauma therapist or clinician new to trauma work, this chapter offers: an evidence-based treatment protocol (Ehring et al., 2014; Teicher & Samson, 2016)
- management of common therapeutic challenges

- guidance on your relationship with your therapist with trauma survivors
- addressing vicarious traumatisation and clinician self-care (Stamm, 2010; Pearlman & Saakvitne, 1995)
- cultural competence considerations
- and troubleshooting common treatment obstacles. This chapter assumes clinical training and uses professional language appropriate for practising clinicians.
- PTSD treatment has evolved with growing evidence base clarifying what works. Effective trauma treatment requires appropriate training in evidence-based protocols
- understanding of trauma's neurobiological impacts
- capacity to provide a safe therapeutic environment
- ability to manage intense affect and therapeutic relationship
- and commitment to ongoing professional development. Trauma work is rewarding but demanding
- this chapter supports your clinical effectiveness whilst protecting your wellbeing.

Core Clinical Competencies for Trauma Treatment

- Effective trauma treatment requires specific competencies beyond general psychotherapy training. Essential competencies include: thorough trauma assessment and differential diagnosis
- knowledge of PTSD neurobiology and psychophysiology
- proficiency in at least one evidence-based trauma treatment (PE, CPT, or EMDR) (Shapiro, 2018)
- skills in affect regulation and distress tolerance (Linehan, 2015)
- ability to work with dissociation
- cultural humility and competence
- understanding of complex trauma and developmental impacts
- capacity to manage therapeutic relationship complexities
- and recognition of your scope of practise limits.

A comprehensive trauma assessment goes beyond confirming a PTSD diagnosis.

- Assess: trauma history across lifespan
- current symptoms across all domains (intrusion, avoidance, cognition/mood changes, arousal)
- functional impairment
- comorbidities, especially depression, substance use, personality pathology
- suicide risk
- dissociative symptoms
- social support
- cultural context
- and treatment history.

Use structured assessments like CAPS-5 or PCL-5 rather than relying solely on clinical interview; research shows structured assessment improves diagnostic accuracy and treatment monitoring.

Understanding trauma neurobiology informs treatment and psychoeducation.

- PTSD involves an overactive amygdala producing exaggerated threat detection
- an underactive prefrontal cortex reducing top-down regulation (Foa & Kozak, 1986)
- an altered HPA axis affecting stress response
- hippocampal changes affecting memory contextualization
- and autonomic nervous system dysregulation.
- This knowledge helps you: explain symptoms to clients
- select appropriate interventions targeting specific neurobiological systems
- and avoid pathologising normal trauma responses.

Proficiency in an evidence-based treatment requires formal training beyond reading manuals.

Seek training from recognised programmes offering supervision and competency evaluation.

- Evidence-based PTSD treatments include Prolonged Exposure (PE) involving imaginal and in vivo exposure
- Cognitive Processing Therapy (CPT) using cognitive restructuring (Resick & Schnicke, 2016)
- Eye Movement Desensitisation and Reprocessing (EMDR) utilising bilateral stimulation (Shapiro, 2018)
- and Trauma-Focused CBT (TF-CBT) for children.

For Complex PTSD, consider phase-based approaches, Schema Therapy, DBT skills, or Compassion-Focused Therapy as adjuncts or alternatives. (Herman, 2015; Teicher & Samson, 2016)

Establishing your relationship with your therapist with Trauma Survivors

your relationship with your therapist predicts treatment outcomes powerfully, particularly in trauma treatment, where the relationship provides a safe base for difficult work. However, trauma histories, especially involving interpersonal trauma, create specific alliance challenges. Understanding these challenges and responding therapeutically strengthens the alliance rather than viewing difficulties as resistance or pathology.

Trust difficulties are universal in trauma survivors.

Clients with trauma histories, particularly relational trauma, approach therapy with justified wariness.

PAUSE POINT: Ground Yourself

- • Notice 5 things you can SEE

They've learned through experience that people can be dangerous, that vulnerability leads to harm, or that no one is trustworthy.

This isn't paranoia; it is an adaptive response to real experiences.

- Build trust through consistency and reliability
- transparency about your approach
- demonstrating competence
- admitting mistakes openly
- and earning trust gradually through behaviour rather than demanding it.

Attachment patterns affect the therapeutic relationship profoundly.

- Clients with anxious attachment: seek excessive reassurance
- monitor for rejection constantly
- experience intense distress around session endings or breaks
- fear abandonment by you
- and might call/text excessively.
- Respond with consistent availability within appropriate boundaries
- explicit reassurance about ongoing treatment
- clear communication about breaks
- and gradual building of capacity to tolerate separation.

Avoid: frustration with their need for reassurance or interpreting it as manipulation.

- Clients with avoidant attachment: maintain emotional distance
- minimise problems
- resist vulnerability
- intellectualise rather than feel
- and might miss sessions or terminate prematurely when closeness threatens. Respond with respect for pacing
- gentle invitation towards emotional experiencing without pressure
- normalising vulnerability
- and explicit appreciation when they do share. Avoid: pushing too hard for emotional disclosure or interpreting distance as a lack of engagement.
- Clients with disorganised attachment: exhibit contradictory behaviour
- alternate between pursuing and rejecting you
- test whether you will abandon them
- and demonstrate intense ambivalence about treatment.
- Respond with recognition of their contradictory needs

- explicit naming of the pattern without criticism
- consistent presence through fluctuations
- and understanding that testing reflects attachment wounds, not personal rejection.

Avoid: taking behaviour personally or becoming inconsistent in response to their inconsistency.

Transparency supports alliance with trauma survivors. Explain your reasoning, describe what is happening in treatment, share your clinical formulation collaboratively, and demystify therapy. Trauma often involves secrecy and power imbalances; therapeutic transparency provides corrective experience. When you make mistakes (and you will), acknowledge them directly, apologise appropriately, and repair the rupture. These repairs strengthen the alliance more than perfect practise would.

Common your relationship with your therapist Challenges and Solutions

Challenge One: Idealisation followed by devaluation.

Client initially views you as a perfect, wonderful therapist who will save them, then becomes intensely disappointed or angry when you inevitably fail to meet idealised expectations.

This reflects splitting and unstable self/other representations common in Complex PTSD and borderline features. (Coventry et al., 2020; Teicher & Samson, 2016)

Solution: Address idealisation early: I am glad you feel comfortable here, though I want to note I am human and will make mistakes.

When devaluation occurs, name it non-defensively: I notice your feelings about therapy have shifted.

Can we explore what happened?

Maintain consistent boundaries and stance through both phases, demonstrating that your care does not fluctuate with their perception.

Challenge Two: Eroticized transference.

The client develops romantic or sexual feelings towards you, which is particularly complex when trauma involves sexual abuse.

- Client might: make inappropriate comments
- dress seductively
- express attraction directly
- or request boundary violations.

Solution: Address directly but compassionately: I notice some romantic feelings may be present.

It is common and understandable, but our relationship needs to remain professional to be helpful.

Let's explore where these feelings come from and what needs they represent.

Maintain firm boundaries whilst exploring meanings.

If you feel unable to manage this therapeutically, consult a supervisor or refer.

Never engage inappropriately, regardless of the client's pursuit.

Challenge Three: Excessive dependency.

Client calls constantly between sessions, requests extra sessions, cannot function without your input, or becomes severely distressed by normal breaks.

Solution: Establish clear boundaries from the outset: session frequency, phone contact policies, and break schedules.

When dependency emerges, address it therapeutically: Let's explore what makes it so difficult when we're not in session.

Build their independent coping whilst providing appropriate availability.

Avoid: becoming overly available, which reinforces dependency, or rigidly withdrawing, which recreates abandonment.

Challenge Four: Hostile or attacking behaviour.

Client becomes angry, critical, or hostile towards you.

- They might: attack your competence
- accuse you of not caring
- become verbally aggressive
- or threaten to leave treatment.

Solution: Stay calm and non-defensive.

Explore: Something I did upset you; can you help me understand what happened?

Validate feelings whilst maintaining boundaries: I understand you are angry, and that's important to address, but I need you to speak to me respectfully.

Recognise that hostility often masks fear or hurt.

If safety is threatened, set firmer boundaries or end treatment with appropriate referral.

Challenge Five: Testing behaviour.

Client tests whether you are trustworthy by missing appointments, not following through on homework, revealing minimal information, making small rule violations, or creating crises.

Solution: Recognise testing as attachment-based rather than wilful resistance.

Respond consistently and predictably to tests, demonstrating you are different from past harmful people.

Name pattern when appropriate: I wonder if you are testing whether I'll give up on you.

I am committed to working with you even when it is difficult.

Pass tests by maintaining engagement whilst holding appropriate boundaries.

Challenge Six: Dissociation during sessions.

Client spaces out, appears absent, or cannot recall session content.

Solution: Assess dissociation formally and regularly.

Teach grounding techniques for use during sessions.

Check in frequently: Are you with me right now?

If dissociation occurs, gently ground before continuing therapeutic work.

Adjust pace, overwhelming material triggers dissociation.

Consider trauma-focused treatment for dissociation (e.g., EMDR with dissociation protocol) if severe. (Shapiro, 2018)

Work on dual awareness, being able to hold both present safety and trauma memory simultaneously.

Treatment Planning and Case Formulation

- Comprehensive case formulation guides treatment decisions. Effective formulation includes predisposing factors (developmental history, pre-trauma vulnerabilities, prior trauma)
- precipitating factors (index trauma, why PTSD developed)
- perpetuating factors (maintaining PTSD: avoidance, negative cognitions, lack of support, ongoing stress)
- and protective factors (strengths, supports, motivation). This formulation, shared collaboratively with the client, creates a roadmap for treatment.

Distinguish standard PTSD from Complex PTSD in treatment planning. (Mavranezouli et al., 2020; Teicher & Samson, 2016)

- Standard PTSD: focal trauma-focused treatment
- relatively brief treatment (12-20 sessions often sufficient)
- a primary focus on trauma processing
- and good prognosis with an evidence-based treatment.

Complex PTSD: (Karatzias et al., 2019; Teicher & Samson, 2016)

- Complex PTSD: phase-based approach (Herman, 2015; Teicher & Samson, 2016)
- extended treatment timeline
- stabilisation before trauma processing
- attention to emotion dysregulation, self-concept, and relationships
- and integration of multiple modalities.

Attempting intensive trauma processing without adequate stabilisation in Complex PTSD typically fails or worsens symptoms. (Lewis et al., 2020; Teicher & Samson, 2016)

- Phase-based treatment for Complex PTSD: Phase One (Stabilisation): ensure safety
- build emotion regulation skills (Linehan, 2015)
- address substance use or self-harm if present
- establish your relationship with your therapist
- create crisis plan
- and build life stability.

Duration: weeks to months.

- Phase Two (Trauma Processing): process traumatic memories
- challenge negative cognitions
- address the meaning of trauma
- work on specific trauma-related difficulties.

Duration: months.

- Phase Three (Integration/Reconnection): consolidate gains
- build life beyond trauma
- work on relationships and meaning
- plan termination.

Duration: months.

Do not rigidly adhere to phases; some movement between them occurs naturally.

Monitor progress systematically.

Use standardised measures (PCL-5, PHQ-9, WSAS) every 4-6 sessions minimum.

Track: symptom severity, functional impairment, quality of life, and treatment targets.

- If progress stalls, reassess formulation
- consider complicating factors
- adjust treatment approach
- increase or decrease intensity
- or consult a colleague.
- Lack of progress might indicate insufficient dose
- wrong treatment for this client
- untreated comorbidity, ongoing trauma (Najavits, 2002)
- or need for a different approach.

Do not persist with ineffective treatment; adapt or refer.

Managing Challenging Clinical Situations

Challenge: Client refuses trauma-focused treatment.

They want symptom management without addressing trauma directly.

Solution: Explore resistance compassionately; fear of trauma work is normal and understandable.

Provide psychoeducation about evidence-based showing trauma-focused work produces better outcomes.

Consider: Is stabilisation adequate?

Are there cultural factors affecting willingness?

Is avoidance too entrenched to confront immediately?

If the client maintains refusal after a thorough discussion, respect autonomy whilst continuing to offer trauma-focused treatment.

Symptom management alone typically produces limited, temporary gains, but forced treatment violates collaboration and consent.

Challenge: Client deteriorates during trauma processing.

Symptoms worsen; functioning declines, self-harm increases, or suicidal ideation intensifies.

Solution: Return to stabilisation immediately.

Do not push through deterioration, assuming it is necessary suffering, which risks re-traumatisation and treatment dropout.

Assess: Was stabilisation truly adequate?

Is the pace too fast?

Are there current stressors amplifying vulnerability?

Is dissociation interfering?

Rebuild the foundation before resuming trauma work.

Some temporary worsening is expected, but sustained deterioration indicates problems requiring adjustment.

Challenge: Client reports recovering memories of previously forgotten trauma.

Approach very carefully, given memory's malleability and controversy around recovered memories.

Neither assume memories are true nor definitely false; both positions are problematic.

Believe the client's distress is regardless of memory accuracy.

- Avoid: suggestive questioning
- confirming or denying memory accuracy
- encouraging memory recovery as a treatment goal (Bisson et al., 2019)
- or investigating historical accuracy.

Focus on current symptoms: emotion processing, functional improvement, and therapeutic relationship.

If legal issues emerge, refer to appropriate legal resources.

Consult ethics guidelines and a legal consultant if needed.

Challenge: Client threatens suicide.

Conduct a thorough risk assessment: intent, plan, means, protective factors, history of attempts, current symptoms, social support, and substance use.

Low risk: increase contact frequency, ensure crisis plan, address factors increasing risk, maintain treatment focus.

Moderate risk: similar to low risk, plus consider family involvement, remove means, if possible, and possibly daily contact.

High risk with imminent danger: hospitalisation if the client cannot contract for safety or lacks protective factors.

Do not avoid addressing suicidality directly; research shows asking about suicide does not increase risk, and appropriate intervention saves lives.

Document risk assessment thoroughly.

Challenge: Client discloses ongoing abuse.

Take immediate action to ensure safety.

For child abuse: mandatory reporting applies; report to the appropriate authorities per your jurisdiction.

- For adult intimate partner violence: safety assessment and planning
- provide domestic violence resources
- support the client's autonomy while ensuring they understand danger
- avoid mandating leaving (which can increase risk)
- document carefully
- and offer ongoing support.

Do not: ignore ongoing abuse to focus on past trauma; current trauma takes precedence.

Trauma treatment cannot progress whilst trauma continues.

Evidence-Based Treatment Protocols: Implementation Guidance

Prolonged Exposure (PE): Highly effective for PTSD involving clear trauma memories.

PAUSE POINT: Ground Yourself

- • Notice 5 things you can SEE

- Components: psychoeducation
- breathing retraining
- imaginal exposure (repeated retelling of trauma)
- in vivo exposure (approaching avoided situations)
- processing.

Implementation tips: Explain the rationale thoroughly; clients need to understand why exposure works.

Start imaginal exposure early (session 3-4); do not spend too many sessions on psychoeducation.

Ensure the client provides a detailed narrative, including sensory details, thoughts, and emotions.

Process after exposure: What did you notice?

What surprised you?

How was it different from the feared outcome?

Assign regular between-session exposure practice; the treatment effect depends on repetition.

- PE adaptations for complex cases: Slow pace for complex trauma
- address emotion regulation deficits before starting
- manage dissociation carefully
- process multiple traumas sequentially
- extend treatment duration. Contraindications: severe dissociation
- active self-harm
- severe substance dependence (Lader, 2011; Ashton, 2002)
- imminent safety threats
- or cognitive impairment preventing engagement. If contraindicated, address contraindications first or select alternative treatment.

Cognitive Processing Therapy (CPT): Excellent for addressing stuck points and negative cognitions. (Resick & Schnicke, 2016)

- Components: psychoeducation
- written trauma account (optional)
- identifying stuck points
- Socratic questioning
- challenging questions
- and patterns of problematic thinking worksheets.

Implementation tips: Stuck points are key; identify them early and return to them throughout.

Common stuck points: safety (the world is dangerous), trust (no one can be trusted), power/control (I am helpless), esteem (I am worthless), intimacy (relationships aren't safe).

Use Socratic questioning rather than directly challenging.

What evidence supports/contradicts this?

What would you tell a friend who thinks this?

Assign homework consistently; practice occurs between sessions.

CPT adaptations: For clients who cannot write a trauma account, use imaginal exposure, or skip the written account entirely, stuck point work is an essential component. For multiple traumas, address sequentially or identify overarching stuck points that apply across traumas. For complex trauma, extend treatment and combine with emotion regulation skills. Consider cultural factors in stuck points; some beliefs are culturally normative rather than trauma-specific. (Linehan, 2015)

EMDR: Effective across trauma types. (Shapiro, 2018)

- Eight phases: history taking
- preparation
- assessment
- desensitization
- installation
- body scan
- closure
- revaluation.

Implementation tips: Adequate preparation is crucial; ensure the client has grounding skills and a safe place visualization before processing.

Standard protocol: identify target memory, negative cognition, positive cognition, emotions, body sensations, and SUDs rating.

Begin bilateral stimulation whilst the client focuses on memory. (Shapiro, 2018)

Stop every 15-30 seconds: What do you notice now?

Follow the client's processing without directing.

Process until SUDs reach 0-1 and positive cognition feels completely true (VOC 6-7).

EMDR adaptations: For dissociation, use a modified protocol with more grounding, a slower pace, and potentially fractionated processing. For complex trauma, prepare thoroughly with resourcing before trauma processing. For recent trauma, use the recent event protocol. For attachment trauma, consider integrating Schema Therapy concepts. Training is essential. EMDR appears simple but requires supervised practice to implement effectively. (Shapiro, 2018)

Working with Comorbidities

Depression and PTSD commonly co-occur.

Assess carefully whether depression is independent or secondary to PTSD.

If secondary (developed after trauma, improves when PTSD improves), treat PTSD primarily; depression often improves with trauma treatment.

If independent or severe, consider concurrent antidepressant and/or adding behavioural activation. (NICE, 2018; Baldwin et al., 2014)

Monitor suicide risk closely as both conditions increase risk.

Do not delay trauma treatment waiting for depression to improve unless depression prevents engagement; treating PTSD often improves depressive symptoms.

Substance use disorders and PTSD: extremely common, complex comorbidity. (Najavits, 2002)

Two primary approaches: sequential (treat substance use first, then PTSD) or integrated (treat simultaneously).

Evidence increasingly supports integrated treatment when possible.

For active severe dependence requiring detox, address substance use first. (Lader, 2011; Ashton, 2002)

For problematic but not severe use, integrated trauma and substance treatment works well.

Key principle: help the client understand the functional relationship, substances manage PTSD symptoms but maintain them long-term.

Trauma treatment reduces the need for substances.

Sobriety allows trauma processing.

Each supports the other.

Personality disorders and PTSD: Complex PTSD shares features with borderline, avoidant, and dependent personality disorders. (Cusack et al., 2016; Teicher & Samson, 2016)

Question whether personality pathology is independent or represents complex trauma effects.

Often, treating developmental trauma addresses personality features. (Teicher & Samson, 2016)

- For true personality disorder, integrate approaches, DBT or Schema Therapy for borderline features
- trauma-focused treatment for PTSD
- and work on interpersonal patterns.

Long-term treatment is required.

Maintain clear boundaries given relationship difficulties.

Psychotic disorders: PTSD can involve psychotic features (flashbacks can resemble hallucinations). Genuine psychotic disorder complicates trauma treatment. Ensure psychotic symptoms are stabilised before intensive trauma work. Coordinate with the psychiatrist. Standard trauma protocols might overwhelm; use gentler approaches, slower pace, more support. Some evidence suggests trauma treatment is possible with psychotic disorders when carefully implemented.

Cultural Competence in Trauma Treatment

Cultural humility is essential in trauma treatment.

Recognise that your cultural lens shapes your understanding of trauma, healing, and appropriate treatment.

What constitutes trauma varies culturally.

Collectivist cultures might prioritise family harmony over individual healing.

Some cultures somatise distress rather than psychologize.

Trauma responses considered pathological in Western psychiatry might be culturally normative elsewhere.

Approach each client with curiosity about their cultural context rather than assuming Western conceptualizations apply universally.

Assess cultural factors explicitly: What is the client's cultural background?

What are cultural beliefs about trauma and mental health?

What cultural resources support healing (community, spirituality, traditional practices)?

Are there cultural barriers to treatment (stigma, collectivist versus individualist values, gender roles)?

What is the acculturation level of an immigrant?

Has the client experienced discrimination, microaggressions, or systemic trauma?

Include cultural formulation in case conceptualisation, culture isn't an addition to treatment but integral to understanding the client's experience.

Historical trauma affects communities collectively, including colonisation, slavery, genocide, and forced assimilation.

Indigenous peoples, African Americans, and other oppressed groups carry intergenerational trauma transmitted culturally and possibly epigenetically.

Individual PTSD treatment without acknowledging collective trauma misses crucial context.

- Integrate: acknowledgement of historical trauma

PAUSE POINT: Ground Yourself

- Notice 5 things you can SEE
- validation of ongoing systemic oppression

- attention to cultural identity as a source of resilience (Bonanno, 2004)
- and connection to community healing traditions when appropriate.

Language matters. Working through an interpreter adds complexity but shouldn't prevent treatment. Use professional trauma-trained interpreters when possible. Brief interpreter on trauma content beforehand. Be aware that trauma concepts might not translate directly; PTSD as a diagnostic category is a Western construct. Some cultures have different frameworks for understanding trauma's impacts. Work within the client's framework whilst offering an evidence-based treatment adapted appropriately.

LGBTQ+ clients require affirming care.

- Use correct pronouns
- do not assume heterosexuality
- understand minority stress
- recognise that discrimination, family rejection, and hate crimes constitute identity-based trauma
- address internalized homophobia/transphobia therapeutically
- and connect clients with LGBTQ+ affirming resources.

Non-affirming treatment harms LGBTQ+ clients and violates ethical principles.

If you cannot provide affirming care due to personal beliefs, refer to an affirming provider rather than attempting conversion or denying identity validity.

Vicarious Traumatisation and Clinician Self-Care (Stamm, 2010; Pearlman & Saakvitne, 1995)

Vicarious traumatisation (VT), trauma symptoms developing from exposure to clients' trauma material, is an occupational hazard in trauma work. (Stamm, 2010; Pearlman & Saakvitne, 1995)

VT differs from burnout (exhaustion from workload) and compassion fatigue (emotional exhaustion from empathising).

- VT specifically involves intrusive thoughts about clients' traumas
- hypervigilance about dangers you didn't previously notice (Porges, 2011; Yehuda & Seckl, 2011)
- a changed worldview (world seems more dangerous)
- emotional numbing
- and trauma dreams involving clients' material.

VT is a normal response to difficult work, not personal weakness.

Preventing and addressing VT requires a multilevel approach.

- Individual strategies: regular personal therapy

- strong separation between work and home
- engaging in activities providing meaning beyond trauma work
- physical self-care (exercise, sleep, nutrition)
- creative outlets
- spiritual practices if relevant
- and limiting trauma caseload percentage.
- Professional strategies: regular supervision discussing both clinical issues and VT
- consultation groups with colleagues
- ongoing training maintaining sense of competence
- varying your caseload
- and taking breaks from trauma work periodically.
- Organisational strategies: employers should provide trauma-informed supervision
- reasonable caseloads
- administrative support, reducing burden
- opportunities for training
- space for processing difficult cases
- and a culture acknowledging VT without shame. If your organisation does not support trauma workers adequately, advocate for changes or consider alternative settings. You cannot provide optimal trauma care whilst sacrificing your wellbeing, that's unsustainable and ultimately harms clients.

Monitor yourself for VT symptoms regularly.

- If you notice: dreading seeing trauma clients
- intrusive thoughts about their traumas
- avoidance of trauma material in sessions
- emotional numbing
- increased cynicism
- sleep disturbance
- or relationship problems attributable to work, address immediately.
- Increase supervision
- reduce trauma caseload temporarily
- ensure adequate self-care
- consider personal therapy
- and do not ignore symptoms, hoping they'll resolve.

VT untreated worsens and can end careers; early intervention prevents serious impairment.

Ethical Considerations in Trauma Treatment

Boundary management requires particular attention in trauma work.

Clients with attachment wounds might push boundaries, testing your reliability or seeking corrective relationship experience.

Maintain consistent professional boundaries whilst being warm and genuine.

Clear boundaries provide the safety trauma survivors need; they demonstrate predictability, structure, and safety.

When boundary violations occur (client or therapist), address them immediately and repair explicitly.

Boundary crossings (minor, non-harmful) might be therapeutically indicated sometimes (limited self-disclosure, attending an important client event) but should be intentional, discussed, and documented.

Informed consent is an ongoing process in trauma work.

- Initially, explain PTSD treatment approaches
- describe potential benefits and risks
- clarify your qualifications
- discuss session structure and expectations
- explain limits of confidentiality
- and address questions.
- Throughout treatment: obtain consent for specific interventions, especially trauma processing
- check consent continues
- explain changes in treatment approach
- and recognise the client can withdraw consent.

Trauma survivors have had consent violated, therapeutic consent process itself can be healing when done properly.

Mandatory reporting creates ethical complexity.

You must report child abuse and often elder/dependent adult abuse, per jurisdiction.

However, reporting might rupture the your relationship with your therapist if the client feels betrayed.

- When possible, explain mandatory reporting limits during informed consent before disclosure
- explore the situation thoroughly before determining if the reporting threshold is met
- involve the client in the reporting process (reporting with them rather than on them when safe)
- and maintain a therapeutic relationship post-report, acknowledging rupture whilst explaining legal requirements.

This balances legal duties with the therapeutic relationship.

Competence requires ongoing attention.

Only provide treatment you are qualified to deliver.

Seek appropriate training and supervision when working with populations or presenting problems outside your expertise.

Recognise your limitations: if the client needs intensive trauma treatment and you are not trained, refer.

If the client has a comorbidity you cannot address, coordinate with other providers, or refer. (Najavits, 2002)

If cultural factors require understanding your lack, seek consultation or refer to a culturally matched provider.

Practising outside competence harms clients and violates ethical codes.

Documentation in trauma cases requires care.

- Document: assessment findings
- treatment plan
- interventions provided
- client response
- risk assessment
- and significant clinical decisions.

However, be judicious about trauma details in records; include what's clinically necessary, but recognise records might be subpoenaed.

Client's safety and privacy matter.

Note: Client discussed childhood trauma without documenting graphic details.

If providing forensic evaluation, documentation requirements differ; seek specialised training.

Know your jurisdiction's laws regarding records, retention, and access.

Concluding Recommendations for Clinicians

Trauma work is a profound privilege; clients trust you with their most painful experiences, allow you to witness their courage, and invite you into their healing.

- This work requires: clinical competence maintained through training and supervision
- emotional capacity to hold pain without fixing or fleeing
- humility about what you do not know
- respect for clients' resilience and agency (Bonanno, 2004)
- and commitment to your own well-being.

The evidence shows trauma treatment works when delivered competently.

Your role as a clinician is essential to recovery; your knowledge, skill, consistency, and care provide the foundation clients need to heal from devastating experiences. (Watkins et al., 2018)

Continue learning throughout your career.

Trauma research evolves constantly with new approaches, refinements to existing treatments, and a deeper understanding of trauma's impacts.

Attend conferences, read current literature, pursue advanced training, and engage with colleagues.

Maintain curiosity and openness whilst grounding yourself in evidence-based.

Balance fidelity to protocols with flexibility for individual clients.

Remember that behind every trauma diagnosis is a person with a unique history, strengths, and goals.

Treat the person, not just the disorder.

Finally, recognise impact of your work extends beyond individual clients.

Each person you help heal from trauma creates ripples; they form healthier relationships, parent more effectively, contribute to communities, and avoid passing trauma to the next generation.

Your work in preventing the transmission of trauma across generations represents a profound contribution to reducing suffering.

On difficult days when work feels overwhelming, remember you are not just treating symptoms, you are helping people reclaim lives trauma tried to take from them.

Chapter Twenty: Combat and Military Trauma - Unique Considerations for Veterans (Seal et al., 2007)

- Military trauma involves unique contextual factors (Seal et al., 2007)
- Service culture affects help-seeking and treatment
- Evidence-based approaches work for combat veterans (Seal et al., 2007)
- Recovery honours your service and sacrifice (Brewin et al., 2017)

Combat-related PTSD presents unique challenges and considerations distinct from civilian trauma. Military service members and veterans experience trauma within specific cultural, operational, and organisational contexts that profoundly influence symptom presentation, help-seeking behaviours, and treatment needs. Understanding these unique factors proves essential for effective treatment of military populations. This chapter addresses combat exposure and deployment-related trauma, moral injury, military sexual trauma, transition challenges from military to civilian life, veteran-specific resources, and adaptations of evidence-based treatments for military populations. (Seal et al., 2007)

The Nature of Combat Trauma: Characteristics of Military-Related PTSD

Combat trauma differs from many civilian traumas in several important ways that affect PTSD presentation and treatment.

Combat typically involves repeated, prolonged trauma exposure rather than single incidents.

Deployment lengths of 6 to 15 months or longer mean sustained threat exposure, chronic stress, and accumulated traumatic events.

Unlike single-incident civilian trauma, where recovery can begin immediately after the event, combat veterans experienced months of ongoing danger where the threat never fully abated. (Seal et al., 2007)

This chronic nature often produces more severe and complex PTSD presentations. (Ford et al., 2019; Teicher & Samson, 2016)

Combat exposure encompasses diverse traumatic experiences including direct combat firefights, incoming mortar or rocket attacks, witnessing serious injury or death of fellow service members, killing or believing you killed enemy combatants, encountering dead bodies or human remains, caring for wounded or dying comrades, participating in or witnessing atrocities, being injured oneself, close calls with death, handling human remains, and encountering child casualties. Many veterans experience multiple types of trauma during a single deployment, creating complex symptom patterns where different memories trigger distinct trauma responses. (Seal et al., 2007)

The unpredictability and lack of control characterising modern warfare, particularly operations in Iraq and Afghanistan, created sustained hypervigilance. (Porges, 2011; Yehuda & Seckl, 2011)

Improvised explosive devices, roadside bombs, suicide attacks, and asymmetric warfare meant threats could emerge anywhere, anytime, from anyone.

This unpredictability produces especially severe hyperarousal symptoms that persist long after returning home.

Veterans describe never feeling truly safe, constantly scanning for threats, struggling to relax even years after deployment. (Seal et al., 2007)

This chronic hypervigilance exhausts psychological and physical resources, significantly impairing quality of life. (Porges, 2011; Yehuda & Seckl, 2011)

Moral Injury: When Trauma Violates Core Values

Moral injury, whilst distinct from PTSD, frequently co-occurs with combat-related PTSD and significantly complicates treatment.

Moral injury occurs when someone perpetrates, witnesses, or fails to prevent actions that violate deeply held moral or ethical beliefs.

Combat situations frequently create moral dilemmas with no good choices, where following orders, surviving, or protecting comrades requires actions conflicting with peacetime moral codes.

- Examples include killing or harming civilians, including children, even when operationally necessary (Cohen et al., 2016; Cohen & Mannarino, 2008)
- participating in or witnessing abuse of prisoners
- making decisions resulting in deaths of civilians or fellow service members
- following orders perceived as unethical
- failing to save wounded comrades
- or witnessing atrocities without the ability to intervene.

Moral injury produces profound guilt, shame, self-condemnation, and loss of trust in oneself, others, and moral institutions.

Whilst PTSD centres on threat and fear responses, moral injury revolves around guilt, shame, and existential questions about one's fundamental goodness.

Veterans with moral injury might believe they are irredeemably bad, unworthy of forgiveness, or permanently tainted by their actions. (Seal et al., 2007)

These beliefs create intense suffering and hopelessness that standard PTSD treatments inadequately address.

Moral injury requires specific therapeutic approaches addressing guilt, shame, forgiveness, and meaning-making rather than solely fear reduction.

Military Culture and Help-Seeking Barriers

Military culture profoundly influences how service members and veterans perceive and respond to PTSD symptoms. (Seal et al., 2007)

Cultural values emphasising strength, self-reliance, stoicism, and mission accomplishment create powerful barriers to acknowledging psychological difficulties and seeking help.

Admitting mental health struggles might feel like weakness, failure, or letting down one's unit.

Service members fear that seeking help will result in being seen as unreliable, losing the trust of comrades, being removed from deployment or duties, damaging career prospects, or appearing weak to peers and leadership.

These concerns are not entirely unfounded; historically, mental health problems could derail military careers, and stigma within units remains substantial.

Unit cohesion, whilst protective during deployment, can paradoxically impair help-seeking.

The intense bonds formed in combat create powerful loyalty and reluctance to burden brothers and sisters in arms with psychological problems.

Veterans might avoid treatment to maintain the image of coping well, not wanting to appear weaker than comrades who seem unaffected. (Seal et al., 2007)

Alternatively, entire units might normalise significant symptoms, creating group denial where serious PTSD is dismissed as normal stress.

Breaking through this cultural resistance requires understanding and respecting military values whilst reframing treatment as strength rather than weakness, emphasising that seeking help demonstrates courage and commitment to optimal functioning, enables continued service to others, and honours those who served by taking care of oneself.

Transition Challenges: From Military to Civilian Life

Transitioning from military to civilian life presents significant challenges even for veterans without PTSD. (Seal et al., 2007)

For those with combat trauma, this transition compounds difficulties.

The military provides clear structure, defined roles, strong social bonds, shared purpose, and mission-oriented existence.

Civilian life often feels chaotic, meaningless, isolating, and overwhelmingly complex after military service.

Veterans describe feeling lost without the structure and purpose military service provided, struggling to find meaning in civilian employment that seems trivial compared to combat missions, missing the camaraderie and trust of military units, feeling misunderstood by civilians who cannot relate to military experiences, and experiencing difficulty with civilian social norms and communication styles. (Seal et al., 2007)

PTSD symptoms complicate transition further by creating hypervigilance in civilian environments perceived as dangerously uncontrolled, avoidance of crowds and public places, irritability and anger damaging civilian relationships, difficulty trusting civilian employers and institutions, and numbing or detachment preventing connection with civilian life. Supporting successful transition requires addressing both PTSD symptoms and broader adjustment challenges, helping veterans find new purpose and meaning, develop civilian social connections, translate military skills to civilian contexts, and navigate practical challenges like employment, education, and benefits. (Porges, 2011; Yehuda & Seckl, 2011)

Military Sexual Trauma: A Hidden Epidemic

Military sexual trauma, sexual assault or severe sexual harassment occurring during military service, affects significant numbers of service members and creates particularly severe PTSD.

Approximately 23 per cent of women veterans and 1 per cent of male veterans report military sexual trauma. (Seal et al., 2007)

These numbers likely underestimate true prevalence due to underreporting driven by fear of retaliation, disbelief, or career consequences.

Military sexual trauma differs from civilian sexual assault in several ways that complicate recovery. (Cloitre et al., 2020)

Perpetrators are often fellow service members, sometimes within the survivor's chain of command, creating ongoing contact impossible to avoid.

Reporting may result in retaliation, ostracism, or being blamed whilst perpetrators face minimal consequences.

Military culture's emphasis on unit cohesion can pressure survivors to remain silent to avoid disrupting the unit.

Survivors might continue serving alongside perpetrators, re-traumatised daily by forced proximity.

The betrayal inherent in military sexual trauma profoundly damages trust and safety.

Survivors trusted their military family to protect them, and that trust was catastrophically violated.

This betrayal creates unique challenges for treatment, particularly in developing therapeutic relationships and trusting institutions.

Military sexual trauma survivors often experience both PTSD from the assault itself and separate PTSD from combat or other military trauma, requiring treatment addressing multiple traumas. (Seal et al., 2007)

Shame and self-blame are particularly intense, with survivors internalising messages that they somehow invited or deserved the assault, failed to prevent it, or overreacted by reporting it.

Adapting Evidence-Based Treatments for Veterans (Seal et al., 2007)

Evidence-based PTSD treatments, Prolonged Exposure, Cognitive Processing Therapy, and EMDR, are effective for combat veterans when appropriately adapted to military populations. However, standard protocols require modifications addressing unique aspects of military trauma. Therapists treating veterans should understand military culture, structure, terminology, and deployment experiences to build credibility and rapport. Using military language appropriately, respecting military service and sacrifice, and demonstrating knowledge of military operations facilitates engagement. Veterans are more likely to trust and engage with therapists who understand their experiences. (Shapiro, 2018)

Prolonged Exposure for combat veterans involves in vivo exposure to safe situations avoided due to trauma, such as crowded places, loud noises, or driving, and imaginal exposure processing combat memories through repeated, detailed recounting. (Foa et al., 2007; Powers et al., 2010)

Veterans might initially resist imaginal exposure, viewing it as dwelling on the past or wallowing rather than moving forward. (Seal et al., 2007)

Framing exposure as courage to face difficult memories rather than weakness helps overcome resistance.

For moral injury, Cognitive Processing Therapy's focus on challenging guilt and shame-based thoughts proves particularly valuable, addressing stuck points like 'I should have saved him,' 'I am a murderer,' or 'I don't deserve to be happy.' Processing these beliefs requires careful, nuanced work acknowledging the genuine moral complexity of combat whilst helping veterans develop more balanced, compassionate perspectives. (Resick & Schnicke, 2016)

Veteran-Specific Resources and Support Systems

Veterans in the United Kingdom have access to several dedicated resources. (Seal et al., 2007)

Combat Stress, the UK's leading military charity specialising in mental health, provides clinical treatment, residential courses, community outreach, and 24-hour helpline support specifically for veterans with PTSD. (Seal et al., 2007)

Veterans' Gateway offers a single point of contact connecting veterans and their families to support services across health, housing, employment, benefits, and social care. (Seal et al., 2007)

NHS veterans' mental health services provide priority access to mental health treatment for service leavers and veterans, with specialist trauma services available in many regions. (Seal et al., 2007)

Help for Heroes supports wounded, injured, and sick veterans and their families through recovery programmes addressing physical and psychological injuries. (Seal et al., 2007)

Peer support proves particularly valuable for veterans, who often feel civilians cannot understand their experiences. (Seal et al., 2007)

Veteran-specific support groups, facilitated or peer-led, provide a community with others who share military experiences and trauma exposure.

Many veterans find that connecting with fellow veterans reduces isolation and provides understanding unavailable elsewhere. (Seal et al., 2007)

Transition support programmes help veterans navigate the shift from military to civilian life, addressing employment, education, housing, benefits, and social integration alongside mental health treatment. (Seal et al., 2007)

Comprehensive transition support improves outcomes by addressing the broader context affecting recovery. (Watts et al., 2013)

Recovery from combat-related PTSD is achievable with appropriate treatment and support. (van Dis et al., 2020)

Evidence-based treatments work for veterans when delivered by knowledgeable clinicians in military-informed ways. (Seal et al., 2007)

Acknowledging unique aspects of military trauma, respecting military service and sacrifice, addressing moral injury alongside fear-based PTSD, supporting successful transition to civilian life, and connecting veterans with military-specific resources creates comprehensive recovery pathways. (Seal et al., 2007)

PAUSE POINT: Ground Yourself

- • Notice 5 things you can SEE

Veterans who have served their country deserve expert, compassionate care addressing the full complexity of their trauma experiences. (Seal et al., 2007)

Chapter Twenty-One: Medical Trauma and Healthcare-Related PTSD

Medical trauma, PTSD from medical events, is under-recognised yet common, affecting patients experiencing life-threatening illness, intensive medical procedures, traumatic childbirth, or prolonged hospitalisation.

- Medical PTSD develops from experiences like cancer diagnosis and treatment
- heart attacks
- stroke
- ICU stays
- organ transplants, traumatic births, paediatric illness or injury

- and medical errors causing harm.

Understanding medical trauma helps patients, families, and healthcare providers recognise and address this specific PTSD form.

What Medical Events Cause PTSD

Medical trauma involves a life threat perceived during a medical crisis or treatment.

- PTSD develops when medical experience involves believing you might die
- intense pain or distress
- feeling helpless or out of control
- invasive procedures
- witnessing frightening medical equipment or procedures
- being restrained or sedated against your will
- or poor communication, leaving you terrified.

The objective medical severity does not always predict PTSD; the subjective experience of fear and helplessness matters most.

Someone might develop PTSD from a seemingly routine procedure if they felt terrified and helpless during it.

Intensive Care Unit (ICU) stays are particularly predisposed to PTSD.

- ICU patients experience: life-threatening illness or injury
- delirium and hallucinations from medications
- mechanical ventilation, feeling like suffocation
- being unable to communicate
- painful procedures without adequate sedation
- and fragmented memories of terrifying experiences.

ICU survivors often have no memory of objective events but retain an emotional imprint of terror.

Post-ICU PTSD affects 10-50 per cent of ICU survivors, depending on the study.

Symptoms include intrusive memories of ICU experiences, avoidance of healthcare, hypervigilance about health, and anxiety about medical settings. (Van der Kolk et al., 1996)

Cancer diagnosis and treatment create trauma through initial diagnosis shock, threatening mortality, painful and invasive treatments, loss of control over the body, uncertain prognosis, and prolonged treatment, causing cumulative stress.

Cancer-related PTSD might focus on specific traumatic moments (hearing diagnosis, particular procedure) or the chronic stress of the entire cancer experience.

Survivors might avoid follow-up care due to trauma from treatment, paradoxically increasing health risks.

Paediatric cancer affects both the child and parents; witnessing the child's suffering creates parental PTSD.

Traumatic childbirth affects approximately 4–9 per cent of mothers who develop full PTSD.

Birth trauma might involve unexpected complications, emergency C-section, severe pain, feeling ignored by medical staff, lack of control during birth, infant health crises, or maternal near-death experiences.

Partners witnessing traumatic birth can also develop PTSD from fear of losing the partner or the baby.

Postpartum PTSD is often misdiagnosed as postpartum depression; symptoms of intrusion, avoidance, and hyperarousal distinguish PTSD.

Affects bonding with the infant and willingness to have additional children. (Cohen et al., 2016; Cohen & Mannarino, 2008)

- Medical errors and negligence create particularly complex trauma involving life threat from preventable harm
- betrayal of trust in the healthcare system
- anger and moral injury
- and difficulty seeking necessary medical care due to fear.

Medical error victims might avoid healthcare entirely, struggle with litigation trauma, experience prolonged distress from knowing harm was preventable, and face invalidation from providers minimising their experience.

This trauma requires addressing both PTSD symptoms and justified anger and loss of trust.

Symptoms and Challenges of Medical PTSD

Medical PTSD symptoms mirror standard PTSD, but with a medical context.

- Intrusion involves flashbacks to medical procedures (Van der Kolk et al., 1996)
- nightmares about illness or treatment (Ross et al., 1989)
- intrusive memories of the diagnosis moment (Van der Kolk et al., 1996)
- and physical reactions to medical reminders (nausea, thinking about chemotherapy, panic remembering ICU).
- Avoidance includes avoiding medical appointments even when necessary
- not discussing medical experience
- avoiding hospitals or medical shows
- and emotional numbing about health.
- Negative cognitions involve beliefs like: My body betrayed me

- I will never be healthy
- Doctors cannot be trusted
- I am irreparably damaged.
- Hyperarousal includes: hypervigilance about physical symptoms (Porges, 2011; Yehuda & Seckl, 2011)
- panic at minor symptoms
- difficulty sleeping in medical settings
- and exaggerated startle to medical sounds.

Medical PTSD creates a dangerous cycle: trauma from a medical event causes avoidance of healthcare, leading to delayed care for new problems, potentially causing worse medical outcomes requiring more traumatic treatment, increasing PTSD.

Breaking this cycle requires treating PTSD whilst ensuring necessary medical care continues.

Collaboration between mental health and medical providers optimises outcomes.

Children with medical trauma show: (Cohen et al., 2016; Cohen & Mannarino, 2008)

- Children with medical trauma show: regression in development (Cohen et al., 2016; Cohen & Mannarino, 2008)
- separation anxiety
- behavioural problems
- nightmares (Ross et al., 1989)
- avoidance of anything medical-related
- and extreme distress at doctor visits, even for routine care.

Parents' own distress affects children's adjustment, and parental PTSD from the child's medical trauma impairs their ability to support the child's recovery. (Cohen et al., 2016; Cohen & Mannarino, 2008)

Family-based treatment addresses both the child's trauma and parents' distress.

- Chronic illness creates ongoing trauma reminders through repeated medical procedures
- unpredictable symptom flares
- medication side effects
- functional limitations, and an uncertain future.

Standard trauma treatment emphasises processing past trauma, but chronic illness involves current ongoing stressors.

- Treatment adapts by building coping skills for managing ongoing medical stress
- processing specific traumatic medical events while acknowledging continuing challenges
- developing meaning despite illness

- and maintaining quality of life alongside medical management.

Treatment for Medical PTSD

Standard evidence-based PTSD treatments adapt well for medical trauma.

Prolonged Exposure involves imaginal exposure to traumatic medical memories (recounting diagnosis, surgery, ICU stay) and in vivo exposure to avoided medical situations (hospitals, doctor offices, medical equipment).

Patients initially fear that revisiting medical trauma will overwhelm them, but repeated exposure reduces distress whilst maintaining the ability to access necessary medical care.

Cognitive Processing Therapy addresses beliefs medical trauma creates: (Resick & Schnicke, 2016)

- Cognitive Processing Therapy addresses beliefs medical trauma creates: My body cannot be trusted (Resick & Schnicke, 2016)

PAUSE POINT: Ground Yourself

- • Notice 5 things you can SEE

- I am fragile and might die any moment
- Medical professionals do not care about me
- I caused my illness through my actions.

Challenging these beliefs whilst acknowledging medical realities (yes, health is uncertain; no, this does not mean constant catastrophic thinking is helpful) creates a balanced perspective.

Particularly important for patients with chronic illness who must hold both uncertainty and the ability to live fully despite it.

EMDR works well for discrete medical traumas like traumatic birth or a specific, frightening procedure. (Shapiro, 2018)

Targeting the worst moments of medical experience whilst developing resources and positive cognitions supports processing.

Some patients process the entire medical experience; others target specific memories, causing most distress.

Flexibility in approach matches individual needs.

Trauma-focused CBT for children adapts to paediatric medical trauma. (Bisson et al., 2013; NICE, 2018)

- Involves: age-appropriate psychoeducation
- gradual exposure using play, drawing, or narrative
- parent involvement addressing parental distress
- and coordination with the medical team.

The goal is to reduce children's medical PTSD whilst supporting continued necessary medical care without re-traumatisation. (Cohen et al., 2016; Cohen & Mannarino, 2008)

Coordination with the medical team enhances treatment.

- Inform medical providers about PTSD so they can: provide trauma-informed care during appointments
- explain procedures beforehand
- allow patient control where possible
- and offer anxiolytic medication for procedures triggering severe anxiety.

Some healthcare systems offer psychological consultation in medical settings, addressing trauma during ongoing care.

Prevention of Medical PTSD

Healthcare systems can reduce medical PTSD through trauma-informed practices.

- Effective prevention includes adequate pain management during procedures
- clear communication about what to expect
- involving patients in decisions, maximising autonomy
- providing psychological support during treatment
- screening for distress and early intervention
- and validating patient experiences.

ICU diaries, written records of ICU stay, help patients understand what happened, reduce post-ICU PTSD.

Early intervention after a traumatic medical event prevents chronic PTSD.

- Psychological first aid immediately post-trauma
- screening for acute stress disorder
- providing psychoeducation about normal trauma responses
- and ensuring access to mental health care if symptoms persist all support recovery. (Ehring et al., 2014)

Do not wait for symptoms to become chronic; early treatment produces better outcomes.

For patients with chronic illness requiring ongoing medical care, psychological support throughout treatment prevents cumulative trauma.

Integrating mental health care with medical treatment, teaching coping skills before traumatic procedures, processing difficult experiences soon after they occur, and addressing medical anxiety as it develops all prevent medical PTSD from developing or worsening.

Medical PTSD is legitimate trauma deserving recognition and treatment.

Having PTSD from medical experience does not diminish your strength; it reflects a normal response to life-threatening or overwhelming medical events.

Treatment allows you to process medical trauma whilst maintaining necessary healthcare.

Recovery means living fully despite medical history, managing health proactively without terror, and building life beyond illness or injury. (Coventry et al., 2020)

You deserve both good physical health care and mental health support; they work together to support your overall well-being.

Chapter Twenty-Two: First Responder and Emergency Services Trauma

First responders, police, firefighters, paramedics, emergency dispatchers, and emergency room staff face repeated trauma exposure, creating cumulative PTSD risk. (Haugen et al., 2012)

Unlike single-incident trauma, first responder trauma accumulates across years through: (Haugen et al., 2012)

- Unlike single-incident trauma, first responder trauma accumulates across years through: witnessing death and severe injury repeatedly (Haugen et al., 2012)
- responding to child deaths and abuse
- making life-or-death decisions under pressure
- experiencing a threat to own safety
- and lacking time to process before the next call.

Understanding first responder PTSD's unique aspects supports prevention, early intervention, and treatment for this population serving communities whilst managing extraordinary stress.

Cumulative Trauma in Emergency Services

First responder trauma differs from civilian trauma through cumulative exposure. (Haugen et al., 2012)

A single traumatic call might not cause PTSD, but hundreds of calls over the years create vulnerability.

- Particularly traumatic calls include child deaths from any cause
- mass casualty incidents
- line-of-duty deaths of colleagues
- violence against responders
- prolonged rescue attempts ending in death
- and calls involving people the responder knows personally.

These events layer upon routine exposure to human suffering, creating a cumulative toll.

Occupational culture affects help-seeking.

- First responder culture values: toughness and ability to handle stress
- helping others whilst minimising own needs
- not showing weakness to colleagues
- and belief that trauma exposure is just part of the job.

This culture delays treatment whilst symptoms worsen.

Fear that mental health treatment affects career, concerns about confidentiality, and belief that PTSD equals inability to do the job all prevent responders from accessing needed care.

Changing culture to normalise mental health treatment as professional self-care rather than weakness supports earlier intervention.

Compassion fatigue and burnout compound PTSD.

Compassion fatigue involves emotional exhaustion from constantly empathising with suffering.

Burnout involves exhaustion from job demands.

- Both interact with PTSD, creating a compound effect: PTSD symptoms increase stress
- stress worsens PTSD
- compassion fatigue reduces motivation for self-care
- burnout depletes resources for coping.

Addressing all three issues simultaneously rather than treating PTSD in isolation produces better outcomes.

Hypervigilance serves a protective function on duty, but creates problems off duty. (Porges, 2011; Yehuda & Seckl, 2011)

First responders must maintain heightened awareness, scanning for dangers, responding rapidly to threats, and making split-second decisions. (Haugen et al., 2012)

This necessary occupational hypervigilance becomes chronic, preventing relaxation off duty. (Porges, 2011; Yehuda & Seckl, 2011)

- Responders might: scan environments constantly, even during leisure
- sleep poorly due to arousal
- startle excessively
- experience road rage from aggressive driving habits
- and struggle to transition from work mode to family mode.

Learning to intentionally shift between professional vigilance and off-duty relaxation is a recovery challenge. (Mavranezouli et al., 2020)

Secondary trauma affects dispatchers and communication centre staff who hear but cannot see incidents, creating unique distress.

- Dispatchers experience listening to callers in crisis without visual information
- making critical decisions affecting outcomes
- bearing responsibility if help does not arrive in time
- and accumulating hundreds of traumatic calls without physical action.

Dispatcher PTSD is under-recognised but rates approach those of field responders.

Recognition and treatment access for dispatchers remains inadequate despite significant risk.

Treatment Adapted for First Responders (Haugen et al., 2012)

Evidence-based PTSD treatments work for first responders with adaptations respecting the occupational context. (Haugen et al., 2012)

Prolonged Exposure processes accumulated traumatic calls sequentially or target the worst incidents, causing the most distress. (Foa et al., 2007; Powers et al., 2010)

Responders benefit from understanding that processing trauma does not eliminate the ability to respond professionally; it enhances it by reducing intrusive symptoms that impair functioning.

Some responders fear treatment will make them too emotional for the job, but evidence shows trauma treatment improves occupational functioning.

Cognitive Processing Therapy addresses the beliefs first responders develop: (Resick & Schnicke, 2016)

- Cognitive Processing Therapy addresses the beliefs first responders develop: I should have done more (guilt over outcomes beyond their control)
- I failed because the person died despite my efforts (unrealistic responsibility)
- I cannot be close to family because of what I have seen (isolation)

- or I am damaged beyond repair (hopelessness).

Challenging these beliefs whilst acknowledging occupational realities (yes, you cannot save everyone; no, this does not mean you failed) creates a balanced perspective supporting continued service without constant guilt.

Peer support programmes leverage the first responder culture, valuing peer connection.

Critical Incident Stress Management (CISM) provides structured peer support after major incidents.

Peer support teams, fellow responders with mental health training, offer support, reduce isolation, normalise reactions, and facilitate professional treatment referrals when needed.

Peer support complements but does not replace professional mental health treatment.

Some responders prefer professional treatment; others benefit from peer support first, then professional care if symptoms persist.

Organisational interventions support individual treatment.

- Departments can: provide confidential mental health services through employee assistance programmes
- normalise treatment through leadership messaging
- offer on-site psychological support
- allow mental health days
- reduce stigma through education
- and screen for PTSD proactively.

Organisations that support mental health retain employees, reduce disability claims, and improve morale.

Return to duty after treatment requires coordination.

Some responders take leave during intensive treatment; others work while attending therapy.

A phased return, allowing a gradual increase in call exposure, might help some.

The treatment goal is maintaining the ability to serve effectively whilst managing symptoms, not forcing a choice between mental health and career.

Many responders successfully treat PTSD whilst continuing their careers, often becoming better responders through increased self-awareness and empathy.

Prevention and Early Intervention

Prevention strategies reduce first responder PTSD incidence.

Pre-deployment resilience training teaching stress management, coping skills, and recognising warning signs supports mental health throughout a career. (Bonanno, 2004)

Regular psychological screening identifies emerging problems early, allowing intervention before symptoms become chronic.

Adequate staffing, preventing an overwhelming workload, reduces chronic stress, compounds trauma exposure.

Organisational culture normalising mental health treatment through leadership example increases help-seeking.

Critical Incident Stress Debriefing (CISD) after major incidents aims to prevent PTSD, but evidence is mixed; some studies show benefit, others show no effect or potential harm.

- Current best practice involves psychological first aid immediately after the incident
- monitoring for acute stress symptoms
- education about normal reactions
- and referral for treatment if symptoms persist beyond one month.

Mandatory group debriefing is not universally helpful, but voluntary access to support is valuable.

Work-life balance protects against PTSD by providing recovery time between shifts. (Karatzias et al., 2019)

Adequate time off, limiting mandatory overtime, encouraging use of vacation time, and respecting off-duty boundaries all support resilience. (Bonanno, 2004)

Responders who maintain lives outside work, including hobbies, relationships, and non-work identity, show better mental health than those whose identity centres entirely on the first responder role.

Self-care practices reduce cumulative trauma effects.

Physical fitness, adequate sleep, healthy eating, and avoiding excessive alcohol all buffer stress.

Social connection with non-responder friends and family provides perspective and emotional support.

Engaging in activities providing meaning beyond work maintains a sense of purpose.

Processing difficult calls with trusted colleagues provides informal support.

These practices do not prevent PTSD entirely but reduce risk and enhance resilience. (Bonanno, 2004)

Special Populations

- Volunteer firefighters and emergency medical technicians face unique stressors from: maintaining regular employment whilst responding to emergencies
- less training and support than career responders
- responding in their own communities involving people they know
- and balancing volunteer service with family and work obligations.

Volunteers need access to mental health support equivalent to career responders, but often lack organisational resources.

Emergency room (ER) or Accident and Emergency Department (AED) staff, including nurses, physicians, and technicians, experience repeated trauma exposure similar to field responders but different context.

- ER/AED trauma involves treating severe injuries and dying patients
- making rapid critical decisions, violence from patients or families
- moral distress from inadequate resources
- and systemic healthcare stressors compounding trauma.

ER/AED staff need recognition that healthcare-related PTSD deserves treatment and organisational support.

Communications officers and dispatchers deserve separate recognition given their unique role.

Auditory trauma from hearing but not seeing incidents, responsibility for outcomes, helplessness, listening to suffering without physical intervention, and repetitive exposure to crisis calls create PTSD risk requiring targeted support.

Dispatcher-specific treatment programmes address auditory trauma and unique occupational stressors that this population faces.

Military medics and corpsmen experience a combination of combat and medical trauma.

Treating wounded comrades under fire, making triage decisions, witnessing preventable deaths from delayed evacuation, and moral injury from being unable to save everyone create complex trauma.

Military medics need treatment addressing both combat exposure and repeated medical trauma, including moral injury specific to battlefield medicine.

First responders serve communities by running towards danger when others flee. (Haugen et al., 2012)

This service carries a psychological cost through cumulative trauma exposure.

PTSD is not a weakness or failure; it is a normal response to abnormal repeated stress.

Treatment works, allowing responders to continue serving whilst managing symptoms effectively.

Recovery means maintaining the ability to do this crucial work whilst protecting your own mental health. (Lewis et al., 2020)

You cannot serve communities well whilst sacrificing your wellbeing; effective service requires taking care of yourself.

Seeking help demonstrates professionalism and commitment to maintaining peak performance.

You deserve support equal to the service you provide.

Chapter Twenty-Three: Conclusion, Moving Forward in Recovery (Bisson et al., 2019)

You have journeyed through this comprehensive guide exploring every aspect of PTSD and Complex PTSD, from understanding symptoms to mastering advanced coping techniques, from navigating relationships to building meaning, from accessing treatment to supporting your recovery team. This conclusion synthesises key themes, offers final guidance, and reminds you of the most important truth: recovery is possible, and you deserve to heal. (Cusack et al., 2016; Teicher & Samson, 2016)

Core Messages of This Guide

PTSD is not your fault.

Trauma happened to you; you did not cause it or deserve it.

PTSD represents a normal response to abnormal experiences, your brain and body responding exactly as they should to an overwhelming threat.

Shame about having PTSD is unwarranted.

You are not weak, broken beyond repair, or permanently damaged.

You are a person who survived trauma and is now managing its aftermath with courage and resilience. (Bonanno, 2004)

Recovery is possible. (Watkins et al., 2018)

- Throughout this guide, you have encountered evidence repeatedly: PTSD treatment works
- symptoms decrease
- functioning improves

- relationships heal
- meaning emerges
- and life beyond trauma becomes possible.

Recovery is not eliminating all symptoms or forgetting that trauma occurred. (Ozer et al., 2003)

Recovery means building a life where trauma is part of your history rather than the dictator of your present. (Guay et al., 2006)

Thousands of people have recovered from PTSD as severe as yours.

Their recovery demonstrates that your recovery is achievable. (Charuvastra & Cloitre, 2008)

Treatment works but requires engagement.

Evidence-based treatments, Prolonged Exposure, Cognitive Processing Therapy, EMDR, produce significant symptom reduction in 60–80 per cent of people who complete them. (Shapiro, 2018)

- However, treatment requires active participation: attending sessions consistently
- completing homework assignments
- using skills between sessions
- tolerating temporary discomfort during trauma processing
- and persisting through challenges.

Treatment is not a passive process where the therapist fixes you.

It is a collaborative journey where you do hard work with expert guidance.

Your commitment determines outcomes.

Recovery is not linear. (Neff & Germer, 2018)

You will experience setbacks, plateaus, and fluctuations.

Good weeks will be followed by difficult days.

Progress will feel slow sometimes.

This is absolutely normal and does not indicate treatment failure.

Recovery resembles a staircase with steps and landings, not a smooth upward line. (Gilbert, 2011)

Each setback you overcome builds resilience. (Bonanno, 2004)

Each plateau preceding the next improvement phase requires patience.

Trust the process even when progress is not obvious day-to-day.

Zoom out to see the trajectory over months, which is where progress appears.

You are not alone.

Millions of people worldwide live with PTSD.

Many have recovered or are recovering.

Community exists, support groups, online forums, and peers who understand your struggles.

Professional help is available through therapists, psychiatrists, and healthcare providers specialising in trauma.

Loved ones, when educated about PTSD, can provide crucial support.

You do not have to face this alone.

Reaching out for help demonstrates strength, not weakness.

Multiple paths lead to recovery. (ISTSS, 2019)

This guide presented comprehensive information, but recovery is individual. (Cloitre et al., 2012)

What works for you might differ from what works for others.

Some people respond best to PE; others to CPT or EMDR. (Shapiro, 2018)

Some benefit from medication; others manage without it.

Some find meaning through spirituality, others through secular approaches.

Your recovery path is yours to discover with professional guidance. (Brand et al., 2019)

Trust yourself whilst staying open to evidence-based recommendations.

Self-compassion supports recovery. (Ross et al., 2017)

Throughout recovery, practice treating yourself as you would treat a dear friend facing similar struggles. (Fenster et al., 2018)

Respond to setbacks with kindness rather than criticism.

Acknowledge how hard you are working.

Celebrate small victories.

Forgive yourself for symptoms you cannot control yet.

Self-criticism maintains suffering, whilst self-compassion creates an internal environment supporting healing.

This is not self-indulgence; it is an essential healing practice.

Practical Steps Moving Forward

IF YOU HAVE NOT STARTED TREATMENT: Your first step is accessing professional help.

Contact your GP for an NHS referral, call IAPT for self-referral, or search for a private trauma therapist if that is an option with Talking Therapies UK (www.TalkingTherapies.co.uk).

Complete PCL-5 screening to document symptoms.

Do not wait for symptoms to become unbearable; early treatment produces better outcomes.

Starting treatment feels daunting, but it is the single most important step you can take towards recovery. (Lanius et al., 2018)

Thousands of people have sat in a therapist's office for the first time, feeling terrified and uncertain.

That courage to begin leads to healing.

IF YOU ARE IN TREATMENT: Continue showing up even when difficult.

Complete homework assignments.

Communicate with the therapist about what is and is not working.

practise skills daily rather than only when in crisis.

Trust the process whilst staying actively engaged.

Monitor your progress through symptom tracking, seeing improvements you might miss subjectively.

Celebrate milestones, completing trauma narrative, facing avoided situations, and sleeping through the night.

If progress stalls, discuss with the therapist rather than assuming treatment is not working.

IF YOU HAVE COMPLETED TREATMENT: Maintain gains through continued skill practise, ongoing self-care, and addressing stressors promptly.

Recovery does not mean you will never have difficult moments; it means you have tools to manage them effectively. (Monson & Shnaider, 2014)

Stay connected with support.

Pursue meaningful activities.

Build a life aligned with your values.

Consider giving back through peer support, advocacy, or helping others when ready.

Monitor for warning signs of relapse, accessing booster sessions if needed.

You worked hard for recovery, maintain it intentionally. (Foa et al., 2019)

IF YOU ARE SUPPORTING SOMEONE WITH PTSD: Educate yourself using reputable resources like this guide.

Listen without judgment.

Ask what helps rather than assuming.

Respect their pace and boundaries.

Encourage treatment whilst understanding you cannot force it.

Take care of your own well-being; supporting trauma survivors affects you.

Celebrate their progress.

Be patient through setbacks.

Remember: your role is a supportive presence, not a therapist.

Professional help provides treatment; you provide a caring relationship.

FOR EVERYONE: Build life beyond trauma.

Recovery is not just symptom reduction; it is creating a fulfilling, meaningful life. (APA, 2017)

Pursue relationships, activities, and goals that matter to you.

Develop identity beyond trauma survivor.

Engage with the community.

Contribute to others when able.

Find or create meaning.

Live in ways honouring yourself and your values.

Trauma took things from you; recovery allows you to build something new, incorporating both your pain and your growth. (NICE, 2018)

PAUSE POINT: Ground Yourself

- • Notice 5 things you can SEE

Resources Summary

This guide provided extensive resources throughout. Key resources to bookmark include Appendix A (organisations and contacts), Appendix B (worksheets for daily use), Appendix C (FAQ answering common questions), and Appendix J (building a recovery team). Keep this guide accessible as a reference throughout recovery. Different sections become relevant at different recovery stages; material not applicable now might prove invaluable later. Photocopy worksheets. Share relevant chapters with loved ones or the treatment team. Return to sections addressing current challenges as they arise.

Hope for the Future

Recovery transforms not just symptoms but perspective on life. Many trauma survivors report that whilst they would never choose trauma, recovery process taught them valuable things: (Forbes et al., 2020)

- Recovery transforms not just symptoms but perspective on life. Many trauma survivors report that whilst they would never choose trauma, recovery process taught them valuable things: deeper appreciation for life's fragility and preciousness (Schnyder et al., 2015)
- enhanced empathy and compassion for others' suffering
- recognition of their own strength and resilience (Bonanno, 2004)
- clearer priorities and values
- more authentic relationships based on genuine connection rather than superficial interaction
- spiritual or existential growth
- and capacity to help others facing similar struggles. These gifts come not from trauma itself but from recovery work you do, processing trauma whilst building a new life. post-traumatic growth is not required for recovery. You do not need to find a silver lining, become grateful for trauma, or transform pain into purpose. Some people experience significant growth (Tedeschi & Calhoun, 2004)
- others simply recover without major transformations beyond symptom reduction. Both are valid outcomes. What matters is that you heal and live life consistent with your

values, whether that involves profound growth or simply getting back to who you were before trauma. Your future is not limited by your trauma. PTSD creates significant impairment and suffering, but recovery opens possibilities you might not see currently. People with PTSD history pursue education, build careers, create families, maintain loving relationships, contribute to communities, and achieve goals across every domain. Your trauma is part of your story, not the entire book. Chapters ahead remain unwritten. You are an author with the power to craft a future reflecting who you want to become, not just who trauma tried to make you. Research continues to advance PTSD understanding and treatment. New interventions are developed, existing treatments refined, neurobiology better understood, and prevention strategies improved. The future holds promise for even more effective treatments, better accessibility, reduced stigma, and enhanced support systems. Your decision to work on recovery now positions you to benefit from ongoing advances whilst your current treatment produces real improvement. You deserve recovery. This deserves emphasis because trauma often creates beliefs that you do not deserve healing, happiness, or good things. Those beliefs are trauma-generated lies. You deserve recovery as much as anyone else with any other medical condition deserves treatment. You deserve relationships that support and nurture you. You deserve to feel safe in your body and life. You deserve to sleep peacefully, experience joy, pursue goals, and live without constant fear. Recovery is your right, not a privilege you must earn. Start from that truth. (Resick et al., 2017)

Final Words

This guide provided comprehensive information about PTSD, Complex PTSD, and recovery. (Maercker et al., 2022; Teicher & Samson, 2016)

Information alone does not create healing; action does.

Reading this guide is the important first step; applying knowledge through treatment, skill practice, and committed recovery work creates actual change. (Hyland et al., 2021)

Knowledge empowers you to make informed treatment decisions, understand what you are experiencing, communicate effectively with providers, and navigate your recovery journey with confidence. (Karatzias et al., 2017)

But knowledge must translate to action.

Recovery requires courage. (Courtois & Ford, 2013)

Facing trauma memories instead of avoiding them takes bravery.

Trusting people again after betrayal requires courage.

Hoping for a better future after despair demands courage.

Showing up to therapy week after week, even when difficult, demonstrates courage.

Practising skills during overwhelming moments takes courage.

Asking for help when independent survival was your strategy requires courage.

You have survived trauma that would break many people.

That survival proves you possess the courage needed for recovery. (Brewin et al., 2017)

Trust that courage will carry you through treatment just as it carried you through trauma.

You are stronger than you know.

Trauma did not break you; you are here, reading this, working towards recovery. (Ford et al., 2019)

That demonstrates extraordinary resilience. (Bonanno, 2004)

The fact that you are struggling with PTSD does not contradict your strength; it reflects a normal response to abnormal experiences.

Strength is not the absence of symptoms or struggle.

Strength is continuing forward despite symptoms, seeking help despite stigma, trying despite setbacks, and hoping despite suffering.

You demonstrate that strength daily, even if you do not recognise it.

Recovery is a journey, not a destination. (Cloitre et al., 2020)

There is no finish line where you are completely healed and never struggle again.

Recovery is an ongoing process of managing symptoms, building skills, maintaining gains, and living fully despite trauma history. (Watts et al., 2013)

Some days will be easier than others.

That is not failure, which is life.

What changes through recovery is not that life becomes perfect but that you develop the capacity to handle life's inevitable challenges without being overwhelmed by trauma responses. (van Dis et al., 2020)

You build resilience that allows you to weather storms whilst maintaining functioning and well-being. (Bonanno, 2004)

The path ahead contains challenges but also holds promise. Each step forward, no matter how small, moves you towards the life you deserve. Every skill you practise, every therapy session you attend, every moment you choose hope over despair contributes to your healing. Your recovery inspires others, both those currently struggling who need to see recovery is possible, and those who love you who want nothing more than to see you well. (Ehring et al., 2014)

Begin where you are. Use what you have. Do what you can. That is enough. You are enough. Recovery awaits. Take the first step, then the next, then the next. Trust the process. Trust yourself. Trust that healing is possible even when you cannot see it yet. Thousands have walked this path before you and found their way through. You can too. Your recovery story is waiting to be written. Begin today. (Coventry et al., 2020)

Appendix A: Resources and Further Reading

This appendix provides additional resources to support your recovery journey beyond this guide. The resources listed represent high-quality, evidence-based information from reputable organisations and authors. This list isn't exhaustive but provides solid starting points for further exploration. (Mavranezouli et al., 2020)

Recommended Books

A comprehensive Dialectical Behavioural Therapy Skills Manual, Jayden James, 2025

Professional Organisations and Information Sources

Talking Therapies UK – www.TalkingTherapies.co.uk

The National Institute for Health and Care Excellence provides clinical guidelines for PTSD treatment in the UK.

The British Association for Behavioural and Cognitive Psychotherapies maintains therapist directories and patient information.

Mind, the mental health charity, offers extensive information about PTSD and other conditions.

Combat Stress provides specialist treatment for veterans. The PTSD UK charity offers support specifically for PTSD. Victim Support provides support for crime and trauma victims. (Seal et al., 2007)

Rape Crisis centres provide specialist support for sexual violence survivors.

The National Centre for PTSD in the United States maintains extensive public education materials freely available online.

Crisis and Emergency Resources

If you are experiencing suicidal thoughts or mental health crisis, immediate help is available.

In the UK, call 999 for immediate emergency or 111 for urgent medical advice.

The Samaritans provide 24/7 emotional support at 116 123.

Shout provides text-based crisis support by texting 85258.

Your local NHS trust has crisis resolution teams available 24/7, contact details should be provided by your GP or mental health service.

Many areas have crisis cafes or safe havens providing face-to-face support during a crisis outside of traditional office hours.

These resources provide immediate support when you need it most urgently.

Mobile Apps and Digital Resources

Several evidence-based mobile applications provide structured self-help for PTSD, offering psychoeducation, symptom tracking, and coping tools based on CBT principles. These apps are designed to complement professional treatment rather than replace it, but can provide valuable self-help tools. Many are available free of charge and do not require account creation.

Mindfulness and meditation applications offer guided meditation and mindfulness exercises that can support PTSD recovery. Whilst not PTSD-specific, these provide accessible mindfulness training that reduces symptoms and improves emotion regulation. Many offer free content alongside paid subscriptions. (Karatzias et al., 2019)

Mood and symptom tracking apps can help monitor symptoms, identify triggers, track treatment progress, and recognise patterns. Regular tracking provides objective data about how you are doing, which can be more accurate than subjective feelings, and helpful for discussing progress with therapists.

Online platforms like www.TalkingTherapies.co.uk provide structured, therapist-assisted online programmes for anxiety and trauma. Some services are free through the NHS; others require payment. These programmes deliver an evidence-based treatment remotely, increasing accessibility for people unable to access in-person therapy.

Appendix B: Worksheets and Practical Exercises

Thought Record Template

Use this template to practise cognitive restructuring as described in Chapter 5. Complete one thought record whenever you notice significant distress or strong negative emotions.

Situation: Describe the situation that triggered distress. What happened? When? Where? Who was involved? Be specific and factual.

Automatic Thoughts: What thoughts went through your mind? What did the situation mean to you? What were you predicting would happen? What did it say about you, others, or the world?

Emotions: What emotions did you feel? Rate intensity 0-100 for each emotion.

Physical Sensations: What did you notice in your body? Tension? Heart racing? Stomach discomfort?

Evidence For the Thought: What facts support this thought being accurate? Be specific about concrete evidence.

Evidence Against the Thought: What facts suggest this thought might not be completely accurate? What would you tell a friend who had this thought? What have you learned previously that contradicts this thought?

Alternative Thoughts: Based on examining evidence, what's a more balanced way to view this situation? What else could this mean? What's another explanation?

Outcome: Re-rate emotion intensity 0-100. How strongly do you now believe the original thought? What will you do differently based on this analysis?

Exposure Hierarchy Template (For Use with Therapist Guidance)

Use this template to create your personalised exposure hierarchy for systematic exposure work as described in Chapter 6 (Facing Your Fears—Advanced Graded Exposure Strategies). Consult with your therapist for guidance on using this tool. List situations you have been avoiding, rate each for the anxiety it provokes, and then approach them systematically from least to most anxiety-provoking.

Instructions: Generate a comprehensive list of avoided situations related to your trauma. Include places, activities, people, objects, times of day, sensations, or anything else you avoid because it triggers trauma-related distress. Do not censor yourself; include everything you are avoiding, even if it seems minor. Aim for at least 10-15 items to create a good hierarchy.

For each item, rate: How much anxiety/distress does thinking about doing this create? Use 0-100 scale where 0 is completely comfortable and 100 is maximum possible distress. Be honest, there's no benefit to minimising your distress.

Organise items by rating, from lowest to highest. Your hierarchy should have items spread across the range, some low anxiety items (20-40), some moderate (40-70), and some high anxiety items (70-90+). If everything is rated very high, try breaking situations into smaller steps to create lower-rated entry points.

For each item, make it concrete and specific: Not 'Go to shops' but 'Go to local Tesco at quiet time for 15 minutes.' Not 'See friends' but 'Have coffee with Sarah for one hour at café.' Specificity allows you to plan exactly what you'll do and know clearly when you have accomplished it.

Start with an item rated around 30-50, challenging enough to require courage but manageable enough that you can realistically attempt it. Do not start with your highest-rated item. Build up gradually, mastering easier items before advancing to harder ones.

Weekly PTSD Symptom Tracking Log

Track your symptoms weekly to monitor progress over time. Rate each symptom cluster's average severity for the past week using 0-10 scale (0 = not present, 10 = extremely severe/constant).

Intrusive Symptoms: Rate frequency and distress from intrusive memories, nightmares, flashbacks, and distressing reactions to reminders. How often did intrusive symptoms occur? How distressing were they when they occurred? (Van der Kolk et al., 1996)

Avoidance: Rate how much you avoided trauma-related thoughts, feelings, conversations, activities, places, or people. How much of your life is restricted by avoidance?

Negative Thoughts and Mood: Rate severity of negative beliefs about yourself/others/world, persistent negative emotions (fear, anger, guilt, shame), emotional numbness, loss of interest in activities, and feeling detached from others.

Hyperarousal: Rate severity of hypervigilance, exaggerated startle response, irritability/anger, difficulty concentrating, and sleep disturbance. (Porges, 2011; Yehuda & Seckl, 2011)

Overall Functioning: Rate how much PTSD interfered with work/education, relationships, self-care, and ability to enjoy life.

Notes: Record any significant events, treatment activities completed (therapy sessions, exposure exercises, practice), and anything else relevant to understanding symptom patterns.

Review your tracking monthly. Compare current ratings to previous weeks. Look for overall trends rather than week-to-week fluctuations. Are symptoms generally decreasing even if progress isn't linear? Are some symptom clusters improving more than others? Is there correspondence between treatment activities and symptom changes? This data helps you and your therapist assess progress and adjust treatment as needed.

Grounding Techniques Quick Reference

Use these grounding techniques when experiencing flashbacks, dissociation, overwhelming emotions, or severe anxiety. Grounding brings you back to present moment and your physical body. practise these when calm so they are familiar during crisis. (Van der Kolk et al., 1996)

5-4-3-2-1 Technique: Name 5 things you can see (describe them in detail). Name 4 things you can physically touch (actually touch them and describe texture, temperature). Name 3 things you can hear (listen carefully for nearby and distant sounds). Name 2 things you can smell (if no smells available, name 2 favourite smells). Name 1 thing you can taste (or describe favourite taste). This engages all senses to anchor you in present.

Physical Grounding: Press feet firmly into floor and notice the sensation. Hold ice cubes and focus on cold sensation. Splash face with cold water. Do jumping jacks or run in place. Stretch muscles systematically. Hold an object (stone, stress ball) and describe its every characteristic. These physical sensations demand present attention and interrupt dissociation.

PAUSE POINT: Ground Yourself

- • Notice 5 things you can SEE

Mental Grounding: Describe your surroundings in detail as if to someone who cannot see them. Count backwards from 100 by 3s or 7s. Recite something memorized (poem, song lyrics, multiplication tables, prayer). Name categories of things (types of trees, countries, foods) as many as you can generate. These cognitive tasks require present thinking and interrupt trauma-related thoughts.

Self-Soothing: Say aloud reassuring statements: 'I am safe now. That was then, this is now. I am in [current year] in [location]. The trauma is over.' Use kind, compassionate tone with yourself. Imagine comforting presence or safe place in detail. These provide emotional grounding alongside physical and mental techniques.

Breathing Anchor: Focus entirely on your breathing. Count breaths (inhale-1, exhale-2, inhale-3, exhale-4, up to 10, repeat). Or breathe in for 4 counts, hold 4, exhale 6, pause 2, repeat. Breathing provides always-available anchor to present moment.

Values Clarification Exercise

Use this exercise to identify your core values as discussed in Chapter 10. Understanding your values provides direction for building meaningful life after trauma.

Step 1 - Brainstorm: Review the following life domains and note what's important to you in each area. Do not censor or judge, just note what comes to mind. Not all domains will be equally important; that's fine.

Relationships and Family: What kind of partner, parent, friend, or family member, do you want to be? What qualities matter in relationships? Examples: being loving, being dependable, being present, being vulnerable, providing support, maintaining connection.

Personal Growth and Learning: What matters regarding developing yourself? Examples: continuous learning, self-awareness, developing skills, embracing challenges, spiritual development, emotional growth.

Work and Career: What matters about how you work? Examples: excellence, contribution, creativity, leadership, collaboration, integrity, work-life balance.

Health and Wellbeing: What's important about caring for yourself? Examples: physical fitness, mental health, energy, longevity, vitality, self-care.

Leisure and Recreation: What matters about how you spend free time? Examples: fun, adventure, creativity, relaxation, experiencing beauty, playfulness.

Community and Citizenship: What's important about your role in broader community? Examples: contributing to society, environmental stewardship, social justice, helping others, leaving positive legacy.

Step 2 - Identify Patterns: Look across all domains for themes. Which words or concepts appear repeatedly? Which feel most emotionally resonant when you read them? These recurring themes likely represent your core values.

Step 3 - Prioritize: From your list, identify 3-5 values that feel most central to who you want to be. These become your core values, your compass points for decision-making and goal setting.

Step 4 - Define Personally: For each core value, write what it specifically means to you. Connection might mean different things to different people. Define it in your words so you have cleared an understanding of what you are committing to.

Step 5 - Identify Actions: For each core value, list concrete actions that would reflect living according to that value. Be specific: Spend dedicated one-on-one time with each child weekly rather than vague be a good parent.

Safety Plan Template

If you experience thoughts of self-harm or suicide, having a safety plan provides concrete steps to follow during crisis. Complete this plan when you are thinking clearly, then keep it accessible for when you need it.

Warning Signs: List thoughts, images, moods, situations, and behaviours that indicate crisis is developing. Examples: Thinking I am a burden, isolating myself completely, Feeling completely hopeless, Specific plans about self-harm.

Internal Coping Strategies: List things you can do on your own without contacting anyone to manage distress. Examples: Use grounding techniques, go for walk, Listen to calming music, Write in journal, practise progressive muscle relaxation, Watch favourite comedy.

People and Social Settings That Provide Distraction: List people you can contact for distraction or support, and places you can go to be around others without necessarily discussing crisis. Examples: Call Sarah and chat about normal things, go to library or cafe, Visit parents, Attend a support group meeting.

People to Contact for Help: List specific people you can talk about crisis and ask for help. Include names and phone numbers. Examples: Trusted friend with name and number,

Family member with name and number, Sponsor with name and number, Therapist with name and emergency contact number.

Professional and Agency Contacts: List crisis services and how to reach them. Examples: Samaritans 116 123, Crisis team local number, Therapist emergency line number, NHS 111, 999 for emergency.

Making Environment Safe: List steps to reduce access to means of self-harm during crisis. Examples: Give medications to partner to store securely, remove specific dangerous items, Stay in public spaces rather than isolating, Ask someone to stay with me.

Reasons for Living: List specific reasons you want to stay alive, even when crisis makes them hard to access emotionally. Be concrete: My children need me, I want to see my niece grow up, my dog depends on me, I have important work to do, There are places I still want to visit, I have survived other crises and they passed. Read this list during crisis to reconnect with reasons to persist. (Cohen et al., 2016; Cohen & Mannarino, 2008)

Sleep Diary Template

Track your sleep for at least two weeks to identify patterns and assess whether sleep hygiene changes improve sleep. Complete the diary each morning. (Perlis et al., 2005)

Date: Record the date.

Bedtime: What time did you get into bed intending to sleep?

Sleep Onset: Approximately what time did you actually fall asleep? If you do not know exactly, estimate.

Night Wakings: How many times did you wake during the night? How long were you awake each time? Estimate if uncertain.

Wake Time: What time did you wake up for the day, not counting brief wakings where you returned to sleep?

Out of Bedtime: What time did you actually get out of bed?

Total Sleep Time: Calculate approximate hours of actual sleep, not just time in bed.

Sleep Quality: Rate 1-10 how restful or refreshing your sleep felt.

Daytime Naps: Note any naps, including duration.

Factors: Note anything that might have affected sleep: caffeine intake and timing, alcohol, exercise and timing, stress levels, nightmares with how many and how disturbing, medications, evening activities. (Ross et al., 1989)

After two weeks, review your diary: What's your average total sleep time? Are there patterns to good versus poor nights? Do certain factors like caffeine, evening activities, or stress correlate with sleep problems? This information helps identify what changes might improve your sleep.

Appendix C: Frequently Asked Questions About PTSD

This appendix addresses common questions people have about PTSD that may not have been fully covered in the main chapters.

Can I have PTSD if I was not directly threatened or injured?

Yes.

PTSD can develop from witnessing trauma happening to others, learning that trauma happened to close family or friends, or repeated exposure to traumatic material common for first responders, journalists, or certain professionals. (Haugen et al., 2012)

You do not need to have been personally physically harmed.

Psychological threat, witnessing others' suffering, or vicarious trauma through repeated exposure can all produce PTSD.

The impact on you is what matters, not external judgments about whether your experience counts as traumatic enough.

How long does PTSD recovery take? (Lewis et al., 2020)

Recovery timelines vary substantially based on trauma type, severity, chronicity, treatment accessed, life circumstances, and individual factors. (Bisson et al., 2019)

With an evidence-based treatment, many people experience a significant improvement within 3-6 months.

Others, particularly those with complex trauma or limited access to treatment, may require years.

Do not compare your timeline to others.

Focus on your own progress, however gradual.

Consistent treatment engagement and practise of skills produces better outcomes than duration alone determines.

Will I ever be completely normal again?

Trauma changes people and returning exactly to your pre-trauma state is often unrealistic.

However, recovery does not require returning to pre-trauma functioning. (Cusack et al., 2016)

It means reducing symptoms to manageable levels, reclaiming meaningful life activities, rebuilding relationships, and developing sense of purpose despite what you experienced.

Many people with PTSD achieve full recovery by this definition, symptoms no longer significantly impair functioning and quality of life is good. (Watkins et al., 2018)

Some people continue experiencing mild residual symptoms but manage them effectively.

Either outcome represents successful recovery, even if you are somewhat changed by what you experienced. (Ozer et al., 2003)

Can PTSD come back after recovery? (Guay et al., 2006)

Symptoms can recur during high-stress periods, around anniversary dates, or if you experience new trauma.

This does not mean all progress is lost.

Think of it like physical fitness, if you stop exercising after getting fit, you lose some fitness, but you regain it faster than you initially built it because your body remembers.

Similarly, if symptoms increase after recovery, you have skills and knowledge to address them more quickly than initially. (Charuvastra & Cloitre, 2008)

Regular maintenance of coping strategies and awareness of warning signs helps prevent significant relapse.

If symptoms do return problematically, brief booster treatment often effectively addresses them.

Should I tell people about my trauma?

This is a personal decision with no single right answer.

Disclosure has potential benefits: reducing isolation, accessing support, and diminishing shame through sharing.

However, it also carries risks: some people respond unhelpfully with judgment, excessive questioning, or inability to understand.

Consider: Who would benefit from knowing?

What do you hope to gain from disclosure?

How safe is this person?

Have they demonstrated trustworthiness previously?

You can disclose selectively, telling some people but not others, or sharing general information without graphic details.

You do not owe anyone your trauma story.

Disclosure should serve your needs, not others' curiosity.

Do I need to remember everything that happened?

No.

Some trauma memories remain fragmented or partially inaccessible, and that's acceptable.

You do not need perfect, complete memory to recover.

Treatment focuses on processing what you do remember and addressing how trauma affects you currently, not excavating every detail.

Be cautious about aggressive attempts to recover supposed repressed memories, as these techniques can actually create false memories.

Work with what you naturally remember, process that, and address current symptoms.

If additional memories emerge naturally during treatment, you can process those as well.

What if my family does not believe trauma affected me significantly?

Unfortunately, family members sometimes minimise trauma's impact due to not understanding PTSD, their own discomfort with acknowledging what happened, or their role in the trauma if it was family-inflicted.

Their belief or understanding isn't required for you to recover.

Seek support from people who do understand, therapists, support groups, friends.

You might provide psychoeducation to family members about PTSD to increase understanding, but you cannot force them to accept something they resist.

Focus your energy on your recovery rather than on convincing sceptical family members. (Neff & Germer, 2018)

Your experience is valid regardless of whether they acknowledge it.

Can exercise really help with PTSD?

Yes, research supports exercise as valuable component of PTSD treatment, though not replacement for trauma-focused therapy.

Regular physical activity reduces anxiety and depression, improves sleep, enhances mood, provides sense of control and accomplishment, and helps regulate the heightened physiological arousal characteristic of PTSD.

Aim for at least 150 minutes of moderate aerobic activity weekly plus strength training twice weekly.

Find activities you enjoy or can tolerate to increase adherence.

Even brief exercise sessions provide benefit, you do not need intensive gym workouts.

Walking, swimming, cycling, dancing, yoga, or any physical activity you'll do consistently helps.

What if exposure therapy makes me feel worse?

Exposure therapy deliberately provokes anxiety by confronting avoided memories and situations, so increased distress during treatment is expected and does not indicate the treatment is harming you.

The distress is temporary and part of how exposure works, anxiety naturally decreases with continued exposure.

However, discuss your distress with your therapist.

They can: adjust the pace, provide additional support, check whether you are engaging appropriately with exposure versus just enduring it, or determine whether your distress level is within expected range or unusually severe.

Most people find exposure challenging but manageable, and symptoms improve significantly after completing treatment.

If you have given it genuine effort with skilled therapist and find it genuinely intolerable, alternative treatments exist.

Is medication necessary for PTSD recovery? (Gilbert, 2014)

No.

Psychological therapy alone is effective for many people with PTSD.

- However, medication can be helpful, particularly when: symptoms are very severe and interfering significantly with functioning
- depression is also present and severe
- psychological treatment alone hasn't been sufficient
- or you prefer combination treatment.

Medication and therapy together often work better than either alone, but therapy should be prioritised as first-line treatment.

Discuss with healthcare providers whether medication might benefit your specific situation, but do not feel medication is mandatory for recovery. (ISTSS, 2019)

Why do I feel guilty about recovering?

Survivor's guilt, feeling guilty about recovering, surviving, or moving on, is common, particularly when others died in the trauma, when you believe you didn't do enough to help others, or when recovering feels like betraying those who suffered.

This guilt, whilst understandable, isn't rational or helpful.

Your recovery does not diminish others' suffering or honour their memory less. (Cloitre et al., 2012)

In fact, living well often honours those who didn't survive better than suffering indefinitely.

You can hold space for grief about others whilst also working towards your own wellbeing.

The two aren't incompatible.

Process this guilt in therapy, challenge thoughts that recovery is betrayal, and permit yourself to heal. (Brand et al., 2019)

How do I stop using alcohol or drugs to cope with PTSD?

Substance use as PTSD coping is common but problematic; it provides short-term relief whilst maintaining symptoms long-term and creating additional problems. (Clark, 1999)

- Stopping requires: recognising that the substances aren't actually helping long-term
- developing alternative coping strategies before discontinuing substances
- accessing appropriate support for substance use, whether through addiction services, mutual support groups like AA or NA, or integrated PTSD-substance use treatment
- and addressing both PTSD and substance use simultaneously rather than trying to treat them separately.

If you are physically dependent on alcohol or other substances, withdrawal can be dangerous and should be medically supervised. (Ashton, 2002)

Consult healthcare providers about safe approaches to reducing or stopping substance use whilst addressing underlying PTSD.

Can PTSD cause physical health problems?

Yes.

PTSD increases risk for numerous physical health conditions, including cardiovascular disease, chronic pain, autoimmune disorders, gastrointestinal problems, and generally weakened immune function.

The chronic stress and inflammation associated with PTSD take a measurable physical toll.

- This does not mean PTSD causes every physical symptom you experience, but it is important to: attend to both mental and physical health

- inform physicians about PTSD so they can consider how it might affect physical health
- not dismiss physical symptoms as only psychological
- and recognise that treating PTSD can improve physical health outcomes.

Physical and mental health are interconnected, and addressing both comprehensively produces the best outcomes.

What if I cannot afford private therapy, and NHS waiting times are very long?

Long waiting times for NHS services are a frustrating reality in many areas.

- Whilst waiting, use self-help resources extensively, including this guide, recommended books, and apps
- join support groups for peer support
- practice strategies independently
- work on general life stability
- and contact your GP regularly to check on wait times and advocate for urgent referral if symptoms worsen.

Some charities provide free trauma therapy, research organisations serving populations you belong to whether veterans, sexual assault survivors, or domestic violence survivors. (Seal et al., 2007)

Consider whether you can afford even occasional private sessions to provide some support whilst waiting.

Online therapy is often more affordable than in-person private treatment.

Some therapists offer sliding scale fees.

Be persistent in seeking resources and do not give up hope of accessing help.

Should I read books or watch films about trauma?

This depends on your current state and the specific content.

Some people find reading or watching media about trauma validating and educational, whilst others find it triggering and overwhelming.

- Consider: your current symptom severity and stability
- whether the content is educational versus sensationalised
- your purpose in consuming this media
- and your capacity to manage any distress it provokes.

If you are early in recovery and highly symptomatic, avoiding trauma-related media might be wise. (Ross et al., 2017)

Later in recovery, when more stable, you might find educational content helpful. (Fenster et al., 2018)

Always prioritise your wellbeing over consuming any media.

You do not need to expose yourself to every trauma story to validate your own experience.

Is it normal to feel angry at people who have not experienced trauma?

Yes, this anger is common and understandable.

You might feel angry that others complain about minor problems, that they cannot understand what you have experienced, that life continues normally for them whilst you struggle, or that they make insensitive comments about trauma.

This anger often reflects grief about what trauma took from you, frustration with the isolation of your experience, and a sense of fundamental divide between those who understand trauma and those who do not.

Anger is a valid emotional response, though acting on it harmfully isn't helpful.

Process this anger in therapy.

Challenge thoughts that divide the world rigidly into those who get it and those who do not; there's a spectrum of understanding.

Practice compassion for yourself and others whilst maintaining boundaries with genuinely insensitive people.

Remember that everyone struggles with something, even if their struggles look different from yours.

Can children develop PTSD? (Cohen et al., 2016; Cohen & Mannarino, 2008)

Yes, children can develop PTSD, though their symptoms might look different from adult PTSD. (Cohen et al., 2016; Cohen & Mannarino, 2008)

Young children might show regression to earlier developmental stages, like bedwetting or baby talk, separation anxiety, nightmares, behavioural problems, or re-enacting trauma through play. (Ross et al., 1989)

Older children and adolescents might display symptoms more similar to adults but also show risk-taking behaviours, school problems, aggression, or withdrawal. (Ashton, 2002)

Children need specialised, developmentally appropriate treatment that often involves play therapy for younger children and includes parents or caregivers. (Cohen et al., 2016; Cohen & Mannarino, 2008)

Early intervention for childhood trauma can prevent long-term effects and support healthy development.

If you suspect your child has PTSD, seek evaluation from a mental health professional specialising in childhood trauma.

what is moral injury, and how does it relate to PTSD?

Moral injury occurs when you participate in, witness, or fail to prevent actions that violate your deeply held moral beliefs and values.

Common in military combat, but also occurs in other contexts like healthcare, first response, or any situation where you make impossible choices with terrible consequences.

Moral injury involves profound guilt, shame, and loss of trust in yourself, others, or the moral order of the world.

It often co-occurs with PTSD but is conceptually distinct.

PTSD centres on fear and threat, whilst moral injury centres on violation of values.

Treatment addresses both the trauma symptoms and the moral and existential dimensions, processing what happened, exploring the moral complexity of impossible situations, addressing self-condemnation, and rebuilding a sense of moral identity.

Specialised approaches for moral injury are developing and might be particularly helpful if moral injury is a prominent component of your suffering.

How can I support someone I love who has PTSD?

Supporting someone with PTSD requires patience, education, and appropriate boundaries.

Educate yourself about PTSD to understand what they are experiencing.

Provide a supportive presence without pressure, let them know you are available whilst respecting when they need space.

Avoid pushy questions about the trauma; let them share when ready.

Do not minimise their symptoms or tell them to just get over it.

Encourage professional treatment whilst respecting their autonomy.

Be patient with symptoms like irritability, emotional numbness, or avoidance; these are symptoms, not personal rejection.

Maintain your own well-being; you cannot help if you are depleted.

Set appropriate boundaries; being supportive does not mean tolerating abuse.

Consider seeking your own support through therapy or a support group for loved ones of trauma survivors.

Remember that recovery is their responsibility, not yours, you can support, but you cannot rescue them. (Lanius et al., 2018)

Is it better to talk about the trauma or avoid thinking about it?

Neither extreme is ideal.

Constant rumination about trauma without processing it maintains symptoms, whilst rigid avoidance also maintains symptoms by preventing processing.

An effective approach involves structured processing of trauma memories in appropriate contexts like therapy, practising coping with trauma-related distress, and gradually reducing avoidance, whilst also building a meaningful life beyond trauma that does not centre entirely on trauma processing.

You need balance: sufficient engagement with trauma to process it effectively without it consuming your entire existence.

Think of it as dedicating specific times to trauma work, therapy sessions, homework assignments, and exposure exercises, whilst also investing in non-trauma aspects of life.

This balanced approach allows healing whilst maintaining overall functioning and quality of life.

Where can I find a support group?

Support groups provide peer support from others with similar experiences.

To find groups: contact mental health charities like Mind, PTSD UK, or trauma-specific organisations relevant to your experience, like Combat Stress for veterans or Rape Crisis for sexual assault survivors. (Seal et al., 2007)

Ask your GP or therapist for local support group referrals.

Search online for support groups in your area.

Consider online support groups if local options aren't available; many operate through forums, video conferencing, or social media groups.

When selecting a support group, assess whether it is facilitated by a trained professional or peer-run, whether it feels safe and supportive rather than competitive or triggering, whether participants are at a similar stage of recovery, and whether the format works for you. (Monson & Shnaider, 2014)

Try several groups if needed to find a good fit.

Support groups complement individual therapy but do not replace professional treatment for most people.

Appendix D: Glossary of Terms

This glossary defines key terms used throughout this guide to ensure a clear understanding of concepts.

Acute Stress Disorder (ASD): A condition that occurs in the first month after trauma exposure, with symptoms similar to PTSD. Many people with ASD develop PTSD if symptoms persist beyond one month.

Avoidance: Deliberate or automatic efforts to avoid trauma-related thoughts, feelings, conversations, activities, places, or people. One of the core symptom clusters of PTSD and a major maintaining factor.

Cognitive Behavioural Therapy (CBT): A structured psychological treatment focusing on the relationship between thoughts, feelings, and behaviours. Evidence-based for many conditions, including PTSD.

Cognitive Processing Therapy (CPT): A Specific type of trauma-focused CBT involving writing trauma accounts and systematically challenging unhelpful trauma-related beliefs. Strong evidence base for PTSD treatment. (Resick & Schnicke, 2016)

Cognitive Restructuring: Process of identifying and challenging unhelpful thinking patterns and developing more balanced, accurate thoughts.

Complex PTSD (C-PTSD): PTSD variant resulting from prolonged, repeated trauma, particularly in childhood or captivity. Includes core PTSD symptoms plus difficulties with emotion regulation, self-concept, and relationships.

Dissociation: Disconnection from thoughts, feelings, memories, surroundings, or sense of self. Exists on a spectrum from mild spacing out to severe detachment or amnesia.

Eye Movement Desensitisation and Reprocessing (EMDR): Evidence-based trauma treatment involving recalling trauma memories whilst engaging in bilateral stimulation like eye movements. Effective for PTSD with strong research support. (Shapiro, 2018)

Exposure Therapy: Treatment approach involving systematic, gradual confrontation of feared or avoided situations, memories, or sensations to reduce anxiety and avoidance. Core component of many trauma-focused treatments.

Flashback: Vivid, intrusive re-experiencing of trauma where you feel as if the trauma is happening again in the present. Can include sensory, emotional, and physical aspects of the original experience.

Grounding: Techniques to anchor yourself in the present moment and physical reality, particularly useful during flashbacks, dissociation, or overwhelming distress. (Van der Kolk et al., 1996)

Hyperarousal: State of increased physiological and psychological activation, including heightened startle response, hypervigilance, irritability, difficulty concentrating, and sleep disturbance. Core PTSD symptom cluster. (Porges, 2011; Yehuda & Seckl, 2011)

Hypervigilance: Excessive watchfulness for threats, scanning the environment constantly, and difficulty relaxing. A common PTSD symptom that exhausts and maintains anxiety. (Porges, 2011; Yehuda & Seckl, 2011)

Intrusion: Unwanted, involuntary trauma-related thoughts, memories, images, or nightmares that invade awareness. Core PTSD symptom cluster. (Ross et al., 1989)

Moral Injury: Psychological and spiritual impact of participating in, witnessing, or failing to prevent actions that violate deeply held moral beliefs. Often co-occurs with PTSD but is conceptually distinct, involving profound guilt, shame, and loss of trust.

Prolonged Exposure (PE): Evidence-based PTSD treatment involving systematic, repeated confrontation of trauma memories through imaginal exposure and a gradual approach to avoided situations through in vivo exposure.

Re-experiencing: Core PTSD symptom cluster including intrusive memories, nightmares, flashbacks, and intense psychological or physiological distress when exposed to trauma reminders. (Van der Kolk et al., 1996)

Relapse: Return of significant symptoms after a period of recovery. In PTSD, relapse does not erase all progress but indicates the need for renewed intervention and application of coping strategies. (Foa et al., 2019)

Safety Behaviour: Actions taken to prevent feared outcomes or reduce anxiety in situations perceived as threatening. Whilst providing temporary relief, safety behaviours maintain anxiety by preventing learning that feared outcomes will not occur. (Clark, 1999)

Trauma: Event or series of events involving actual or threatened death, serious injury, or sexual violence, experienced directly, witnessed, or learned about happening to close others. Produces an overwhelming emotional response.

Trauma-Focused Cognitive Behavioural Therapy (TF-CBT): Evidence-based treatment for traumatised children and adolescents, combining CBT techniques with trauma processing and parent involvement. Adapted for developmental stages.

Trigger: Reminder of trauma that provokes distressing emotional, cognitive, or physical reactions. Can be external, like places or sounds, or internal, like thoughts or body sensations.

Vicarious Trauma: Trauma symptoms that develop from repeated exposure to others' traumatic material, common in helping professionals, journalists, or first responders. Also called secondary traumatic stress. (Haugen et al., 2012)

Window of Tolerance: Optimal zone of arousal where you can function effectively, process information, and regulate emotions. Trauma often narrows this window, causing fluctuation between hyperarousal and hypoarousal. (Ashton, 2002)

Appendix E: What to Expect, Sample Treatment Timeline

This appendix provides a general timeline of what PTSD recovery might look like. Remember that everyone's journey is unique; your timeline may be faster or slower, and that's normal and acceptable. This is intended as a rough guide to help you understand typical treatment progression, not a rigid schedule you must follow. (APA, 2017)

Weeks 1-2: Initial Assessment and Preparation Phase

The first sessions focus on comprehensive assessment and preparing for trauma work. Your therapist conducts a detailed evaluation of your trauma history, current symptoms, life circumstances, strengths, and treatment goals. They provide psychoeducation about PTSD, explain how the specific treatment approach works, and address your questions and concerns. This foundation-building is crucial; adequate preparation supports more effective trauma processing later.

You might begin learning preliminary coping skills during this phase: basic relaxation techniques, grounding skills, or emotion regulation strategies. These provide tools to manage distress as treatment intensifies. You will also discuss what to expect, clarify the treatment plan, and establish a therapeutic relationship. Do not rush through this phase wanting to jump straight to trauma processing; solid preparation prevents problems later.

Homework during this phase typically includes reading psychoeducational materials, tracking symptoms to establish a baseline, practising initial coping skills, and perhaps beginning to identify avoided situations or unhelpful thoughts. Expect to invest 2-3 hours weekly in homework beyond the therapy session itself.

Weeks 3-4: Beginning Trauma-Focused Work

Trauma-focused work begins, though the specific approach depends on your treatment modality. In CPT, you might write your first trauma account and begin identifying stuck points, problematic beliefs maintaining distress. In PE, you begin imaginal exposure, recounting the trauma memory in session. In EMDR, you begin the desensitisation phase, processing trauma memories with bilateral stimulation. The work becomes more emotionally demanding during this phase. (Shapiro, 2018)

- Expect increased distress as you begin confronting what you have been avoiding. This temporary worsening is expected
- it is part of how trauma-focused treatment works, not evidence that treatment is harming you. Your therapist supports you through this difficult phase, helping you tolerate distress whilst engaging fully with the processing work. Do not judge your ability to tolerate this distress as weakness

- confronting trauma requires courage.

Homework intensifies, you might practise imaginal exposure between sessions, continue writing trauma accounts, complete thought records, challenge stuck points, or practise bilateral stimulation. You'll also likely begin in vivo exposure, gradually approaching avoided situations. This between-session work is where much therapeutic benefit occurs, so prioritise completing homework assignments despite discomfort. (Shapiro, 2018)

Weeks 5-8: Intensive Processing Phase

This middle phase involves intensive trauma processing. Sessions focus heavily on confronting trauma memories, challenging unhelpful beliefs, and conducting exposure exercises. The work is demanding, and you might feel worse before feeling better. Many people find this phase most difficult. You are working hard, experiencing distress, but haven't yet experienced significant relief. This is when people most commonly consider quitting treatment, but persisting through this phase is crucial.

Continue practising exposure both in imagination and in real-world situations. Your exposure hierarchy guides a systematic approach to avoiding situations. Each successful exposure, staying in the situation until anxiety naturally decreases, teaches your brain that these situations are safe, gradually reducing symptoms. Similarly, repeated processing of trauma memories in therapy reduces their emotional intensity over time.

Track your progress formally using symptom measures. Sometimes improvement is occurring even when it does not feel like it subjectively. Objective tracking reveals changes you might not notice otherwise. If you are not seeing any improvement by week 6-7, discuss this with your therapist. They might adjust the approach, increase session frequency, or determine whether additional interventions are needed.

Self-care becomes particularly important during this intensive phase. Maintain regular sleep schedules, eat adequately, engage in physical activity, stay connected with a support system, and use coping skills learned in treatment. Balance the difficult trauma work with activities that provide relief, pleasure, or meaning. You need positive experiences to sustain you through this challenging period.

Weeks 9-12: Consolidation and Continued Progress

By this phase, many people begin experiencing noticeable symptom relief. Intrusive memories become less frequent or less distressing. You can engage in more activities without overwhelming anxiety. Sleep might improve. Relationships function better. These improvements motivate continued effort even though work remains to be done. (Van der Kolk et al., 1996)

Continue trauma processing, but also begin consolidating gains. What have you learned? What skills are most helpful? What progress have you made? How will you maintain improvements? Sessions might shift somewhat from intensive processing towards integration, applying what you have learned, addressing residual difficulties, and planning for continued progress after treatment ends.

If you are completing structured 12-session treatments like CPT, sessions near the end focus on relapse prevention. You develop a written plan for maintaining progress, identifying warning signs, and addressing future challenges. You might complete final trauma accounts or exposure exercises addressing any remaining avoided situations.

Some people complete treatment around this timeframe with a significant improvement. Others need additional sessions to address remaining symptoms or complex presentations. Discuss with your therapist whether continuing treatment would benefit you. If symptoms have improved substantially and you have the skills to maintain gains, you might complete treatment. If significant symptoms persist, continue working.

Weeks 13-20: Extended Treatment if Needed.

- If you continue beyond 12 weeks, treatment addresses: remaining symptoms requiring additional processing
- comorbid conditions needing attention
- life circumstances complicating recovery (NICE, 2018)
- or building additional skills. Extended treatment allows a more gradual pace for people who need it, particularly those with complex trauma, severe symptoms, or limited support.

Sessions might involve processing additional trauma memories if you experienced multiple traumas. They might address ongoing life stressors interfering with recovery. They might focus on relationship skills, emotion regulation, or other areas where difficulties persist. The work continues, but you might feel less intensely focused on trauma processing as you have already made progress in that domain. (Forbes et al., 2020)

Continue monitoring progress and adjusting approach as needed. By this point, you should be seeing substantial improvement, even if recovery isn't complete. If you have made minimal progress despite sustained treatment engagement, discuss with your therapist whether a different approach might be more effective or whether factors outside therapy are maintaining symptoms. (Schnyder et al., 2015)

Post-Treatment: Months 6-12 and Beyond

Treatment formally ends, but recovery continues. The first months after treatment completion are crucial for consolidating gains and preventing relapse. Continue practising skills learned in treatment even though you are not meeting with the therapist regularly. Maintain healthy routines, use coping strategies when distress arises, continue exposure to previously avoided situations, and stay connected with a support system. (Resick et al., 2017)

Monitor for warning signs that symptoms are returning. If you notice increases in avoidance, intrusive symptoms, or other PTSD manifestations, implement your relapse prevention plan immediately. Contact your therapist for booster sessions if needed; brief additional treatment often prevents full relapse. Think of this as ongoing maintenance rather than treatment failure.

Continue building life beyond trauma. Set new goals unrelated to PTSD recovery. Pursue interests and relationships. Engage meaningfully with your values. Recovery isn't just about symptom absence; it is about building a satisfying life. The months and years after treatment provide an opportunity to consolidate your new identity as someone who experienced trauma and recovered, rather than someone whose life centres entirely on trauma and recovery. (Maercker et al., 2022)

Many people continue improving even after treatment ends as they apply skills in daily life and build momentum towards wellbeing. The treatment provided foundation and tools; ongoing life provides a practice field for continued growth. Trust the process and your capacity to manage challenges that arise.

Important Note: This timeline represents typical progress for someone engaging in weekly trauma-focused therapy with good adherence to treatment.

Your timeline might differ substantially based on trauma complexity and severity, presence of comorbid conditions, life circumstances and stressors, frequency of sessions, specific treatment approach, quality of therapeutic relationship, support system strength, and individual factors affecting processing.

Some people improve faster; others require more time.

Neither reflects on your worth or effort, focus on your personal progress rather than comparing to idealised timelines.

Appendix F: A Letter to Loved Ones, Understanding and Supporting Someone with PTSD

If someone you care about has PTSD, this letter helps you understand what they are experiencing and how you can provide meaningful support. PTSD profoundly affects not just the person who experienced trauma but their relationships, family, and support network. Educating yourself and learning how to help effectively benefits everyone involved.

What PTSD Is and Is Not

PTSD is a mental health condition that develops after experiencing or witnessing a traumatic event. It is a normal response to abnormal circumstances, the brain's attempt to process and cope with overwhelming experiences. PTSD is not: weakness, character flaw, attention-seeking, exaggeration, excuse for bad behaviour, or something people can just get over by trying harder or thinking positively.

Your loved one likely experiences: intrusive memories or nightmares about the trauma; flashbacks where they feel the trauma is happening again; intense anxiety or distress when reminded of trauma; avoidance of trauma-related people, places, activities, or conversations; negative thoughts about themselves, others, or the world; emotional numbness or difficulty experiencing positive emotions; irritability or anger outbursts; hypervigilance and exaggerated startle response; difficulty concentrating; and sleep disturbance. These symptoms genuinely impair functioning; they are not chosen or controllable through willpower alone. (Van der Kolk et al., 1996)

Understanding that PTSD is a real medical condition requiring treatment helps you respond with compassion rather than frustration. Your loved one isn't choosing to struggle; they are managing difficult condition that affects their brain's threat detection and stress response systems.

How PTSD Affects Your Loved One and Your Relationship

PTSD affects relationships in numerous ways that might be confusing or hurtful if you do not understand their origin.

Your loved one might withdraw emotionally, seeming distant or uninterested.

They might avoid activities you previously enjoyed together because these trigger trauma memories.

They might seem irritable or angry more often.

They might be unable to remember notable events or conversations.

They might have difficulty trusting you or others.

They might struggle to express affection or maintain intimacy.

These changes are not about you or their feelings for you; they are symptoms of PTSD. The emotional numbness makes it hard to feel a connection even when they want to. The hypervigilance makes relaxation and intimacy difficult. The avoidance extends to emotional vulnerability. Recognising these as symptoms rather than personal rejection helps you respond supportively rather than taking them personally. (Porges, 2011; Yehuda & Seckl, 2011)

Your relationship might also experience positive changes: many people report developing greater appreciation for each other, a deeper emotional connection through facing challenges together, clearer communication about needs, and stronger relationship resilience. Recovery from PTSD can strengthen relationships that navigate this challenge together, though the journey is difficult. (Hyland et al., 2021)

What Helps: Do These Things

Educate yourself about PTSD. Understanding the condition helps you respond appropriately and reduces misunderstandings. Read about PTSD, attend family sessions if your loved one's therapist offers them, and talk to your loved one about their experience when they are willing.

Provide patient, supportive presence without pressure. Let them know you are available whilst respecting when they need space. Simple presence, being there without demanding they talk or feel certain ways, provides powerful support. Say things like: I am here for you, take your time, I care about you, how can I support you right now?

Listen without judgment when they do share. If they talk about the trauma or their symptoms, listen attentively without interrupting, advising unless requested, or minimising their experience. Acknowledge their feelings: That sounds difficult. I can see this is painful for you. Thank you for trusting me with this.

Encourage professional treatment whilst respecting their autonomy. PTSD responds well to an evidence-based treatment, and professional help significantly improves outcomes. Express support for them seeking help: I think therapy could really help you. I will support you in finding treatment. Would you like help researching therapists? However, respect that they choose whether and when to seek treatment. You cannot force someone into recovery. (Karatzias et al., 2017)

Maintain normal routines and activities where possible. Whilst accommodating PTSD symptoms is important, maintaining some normalcy helps. Continue doing activities you enjoy together when they are able. Maintain household routines. Engage in regular activities that provide structure and positive experiences. Life should not centre entirely on PTSD and recovery. (Courtois & Ford, 2013)

Take care of yourself. Supporting someone with PTSD is emotionally demanding. You need your own support system, self-care practices, and outlets for stress. Consider your own therapy or a support group for loved ones of trauma survivors. Maintain friendships and activities that sustain you. Set appropriate boundaries to prevent depletion. You cannot help effectively if you are exhausted and depleted.

Celebrate progress, however little. Notice and acknowledge improvements: You went to the supermarket today, that's great progress. I noticed you seemed more engaged today. I am proud of you for staying in therapy even when it is hard. These acknowledgments reinforce progress and encourage.

What Does Not Help: Avoid These Things

Do not minimise or dismiss their symptoms. Saying things like: It wasn't that bad, Others have it worse, just get over it, stop dwelling on the past, or You should be over this by now are profoundly unhelpful and damaging. These statements communicate that you do not understand PTSD and that they cannot trust you with their struggles.

Do not pressure them to talk about the trauma. Whilst you might be curious or think talking would help, forced disclosure can be retraumatising. Let them share when and if they choose to. Respect if they prefer not to discuss details with you, even if they are discussing them in therapy. They might need professional context to process trauma safely.

Do not take their symptoms personally. When they withdraw, seem distant, or are irritable, remind yourself that these are PTSD symptoms, not statements about their feelings for you. Responding with hurt or anger escalates conflict and increases their distress. Instead, recognise the symptoms for what they are and respond with patience.

Do not enable avoidance. Whilst supporting them through difficulties is important, doing everything for them or allowing them to avoid all challenges maintains PTSD rather than supporting recovery. Gentle encouragement to face manageable challenges, with support, helps more than removing all obstacles from their path. (Brewin et al., 2017)

Do not make their recovery your responsibility. You can support recovery, but you cannot recover for them. They need to do the work of treatment, practise skills, and face challenges. Attempting to take responsibility for their recovery creates an unhealthy dynamic and prevents them from developing their own agency in the process. (Ford et al., 2019)

Do not give up on them or the relationship. Recovery takes time and isn't linear. There will be setbacks, difficult periods, and moments when progress seems impossible. Your continued presence and support throughout these difficulties provide a foundation for recovery. However, this does not mean tolerating abuse; there's a difference between patience with symptoms and accepting harmful behaviour. (Cloitre et al., 2020)

Understanding Specific Symptoms and How to Respond

Flashbacks: If your loved one is having flashbacks, they are re-experiencing the trauma as if it is happening now. Do not touch them suddenly, as this might be perceived as a threat. Speak calmly and gently. Help them get grounded in the present: What's the date today? Look around and name five things you see. You are safe now; you are in our home. If they have discussed what helps during flashbacks, do that. After the flashback passes, provide reassurance and normalcy. (Van der Kolk et al., 1996)

Nightmares: PTSD nightmares are intensely distressing and disrupt sleep for both the person experiencing them and partners sharing a bed. If they wake from a nightmare, provide calm reassurance without excessive questioning about the content. Help them use grounding techniques. Respect if they need some practices that improve sleep, like separate sleeping arrangements temporarily. This isn't rejection of you; it is a pragmatic response to sleep disruption. (Ross et al., 1989)

Hypervigilance: Your loved one might seem constantly on edge, scanning for threats, unable to relax with their back to the doors, or startling easily. Do not tease them about this or try to startle them as a joke. Provide predictability and safety. Warn them before approaching from behind. Keep the environment calm when possible. Understand that this heightened vigilance is exhausting for them even when nothing threatening is occurring. (Porges, 2011; Yehuda & Seckl, 2011)

Emotional Numbness: If your loved one seems emotionally flat or unable to experience joy, understand this is a symptom rather than a lack of caring. They are not choosing to feel nothing. Continue providing opportunities for positive experiences without pressure to respond in particular ways. Sometimes engaging in activities helps emotions return even when they do not want to participate initially.

Irritability and Anger: PTSD often involves heightened irritability and anger that seems disproportionate to triggers. These anger outbursts reflect dysregulated arousal and stress response, not their actual feelings about minor frustrations. Do not escalate conflicts by responding with your own anger. Set boundaries about acceptable behaviour whilst having compassion for the underlying distress. If anger becomes abusive, that requires professional intervention and potentially safety planning. (Stanley & Brown, 2012)

Taking Care of Your Own Wellbeing

Supporting someone with PTSD affects you emotionally and practically. Secondary traumatic stress, developing trauma symptoms yourself from supporting someone with trauma, is a real possibility, particularly if you hear traumatic details. Compassion fatigue, emotional exhaustion from sustained caregiving, commonly affects partners and family members of people with PTSD. Protect your own mental health.

- Seek your own support. This might include: your own therapy to process emotions and develop coping strategies
- a support group for loved ones of trauma survivors where you can share experiences with others facing similar challenges
- maintaining friendships and social connections outside your relationship with the person with PTSD
- and connecting with family members also affected by your loved one's PTSD.

Set appropriate boundaries. You can be supportive whilst also maintaining limits on your time, energy, and emotional resources. It is acceptable to say: I need some time for myself today, I cannot talk about this right now, I need you to use your coping skills rather than relying entirely on me, or I am willing to support you but not to do everything for you. These boundaries aren't selfish; they are necessary for sustainable support.

Maintain your own activities, interests, and identity. Your life shouldn't consist solely of supporting your loved one. Continue pursuing your interests, seeing friends, engaging in hobbies, and maintaining aspects of life that sustain you. This provides both respite from caregiving and models healthy living for your loved one.

Recognise when professional help is needed for you. If you are experiencing significant depression, anxiety, relationship distress, or other difficulties yourself, do not hesitate to seek professional support. Supporting someone with PTSD is legitimately difficult, and seeking help for yourself isn't a weakness; it is wise self-care that ultimately benefits everyone.

Hope for the Future

PTSD is treatable.

With evidence-based treatment and support, most people experience a significant improvement.

Recovery takes time and effort, but it is genuinely possible. (Watts et al., 2013)

Your support throughout this journey matters profoundly.

Many relationships emerge stronger after navigating PTSD recovery together. (van Dis et al., 2020)

The challenges you face together can deepen your connection, increase mutual understanding, and create resilience that benefits you both throughout life. (Bonanno, 2004)

Continue learning, practising patience, taking care of yourself, and maintaining hope.

Your loved one can recover, and you can support them effectively whilst maintaining your own wellbeing.

Appendix G: Information for Healthcare Providers

This appendix guides healthcare providers, GPs, nurses, emergency department staff, and other medical professionals who encounter patients with PTSD in their practice. Whilst mental health specialists provide definitive PTSD treatment, general healthcare providers play a crucial role in identification, initial response, appropriate referral, and ongoing medical care for patients with PTSD.

Screening and Identification

- Many people with PTSD present to general medical settings rather than mental health services, often with physical symptoms or indirect presentations. Maintain high index of suspicion for PTSD in patients who have history of trauma exposure, including combat, assault, serious accidents, or other traumatic events
- present with medically unexplained physical symptoms particularly pain, gastrointestinal complaints, or cardiovascular symptoms
- have sleep complaints particularly nightmares (Ross et al., 1989)
- show excessive anxiety or hypervigilance during medical examinations (Porges, 2011; Yehuda & Seckl, 2011)
- avoid certain medical procedures or appointments
- or have comorbid depression, anxiety, or substance use.

Brief screening tools facilitate identification. The Primary Care PTSD Screen (PC-PTSD-5) consists of five yes-or-no questions covering PTSD symptom clusters and takes under two minutes to administer. Positive screen warrants more comprehensive assessment or referral to mental health services. Incorporate trauma screening into routine care where appropriate, particularly when patients present with symptoms suggestive of PTSD.

Trauma-Informed Care Principles

- Trauma-informed care recognises the widespread impact of trauma and integrates this understanding into all aspects of service delivery. Key principles include: safety, ensuring physical and emotional safety in healthcare environment
- trustworthiness and transparency, clear communication about procedures and decisions
- peer support, facilitating connections with others who have experienced trauma
- collaboration and mutuality, shared power and decision-making with patients
- empowerment, recognising patient strengths and building on them
- and cultural, historical, and gender considerations, recognising role of cultural trauma, discrimination, and systemic oppression.
- Implement trauma-informed practices in your clinical work: explain all procedures before implementing them to reduce unpredictability and loss of control
- obtain explicit consent for examinations particularly those involving touching
- provide choices wherever possible to restore sense of agency
- recognise that certain medical procedures might be triggering particularly for sexual trauma survivors
- allow patients to have support person present during difficult procedures
- and maintain professional boundaries whilst demonstrating respect and compassion.

Be mindful of language. Avoid phrases that minimise trauma, like: It could have been worse, at least you survived, or You should be over this by now. Instead, use: That sounds really difficult. Thank you for sharing this with me. It makes sense that you are struggling with this, or how can I help? Validate patients' experiences rather than questioning or dismissing them.

Appropriate Referral and Treatment Recommendations

When you identify PTSD, provide an appropriate referral to mental health services.

In NHS settings, refer to IAPT services for evidence-based psychological therapy or to secondary mental health services (Community Mental Health Teams) for severe or complex presentations.

- Explain to patients: PTSD is a treatable condition with effective treatments available
- psychological therapy is recommended first-line treatment
- what to expect from the referral process
- and that treatment works even for people who have experienced severe trauma.

Educate patients about PTSD using accessible language. Explain that PTSD is a normal response to abnormal events, not personal weakness. Describe common symptoms so they understand their experiences are recognised trauma responses. Provide written information about PTSD and where to access help. This psychoeducation often reduces stigma and increases treatment engagement.

Consider medication when appropriate. Whilst psychological therapy is first-line treatment, SSRIs like sertraline or paroxetine can be helpful, particularly when: (NICE, 2018; Baldwin et al., 2014)

- Consider medication when appropriate. Whilst psychological therapy is first-line treatment, SSRIs like sertraline or paroxetine can be helpful, particularly when: symptoms are severe (NICE, 2018; Baldwin et al., 2014)
- depression is prominent
- psychological therapy isn't accessible or hasn't been effective
- or the patient prefers medication. Prescribe adequate doses for adequate duration
- typical antidepressant dosing and timeline apply. Monitor response and side effects regularly. (NICE, 2018; Baldwin et al., 2014)

Avoid prescribing benzodiazepines for PTSD. Despite being commonly requested for anxiety, benzodiazepines do not effectively treat PTSD, can interfere with trauma-focused psychological treatment, carry dependence risks, and are associated with worse long-term outcomes. If the patient is already taking benzodiazepines, work towards a gradual taper whilst introducing more effective treatments. (Ashton, 2002; Lader, 2011; NICE, 2018)

Managing Physical Health Needs

PTSD significantly impacts physical health. Patients with PTSD have elevated rates of cardiovascular disease, chronic pain, gastrointestinal disorders, autoimmune conditions, and general medical morbidity. The chronic stress and inflammation associated with PTSD take a measurable physical toll. Provide comprehensive medical care, attending to both mental and physical health needs.

Do not assume physical symptoms are purely psychological. Patients with PTSD experience genuine physical health problems requiring medical investigation and treatment. Conduct an appropriate workup for physical symptoms whilst recognising that PTSD might contribute to symptom severity or presentation. Integrated care addressing both physical and mental health produces the best outcomes.

Screen for health behaviours affecting prognosis. PTSD increases risk for: tobacco use, excessive alcohol consumption, substance misuse, sedentary lifestyle, poor nutrition, and inadequate sleep. Address these through health promotion, appropriate referrals to substance use services when needed, and emphasising that improving these behaviours supports both physical and mental health recovery. (Ehring et al., 2014)

Recognise when medical procedures might be particularly challenging. Patients with PTSD, particularly sexual trauma survivors, may find certain examinations extremely distressing. Approach procedures like pelvic exams, dental work, or procedures requiring sedation with extra care. Explain thoroughly, obtain explicit consent, provide choices, allow a support person, and recognise that avoidance of medical care might reflect trauma-related distress rather than noncompliance.

Working with Patients in Crisis

Patients with PTSD are at elevated risk for suicidal thoughts and behaviours. Assess suicide risk explicitly and thoroughly. Do not avoid asking about suicide for fear of planting the idea; directly asking does not increase risk and allows appropriate intervention. Use validated assessment tools and clinical judgment to determine the appropriate level of care.

- For patients in acute crisis: ensure immediate safety
- conduct a comprehensive risk assessment
- connect with crisis services, whether crisis resolution teams, liaison psychiatry, or emergency department
- do not send high-risk patients away without appropriate safety planning and follow-up (Stanley & Brown, 2012)
- and involve family or support network when appropriate, with patient consent.

Healthcare providers encounter PTSD regularly across all medical settings.

Your role in identification, appropriate referral, provision of trauma-informed care, and ongoing support for physical health needs is crucial.

Continue professional development in trauma-informed practice, maintain updated knowledge of local referral pathways and resources, and recognise the privilege and responsibility of supporting patients through trauma recovery. (Coventry et al., 2020)

PAUSE POINT: Ground Yourself

- • Notice 5 things you can SEE

Your compassionate, informed care makes a substantial difference in patient outcomes.

Appendix H: Stories of Recovery, Hope from Others Who Have Been There (Mavranezouli et al., 2020)

This appendix shares composite recovery stories based on typical experiences of people who have successfully recovered from PTSD. These are not specific individuals but represent common patterns, challenges, and successes in PTSD recovery. Reading others' recovery stories often provides hope, validation, and practical insights for your own journey. (Karatzias et al., 2019)

Sarah: Recovery from Sexual Assault (Lewis et al., 2020)

Sarah developed PTSD after a sexual assault in her early twenties. Initially, she tried to carry on as if nothing had happened, but symptoms escalated: intrusive memories, nightmares, avoidance of dating and intimacy, hypervigilance, particularly around men, and profound shame. For two years, she struggled alone, believing she should be able to cope without help. Finally, at a friend's urging, she contacted sexual assault support services and began trauma-focused therapy. (Van der Kolk et al., 1996)

Treatment was challenging. Sarah found cognitive processing therapy difficult, particularly writing about the assault and challenging beliefs that she was to blame. She frequently wanted to quit, but continued with therapist support. After several months of treatment, she began experiencing relief. Intrusive memories decreased. She could think about the assault without being overwhelmed. The shame began lifting as she recognised the assault wasn't her fault. (Van der Kolk et al., 1996)

Five years later, Sarah reports full recovery. She's in a healthy relationship, has rebuilt trust in herself and others, and rarely experiences PTSD symptoms. She volunteers with sexual assault services, supporting other survivors. The assault remains part of her history but does not define her present. She describes recovery as the hardest thing she's ever done and the most worthwhile. (Bisson et al., 2019)

James: Recovery from Combat Trauma (Cusack et al., 2016)

James served multiple tours in Afghanistan and witnessed events he struggled to process. After discharge, he experienced severe hypervigilance, anger problems affecting his marriage, nightmares, and emotional numbness. He initially resisted treatment, viewing seeking help as a weakness. His wife's ultimatum, get help or lose the marriage, finally motivated engagement with veteran mental health services. (Ross et al., 1989)

Prolonged exposure therapy helped James process combat memories he'd avoided for years. Group therapy with other veterans reduced isolation and provided peer support. He learned anger management strategies and communication skills for his marriage. Medication helped manage depression that emerged alongside PTSD. Recovery was gradual and nonlinear with setbacks, particularly around anniversaries of traumatic events. (Foa et al., 2007; Powers et al., 2010)

Three years into recovery, James functions well. He maintains employment, has repaired his marriage, and mentors newly discharged veterans. Symptoms occasionally resurface during stress, but he manages them effectively. He wishes he had sought help sooner rather than suffering unnecessarily for years. His advice: combat trauma is an injury requiring treatment like any other wound, and seeking treatment demonstrates strength, not weakness. (Seal et al., 2007)

Maria: Recovery from Childhood Abuse (Watkins et al., 2018; Teicher & Samson, 2016)

Maria experienced prolonged childhood abuse, resulting in Complex PTSD. Her symptoms included difficulty regulating emotions, relationship problems, negative self-concept, dissociation, and depression. She'd been in various therapies over the years with limited improvement until finding a therapist specialising in complex trauma who provided phase-based treatment. (Teicher & Samson, 2016)

Initial treatment focused on stabilisation, building emotion regulation skills, reducing self-harm, and establishing safety before trauma processing. This stabilisation phase took a year. Trauma processing followed, addressing multiple traumatic memories from childhood. Finally, integration work helped Maria rebuild her identity beyond trauma survivor and develop healthier relationship patterns. Total treatment spanned several years. (Linehan, 2015)

Recovery hasn't been the complete elimination of all difficulties; Maria still experiences occasional dissociation and relationship challenges, but her life is immeasurably better. She maintains steady employment, has fulfilling friendships, and experiences joy regularly. Most importantly, she has developed compassion for herself and no longer believes the abuse defined her worth. Recovery from complex trauma takes time, but it is genuinely possible even from severe childhood trauma. (Ozer et al., 2003)

David: Recovery from a Serious Accident (Guay et al., 2006)

David developed PTSD after a near-fatal car accident where he sustained serious injuries, and his passenger died.

He experienced intrusive memories of the crash, avoided driving, had panic attacks in vehicles, and struggled with survivor's guilt. (Van der Kolk et al., 1996)

Treatment involved EMDR, which helped process the accident memory and reduce its emotional intensity. (Shapiro, 2018)

He also worked through complicated grief about his passenger's death and challenged beliefs that he should have prevented the accident.

Gradually, he reintroduced driving through systematic exposure, beginning with quiet streets and building to motorways.

After one year of treatment, David drives comfortably, has processed his grief, and no longer experiences regular intrusive memories. (Van der Kolk et al., 1996)

The accident changed him; he's more cautious and appreciates life's fragility, but he's moved forward rather than remaining trapped by trauma.

These stories demonstrate that recovery is possible across different trauma types and presentations. Recovery requires courage, persistence, an appropriate treatment, and support, but it is genuinely achievable. If these individuals recovered, you can too. Your story might look different, your trauma, your symptoms, your path, and your timeline are uniquely yours, but recovery remains possible. Keep moving forward. (Charuvastra & Cloitre, 2008)

Recovery awaits you, too. Begin your journey today. (Neff & Germer, 2018)

Appendix I: Coping Statements and Affirmations for Difficult Moments

During distressing moments, flashbacks, panic attacks, overwhelming emotions, or intrusive thoughts, having prepared coping statements can help you regulate distress and maintain perspective. This appendix provides coping statements you can use or adapt for your needs. Write your favourites on cards to carry with you, save them in your phone, or post them where you will see them regularly. (Van der Kolk et al., 1996)

Grounding and Present-Moment Statements

I am safe right now in this moment.
That was then, this is now. The trauma is over.
I am in the current year, in my home, and I am safe.
My body is reacting to a memory, not a current threat.
This feeling will pass. Feelings always pass.
I can handle this moment. I just need to get through right now.
I am here, in the present. I am grounded.
These are symptoms of PTSD, not actual danger.
I have survived this before, and I will survive it again.
I am stronger than this moment of difficulty.

Self-Compassion and Encouragement Statements

I am doing the best I can with what I have right now.
Recovery is not linear. Setbacks are part of the process, not (Gilbert, 2014)

evidence of failure.

I deserve compassion, especially from myself.
It is okay to struggle. Struggling does not make me weak.
I am brave for facing this rather than avoiding it.
I have come so far already, even when progress feels invisible.
I am allowed to take this at my own pace.
Healing takes time. I can be patient with myself.
I am more than this trauma. I contain multitudes.
I am worthy of peace, happiness, and love.
Every small step forward matters.
I am doing important, challenging work. That deserves

acknowledgment.

Challenging Fear and Anxiety Statements

I have felt this way before, and it passed. This will pass too.
Anxiety is uncomfortable but not dangerous.
I can tolerate discomfort. I do not need to escape immediately.
This feeling has a beginning, middle, and end. I am in the middle.

It will end.

I can sit with this anxiety without letting it control my choices.
My thoughts are not facts. Anxiety tells lies.
I am safe even though my body feels afraid.
I can cope with uncertainty. I have done it before.
The worst is behind me, not ahead of me.
I am building courage by facing my fear.

Challenging Guilt and Shame Statements

What happened to me was not my fault.
I did the best I could in an impossible situation.
Surviving was enough. I did not need to do more.
Having these reactions does not make me broken or damaged.
I deserve to heal, regardless of what happened.
My worth is not determined by what happened to me or how I

responded.

I can forgive myself for not having the resources or knowledge I

have now.

Shame is a feeling, not a truth about who I am.
I am worthy of love and belonging exactly as I am.
I am not defined by my worst moments or experiences.

Motivational Statements for Persisting with Recovery (ISTSS, 2019)

Recovery is possible. Others have done this, and so can I. (Cloitre et al., 2012)
Every time I practise a skill, I get stronger.
Discomfort in treatment means I am doing the work, not that

treatment is failing.

I am investing in my future by doing this challenging work now.
I owe it to myself to keep trying.
I deserve a life not dominated by trauma.
Each small victory matters. I am making progress.
I am reclaiming my life piece by piece.
Giving up guarantees things stay the same. Continuing creates the

possibility of change.

> I have already come further than I thought possible.
> I am not doing this perfectly, and that is perfectly fine.
> My future self will thank me for not giving up.

How to Use These Statements Effectively

Select statements that resonate with you personally. Not every statement will feel meaningful or helpful; that is normal. Identify 5-10 statements that genuinely help you and focus on those.

practise statements when you are calm, not just during a crisis. Read them daily, say them aloud, write them repeatedly. This practise makes them more accessible when you need them during distress. Your brain needs to be familiar with these statements to retrieve them during a crisis.

Personalise statements to make them more powerful. Change wording to match how you naturally speak. Add specific details relevant to your situation. Create your own statements based on what you are learning in therapy or from your own experience.

Use statements actively during distress. When you notice difficult thoughts or feelings, deliberately recall and repeat appropriate statements. Say them aloud if possible; speaking engages more of your brain than just thinking. Repeat statements multiple times until you feel some shift in emotional intensity.

Combine statements with other coping strategies. Use grounding statements whilst also engaging in physical grounding techniques. Use anxiety statements whilst practising breathing exercises. Statements support other skills rather than replacing them.

Be patient with yourself if statements feel false or unhelpful initially. When you are very distressed or deeply believe negative thoughts, positive statements can feel hollow. Continue using them anyway. Over time and with repetition, they become more believable and effective.

Appendix J: Building Your Recovery Team, Who Can Help and How (Brand et al., 2019)

Recovery from PTSD rarely happens in isolation. Most people benefit from a team of supporters, professionals, and resources working together to facilitate healing. This appendix helps you identify and build your personal recovery team, the network of people and resources supporting your journey. (Ross et al., 2017)

Professional Team Members

Trauma Therapist: The cornerstone of your professional team. Provides evidence-based trauma-focused treatment, guides you through processing trauma memories, teaches coping skills, and supports you through recovery challenges. Choose a therapist specifically trained in trauma treatment who uses an evidence-based approach like CPT, PE, EMDR, or CT-PTSD. The therapeutic relationship significantly predicts outcomes, so finding a therapist you feel safe with and understood by is crucial. (Shapiro, 2018)

Psychiatrist or Prescriber: If you use medication for PTSD or comorbid conditions, maintain regular contact with the prescriber. They monitor medication effectiveness, adjust dosing as needed, assess side effects, and ensure medication supports rather than complicates recovery. Coordinate between the therapist and prescriber so they work together towards your goals. (Fenster et al., 2018)

General Practitioner or Primary Care Physician: Your GP provides ongoing medical care, monitors physical health impacts of PTSD, coordinates care between specialists, and serves as the first point of contact when symptoms worsen or new problems emerge. Keep your GP informed about your PTSD treatment and any changes in symptoms.

Support Group Facilitator or Peer Support Worker: If you attend a support group, the facilitator provides structure, ensures safety, and guides group process. Peer support workers, people with lived experience of trauma who have trained to support others, offer a unique understanding and hope from someone who has been there.

Case Manager or Care Coordinator: If you have complex needs, a case manager helps navigate services, coordinate between providers, connect you with resources, and ensure holistic care. They advocate for you within healthcare systems and help address practical barriers to recovery. (Lanius et al., 2018)

Personal Support Team Members

Trusted Friends: Friends who understand trauma, respect your boundaries, provide emotional support, and engage in positive activities with you are invaluable. You do not need many, even one or two close friends with whom you can be honest about struggles, to make a substantial difference. Choose friends who listen without judgment, respect your pace, and maintain appropriate boundaries between support and co-dependency.

Family Members: A supportive family can provide practical help, emotional support, and continuity throughout recovery. However, not all families are supportive, particularly if family members were involved in trauma or do not understand PTSD. Be selective about which family members you involve in your recovery. Seek those who demonstrate care, respect boundaries, and respond helpfully to your needs. (Monson & Shnaider, 2014)

Partner or Spouse: If you are in a relationship, your partner plays a significant role in recovery. (Foa et al., 2019)

They witness daily struggles, provide intimate support, and are affected by your symptoms.

Honest communication about what helps and what does not, education about PTSD, participation in couples therapy if needed, and maintenance of the relationship alongside recovery work all support a positive outcome. (APA, 2017)

Remember that your partner has their own needs and feelings about the situation; their support requires mutual care, not just one-way assistance.

Peer Supporters with Lived Experience: Other trauma survivors, whether met through a support group or naturally in life, provide a unique understanding that people without trauma experience cannot fully offer. They have walked this path and survived. They understand in ways others do not. Connection with peers reduces isolation and provides hope that recovery is possible; if they recovered, you can too. (NICE, 2018)

Recovery Mentor or Sponsor: Some people benefit from a formal mentorship relationship with someone further along in recovery who can provide guidance, accountability, and encouragement. This is common in 12-step programmes but can be arranged informally through a support group or a treatment programme. Choose mentors who model the recovery you aspire to and who respect your autonomy. (Forbes et al., 2020)

Complementary Support and Resources

Support Groups: Whether in-person or online, facilitated or peer-led, support groups provide a community with others facing similar challenges. Groups reduce isolation, normalise struggles, provide practical tips from those with lived experience, and create accountability for recovery efforts. Try several groups to find one that feels right for you. (Schnyder et al., 2015)

Helplines and Text Services: Crisis helplines like Samaritans, text services like Shout, and specialised trauma helplines provide immediate support during a crisis or when regular support is not available. Having these numbers readily accessible, saved in your phone, written on cards in your wallet, ensures help is available when needed urgently.

Self-Help Resources: Books, workbooks, apps, websites, podcasts, and online courses provide education, strategies, and ongoing learning to supplement professional treatment. Quality self-help resources extend therapy between sessions and provide tools you can use independently. Choose evidence-based resources from reputable sources rather than unverified information online.

Physical Health Team: Physiotherapists, personal trainers, yoga instructors, massage therapists, or other movement and body-focused practitioners support physical aspects of recovery. Regular physical activity and body awareness practices significantly benefit PTSD recovery. Find practitioners who understand trauma and can work appropriately with trauma survivors. (Resick et al., 2017)

Spiritual or Religious Community: For those with religious or spiritual orientation, faith communities can provide meaning, community, support, and practices that facilitate healing. Religious leaders, spiritual directors, or faith-based counsellors might complement professional treatment. However, ensure any spiritual guidance supports your recovery rather than promoting guilt or shame about trauma. (Maercker et al., 2022)

Building and Maintaining Your Team

Assess your current supports. Who do you already have in your life who could support recovery? Are there gaps, areas where you need support but do not currently have it? Do not expect one person to meet all your needs. Different team members serve different functions. Your therapist provides professional expertise. Friends provide social connections. A support group provides peer understanding. Family provides practical help. Building a comprehensive team ensures your varied needs are met. (Hyland et al., 2021)

Communicate clearly about your needs. People who care about you want to help, but often do not know how. Tell them specifically what helps: I need someone to listen without giving advice, I need help with childcare so I can attend therapy, and I need you to check in if you haven't heard from me in a few days. Clear communication helps people provide useful support rather than well-intentioned but unhelpful assistance.

Set and maintain boundaries. Recovery teams work best when everyone understands their role and respects appropriate limits. Your therapist shouldn't be your friend. Your friends shouldn't be your therapists. Partners need their own support. Support group members maintain confidentiality. Clear boundaries prevent burnout, maintain healthy relationships, and ensure sustainable support over time. (Karatzias et al., 2017)

Regularly evaluate and adjust your team. Your needs change throughout recovery. Early in recovery, you might need intensive professional support. Later, you might focus more on peer support and building non-trauma-related connections. Some relationships that supported you initially might need to change as you grow. It is acceptable to change therapists, leave support groups that no longer serve you, or shift relationship dynamics. Your team should evolve as you do. (Courtois & Ford, 2013)

Express appreciation to your team. People supporting you are choosing to invest time, energy, and care in your well-being. Acknowledge this. Thank them. Let them know specifically how they've helped. This appreciation sustains their willingness to continue supporting you and strengthens relationships. Recovery is collaborative; recognise the contributions of those helping you. (Brewin et al., 2017)

Remember that you are the leader of your team. Professionals provide expertise and supporters provide care, but you direct your recovery. You choose which treatments to pursue, which strategies to use, and how to spend your time and energy. Take input from your team but make decisions aligned with your values and goals. This agency is crucial for sustainable recovery; it is your journey, and you are in charge. (Ford et al., 2019)

Building a strong recovery team creates a foundation supporting successful healing. You do not recover in isolation; connection, support, expertise, and community all contribute to positive outcomes. Invest time and effort in building your team. Ask for what you need.

Accept help when offered. Participate in communities. Connect with professionals. Your recovery deserves comprehensive support, and building that support is a worthwhile investment in your healing. (Cloitre et al., 2020)

==

COMPREHENSIVE REFERENCE LIST

Primary Treatment Efficacy & Guidelines

Evidence-based treatment manuals and clinical guidelines establishing standard of care for PTSD treatment.

- Ehlers, A., & Clark, D. M. (2000). A cognitive model of post-traumatic stress disorder. Behaviour Research and Therapy, 38(4), 319-345.
- Foa, E. B., Hembree, E. A., & Rothbaum, B. O. (2007). Prolonged Exposure Therapy for PTSD: Emotional Processing of Traumatic Experiences. Oxford University Press.
- Resick, P. A., & Schnicke, M. K. (2016). Cognitive Processing Therapy for PTSD: A Comprehensive Manual. Center for Mental Health Disparities.
- Cohen, J. A., Mannarino, A. P., & Deblinger, E. (2016). Trauma-Focused CBT for Children and Adolescents (2nd ed.). Guilford Press.
- Shapiro, F. (2018). Eye Movement Desensitization and Reprocessing: Basic Principles, Protocols, and Procedures (3rd ed.). Guilford Press. (Shapiro, 2018)
- American Psychiatric Association. (2013). Diagnostic and Statistical Manual of Mental Disorders (5th ed.). Arlington, VA.
- World Health Organization. (2019). International Classification of Diseases (11th Revision). Retrieved from https://icd.who.int/
- National Institute for Health and Care Excellence. (2018). Post-traumatic stress disorder (PTSD): Management. Clinical Guideline NG116.

Neurobiology & Trauma Processing

Research explaining how trauma affects the brain and nervous system.

- van der Kolk, B. (2014). The Body Keeps the Score: Brain, Mind, and Body in the Healing of Trauma. Viking.
- Porges, S. W. (2011). The Polyvagal Theory: Neurophysiological Foundations of Emotions. W.W. Norton & Company.
- Siegel, D. J. (2012). Developing Mind: How Relationships and the Brain Interact (2nd ed.). Guilford Press.

- Teicher, M. H., & Samson, A. Y. (2016). Annual Research Review: Enduring neurobiological effects of childhood abuse. Journal of Child Psychology and Psychiatry, 57(3), 241-266.
- Yehuda, R., & Seckl, J. (2011). Stress-related psychiatric disorders with short- and long-term perspectives. Current Psychiatry Reports, 13(6), 409-420.

Complex PTSD & Developmental Trauma (Teicher & Samson, 2016)

- Herman, J. L. (2015). Trauma and Recovery (Revised ed.). Basic Books.
- Schachner, D. A., & Shaver, P. R. (2004). Attachment style and loneliness in close relationships. Personal Relationships, 11(2), 253-271.

Cognitive, Emotional, & Behavioural Mechanisms

- Clark, D. M. (1986). A cognitive approach to panic. Behaviour Research and Therapy, 24(4), 461-470.
- Foa, E. B., & Kozak, M. J. (1986). Emotional processing of fear: Exposure to corrective information. Psychological Bulletin, 99(1), 20-35.
- Wells, A. (2009). Metacognitive Therapy for Anxiety and Depression. Guilford Press.
- Gross, J. J., & John, O. P. (2003). Individual differences in two emotion regulation processes. Journal of Personality and Social Psychology, 85(2), 348-362.
- Teasdale, J. D., & Barnard, P. J. (1993). Affect, Cognition, and Change. Lawrence Erlbaum.

Specific Treatment Elements & Techniques

- Linehan, M. M. (2015). DBT Skills Training Manual (2nd ed.). Guilford Press.
- Najavits, L. M. (2002). Seeking Safety: A Treatment Manual for PTSD and Substance Abuse. Guilford Press.
- Bisson, J. I., Roberts, N. P., Andrew, M., Cooper, R., & Lewis, C. (2013). Psychological therapies for chronic PTSD in adults. Cochrane Database, 12, CD003388.

Sleep, Nightmares & Physical Symptoms (Ross et al., 1989)

- Ross, R. J., Ball, W. A., Sullivan, K. A., & Caroff, S. N. (1989). Sleep disturbance as the hallmark of PTSD. American Journal of Psychiatry, 146(6), 697-707.
- Krakow, B., Hollifield, M., Johnston, L., et al. (2001). Imagery rehearsal therapy for chronic nightmares. JAMA, 286(5), 537-545.

Resilience & Post-Traumatic Growth (Tedeschi & Calhoun, 2004)

- Brewin, C. R., Andrews, B., & Valentine, J. D. (2000). Meta-analysis of risk factors for PTSD. Journal of Consulting and Clinical Psychology, 68(5), 748-766.
- Bonanno, G. A. (2004). Loss, trauma, and human resilience. American Psychologist, 59(1), 20-28.
- Tedeschi, R. G., & Calhoun, L. G. (2004). Post-traumatic growth: Conceptual foundations and empirical evidence. Psychological Inquiry, 15(1), 1-18.

Special Populations & Contexts

- Seal, K. H., Bertenthal, D., Moos, R. H., et al. (2007). Traumatic life experiences and suicide attempt history in combat veterans. Journal of Clinical Psychiatry, 68(7), 1051-1056.
- Haugen, P. T., Evces, M., & Weiss, D. S. (2012). Treating PTSD in first responders: A systematic review. Clinical Psychology Review, 32(5), 370-380.
- Cohen, J. A., & Mannarino, A. P. (2008). Trauma-focused CBT for children and parents. Journal of the American Academy of Child & Adolescent Psychiatry, 47(12), 1402-1409.

Cultural Competence & Intersectionality

- Comas-Díaz, L. (2000). Hispanicity and masculinity. Harvard Review of Psychiatry, 8(6), 289-296.
- Mueser, K. T., Friedman, M. J., & Rosenberg, S. D. (2007). Psychosis and trauma. Comprehensive Psychiatry, 48(2), 145-152.

Evidence Hierarchy Note: This guide prioritises evidence from randomised controlled trials and systematic reviews (Level 1), followed by cohort studies (Level 2), case studies (Level 3), and expert opinion (Level 4). All treatment recommendations are grounded in the peer-reviewed research cited above.

COMPREHENSIVE EVIDENCE-BASED REFERENCE LIST

Every therapeutic claim in this guide is grounded in peer-reviewed research. This reference list prioritizes UK clinical guidance (NICE, British Association for Psychopharmacology) and high-quality research evidence. Pharmacological recommendations are supported by UK-focused sources where available.

UK CLINICAL GUIDELINES (PRIMARY SOURCES)

- National Institute for Health and Care Excellence. (2018). Post-traumatic stress disorder (PTSD): Management. Clinical Guideline NG116. https://www.nice.org.uk/guidance/ng116
- Baldwin, D. S., Anderson, I. M., Nutt, D. J., et al. (2014). Evidence-based pharmacological treatment of anxiety disorders, post-traumatic stress disorder and obsessive-compulsive disorder: A revision of the 2005 guidelines from the British Association for Psychopharmacology. Journal of Psychopharmacology, 28(5), 403-439. (NICE, 2018)
- Ashton, H. (2002). Benzodiazepines: How they work and how to withdraw (The Ashton Manual). http://www.benzo.org.uk/manual/

Prevalence and Epidemiology

- Breslau, N., Kessler, R. C., Chilcoat, H. D., et al. (2005). Trauma and post-traumatic stress disorder in the community: The 1996 Detroit Area Survey of Trauma. Archives of General Psychiatry, 55(7), 626-632.

- Kessler, R. C., Sonnega, A., Bromet, E., et al. (1995). Post-traumatic stress disorder in the National Comorbidity Survey. Archives of General Psychiatry, 52(12), 1048-1060. (Najavits, 2002)

Neurobiology and Brain Mechanisms of Trauma

- LeDoux, J. E. (1998). The Emotional Brain: The Mysterious Underpinnings of Emotional Life. Simon & Schuster.
- Foa, E. B., & Kozak, M. J. (1986). Emotional processing of fear: Exposure to corrective information. Psychological Bulletin, 99(1), 20-35.
- Yehuda, R., & Seckl, J. (2011). Stress-related psychiatric disorders with short- and long-term perspectives: allostatic load as a mechanism. Current Psychiatry Reports, 13(6), 409-420.
- Porges, S. W. (2011). The Polyvagal Theory: Neurophysiological Foundations of Emotions. W.W. Norton & Company.
- Levine, P. A. (2008). Healing Trauma: A Pioneering Program for Restoring the Wisdom of Your Body. Sounds True.
- Van der Kolk, B., Roth, S., Pelcovitz, D., et al. (1996). Dissociation in traumatized adolescents. Journal of Nervous and Mental Disease, 184(12), 727-735.
- Brewin, C. R., Gregory, J. D., Lipton, M., & Burgess, N. (2010). Intrusive images in psychological disorders. Psychological Review, 117(1), 210-232.
- Eichenbaum, H. (2000). A cortical-hippocampal system for declarative memory. Nature Reviews Neuroscience, 1(1), 41-50.

Cognitive Models and Mechanisms

- Ehlers, A., & Clark, D. M. (2000). A cognitive model of post-traumatic stress disorder. Behaviour Research and Therapy, 38(4), 319-345.
- Clark, D. M. (1999). Anxiety disorders: Why they persist and how to treat them. Behaviour Research and Therapy, 37, S5-S27.
- Salkovskis, P. M. (1991). The importance of behaviour in the maintenance of anxiety and panic. Behavioural and Cognitive Psychotherapy, 19(1), 6-19.
- Brewin, C. R., & Holmes, E. A. (2003). Psychological theories of post-traumatic stress disorder. Clinical Psychology Review, 23(3), 339-376.

Treatment Efficacy: Systematic Reviews and Meta-Analyses

- Bisson, J. I., Roberts, N. P., Andrew, M., Cooper, R., & Lewis, C. (2013). Psychological therapies for chronic post-traumatic stress disorder (PTSD) in adults. Cochrane Database of Systematic Reviews, 12, CD003388.
- Foa, E. B., & Rauch, S. A. M. (2004). Cognitive changes in post-traumatic stress disorder: Updated thinking about cognitive models of PTSD. Journal of Cognitive Psychotherapy, 18(3), 281-294.
- Powers, M. B., Halpern, J. M., Ferenschak, M. P., et al. (2010). A meta-analytic review of prolonged exposure for post-traumatic stress disorder. Clinical Psychology Review, 30(6), 635-641.

- Foa, E. B., Franklin, M. E., Moser, J., & Higgs, A. P. (2005). Long-term efficacy of cognitive-behavioral therapy for PTSD. Journal of Consulting and Clinical Psychology, 73(3), 488-494.
- Cusack, K., Jonas, D. E., Forneris, C. A., et al. (2016). Psychological treatments and pharmacotherapies for adults with PTSD: a systematic review update. Journal of General Internal Medicine, 31(3), 339-352.

Evidence-Based Treatment Manuals (Primary Sources)

- Foa, E. B., Hembree, E. A., & Rothbaum, B. O. (2007). Prolonged Exposure Therapy for PTSD: Emotional Processing of Traumatic Experiences. Oxford University Press.
- Resick, P. A., & Schnicke, M. K. (2016). Cognitive Processing Therapy for PTSD: A Comprehensive Manual. Center for Mental Health Disparities.
- Shapiro, F. (2018). Eye Movement Desensitization and Reprocessing: Basic Principles, Protocols, and Procedures (3rd ed.). Guilford Press. (Shapiro, 2018)
- Cohen, J. A., Mannarino, A. P., & Deblinger, E. (2016). Trauma-Focused CBT for Children and Adolescents (2nd ed.). Guilford Press.

Pharmacological Treatments for PTSD (UK-Focused References) (NICE, 2018)

- NICE. (2018). Post-traumatic stress disorder (PTSD): Management. Clinical Guideline NG116. [UK PRIMARY GUIDANCE FOR MEDICATIONS]
- Stein, D. J., Ipser, J. C., & Seedat, S. (2006). Pharmacotherapy for post traumatic stress disorder (PTSD). Cochrane Database of Systematic Reviews, 1, CD002795.
- Raskind, M. A., Peskind, E. R., Kanter, E. D., et al. (2007). Reduction of nightmares and other PTSD symptoms in combat veterans by prazosin. American Journal of Psychiatry, 160(2), 371-373.
- Thompson, C. E., Raskind, M. A., & Peskind, E. R. (2018). Prazosin and PTSD: Basic mechanisms and clinical implications. In Pharmacotherapy for PTSD (pp. 221-241).
- Spiegel, D. A., Wiegel, M., Baker, S. L., & Greene, K. A. I. (2009). Pharmacological augmentation of cognitive behavioral therapy for anxiety disorders. Psychiatry Research, 181(2), 147-159.
- Ashton, H. (2002). Benzodiazepines: How they work and how to withdraw (The Ashton Manual). [UK ESSENTIAL REFERENCE ON BENZODIAZEPINE RISKS]
- Lader, M. (2011). Benzodiazepines revisited—will we ever learn?. Addiction, 106(12), 2086-2109.
- Connor, K. M., Sutherland, S. M., Tupler, L. A., et al. (2006). Fluoxetine in post-traumatic stress disorder: Randomized, double-blind study. British Journal of Psychiatry, 175(5), 443-450.
- Schoenfeld, F. B., Marmar, C. R., & Neylan, T. C. (2004). Current concepts in pharmacotherapy for PTSD. Journal of Clinical Psychiatry, 65 Suppl 1, 45-48.

Sleep Disturbance and Nightmare Treatment (Krakow & Zadra, 2006)

- Ross, R. J., Ball, W. A., Sullivan, K. A., & Caroff, S. N. (1989). Sleep disturbance as the hallmark of PTSD. American Journal of Psychiatry, 146(6), 697-707.

- Krakow, B., & Zadra, A. (2006). Clinical management of nightmares: Imagery rehearsal therapy. Behavioral Sleep Medicine, 4(1), 45-70.
- Riemann, D., Krone, L. B., Wulff, K., & Nissen, C. (2009). Sleep, insomnia, and depression. Neuropsychopharmacology, 45(1), 74-89.
- Perlis, M. L., Jungquist, C., Smith, M. T., & Posner, D. (2005). Cognitive behavioral treatment of insomnia: A session-by-session guide. Springer.

Complex PTSD and Developmental Trauma (Teicher & Samson, 2016)

- Herman, J. L. (2015). Trauma and Recovery: The Aftermath of Violence. Basic Books.
- Teicher, M. H., & Samson, A. Y. (2016). Enduring neurobiological effects of childhood abuse and neglect. Journal of Child Psychology and Psychiatry, 57(3), 241-266.
- Van der Kolk, B., Perry, B. D., & Herman, J. L. (2005). Traumatic antecedents of aggression and violence. Journal of Traumatic Stress, 4(1), 31-45.

Special Populations and Contexts

- Seal, K. H., Bertenthal, D., Moos, R. H., et al. (2007). Traumatic experiences and suicide attempt history in combat veterans. Journal of Clinical Psychiatry, 68(7), 1051-1056.
- Haugen, P. T., Evces, M., & Weiss, D. S. (2012). Treating PTSD in first responders: A systematic review. Clinical Psychology Review, 32(5), 370-380.
- Cohen, J. A., & Mannarino, A. P. (2008). Trauma-focused CBT for children and parents: An empirical update. Journal of the American Academy of Child & Adolescent Psychiatry, 47(12), 1402-1409.

Supporting Evidence: Emotion Regulation, Resilience, and Related Topics (Bonanno, 2004)

- Linehan, M. M. (2015). DBT Skills Training Manual (2nd ed.). Guilford Press.
- Gross, J. J., & John, O. P. (2003). Individual differences in emotion regulation processes. Journal of Personality and Social Psychology, 85(2), 348-362.
- Bonanno, G. A. (2004). Loss, trauma, and human resilience. American Psychologist, 59(1), 20-28.
- Tedeschi, R. G., & Calhoun, L. G. (2004). Post-traumatic growth: Conceptual foundations and evidence. Psychological Inquiry, 15(1), 1-18.
- Najavits, L. M. (2002). Seeking Safety: A Treatment Manual for PTSD and Substance Abuse. Guilford Press.

Evidence Standards and Access

Evidence Hierarchy: *This guide prioritises Level 1 evidence (randomised controlled trials and systematic reviews) and Level 2 evidence (cohort studies). All therapeutic recommendations are grounded in peer-reviewed research. UK sources are prioritised for clinical guidance and pharmacotherapy to ensure relevance to UK NHS practice. When research evidence is limited or conflicting, this is explicitly noted in the text.*

How to Access Full-Text References: *NICE guidelines are freely available at www.nice.org.uk. Many peer-reviewed articles are available through PubMed (pubmed.ncbi.nlm.nih.gov). NHS staff can access articles through NHS library services. Authors often provide copies upon request. Patients can ask their GP or mental health provider for information about specific treatments.*

Additional Contemporary Evidence Base

- American Psychological Association. (2017). Clinical practice guideline for the treatment of posttraumatic stress disorder (PTSD) in adults. APA.
- Bisson, J. I., Berliner, L., Cloitre, M., Forbes, D., Jensen, T. K., Lewis, C., Monson, C. M., Olff, M., Pilling, S., Riggs, D. S., Roberts, N. P., & Shapiro, F. (2019). The International Society for Traumatic Stress Studies new guidelines for the prevention and treatment of posttraumatic stress disorder: Methodology and development process. Journal of Traumatic Stress, 32(4), 475-483.
- Brand, B. L., Schielke, H. J., Brams, J. S., & DiComo, R. A. (2019). Assessing trauma-related dissociation in forensic contexts: Addressing trauma-related dissociation as a forensic psychologist. Psychological Injury and Law, 12(3-4), 298-312.
- Brewin, C. R., Cloitre, M., Hyland, P., Shevlin, M., Maercker, A., Bryant, R. A., Humayun, A., Jones, L. M., Kagee, A., Rousseau, C., Somasundaram, D., Suzuki, Y., Wessely, S., van Ommeren, M., & Reed, G. M. (2017). A review of current evidence regarding the ICD-11 proposals for diagnosing PTSD and complex PTSD. Clinical Psychology Review, 58, 1-15.
- Charuvastra, A., & Cloitre, M. (2008). Social bonds and posttraumatic stress disorder. Annual Review of Psychology, 59, 301-328.
- Cloitre, M., Courtois, C. A., Ford, J. D., Green, B. L., Alexander, P., Briere, J., Herman, J. L., Lanius, R., Stolbach, B. C., Spinazzola, J., van der Kolk, B. A., & van der Hart, O. (2012). The ISTSS expert consensus treatment guidelines for complex PTSD in adults. Journal of Traumatic Stress, 25(6), 615-627.
- Cloitre, M., Shevlin, M., Brewin, C. R., Bisson, J. I., Roberts, N. P., Maercker, A., Karatzias, T., & Hyland, P. (2020). The International Trauma Questionnaire: Development of a self-report measure of ICD-11 PTSD and complex PTSD. Acta Psychiatrica Scandinavica, 141(3), 191-210.
- Courtois, C. A., & Ford, J. D. (Eds.). (2013). Treatment of complex trauma: A sequenced, relationship-based approach. Guilford Press.
- Coventry, P. A., Meader, N., Melber, H., Llewellyn, D. J., Morgan, C., Sherpherd, P., Sherpherd, E., Sherpherd, S., & Bauer, A. (2020). Psychological and pharmacological interventions for posttraumatic stress disorder and comorbid mental health problems following complex traumatic events: Systematic review and component network meta-analysis. PLoS Medicine, 17(8), e1003262.
- Cusack, K., Jonas, D. E., Forneris, C. A., Wines, C., Sonis, J., Middleton, J. C., Feltner, C., Brownley, K. A., Olmsted, K. R., Greenblatt, A., Weil, A., & Gaynes, B. N. (2016). Psychological treatments for adults with posttraumatic stress disorder: A systematic review and meta-analysis. Clinical Psychology Review, 43, 128-141.

- Ehring, T., Welboren, R., Morina, N., Wicherts, J. M., Freitag, J., & Emmelkamp, P. M. G. (2014). Meta-analysis of psychological treatments for posttraumatic stress disorder in adult survivors of childhood abuse. Clinical Psychology Review, 34(8), 645-657.
- Fenster, R. J., Lebois, L. A. M., Ressler, K. J., & Suh, J. (2018). Brain circuit dysfunction in post-traumatic stress disorder: From mouse to man. Nature Reviews Neuroscience, 19(9), 535-551.
- Foa, E. B., Hembree, E. A., Rothbaum, B. O., & Rauch, S. A. M. (2019). Prolonged exposure therapy for PTSD: Emotional processing of traumatic experiences (2nd ed.). Oxford University Press.
- Forbes, D., Bisson, J. I., Monson, C. M., & Berliner, L. (Eds.). (2020). Effective treatments for PTSD: Practice guidelines from the International Society for Traumatic Stress Studies (3rd ed.). Guilford Press.
- Ford, J. D., Courtois, C. A., Steele, K., van der Hart, O., & Nijenhuis, E. R. S. (2019). Treatment of complex posttraumatic self-dysregulation. Journal of Traumatic Stress, 18(5), 437-447.
- Gilbert, P. (2014). The origins and nature of compassion focused therapy. British Journal of Clinical Psychology, 53(1), 6-41.
- Guay, S., Billette, V., & Marchand, A. (2006). Exploring the links between posttraumatic stress disorder and social support: Processes and potential research avenues. Journal of Traumatic Stress, 19(3), 327-338.
- Hyland, P., Shevlin, M., Cloitre, M., Karatzias, T., Vallières, F., McGinty, G., Fox, R., & McHugh Power, J. (2021). The factor structure of the International Trauma Questionnaire in a sample of adults seeking treatment for trauma-related psychological difficulties. Acta Psychiatrica Scandinavica, 143(3), 251-262.
- International Society for Traumatic Stress Studies. (2019). ISTSS PTSD prevention and treatment guidelines: Methodology and recommendations. ISTSS.
- Kang, H., Fischer, I. C., Dickinson, S., Na, P. J., Tsai, J., Tedeschi, R. G., & Pietrzak, R. H. (2024). Posttraumatic growth in U.S. military veterans: Results from the National Health and Resilience in Veterans Study. Psychiatric Quarterly, 95(1), 17-32.
- Karatzias, T., Shevlin, M., Fyvie, C., Hyland, P., Efthymiadou, E., Wilson, D., Roberts, N., Bisson, J. I., Brewin, C. R., & Cloitre, M. (2017). Evidence of distinct profiles of posttraumatic stress disorder (PTSD) and complex posttraumatic stress disorder (CPTSD) based on the new ICD-11 Trauma Questionnaire (ICD-TQ). Journal of Affective Disorders, 207, 181-187.
- Karatzias, T., Murphy, P., Cloitre, M., Bisson, J., Roberts, N., Shevlin, M., Hyland, P., Maercker, A., Ben-Ezra, M., Coventry, P., Mason-Roberts, S., Bradley, A., & Hutton, P. (2019). Psychological interventions for ICD-11 complex PTSD symptoms: Systematic review and meta-analysis. Psychological Medicine, 49(11), 1761-1775.
- Lanius, R. A., Frewen, P. A., Tursich, M., Jetly, R., & McKinnon, M. C. (2018). Restoring large-scale brain networks in PTSD and related disorders: A proposal for neuroscientifically-informed treatment interventions. European Journal of Psychotraumatology, 6(1), 27313.

- Lewis, C., Roberts, N. P., Andrew, M., Starling, E., & Bisson, J. I. (2020). Psychological therapies for post-traumatic stress disorder in adults: Systematic review and meta-analysis. European Journal of Psychotraumatology, 11(1), 1729633.
- Li, S., Shu, H., Wu, Y., Li, F., Yang, J., Luo, L., & Wei, X. (2025). Post-traumatic growth promotes resilience development: A longitudinal mediation model. Journal of Affective Disorders, 368, 727-733.
- Maercker, A., Cloitre, M., Bachem, R., Schlumpf, Y. R., Khoury, B., Hitchcock, C., & Bohus, M. (2022). Complex post-traumatic stress disorder. The Lancet, 400(10345), 60-72.
- Mavranezouli, I., Megnin-Viggars, O., Grey, N., Bhutani, G., Leach, J., Daly, C., Dias, S., Welton, N. J., Katona, C., El-Leithy, S., Greenberg, N., Stockton, S., & Pilling, S. (2020). Cost-effectiveness of psychological treatments for post-traumatic stress disorder in adults. PLoS One, 15(4), e0232245.
- Monson, C. M., & Shnaider, P. (2014). Treating PTSD with cognitive-behavioral therapies: Interventions that work. American Psychological Association.
- Neff, K. D., & Germer, C. K. (2018). The Mindful Self-Compassion Workbook: A proven way to accept yourself, build inner strength, and thrive. Guilford Press.
- Ozer, E. J., Best, S. R., Lipsey, T. L., & Weiss, D. S. (2003). Predictors of posttraumatic stress disorder and symptoms in adults: A meta-analysis. Psychological Bulletin, 129(1), 52-73.
- Resick, P. A., Monson, C. M., & Chard, K. M. (2017). Cognitive processing therapy for PTSD: A comprehensive manual. Guilford Press.
- Ross, D. A., Arbuckle, M. R., Travis, M. J., Dwyer, J. B., van Schalkwyk, G. I., & Bhilai, K. (2017). An integrated neuroscience perspective on formulation and treatment planning for posttraumatic stress disorder: An educational review. JAMA Psychiatry, 74(4), 407-415.
- Schnyder, U., Ehlers, A., Elbert, T., Foa, E. B., Gersons, B. P. R., Resick, P. A., Shapiro, F., & Cloitre, M. (2015). Psychotherapies for PTSD: What do they have in common? European Journal of Psychotraumatology, 6(1), 28186.
- van Dis, E. A. M., van Veen, S. C., Goto, A., Hagenaars, M. A., & Engelhard, I. M. (2020). Long-term outcomes of cognitive behavioral therapy for anxiety-related disorders: A systematic review and meta-analysis. JAMA Psychiatry, 77(3), 265-273.
- Watkins, L. E., Sprang, K. R., & Rothbaum, B. O. (2018). Treating PTSD: A review of evidence-based psychotherapy interventions. Frontiers in Behavioral Neuroscience, 12, 258.
- Watts, B. V., Schnurr, P. P., Mayo, L., Young-Xu, Y., Weeks, W. B., & Friedman, M. J. (2013). Meta-analysis of the efficacy of treatments for posttraumatic stress disorder. Journal of Clinical Psychiatry, 74(6), e541-e550.

www.ingramcontent.com/pod-product-compliance
Lightning Source LLC
LaVergne TN
LVHW082115200926
848484LV00008B/1952